Amid the recent resurgence of interest in the political economy of punishment, this timely and valuable collection brings fresh insights as well as building on established paradigms. The book, which features some of the leading figures in the field, ranges widely across countries and explores a variety of approaches, yet holds nicely together within a coherent shared project. It should reach a wide and attentive audience.

Nicola Lacey, *School Professor of Law, Gender and Social Policy, London School of Economics, UK*

The Political Economy of Punishment Today

Over the last fifteen years, the analytical field of punishment and society has witnessed an increase of research developing the connection between economic processes and the evolution of penality from different standpoints, focusing particularly on the increase of rates of incarceration in relation to the transformations of neoliberal capitalism.

Bringing together leading researchers from diverse geographical contexts, this book reframes the theoretical field of the political economy of punishment, analysing penality within the current economic situation and connecting contemporary penal changes with political and cultural processes. It challenges the traditional and common sense understanding of imprisonment as 'exclusion' and posits a more promising concept of imprisonment as a 'differential' or 'subordinate' form of 'inclusion'.

This groundbreaking book will be a key text for scholars who are working in the field of punishment and society as well as reaching a broader audience within law, sociology, economics, criminology and criminal justice studies.

Dario Melossi is Professor of Criminology in the School of Law of the University of Bologna. After having been Editor-in-Chief of *Punishment and Society* he is currently Editor-in-Chief of the *European Journal of Criminology*.

Máximo Sozzo is Professor of Sociology and Criminology at the Social and Juridical Sciences Faculty of the National University of Litoral (Santa Fe, Argentina). He is also Adjunct Professor at the School of Justice of Queensland University of Technology (Brisbane, Australia).

José A. Brandariz-García is Associate Professor of Criminal Law and Criminology at the University of A Coruña (Spain), and member of the Executive Board of the European Society of Criminology.

Routledge Critical Studies in Crime, Diversity and Criminal Justice

Edited by Sharon Hayes
University of Newcastle, Australia
and
Patricia Faraldo Cabana
University of A Coruña, Spain

The works in this series strive to generate new conceptual and theoretical frameworks to address the legal, organisational and normative responses to the challenges that diversity and intersectionality present to criminal justice systems. This series aims to present cutting edge empirically informed theoretical works from both new and established scholars around the world.

Drawing upon a range of disciplines including sociology, law, history, economics, and social work, the series encourages different approaches to questions of mobility and exclusion with a cross-section of theorists, empiricists, and critical policy researchers. It will be key reading for scholars who are working in criminal justice, criminology, criminal law and human rights, as well as those in the fields of gender and LGBTI studies, migration studies, anthropology, refugee studies and post-colonial studies.

1 **Gender Responsive Justice**
   A Critical Appraisal
   Karen Evans

2 **The Political Economy of Punishment Today**
   Visions, Debates and Challenges
   Edited by Dario Melossi, Máximo Sozzo and José A. Brandariz-García

The Political Economy of Punishment Today

Visions, Debates and Challenges

Edited by
Dario Melossi, Máximo Sozzo
and José A. Brandariz-García

LONDON AND NEW YORK

First published 2018 by Routledge

2 Park Square, Milton Park, Abingdon, Oxon OX14 4RN
605 Third Avenue, New York, NY 10017

Routledge is an imprint of the Taylor & Francis Group, an informa business

First issued in paperback 2021

Copyright © 2018 selection and editorial matter, Dario Melossi, Máximo Sozzo and José A. Brandariz-García; individual chapters, the contributors

The right of Dario Melossi, Máximo Sozzo and José A. Brandariz-García to be identified as the authors of the editorial matter, and of the authors for their individual chapters, has been asserted in accordance with sections 77 and 78 of the Copyright, Designs and Patents Act 1988.

All rights reserved. No part of this book may be reprinted or reproduced or utilised in any form or by any electronic, mechanical, or other means, now known or hereafter invented, including photocopying and recording, or in any information storage or retrieval system, without permission in writing from the publishers.

Notice:
Product or corporate names may be trademarks or registered trademarks, and are used only for identification and explanation without intent to infringe.

Publisher's Note

The publisher has gone to great lengths to ensure the quality of this reprint but points out that some imperfections in the original copies may be apparent.

British Library Cataloguing in Publication Data
A catalogue record for this book is available from the British Library

Library of Congress Cataloging in Publication Data
A catalog record for this book has been requested

ISBN: 978-1-138-68628-1 (hbk)
ISBN: 978-0-367-48191-9 (pbk)

Typeset in Times New Roman
by Wearset Ltd, Boldon, Tyne and Wear

Printed in the United Kingdom
by Henry Ling Limited

Contents

List of figures ix
List of tables x
Notes on contributors xi
Series editor foreword xv
Acknowledgements xviii

The political economy of punishment today: an introduction 1
JOSÉ A. BRANDARIZ-GARCÍA, DARIO MELOSSI AND MÁXIMO SOZZO

1 **Between struggles and discipline: Marx and Foucault on penality and the critique of political economy** 23
DARIO MELOSSI

2 **The renaissance of the political economy of punishment from a comparative perspective** 37
MÁXIMO SOZZO

3 **For and against the political economy of punishment: thoughts on Bourdieu and punishment** 65
IGNACIO GONZÁLEZ-SÁNCHEZ

4 **Do economic depressions reduce the use of fines? Revisiting Rusche and Kirchheimer's *Punishment and Social Structure*** 87
PATRICIA FARALDO CABANA

5 From one recession to another: the lessons of a long-term political economy of punishment. The example of Belgium (1830–2014)   107
CHARLOTTE VANNESTE

6 Political economy of punishment in Australia   137
HILDE TUBEX

7 Punishment in a hybrid political economy: the Italian case (1970–2010)   160
ZELIA A. GALLO

8 'A return to Gulags'? Explaining trends in post-Soviet prison rates   185
GAVIN SLADE

9 Inclusion's dark side: the political economy of irregular migration in Greece   205
LEONIDAS K. CHELIOTIS

10 Reflections on Spanish policies of migration control: a political economic reading on the punishment of migrants   218
JOSÉ A. BRANDARIZ-GARCÍA

Index   238

Figures

4.1	Prison and fine sentences. German Empire: 1882–1932	94
4.2	Convictions to prison, fine and other penalties. German Empire: 1933–first semester 1943	102
5.1	Prison population and significant indicators in successive periods (Belgium, 1831–2014)	109
5.2	Indicators of inequality (Belgium 1951–2013)	114
5.3	Detention rate and ratio average/median income	115
5.4	Detention rate and part of the income of tenth decile	115
5.5	Detention rate and part of the income of first decile	116
5.6	Detention rate and part of population with living allowance	116
5.7	Proportion of votes in Belgium: Right, centre and Left (1951–2011)	119
5.8	Detention rate and part of votes on the Right (1981–2011)	120
5.9	Detention rate and part of votes on the centre (1981–2011)	120
5.10	Varieties of capitalism and varieties of punishment	125
6.1	Australian imprisonment rates	143
6.2	Neoliberal countries	144
6.3	Conservative corporatist countries	145
6.4	Social democratic corporatist countries	146
8.1	Prison rates in selected post-Soviet countries across time	188

Tables

2.1	Incarceration rates (countries included in Cavadino and Dignan (2006b))	48
2.2	Incarceration rates in Latin America	56
4.1	Commitment to prison for non-payment of fines. German Empire: 1926–1931	90
4.2	Commitment to prison for non-payment of fines (total numbers and percentage). German Empire: 1925–1931	92
4.3	Prison and fine sentences (percentages). German Empire: 1920–1932	93
4.4	Prison, fine and other intermediate sentences (percentages). Spain: 1994–2002	95
4.5	Prison and fine sentences (total numbers). Spain: 2007–2015	97
4.6	Prison and fine sentences (percentages). Spain: 2007–2015	98
5.1	Correlations between detention rate and inequality indicators (1973–2014)	117
8.1	Top ten incarcerators in Europe per 100,000 of the population in 2015	188
8.2	Variation across theoretically important factors in Georgia and Kazakhstan affecting prison rates	196
10.1	Evolution of the unemployment rate of the foreign population and evolution of the foreign prison population rate, 2000–2009	220
10.2	Evolution of prison population rate and evolution of certain economic and labour variables, 2000–2009	222
10.3	Evolution of the unemployment rate of the non EU-born population and evolution of the non EU-born resident population, 2009–2016	225
10.4	Evolution of the foreign prison population and evolution of migration law-enforcement activities, 2009–2015	226
10.5	Evolution of the various legal categories of enforced deportations, 2008–2014	227

Contributors

Dario Melossi is Full Professor of Criminology in the School of Law of the University of Bologna. After having being conferred a law degree at this University, he went on to do a PhD in sociology at the University of California, Santa Barbara. He was then Assistant and thereafter Associate Professor in Sociology at the University of California, Davis, until the mid-1990s when he went back to Bologna. He has published *The Prison and the Factory* (London, Macmillan, 1977, together with Massimo Pavarini), *The State of Social Control: A Sociological Study of Concepts of State and Social Control in the Making of Democracy* (Cambridge, Polity Press, 1990) and *Controlling Crime, Controlling Society: Thinking About Crime in Europe and America* (Cambridge, Polity Press, 2008), *Crime Punishment and Migration* (London, SAGE, 2015), plus about 200 other edited books, chapters and articles. He has been Editor of *Studi sulla questione criminale*, is currently Editor-in-Chief of *Punishment and Society*, and is member of the Board of many other professional journals. In 2007 he was conferred the 'International Scholarship Prize' of the Law and Society Association and in 2014 the 'European Criminology Award' of the European Society of Criminology. His most recent publication is entitled *Crime, Punishment and Migration* (2015) and it reflects his current research interests, about the processes of construction of deviance and social control of migration, within the European Union.

Máximo Sozzo is Full Professor of Sociology and Criminology at the National University of Litoral (Argentina). He was a Fellow of the Straus Institute for the Advance Study of Law and Justice at the School of Law of New York University (2010/2011). He has been Visiting Professor at the Universities of Bologna, Toronto, Barcelona and Hamburg, among others. He is Adjunct Professor of the School of Justice at Queensland University of Technology (Australia). He has published widely on criminology and sociology of police and punishment and he is currently researching on the penal policies in post-neoliberal contexts of South America. He has authored and edited ten books and seventy article journals and book chapters, which have been published mainly in Spanish, but also in English, Italian and Portuguese. His most recent books are: *Locura y Crimen. Nacimiento de la intersección entre los dispositivos psiquiátrico y penal* (Didot, Buenos Aires, 2015); *Viagems Culturais e Questao Criminal* (Revan, Rio de Janeiro, 2014) and with Dario Melossi and Richard Sparks (editors): *The Travels of the Criminal Question* (Hart, Oxford, 2011).

José A. Brandariz-García is Associate Professor of Criminal Law and Criminology at the University of A Coruna (Spain), and member of the Executive Board of the European Society of Criminology (2016–2019). He has published widely on penality and criminal justice issues, especially on penal policies, migration control and penal managerialism. He is currently researching on political economy of punishment and the influence of the Great Recession on penality. He has authored and edited almost twenty books and around 100 journal articles and book chapters, which have been published mainly in Spanish, but also in English, French, Italian and Portuguese. His most recent books are *El modelo gerencial-actuarial de penalidad* (Dykinson, Madrid, 2016) *Prácticas y políticas de control migratorio* (authored together with Marta Monclús Masó, Didot, Buenos Aires, 2015) and *El gobierno de la penalidad* (Dykinson, Madrid, 2014). He has also been visiting scholar in several international universities, such as those of Chicago (USA), Freiburg (Germany), Buenos Aires (Argentina), Milan (Italy) and Coimbra (Portugal).

Patricia Faraldo Cabana is Full Professor for Criminal Law at the University of A Coruna, in Spain, and Adjunct Professor at the Queensland University of Technology in Brisbane, Australia. She was European Institutes for Advanced Study (EURIAS) Senior Fellow at the Freiburg Institute for Advanced Studies in Germany in 2015–2016, after being a Marie Curie fellow in 2013–2014 at the Max Planck Institute for Foreign and International Criminal Law also in Germany. She has published ten monographs and co-edited nine collective books. She has written more than 100 articles and book chapters on issues concerning Criminal Law and Criminal Policy in English, Italian, German and Spanish.

Leonidas K. Cheliotis is Assistant Professor of Criminology at the Department of Social Policy, London School of Economics and Political Science. He is also an Editor and Book Review Editor of the *British Journal of Criminology*. He has published widely in the sociology of punishment, and has received various awards for his research, including, most recently, the Adam Podgòrecki Prize by the International Sociological Association, the Outstanding Critical Criminal Justice Scholar Award by the American Academy of Criminal Justice Sciences, and the Critical Criminologist of the Year Award by the American Society of Criminology.

Zelia A. Gallo is Lecturer in Criminal Law and Criminology and Criminal Justice at the Dickson Poon School of Law, King's College London (KCL). Before joining the KCL Law Faculty, she was a Research Fellow in the

London School of Economics and Political Science (LSE) Law Department, where she had previously obtained her PhD with a thesis entitled *The Penality of Politics: Punishment in Contemporary Italy*. She researches and writes about punishment in comparative perspective, focusing on the links between punishment, politics and the political economy.

Ignacio González Sánchez is Visiting Lecturer in the Department of Public Law at Universitat de Girona (Spain). He completed his PhD in Sociology at Universidad Complutense de Madrid (Spain), in 2014. His thesis is entitled *The Neoliberal Penality*, and some of its research was completed throughout visits at the Law School at University of Edinburgh (UK), and the Department of Sociology at the University of California, Berkeley (USA). His research interests involve the sociology of punishment – especially prisons – and sociological theory. He has published some papers on these topics, and edited a collective book on the work of Loïc Wacquant (*Teoría social, marginalidad urbana y Estado penal*, Madrid, Dykinson, 2012).

Gavin Slade is Lecturer in the Legacies of Communism, based at the University of Glasgow, UK. He holds a PhD in Law from the University of Oxford and has held positions at the University of Toronto and Free University of Berlin. His work focuses on criminal justice in the former Soviet Union. His articles have been published in high-ranking criminological and socio-legal journals including the *British Journal of Criminology*, *European Journal of Criminology*, *Theoretical Criminology*, *Law and Society Review* and *Punishment and Society*. In 2013, Oxford University Press published his first book on anti-organised crime policies in post-Soviet Georgia.

Hilde Tubex is Associate Professor and Deputy Head of School, Research at the Law School of the University of Western Australia. Her areas of research expertise are on comparative criminology and penal policy and on the Indigenous overrepresentation in the Australian criminal justice system – she has published widely published on these topics. She received an Australian Research Council (ARC) Future Fellowship studying the difference in imprisonment rates between Australian jurisdictions and to explore the validity of internationally developed explanatory models for the Australian situation. She is currently working on a Criminology Research Grant to develop effective throughcare for Indigenous offenders. Before migrating to Australia, she worked as a researcher/lecturer at the Free University of Brussels (Belgium), and was an advisor to the Belgian Minister of Justice and the Council of Europe.

Charlotte Vanneste has a PhD in Criminology. After serving as Head of the Department of Criminology at the National Institute of Criminalistics and Criminology (NICC) in Brussels (1997–2012), she is now Senior Research Fellow (NICC) and, since 2014, also Associate Professor at the University of Liège (Belgium). Her research focuses for one part on the long-term trends in punishment and their relation with economy. In 2000, she was awarded with the 'Prix Gabriel Tarde' of the French Society of Criminology for her book *Les chiffres des prisons. Des logiques économiques à leur traduction pénale* (Prisons Figures. From Economic Logics to Their Penal Translation) (Paris, L'Harmattan, 2001). She has also edited three books and published a number of journal articles and book chapters, in French, Dutch and English, related to criminal justice decision-making processes, prisons, juvenile justice, policies related to intimate partner violence and the construction of criminal justice statistics.

Series editor foreword

On 21 October 2008, the Australian government sent 600 Defence Force soldiers and detachments into Aboriginal communities in the Northern Territory in what has become known as the 'Northern Territory Intervention'. The intervention was the result of a report issued in 2007 by the Northern Territory Government, which claimed those communities were riddled with child sexual abuse. In addition to law enforcement, a package of changes including those affecting welfare provision and land tenure were also enacted. In the decade since the report was first made available, not one person in the region has been prosecuted for child sexual abuse.

The political economy of punishment in Australia works to discipline those who fail to comply with or fit into its capitalist market regime, targeting the Indigenous rural population in particular, which tends to put kinship, harmony with the natural world and spirituality ahead of market consumption and participation. Since the advent of colonial rule in Australia, which assumed Terra Nullus in the apparent absence of Aboriginal leaders and landowners, in spite of an obvious Indigenous presence, in the last 250 years Aboriginal people have been coerced, exploited, murdered and incarcerated in frightening numbers, their children removed from them, and attempts were made to breed their Aboriginality out of them. In spite of successfully achieving land rights in 1992 in two landmark court cases, there is still no treaty, nor formal constitutional recognition of Australia's First Peoples. Instead, they continue to be punished for being who they are; indeed, increasingly high levels of incarceration despite lessening crime rates is demonstrative of this. The political economy of punishment is important in the context of Indigenous Australians because it serves to demonstrate how disciplinary regimes create and exploit power relations based on economic relations. It allows us to conceptualise punishment and penality in a more critical light than may otherwise be imagined from a mainstream (that is, purely sociological) criminological perspective.

This book is timely, in that Australia is not by any means the only Western market democracy in which the political economy of punishment needs to be studied, as the book's contents very well demonstrate. Its ten chapters explore the political economy of punishment across cultures, both empirically and theoretically, providing much-needed critical analysis of disciplinary regimes around the globe. When it was first proposed for the Routledge Critical Studies in Crime, Diversity and Criminal Justice series, I was thrilled to include such a distinguished collection of authors, some of whom I have worked with and/or admired in the various forums in which they have presented their work over the past few years, including conferences organised by the American Society of Criminology and European Society of Criminology to name just two.

While the political economy of punishment has been the subject of scholarly research for some decades now, this book is the first to provide such a cross-cultural perspective. But more than that, its focus moves from the usual Global North to encompass other regimes and cultures, providing a much-needed voice within the mainstream criminological literature for non-English speaking perspectives. These perspectives provide rich insight into penality in South America, Southern and Western Europe, and the post-soviet region, filling an important gap in the literature and challenging dominant perspectives in the field. In this sense, it encapsulates Connell's conception of 'Southern Theory' outlined in her 2007 book of the same name, by disrupting 'the global dynamics of knowledge in social science'. It also offers an array of original empirical analysis – from the treatment of migrant populations in Greece, to the use of penal fines in Spain and the political economy of punishment in South America – the contribution of which is significant for penality and also for criminology in general.

Insightful chapters by Ignacio González and Dario Melossi help set the theoretical framework for critical analysis of the political economy of punishment. Drawing on the work of Foucault, we are first treated by Melossi to a compelling Neo-Marxist inquiry into the discipline and subordination of outcast populations – an argument that neatly illustrates my earlier comments about post-Colonial treatment of Indigenous Australians. This works beautifully with the later exposition of how Bourdieu's concepts of symbolic violence, bureaucratic field and habitus can usefully inform our study. González's argument that the main challenges to the political economy of punishment – namely, its tendency towards economic determinism and the charge that it 'does not pay enough attention to existing reciprocal influences operating between the productive, penal, political and cultural systems' – can be overcome by bringing together the materialist and symbolic analysis of punishment, is a revelation. Not only does it overcome the charge of essentialism of material relations, suggesting that symbolic frameworks are 'matrices or schemas' that could have been different under different circumstances, the concept of symbolic violence explains how relations of domination are successfully produced and concealed as part of the creation of habitus. These exciting theoretical developments further enhance the originality of the book, and make for necessary reading.

It is no wonder this book has achieved such a high standard – its editors, Dario Melossi, Máximo Sozzo and José A. Brandariz-García between them have produced a highly distinguished body of work on the political economy of punishment, and this work is a serious addition to that, one that I suspect will have positive implications for future research in the field of penality. I hereby commend it to you.

Sharon Hayes
Co-Editor, Routledge Critical Studies in Crime, Diversity and Criminal Justice
Conjoint Fellow, University of Newcastle, Callaghan, Australia

Acknowledgements

This book is the outcome of a series of debates about the analytical tradition of the political economy of punishment and its impact on recent political economic accounts on penality, which were held in international conferences during the last few years. Initially, this project arose out of the international conference *The Political Economy of Punishment Today: Visions, Debates and Challenges*, held at the Law School of the University of A Coruna, Spain, on 17–18 September 2014, which was chaired by the three editors of this volume. Our gratitude goes to the organisers of that conference, the ECRIM research group (University of A Coruna). We owe a debt of gratitude also to the participants, a wide of number of whom have contributed to this book with chapters based on the talks given in A Coruna. Likewise, we are grateful to the institutions that funded the original conference, namely the University of A Coruna and the Council for Culture, Education and Universities of the Galician autonomous government (Spain).

The conversation that has led to this book encouraged us to organise three panel sessions on the political economy of punishment within the annual conferences of the European Society of Criminology held in Oporto (Portugal, September 2015) and Muenster (Germany, September 2016), as well as within the annual meeting of the American Society of Criminology that took place in San Francisco (USA) in November 2014. Thank you to the participants and audience of these sessions who helped us to refine our perspective on the political economy analysis on penality.

Finally, we are deeply grateful to Routledge-Taylor and Francis, especially to our editors, Tom Sutton and Hannah Catterall, for their enthusiasm in accepting this project, their patience in dealing with the preparation of the manuscript, and their constant support and assistance during the editing process.

The political economy of punishment today

An introduction

José A. Brandariz-García, Dario Melossi and Máximo Sozzo

This book seeks to address the tradition and possible current uses of a political economy of punishment. We wish to investigate the arguments and concepts that may be produced from this descriptive and interpretative framework in order to understand penality in our present. At the same time, the volume seeks to portray a 'state of the art' of contemporary debates as well as to establish an agenda of the challenges for this type of research in the broader field of studies on punishment and society. The book brings together researchers based in diverse contexts who have been exchanging views and ideas about this topic in recent years. A crucial moment of this dialogue was the International Conference *Political Economy of Punishment Today. Visions, Debates and Challenges*, held at the Law School of the University of A Coruña, Spain, on 17 and 18 September 2014 and chaired by the editors of this volume. New encounters followed in the American Society of Criminology 2014 annual meeting held in San Francisco (USA), as well as in the European Society of Criminology Conferences held at Porto, Portugal (2015) and Münster, Germany (2016). The outcome of such exchange is this collection of essays in which general theoretical arguments and concepts are discussed but also applied in order to understand different contemporary penal scenarios – from Spain to Australia, from Belgium to Georgia. As such, the collection is thought of as a contribution to an ongoing and growing line of research and debate in the sociology of punishment, hopefully opening possibilities for future developments.

The origins and early developments of the political economy of punishment

Discussions about the relationship between political economy and penality find their roots in the twentieth century, by authors influenced by the tradition of Marxism or, at least, by debate with Marxism. The economic and political turmoil of the 1920s and 1930s, in both Europe and the United States, suggested the importance of such a discussion. Authors steeped in the traditions of the Positivist School and of a criminology attentive to the importance of changing economic conditions had already tackled the issue of the relationships between political economy and crime between the nineteenth and the twentieth centuries (Ferri [1884] 1967; Bonger 1916). In light of the economic devastation brought on the United States by the crisis of 1929 such interest was revived by Thorsten Sellin in his research report on crime in the Depression (Sellin 1937). However, the issue of the specific relationship between penality and the economy had never been thematized as such. The relationship between political economy, crime and punishment had in fact been traditionally conceived according to the so-called 'legal syllogism' (Melossi 1985, p. 170): because punishment was thought of as mere consequence of crime, the relationship between political economy and punishment had to be wholly dependent on the one between political economy and crime. It would have taken a concept of the relative autonomy of penal policies from a mere 'response to crime' in order to think of the relationship between political economy and penality as an autonomous object of investigation. This would not have been the case, in a full-blown way, until the sociology of deviance of the 1960s and its insistence on the centrality of 'labelling' processes and effects.

However, a sceptical approach about the social activity of punishing made possible by a Marxist approach, allowed a young scholar in Weimar Germany who had been involved in prison administration in the 1920s, Georg Rusche, to sketch, for the first time in the history of social sciences, an analysis of the development of penality in relation to the economy that was at least partially independent from the effects of crime.[1] First in two articles (Rusche [1930] 1978, [1933] 1980), then in the basic structure of a volume that would then be completed by Otto Kirchheimer, Georg Rusche indicated that understanding the evolution of punishment over time should be connected to the conditions of the labour market, according to a principle that previous social writers had called 'less eligibility' (Rusche and Kirchheimer [1939] 2003).[2] According to Rusche and Kirchheimer,

> Every system of production tends to discover punishments which correspond to its productive relationships. It is thus neccesary to investigate the origin and fate of penal systems, the use or avoidance of specific punishments and the intensity of penal practices as they are determined by social forces, above all by economic and the fiscal forces.
>
> ([1939] 2003, p. 5)

Because de facto the goal of punishment was deterrence of the lowest social strata of society, the most important goal of political elites was to make sure that punishment would focus on the poorest sectors of society.[3] Penality would therefore follow the relative worth of the working class in a given society and given period, as this was measured by wages and the rate of unemployment. According to a classic view of the labour market (not necessarily Marxist) the intervention of penality would be more generously required, therefore, where destitution was on the rise, also because Rusche implicitly assumed that destitution would be related to increasing criminal activity.

Therefore, if it is not to contradict its goals, the penal system must be such that the most criminally predisposed groups will prefer a minimal existence in freedom, even under the most miserable condition, to a life under the pressure of a penal system.

(Rusche [1930] 1980, p. 42)

Penality would be less required instead where the working class would be tendentially full employed and could count on decent wages. Rusche and Kirchheimer demonstrate the usefulness of this interpretative key through an analysis of the history of legal punishment in Europe and North America, from the late Middle Ages to the 1930s, focusing on the transition from a pre-capitalist to a capitalist mode of production, but also on the transformations of capitalism itself.

The volume by Rusche and Kirchheimer was published at a rather unpropitious time for such concerns, right at the start of the Second World War – even if the reviews that came out of the book were indeed prestigious for the time, they were also critical, pointing to its 'economic determinism' (see Burgess 1940; Hall 1940; Marshall 1940; Riesman 1940). A republication by Russell and Russell in 1968 found quite a different audience, getting in touch probably with the more critical stance that had in the meanwhile developed about social control and its main institutions, such as prisons and mental hospitals.

In the 1970s, analysis developed about the historical roots and origins of penality and specifically of the prison system that also highlighted the importance of the relationship of punishment and more generally of institutions of social control with the capitalist political economy (Ignatieff 1978; Platt 1969). These explorations had in turn a greater or lesser proximity to the seminal work of Rusche and Kirchheimer. In Melossi and Pavarini's ([1977] 1981) version of such endeavour, however, the main concept to be focused on was no longer (or, only secondarily) the labour market – see also on this De Giorgi (2013a, pp. 45–46, 2006, pp. 9–19) and Simon (2013). The main concept was *discipline* as the link that would join together Marx's concept of surplus value and exploitation to the history of penality and more specifically of imprisonment. Particularly salient, in this light, was the work by Thorsten Sellin on the workhouse in early sixteenth century Europe (Sellin 1944) because in these institutions one could find the very seedling of the origins of capitalism, of the 'invention' of capitalism, so to speak (see the chapter by Melossi in this collection). Melossi and Pavarini – as well as, with different emphasis, Stuart Hall from his Birmingham Centre for Contemporary Cultural Studies with *Policing the Crisis* (Hall et al. 1978) – were therefore trying to come to terms with Paul Q. Hirst's critique of the critical criminological enterprise, that he had characterized as the vain attempt to call 'Marxist' something that was instead framed in the hopeless language of 'bourgeois' sociology – see the exchange between Hirst and Taylor and Walton at the end of *Critical Criminology* (Taylor, Walton and Young 1975, pp. 203–243). Marx's central concepts of surplus value, original accumulation and the capitalist organization of work played instead a central role in *The Prison and the Factory*'s reconstruction of the origins of the prison system in Europe and America, in the same way in which Gramsci's concept of hegemony was Stuart Hall's main organizing concept in *Policing the Crisis*. In Melossi and Pavarini's view, discipline was the crucial connector between the centrality of the factory in the early stages of capitalism and the contemporary construction of institutions of social control 'ancillary to the factory', as these had been conceptualized, at first, by Jeremy Bentham in his famous *Panopticon* (Bentham [1787] 1995).

At the same time, as it is well known, Michel Foucault published his book *Discipline and Punish. The Birth of the Prison* ([1975] 1977). The relationship of this book – as in general of this author's work – to Marxist perspectives and vocabularies is complex and has given rise to dissimilar assessments (Garland 1990, pp. 131–155; Melossi 2006 and in this volume, Valverde and O'Malley 2014). In any case, it is relevant that Foucault introduced a complimentary reference to the book of Rusche and Kirchheimer, among the few made to previous analyses on the evolution of penality throughout the book. He points out that, 'Rusche and Kirchheimer's great book, *Punishment and Social Structure*, provides a number of essential reference points' (Foucault [1975] 1977, p. 24). In particular, he considers that they made a significant contribution by separating the evolution of penality from the evolution of crime and ideas about crime and punishment and by stating that mechanisms of punishment should be analysed as producing 'positive' rather than 'negative' effects. And even if '[t]here are no doubt a number of observations about such a strict correlation' (Foucault [1975] 1977, p. 25), nevertheless, at the same time he explicitly supports Rusche and Kirchheimer's main argument:

> But we can surely accept the general proposition that, in our societies, the systems of punishment are to be situated in a certain 'political economy' of the body: even if they do not make use of violent or bloody punishment, even when they use 'lenient' methods involving confinement or correction, it is always the body that is at issue – the body and its forces, their utility and their docility, their distribution and their submission.
>
> (Foucault [1975] 1977, p. 25)

It would seem that Foucault's ambivalence about Rusche and Kirchheimer's book reflected that which he manifested with respect to Marx's legacy in the more general theoretical debates of his time.[4]

In the 1970s Rusche and Kirchheimer's work was translated into quantitative empirical research oriented to test hypotheses about the relationship between the conditions of the labour market and penality by analysing historical series of statistical data in some countries – the United States, Great Britain, France and Italy. The preferred indicator of penality was the incarceration rate and the preferred indicator of the working class situation was the unemployment rate –

although other indicators were also used in more sophisticated versions. This research continued to develop in the 1980s and early 1990s. In general, it showed the existence of positive and significant associations between penal and economic variables (Box 1987; Box and Hale 1982, 1985; Galster and Scaturo 1985; Greenberg 1977, 1980; Hale 1989a, 1989b; Inverarity and McCarthy 1988; Jankovic 1977; Wallace 1980; see Chiricos and DeLone 1992, pp. 427–428; De Giorgi 2006, pp. 19–39).[5]

However, these associations between economic and penal variables did not imply an explanation of this connection. In many cases, the attempts to build such an explanation in this literature were thin and mechanistic (Box 1987; Chiricos and De Lone 1992; Hale 1989b; Melossi 1985; 1998, Sutton 2000). On the contrary, we can highlight the approach by Melossi (1985, 1993, 1994, 1998). Melossi draws on theoretical tools from the interactionist and pragmatist sociology and the more contemporary critical criminology literature on 'crime waves'. For him, the connection between these two elements is produced by a 'discursive chain' that links the ways in which social and economic problems and crime and penal problems are perceived by the elites in diverse moments of the economic cycles. These elites' perceptions connect different fields – from entrepreneurs to politicians to judges – and deploy 'vocabularies of motive', constructing a moral and political climate, that is translated in coherent decisions and actions (Melossi 1985). This point of view implies a strong separation from the metaphor structure/superstructure, even in its more sophisticated re-elaborations in Marxist social and political theory (Melossi 1985; see also Melossi 2003, 2006, 2011, pp. 57–60).

Other subsequent research raised doubts about a simplistic connection between unemployment and imprisonment rates, particularly in relation to the case of the USA during the 1980s and 1990s, when cyclically oscillating unemployment rates were combined with an extraordinary increase of incarceration rates (D'Alessio and Stolzenberg 1995, 2002; Melossi 2003; Sutton 2000, 2004; Western and Beckett 1999). Some authors within this tradition tried to avoid the reductionist translation of the 'situation of the working class' to the unemployment rate (Melossi 2003). John Sutton, in two very influential studies, promoted the simultaneous use of other variables to produce a more complex quantitative analysis of the connection between 'the economy' and penality – like male labour-force participation, inequality, spending on unemployment benefits, unionization of the working class and degree or corporatism of labour market institutions (Sutton 2000, pp. 353–364, 2004, pp. 171–178).

The renewal of the political economy of punishment

During the second half of the 1980s and 1990s, much of the sociology of punishment – especially in the English-speaking world – experienced an important 'culturalist turn'. This theoretical mutation was strongly linked to the crisis of

Marxism as an intellectual tradition – especially after the fall of many of the regimes of so-called 'Real Socialism' (Melossi 2003, p. ix). At the same time, in a paradoxical way, this coincided with the consolidation of a post-Fordist restructuring of the capitalist regime of accumulation and the strong diffusion of neoliberalism as a rationality and political project, with its vast consequences of growing social inequality and exclusion (De Giorgi 2013a, pp. 48, 53–54). These economic, social, cultural and political changes in many countries coincided with the production of a strong – though also unequal – increase in punitiveness in the penal field – for example, in the United States and the United Kingdom.

These transformations have been the object of a new generation of social research developed since the 2000s that returned to the exploration of the relation between political economy and penality. The recent work by Alessandro De Giorgi (2000, 2002, 2006, 2011, 2013a, 2013b) can be highlighted in this direction. De Giorgi departs from the tradition of the political economy of punishment – making one of the most significant contributions to its historization – but sustains the need to update its tools in order to account for the changes in contemporary capitalism. For example, he believes that the 'situation of the lowest socially significant proletarian class' to which Rusche and Kirchheimer referred in their work of the 1930s as a crucial element in understanding the extent and intensity of penality, cannot be simply translated – as was often the case in the literature of the 1970s and 1980s – in the statistical indicator of unemployment, since this makes us lose sight of the extreme diffusion of situations of subordination, insecurity and hyper-exploitation in the post-Fordist labour market. He even advocates including in the understanding of this 'situation' elements that go beyond 'narrow economic dynamics' (De Giorgi 2013a, pp. 54–55, 2013b, pp. 28–29).

In much of his work, De Giorgi (2000, 2002, 2006, 2011) tends to emphasize the existence of a homogeneous tendency towards an exclusive and harsh penal policy at a global level, crossing regional and national borders, as a result of equally convergent mutations of contemporary capitalism. To a certain extent this view persists in his more recent works, when he emphasizes the role of the selectivity – but not the scale – of penality as a feature of severity that can be found both in the United States and Europe – impacting respectively on urban minorities and immigrants coming from the Global South (De Giorgi 2013b, pp. 35–38). However, in dialogue with other recent intellectual productions – as we shall see – he seems to give a greater place to the recognition of penal differences linked to diverse institutional conditions in contemporary capitalist economies (De Giorgi 2013a, pp. 51–52). In any case, he appeals to the need for the political economy of punishment to become 'post-reductionist' and 'culturally sensitive' by being able to 'overcome the false alternative between 'structure' and 'culture', while addressing the important theoretical concerns raised by other critical perspectives in the field of punishment and society' (De Giorgi 2013a, p. 48, 52, 2013b, p. 42). This implies including in the analysis the weight of political, institutional and cultural dimensions, the 'extra-economic' factors (De Giorgi 2013a, p. 54, 2013b, p. 41).[6]

In relation to some of these concerns, there is another series of recent works that has centered around the exploration of the link between political economy and penality, but from a comparative perspective, stressing penal differences and divergences in the contemporary world. This intellectual production calls into question the previous vision – associated with much of the literature since the 1970s – which views capitalism as a homogenous entity across the national and regional borders of the world. John Sutton (2004, pp. 171–172), for instance, in his study of the 'political economy of imprisonment' in 15 affluent capitalist democracies, emphasized the need to take into account the institutional foundations of Western capitalist economies and the consequences of these differences for economic performance, pointing to the uneven capacities for regulating the macro-economy and containing inequality. He distinguished between three groups of nations – 'Anglo-American democracies', 'Scandinavian social democracies' and 'corporatist democracies' – and developed a complex statistical analysis, coming to the conclusion that the determinant element in the level and evolution of imprisonment rates should be sought not so much in business cycles as in the crucial differences between corporate and neoliberal economies.

In this regard, the work of Cavadino and Dignan (2006, 2011, 2014) has been crucial. Unlike Sutton, these authors present few explicit links to the precedents developed in the tradition of the political economy of punishment. They make a comparative study of 12 countries, predominantly of the Global North, based on a classification of types of contemporary capitalist economies – inspired to the work of Esping-Andersen (1990) – that distinguishes 'neoliberal economies' (e.g. USA), 'corporatist conservative economies' (e.g. Germany), 'corporatist social-democratic economies' (e.g. Sweden) and 'corporatist oriental economies' (Japan). For Cavadino and Dignan these 'family groupings' have different levels of punitiveness, measured centrally by the rate of imprisonment. They consider that there may be a significant association of such different levels with the different types of political economy.[7] They argue that the analysis should not stop there and seek to understand this significant association by exploring various possibilities in order to explain it. In their work, they are not conclusive about it. However, after giving up on alternative hypotheses, they point to the crucial role of the 'choices' of the 'penal elite' which directs the exercise of the 'power to punish' – among which judicial decisions stand out. These choices are in turn influenced by 'penal culture and ideologies', always in relation to the broader 'political and cultural mood' (Cavadino and Dignan 2006, pp. 31, 35, 46, 338–339, 2011, pp. 201–203). They also consider that these choices are influenced by certain 'institutional' conditions such as the characteristics of political parties and penal agencies – their greater or lesser degree of bureaucratization and centralization (Cavadino and Dignan 2006, pp. 31–32, 36, 335, 2011, pp. 209–211). They emphasize the role of these elements as mediators of the influences that arise from the specific type of political economy and that would allow their translation into penal practices and outcomes (Cavadino and Dignan 2006, pp. 36, 337). However, in their more recent texts, Cavadino and Dignan also seem to recognize that certain elements may impact on penality, regardless of the type of political economy, going beyond the idea of mediation (2011, p. 209).

Another important contribution in this new emerging comparative research, has been the recent work of Nicola Lacey (2008, 2010a, 2010b, 2011, 2012, 2013). Based on these precedents – and claiming its connection with the tradition of the political economy of punishment – she takes up the distinction generated in the literature on 'varieties of capitalism' (Hall and Soskice 2001) between two types of contemporary capitalist political economy: 'liberal market economies' (LME) and 'coordinated market economies' (CME) – simplifying the classification used by Cavadino and Dignan. She uses this distinction to research comparatively a group of 'advanced capitalist' countries. The variations of incarceration rates previously observed by Cavadino and Dignan can be understood from her point of view as a consequence of the types of political economy. In the CME there is a tendency to create incentives for moderate and inclusionary penal policy whereas in the LME there is a tendency to create incentives for a harsh and exclusionary penal policy. It seems crucial to Lacey to advance beyond description, towards the explanation of this connection and for this she has worked in the elaboration and application to different scenarios of a model of 'interlinking variables', with a strong weight of institutional dimensions (Lacey 2008, p. 56, 2011, p. 216, 2012, pp. 209–210). In this model, she includes the characteristics of the economy, but also of the political system (including electoral arrangements and the strength of professional bureaucracy), of the welfare state, of the constitutional structure (including the distribution of decision-making power, the tenure and selection of the judiciary and prosecutors and the impact of the constitutional framework on what may be criminalized) and finally, the institutional capacity to include those regarded as 'others' (Lacey 2008, pp. 62–169, 2011, pp. 222–235). Lacey repeatedly uses the notion of mediation to express the role played by the variables included in her model beyond the type of political economy (2008, p. 57, 2010a, p. 104, 2011, pp. 215, 217). Nevertheless, at different moments, she also recognizes, as Cavadino and Dignan, their 'independence' (2010a, p. 105, 2013, p. 274)[8] (see on these comparative perspectives, the chapter by Sozzo in this collection).

As we have seen, in the last 15 years there has been a strong renewal of studies that explore the link between political economy and penality, giving rise to a rich variety of alternatives and possibilities.

Great Recession and penality

Political economic analyses of punishment have regained momentum in the recent past, against the backdrop of what has come to be known as the Great Recession. The economic turmoil initiated in 2007–2008, with all its dire consequences in terms of unemployment, inequality and impoverishment, makes up a most suitable case study in order to examine the impact of economic crises on penality.

A broad range of countries has witnessed relevant penal changes since the onset of the financial crisis. As regards to Group of Twenty (G20) nations, incarceration rates have prominently risen in countries such as Australia, Brazil, Indonesia and especially Turkey. Nonetheless, incarceration rates have declined during this period in other jurisdictions, such as Japan, Russia and South Africa.

Recent changes are no less striking in the European Union (EU) context. Even though in some countries (such as Belgium and Portugal) incarceration rates have escalated since the beginning of the economic turmoil, there has been a general downward trend of prison population rates in EU jurisdictions (Dünkel 2016; Karstedt 2013). Unlike the previous phase, incarceration rates have significantly fallen from 2008 to 2016 in Germany, in Spain and most particularly in the Netherlands. This rate has also dwindled in France, Ireland, Italy, UK and the Scandinavian nations (particularly in Finland and Sweden), as well as in a variety of Eastern European countries (Dünkel 2016).

In addition, the downsizing of the US prison system should be particularly highlighted. After more than three decades of exponential growth of prison population rates, which turned the US prison system into a mass incarceration model, the rise of the correctional population slowed down at the turn of the century and finally began to decline since 2008. Although this decrease has been less prominent than those of some EU countries (De Giorgi 2015, Krisberg 2016), it stands in stark contrast with the previous evolution. The US incarceration rate has dwindled from 760 inmates per 100,000 inhabitants in 2008 to 670 inmates per 100,000 inhabitants in 2015.[9]

The US academic literature has widely acknowledged the influence of the economic crisis on this correctional population decline (Austin 2016; Aviram 2015, 2016; Clear and Frost 2014; Gottschalk 2015a). The Great Recession has enabled the claim on the financial unsustainability of the mass incarceration model to gain traction across the US political field. Yet the economic turmoil seems to have operated as a condition of possibility, merely facilitating the influence of other factors on the current prison cycle (Aviram 2015; Clear and Frost 2014).

The significant decline of crime rates appears to be a critical determinant of the current situation, according to some authors (Austin 2016; Clear and Frost 2014; Simon et al. 2008). This widely analysed crime drop began in the mid-1990s (Beckett and Sasson 2004; Van Dijk 2014; Zimring 2007) and it has uninterruptedly continued throughout the economic crisis period (Crutchfield 2014; Rosenfeld and Messner 2013). In fact, from 2008 to 2015 violent crime rates fell by 18.8 per cent – in spite of a slight growth in the last biennium – and property crime rates declined by 22.6 per cent.[10] There does not appear to be, though, a direct relation between this crime drop and the downsizing of the US prison system; on the contrary, this relation has been mediated by the consolidation of certain collective representations on crime and punishment.

The long-lasting period of crime decline, and particularly the persistent drop of violent crime rates, has allowed key political actors to abandon their former punitivist stance (Dagan and Teles 2014, 2016; Schoenfeld 2016), a transformation mirrored in the media field (Beckett *et al.* 2016). What is more, the long cycle of crime drop has had a significant influence on public punitiveness and the fear of crime. In contrast to the conclusions of previous studies on the relation between socio-economic uncertainty and rise of public punitiveness (Chancer and Donovan 1996; Costelloe *et al.* 2009), a number of indicators unambiguously show a decline of both fear of crime and subjective punitiveness in the recent past (Clear and Frost 2014; Gottschalk 2015a; Petersilia 2016). This apparent paradox may surely be explained by the prominence achieved during the current economic context by other collective preoccupations, such as terrorism, immigration or the crisis of the middle classes (Aviram 2015; Schoenfeld 2016; Simon *et al.* 2008).

In short, the reinforced concern over public spending, decisively fostered by the economic recession, together with a persistent crime decline and low levels of public punitiveness have enabled the recent turn of penal policies. In the US case, during the Obama administration a wide number of measures geared towards decreasing the correctional population have been implemented, such as setting prison population caps, strengthening the utilization of both parole and non-custodial sentences, and even closing down correctional facilities (Austin 2016; Clear and Frost 2014; Gottschalk 2013, 2015a). The judiciary power has played a key role in this regard, especially in California (Gottschalk 2015a; Simon 2011, 2014). This has been supplemented with an intense public and political debate on crime and punishment, in which unseen alliances between liberal and conservative sectors have been set in order to downsize the prison system (Beckett *et al.* 2016; Dagan and Teles 2016; Petersilia and Cullen, 2015). The centre of gravity of penal policies seems to have slid towards the so-called 3-Rs, i.e. re-entry, justice reinvestment and reduction of recidivism (Clear and Frost 2014; De Giorgi 2015; Gottschalk 2015a). By contrast, profound penological reforms have been wanting, with the exception of the passage of a number of criminal statutes aimed at scaling down the sentences to be enforced in drug cases (Aviram 2015; Beckett *et al.* 2016; Gottschalk 2015a).

A range of EU countries have also enacted legal and administrative measures seeking to put an end to correctional population growth, such as the UK (FitzGerald and Hale 2013; Matthews 2014) and especially Italy – following the European Court of Human Rights (ECHR) ruling *Torreggiani* v. *Italy*, of 8 January 2013, which obliged Italian law enforcement agencies to significantly reduce prison overcrowding through the release of prisoners and the increasing use of non-custodial sentences.

One compelling question needs to be asked whether the current prison situation will be short-lived or rather will be consistent enough to give rise to a new era of moderate penality. In contrast to optimistic accounts (Aviram 2015; Clear and Frost 2014; Karstedt 2013; Simon 2014), a set of authors have argued that penal policies essentially fuelled by financial concerns (what Aviram 2015, 2016, calls the 'humonetarianism' standpoint) are not suitable to open up a new period of punitive frugality (Beckett et *al.* 2016; Cate and HoSang 2017; De Giorgi 2015; Gottschalk 2015a, 2015b). At least in the US case, as it has been pointed out, penal reforms have had a narrow scope, exclusively affecting the so-called 'non-non-nons' (non-violent, non-serious, non-sexual offenders) (Beckett *et al.* 2016; Gottschalk 2015a; Seeds 2017). Moreover, a perspective focused on the 'dollars and cents' of the correctional system is conspicuously incapable of dismantling deep-seated apparatuses of mass incarceration such as that of the US (Cate and HoSang 2017; Gottschalk 2015a, 2015b; Krisberg 2016; Petersilia and Cullen 2015). Consequently, the US literature (Beckett *et al.* 2016; De Giorgi 2015a; Gottschalk 2015a; Simon 2014) has convincingly claimed that the gargantuan task of constructing the bases of a moderate penality requires an in-depth conversation on the harmful effects of mass imprisonment on inmates, their families, their communities and society in its entirety. This debate is largely still to be carried out, and most likely the recent coming into office of the Trump administration, with all its rhetoric of law and order, criminalization of immigrants, renewed war on terror and privatization of the correctional system, will definitely put this conversation aside.

Even more interestingly, the downward trend affecting many national prison systems challenges conclusions set out by political economy of punishment studies in the 1970s and 1980s[11] – and even some of the arguments elaborated by Rusche and Kirchheimer (Aviram 2015). As is widely known, the Great Recession has had most significant consequences in terms of huge public spending cutbacks, escalating unemployment and precariousness, rising inequality, widespread impoverishment and an increasing exploitation of the workforce. In contrast to what had been theorized by political economy of punishment's analytical frameworks, this direst economic context has not given birth to a rise of punitiveness and the growth of correctional populations – with some exceptions, as we have seen. With regard to neoliberalism, it is evident that the Great Recession has not put an end to neoliberal socio-economic policies. On the contrary, since the onset of the so-called 'age of austerity' (Lapavitsas *et al.* 2012), neoliberalism has made up the theoretical basis of the policies implemented by a wide number of institutions, national and supranational alike, to deal with the consequences of economic turmoil (Dardot and Laval [2009] 2014).

It might be the case that the economic recession has not been the pivotal cause of the current prison cycle (Matthews 2014). It may have played the more humble role of not hindering a trend that began before 2007–2008, and that has been determined by non-economic forces. Whether this perspective is misleading or not, the recent crisis calls for fresh analyses on the political economy of punishment.

Contents of the book

As we already said, this collection combines chapters in which general theoretical arguments and concepts related to the political economy of punishment's tradition and present are discussed with chapters in which they are applied in order to understand different contemporary penal scenarios.

In the chapter following this general introduction, Dario Melossi reconsiders the significance of the discipline of living labour for the political economic analyses on punishment, a topic that had been at the centre of his renowned book, co-authored with Massimo Pavarini, *The Prison and the Factory* ([1977] 1981) as well as, of course, in Michel Foucault's path-breaking work, *Discipline and Punish* ([1975] 1977). Melossi compellingly claims that this perspective eludes the traces of 'economism' embedded in Rusche and Kirchheimer's ([1939] 2003) reading of penality. In his chapter, Melossi emphasizes the relevance of class revolts and struggles in the crisis that has accompanied the overall system of social control and penality since the 1970s. Consequently, drawing partially upon the recently published Foucault's lectures, *The Punitive Society* ([2013] 2015), Melossi argues that, from the perspective of a Marx-oriented political economy of punishment, the teaching of obedience and the subordination of (frequently ethnicized) outcast populations have been, and continue to be, also in post-industrial capitalism, the principal ideological characteristics of the contemporary penal project.

Máximo Sozzo, in the second chapter of the book, examines a body of literature that has recently given way to a renaissance of the political economic analyses on punishment. More precisely, he studies a range of books and essays that have comparatively explored penality in different jurisdictions through the lens, among other viewpoints, of various models of capitalist political economy. For these purposes, Sozzo thoroughly analyses both Michael Cavadino and James Dignan's work (2006, 2011, 2014) and Nicola Lacey's research (2008, 2010a, 2010b, 2011, 2012, 2013). In his chapter, Sozzo explores whether these contributions set a dialogue with the tradition of the political economy of punishment, as well as how they define the disparate schemes of political economy. Moreover, he delves into how these investigations relate such economic models to the penal field. In this framework, Sozzo highlights the strengths of this set of analyses and at the same time points out their shortcomings, crucially among them the pitfalls of taxonomic explorations and their inability to account for recent penal changes witnessed in Global South jurisdictions.

In the next chapter, Ignacio González reviews the political economy of punishment analytical frameworks in light of the French sociologist Pierre Bourdieu's conceptual system. For these purposes, González briefly traces a genealogy of the political economy of punishment tradition and expounds the key critiques elaborated in the academic literature. He subsequently reconsiders these criticisms through the lens of several analytical tools forged by Bourdieu that are increasingly widespread among punishment and society scholarship, namely symbolic violence (Bourdieu [1977] 1979, [1982] 1991), bureaucratic field (Bourdieu (1986, [1993] 1994, [2012] 2014) and habitus (Bourdieu [1980] 1990, [1997] 2000). From this standpoint, González signals that by engaging in dialogue with these concepts, the political economy of punishment tradition may overcome the most challenged aspects of its analytical framework, such as the prevailing role given to the economic field and the predominance of the material dimension of penality over its symbolic dimension.

In the fourth chapter, Patricia Faraldo-Cabana sheds light on a topic hardly researched by the political economy of punishment tradition, i.e. the use of fines as a means of punishment. To this end, Faraldo critically analyses the hypothesis drawn up by Rusche and Kirchheimer in Chapter 10 of *Punishment and Social Structure* ([1939] 2003; a section actually exclusively written by Kirchheimer) on the utilization of pecuniary sentences, especially in periods of economic crisis. Faraldo tests the German authors' hypothesis by examining two case studies on the use of fines, the German criminal justice system during the crisis of 1929 and the Spanish criminal justice system in the context of the financial turmoil initiated in 2008. In these analyses on the penal consequences of both recessions, she takes into consideration the relevance of both the statutorily established fine system and the legal instruments set in place to tackle non-payments of fines. Faraldo thereby contributes to the political economic analysis of fines and of their relation with prison sentences in phases of economic collapse.

Charlotte Vanneste's article (Chapter 5) assumes a long-term perspective, in line with the long economic cycles theories, in which she prominently incorporates the influence of specific political factors. Vanneste elaborates an account of the relation of economic policies and penality in Belgium since the country gained independence in 1830. Her chapter is particularly focused on the transformations of the last four decades, with regard to which she examines the correlation of incarceration rates and economic inequality indexes and changes in electoral results. She complements her analysis by taking into account a set of recent works (such as Cavadino and Dignan 2006, 2014; Lacey 2008; Lappi-Seppälä 2008, 2011a, 2011b, 2014; Sutton 2004) that relate penality to political economic models and types of political systems. Finally, Vanneste concludes her detailed examination of the Belgian penal field by comparatively exploring the economic crisis of 1929 and that of 2008 in terms of their consequences on both the economic sphere and the criminal justice system.

In the sixth chapter, Hilde Tubex delivers a contribution to the studies on sub-national penality by considering the Australian case. She stresses that Australia is characterized by a number of economic traits that, according to the neoliberal penality literature (Wacquant 2009) and to well-known comparative research on penal systems, are correlated with a high degree of punitiveness. Tubex substantiates, however, that penal severity, as measured by incarceration rates, notably varies across Australian jurisdictions. Consequently, she carries out a sophisticated analysis to account for these differences, which delves with several state jurisdictions. Her study, which is largely based in Cavadino and Dignan's (2006) and Lacey's (2008) models, takes into consideration both economic factors and political factors. Moreover, she explores the statistical data on the penal management of indigenous population, which confirm the persistence of a (post-) colonial model of penality in the Australian case.

Zelia A. Gallo draws up in Chapter 7 a political economic reading on penality in the Italian case. She emphasizes that this case, with all its complexity and internal differences, cannot be understood from the viewpoint of most widespread political economy of punishment theories, such as the thesis of post-Fordist penality (De Giorgi 2006) or that of the varieties of capitalism (Lacey 2008, 2011, 2013). Gallo points out therefore that – especially in the Italian case – political variables should be additionally considered, for they supplement the materialist analysis, by bridging the economic field and the penal field. She examines the features of Italian penality, which is characterized by the alternation of punitiveness and moderation, as well as the Italian political economic model and its welfare system. Furthermore, she develops an analytical framework to explicate the impact of political factors on Italian penality, by regarding, among other components, political institutions, political culture and political dynamics. Gallo thereby substantiates that there is nothing inevitable in the couplet political economy-penality.

Chapter 8, authored by Gavin Slade, locates the political economy of punishment analysis within an under-researched geographical area, i.e. the post-Soviet region. This region has experienced over the last quarter of a century, concomitantly with an abrupt transition to market capitalism, an overall trend of prison downsizing – albeit with some meaningful divergences – in contrast to the general rise of punitiveness witnessed in other jurisdictions. After having explored penal changes, particularly related to the use of imprisonment, in the whole post-USSR world, Slade focuses on two peculiar national cases, i.e. punitiveness-increasing Georgia and decarcerating Kazakhstan. He examines in detail the economic liberalization models embraced by both countries. In addition, Slade complements his analytical framework with an institutionalist approach, which unveils the political needs of the Georgian and Kazakh states engendered by such capitalist liberalization and the ways in which the criminal justice system, and especially the prison system, have been determined by these needs.

Leonidas K. Cheliotis reflects in the ninth chapter upon the political economic dimension of migration control and the punishment of – especially irregular – migrants. Drawing on the analysis of the inclusion and exploitation of migrants within the Greek informal economic sector, he explores the relation of migration enforcement policies with their subordinated insertion within the production system. Furthermore, Cheliotis insightfully examines the symbolic dimension of these apparatuses of control and subordination and its effects on the 'host' society in its entirety. He thereby encourages overcoming the critical stance focusing on the allegedly exclusive nature of migration control and the idea of 'Fortress Europe'. Consequently, Cheliotis convincingly claims that the ways in which migrants' inclusion is actually taking place is part of the problem; in other words, it is a core component of the unjust and inhumane treatment exerted on newcomers.

The last chapter of the book revisits the political economy of punishment analysis of migration control policies. José A. Brandariz's chapter draws on this theoretical framework to examine migration penalty in Spain, both before and after the onset of the so-called Great Recession. More precisely, Brandariz tests the suitability of concepts such as less eligibility and the discipline of the (migrant) workforce to account for the evolution of this sphere of the criminal justice during the 2000s. By contrast, he argues that since the beginning of the financial turmoil Spanish migration penalty has been increasingly geared towards a model of managerial criminal justice. This chapter highlights the shortcomings of an exclusively economic account of border control policies, since this analysis requires additional viewpoints, crucially among them the sovereign dimension inherent in migration control and the othering and racialization processes underlying this area of the penal field.

We think that this collection is an important contribution to the future development of exploration of the relation between political economy and punishment in order to understand our penal present.

Notes

1 Émile Durkheim at the end of the nineteenth century, had already developed a sociological approach to punishment independent of crime, although he linked its evolution and function to mutations and reinforcement of the collective consciousness, as a set of moral beliefs and values common to the average members of society, in the framework of the transition from a primitive to a modern society (Durkheim [1893] 1997, [1895] 1982, [1899] 1973).
2 The volume by Rusche and Kirchheimer was intended to be the very first publication by the Frankfurt School of Research in Social Science in their new site in New York at Columbia University. See the Introduction by Dario Melossi (2003) on the genesis and fortune of the book.
3 On this see De Giorgi (2013a, pp. 41–44, 2006, pp. 3–9) and Garland (1990, pp. 83–110).
4 As Foucault states in an interview in 1975,

> there is also a sort of game that I play with this. I often quote concepts, texts and phrases from Marx, but without feeling obliged to add the authenticating label of a footnote with a laudatory phrase to accompany the quotation. As long as one does that, one is regarded as someone who knows and reveres Marx, and will be suitably honoured in the so-called Marxist journals. But I quote Marx without saying so, without quotation marks, and because people are incapable of recognising Marx's texts I am thought to be someone who doesn't quote Marx. When a physicist writes a work of physics, does he feel it necessary to quote Newton and Einstein? He uses them, but he doesn't need the quotation marks, the footnote and the eulogistic comment to prove how completely he is being faithful to the master's thought. And because other physicists know what Einstein did, what he discovered and proved, they can recognise him in what the physicist writes. It is impossible at the present time to write history without using a whole range of concepts directly or indirectly linked to Marx's thought and situating oneself within a horizon of thought which has been defined and described by Marx. One might even wonder what difference there could ultimately be between being a historian and being a Marxist.
>
> (Foucault, M. ([1975] 1980, pp. 52–53)

5 In some examples of this literature the possible mediation of crime rates between economic and penal variables was also analysed. But, in general, it was considered not plausible (Chiricos and DeLone 1992; Melossi 1985, 1998).
6 Other authors have recently produced contributions that have many points in common with De Giorgi's perspective. For example, Robert Reiner has published several texts on the importance of the changes in political economy in order to understand crime control strategies in the present (Reiner 2006, 2007). In the same direction, Wacquant has elaborated an important narrative on penal change, that gives a central role to the impact of the transformations of capitalism from Fordism to Post-Fordism, although he sustained that it 'does not belong to the genre ... of the 'political economy of imprisonment', since – in a rather narrow interpretation – this tradition of research has a 'congenital incapacity to recognize the specific efficacy and the materiality of symbolic power' (Wacquant 2009, p. xvii; see also Wacquant [1999] 2009, 2005, 2013).
7 Cavadino and Dignan recognize the presence of a strong tendency towards the growth of the punitiveness that crosses the national and regional borders, although they state that it is not able to erode the penal differences that persist over time (2006, pp. 32–35, 43–49).
8 Lacey also recognizes – as Cavadino and Dignan – the existence of a tendency towards the increase of punitiveness in the CMEs, but she sustains the persistence of the observed penal differences (2010b, pp. 781–782, 2011, pp. 215–216, 2013, pp. 270–271).
9 Source: Bureau of Justice Statistics. Available at www.bjs.gov [accessed 20 February 2017].
10 Source: FBI. Available at ucr.fbi.gov [accessed 20 February 2017].
11 In this literature a strong link between 'economic crisis', moments of 'depression' or 'recession' and the growth of the extent and intensity of penality was sustained. For example, Melossi said: 'There is no doubt that times of depression are times of punishment' (Melossi 1985, p. 181; see also Allen 1996; Arvanites and Defina 2006). However, Box has mentioned briefly the possibility of the existence of 'anomalies' in this typical relationship (Box 1987, p. 191; see also Box and Hale 1982, 1985). On this point, see also Melossi (2013, p. 429, fn. 5); Crutchfield (2014); FitzGerald and Hale (2013); Gottschalk (2015a); Hale (2013); Reiner (2007); Van Dijk (2014); Weatherburn (1992).

References

Allen, R.C. (1996). Socioeconomic Conditions and Property Crime: A Comprehensive Review and Test of the Professional Literature. *American Journal of Economics and Sociology*, 55 (3), 293–308.

Arvanites, T.M. and Defina, R.H. (2006). Business Cycles and Street Crime. *Criminology*, 44 (1), 139–164.

Austin, J. (2016). Regulating California's Prison Population: The Use of Sticks and Carrots. *The Annals of the American Academy of Political and Social Science*, 664, 84–107.

Aviram, H. (2015). *Cheap on Crime: Recession-Era Politics and the Transformation of American Punishment*. Oakland: University of California Press.

Aviram, H. (2016). The Correctional Hunger Games: Understanding Realignment in the Context of the Great Recession. *The Annals of the American Academy of Political and Social Science*, 664, 260–279.

Beckett, K., Reosti, A. and Knaphus, E. (2016). The End of an Era? Understanding the Contradictions of Criminal Justice Reform. *The Annals of the American Academy of Political and Social Science*, 664, 238–259.

Beckett, K. and Sasson, T. (2004). *The Politics of Injustice*. 2nd edn. Thousand Oaks: Sage.
Bentham, J. ([1787] 1995). *The Panopticon Writings*. London: Verso.
Bonger, W. (1916). *Criminality and Economic Conditions*. Boston: Little, Brown and Company.
Bourdieu, P. ([1977] 1979). Symbolic Power. *Critique of Anthropology*, 4, 77–85.
Bourdieu, P. ([1980] 1990). *The Logic of Practice*. Stanford: Stanford University Press.
Bourdieu, P. ([1982] 1991). *Language and Symbolic Power*. Cambridge: Polity Press.
Bourdieu, P. (1986). The Force of Law: Toward a Sociology of the Juridical Field. *The Hastings Law Journal*, 38, 805–853.
Bourdieu, P. ([1993] 1994). Rethinking the State: Genesis and Structure of the Bureaucratic Field. *Sociological Theory*, 12 (1), 1–18.
Bourdieu, P. ([1997] 2000). *Pascalian Meditations*. Stanford: Stanford University Press.
Bourdieu, P. ([2012] 2014). *On the State*. Cambridge: Polity Press.
Box, S. (1987). *Recession, Crime and Punishment*. London: Rowman & Littlefield.
Box, S. and Hale, C. (1982). Economic Crises and the Rising Prisoner Population in England and Wales. *Crime and Social Justice*, 17, 20–35.
Box, S. and Hale, C. (1985). Unemployment, Imprisonment and Prison Overcrowding. *Contemporary Crises*, 9 (3), 209–228.
Burgess, E. (1940). Book Review: Punishment and Social Structure, by G. Rusche and O. Kirchheimer. *The Yale Law Journal*, 49 (5), 986.
Cate, S. and HoSang, D. (2017). 'The Better Way to Fight Crime': Why Fiscal Arguments Do Not Restrain the Carceral State. *Theoretical Criminology* (forthcoming).
Cavadino, M. and Dignan, J. (2006). *Penal Systems. A Comparative Approach*. London: Sage.
Cavadino, M. and Dignan, J. (2011). Penal comparison: puzzling relations. *In*: Crawford, A., ed., *International and Comparative Criminal Justice and Urban Governance*. Cambridge: Cambridge University Press, 193–213.
Cavadino, M. and Dignan, J. (2014). Political economy and penal systems. *In*: Body-Gendrot, S. Hough, M., Kerezsi, K., Lévy, R. and Snacken. S., eds, *The Routledge Handbook of European Criminology*. Abingdon: Routledge, 280–294.
Chancer, L. and Donovan. P. (1996) A Mass Psychology of Punishment: Crime and the Futility of Rationally Based Approaches. *Social Justice*, 21, 50–72.
Chiricos, T. and DeLone M. (1992). Labor Surplus and Punishment: A Review and Assessment of Theory and Evidence. *Social Justice*, 39 (4), 421–446.
Clear, T.R. and Frost, N.A. (2014). *The Punishment Imperative*. New York: New York University Press.
Costelloe, M.T., Chiricos, T. and Gertz, M. (2009). Punitive Attitudes toward Criminals: Exploring the Relevance of Crime Salience and Economic Insecurity. *Punishment and Society*, 11 (1), 25–49.
Crutchfield, R.D. (2014). *Get a Job: Labor Markets, Economic Opportunity, and Crime*. New York: New York University Press.
D'Alessio, S. and Stolzenberg, L. (1995). Unemployment and the Incarceration of Pretrial Defendants. *American Sociological Review*, 60 (3), 350–359.
D'Alessio, S. and Stolzenberg, L. (2002). A Multilevel Analysis of the Relationship between Labor Surplus and Pretrial Incarceration. *Social Problems*, 49 (2), 178–193.
Dagan, D. and Teles, S.M. (2014). Locked in? Conservative Reform and the Future of Mass Incarceration. *The Annals of the American Academy of Political and Social Science*, 651, 266–276.

Dagan, D. and Teles, S.M. (2016). *Prison Break: Why Conservatives Turned Against Mass Incarceration*. New York: Oxford University Press.
Dardot, P. and Laval, C. ([2009] 2014). *The New Way of the World: On Neoliberal Society*. London: Verso.
De Giorgi, A. (2000). *Zero Tolleranze. Strategie e pratiche della società di controllo*. Roma: Derive Approdi.
De Giorgi, A. (2002). *Il governo della eccedenza. Postfordismo e controllo della moltitudine*. Verona: Ombre Corte.
De Giorgi, A. (2006). *Re-Thinking the Political Economy of Punishment*. Aldershot: Ashgate.
De Giorgi, A. (2011). Post-Fordism and penal change: The new penology as a post-disciplinary social control strategy. *In*: Melossi, D., Sozzo, M. and Sparks, R., eds, *Travels of the Criminal Question. Cultural Embeddedness and Diffusion*. Oxford: Hart, 113–143.
De Giorgi, A. (2013a). Punishment and political economy. *In*: Sparks, R. and Simon, J., eds, *The Sage Handbook of Punishment and Society*. London: Sage, 40–59.
De Giorgi, A. (2013b). Prisons and social structure in late-capitalist societies. *In*: Scott, D., ed., *Why Prison?* Cambridge: Cambridge University Press, 25–43.
De Giorgi, A. (2015). Five Theses on Mass Incarceration. *Social Justice*, 42 (2), 5–30.
Dünkel, F. (2016). The Rise and Fall of Prison Population Rates in Europe. *Criminology in Europe*, 2016/2, 2–5.
Durkheim, E. ([1893] 1997). *The Division of Labor in Society*. New York: Free Press.
Durkheim, E. ([1895] 1982). *The Rules of Sociological Method*. New York: Free Press.
Durkheim, E. ([1899] 1973). Two laws of penal evolution. *Economy and Society*, 2 (3), 285–308.
Esping-Andersen, G. (1990). *The Three Worlds of Welfare Capitalism*. Cambridge: Polity Press.
Ferri, E. ([1884] 1967). *Criminal Sociology*. New York: Agathon Press.
FitzGerald, M. and Hale, C. (2013). The politics of law and order. *In*: Hale, C. et al., eds, *Criminology*. 3rd edn. Oxford: Oxford University Press, 387–407.
Foucault, M. ([1975] 1977). *Discipline and Punish*. New York: Pantheon.
Foucault, M. ([1975] 1980). 'Prison talk'. *In*: Gordon, C., ed., *Power/Knowledge. Selected Interviews and Other Writings, 1972–1977. Michel Foucault*. New York: Pantheon Books, 37–54 (pp. 52–53).
Foucault, M. ([2013] 2015). *The Punitive Society: Lectures at the Collège de France 1972–1973*. Basingstoke: Palgrave Macmillan.
Galster, G. and Scaturo, L. (1985). The US Criminal Justice System: Unemployment and the Severity of Punishment. *Journal of Research in Crime and Delinquency*, 22 (2), 163–189.
Garland, D. (1990). *Punishment and Modern Society*. Chicago: The University of Chicago Press.
Gottschalk, M. (2013). The Carceral State and the Politics of Punishment. *In*: Simon, J. and Sparks, R., eds, *The Sage Handbook of Punishment and Society*. London: Sage, 205–241.
Gottschalk, M. (2015a). *Caught: The Prison State and the Lockdown of American Politics*. Princeton: Princeton University Press.
Gottschalk, M. (2015b). Razing the Carceral State. *Social Justice*, 42 (2), 31–51.
Greenberg, D. (1977). The Dynamics of Oscillatory Punishment Processes. *The Journal of Criminal Law and Criminology*, 68 (4), 643–651.

Greenberg, D. (1980). Penal Sanctions in Poland: A Test of Alternative Models. *Social Problems*, 28 (2), 194–204.

Hale, C. (1989a). Unemployment, Imprisonment and the Stability of Punishment Hypothesis: Some Results using Cointegration and Error Correction Models. *Journal of Quantitative Criminology*, 5 (2), 169–186.

Hale, C. (1989b). Economy, Punishment and Imprisonment. *Contemporary Crises*, 13 (4), 327–349.

Hale, C. (2013). Economic marginalization, social exclusion, and crime. *In*: Hale, C. et al., eds, *Criminology*. 3rd edn. Oxford: Oxford University Press, 289–307.

Hall, J. (1940). Book Review: Punishment and Social Structure, by G. Rusche and O. Kirchheimer. *Journal of Criminal Law and Criminology*, 30 (6), 971–973.

Hall, P.A. and Soskice, D., eds (2001). *Varieties of Capitalism*. Oxford: Oxford University Press.

Hall, S., Critcher, C., Jefferson, T., Clarke, J. and Roberts, B. (1978). *Policing the Crisis. Mugging, the State and Law and Order*. London: Palgrave.

Ignatieff, M. (1978). *A Just Measure of Pain: The Penitentiary in the Industrial Revolution, 1750–1850*. New York: Pantheon.

Inverarity, J. and McCarthy, D. (1988). Punishment and Social Structure Revisited: Unemployment and Imprisonment in the United States, 1948–1984. *The Sociological Quarterly*, 29 (2), 263–79.

Jankovic, I. (1977). Labor Market and Imprisonment. *Crime and Social Justice*, 8, 17–31.

Karstedt, S. (2013). Never Waste a Good Crisis! *Criminology in Europe*, (1), 5–11.

Krisberg, B. (2016). How Do You Eat an Elephant? Reducing Mass Incarceration in California One Small Bite at a Time. *The Annals of the American Academy of Political and Social Science*, 664, 136–154.

Lacey, N. (2008). *The Prisoners' Dilemma. Political Economy and Punishment in Contemporary Democracies*. Cambridge: Cambridge University Press.

Lacey, N. (2010a). American Imprisonment in Comparative Perspective. *Daedalus*, 139 (3), 102–114.

Lacey, N. (2010b). Differentiating among Penal States. *British Journal of Sociology*, 61 (4), 778–794.

Lacey, N. (2011). Why globalization doesn't spell convergence: models of institutional variation and the comparative political economy of punishment. *In*: Crawford, A., eds, *International and Comparative Criminal Justice and Urban Governance*. Cambridge: Cambridge University Press, 214–250.

Lacey, N. (2012). Political Systems and Criminal Justice: The Prisoners' Dilemma after the Coalition. *Current Legal Problems*, 65 (1), 203–239.

Lacey, N. (2013). Punishment, (Neo)Liberalism and Social Democracy. *In*: Sparks, R. and Simon, J., eds, *The Sage Handbook of Punishment and Society*. London: Sage, 260–280.

Lapavitsas, C., Kaltenbrunner, A., Labrinidis, G., Undo, D., Meadway, J., Michell, J., Painceira, J.P., Pires, E., Powell, J., Stenfors, A., Teles, N. and Vatikiotis, L. (2012). *Crisis in the Eurozone*. London: Verso.

Lappi-Seppälä, T. (2008). Trust, welfare, and political culture: explaining differences in national penal policies. *In*: Tonry, M., ed., *Crime and Justice: A Review of Research*, 37, 313–387.

Lappi-Seppälä, T. (2011a). Explaining national differences in the use of imprisonment. *In*: Snacken, S., Dumortier, E., eds, *Resisting Punitiveness in Europe? Welfare, Human Rights and Democracy*. London: Routledge, 35–72.

Lappi-Seppälä, T. (2011b). Explaining Imprisonment in Europe. *European Journal of Criminology*, 8 (4), 303–328.

Lappi-Seppälä, T. (2014). Imprisonment and penal demands. Exploring the dimensions and drivers of systemic and attitudinal punitivity. *In*: Body-Gendrot, S., Hough, M., Kerezsi, K., Lévy, R. and Snacken, S., eds, *The Routledge Handbook of European Criminology*. London: Routledge, 295–336.

Marshall, T.H. (1940). Book Review: Punishment and Social Structure, by G. Rusche and O. Kirchheimer, *The Economic Journal*, 50 (197), 126–127.

Matthews, R. (2014). *Realist Criminology*. London: Palgrave Macmillan.

Melossi, D. (1985). Punishment and Social Action: Changing Vocabularies of Punitive Motive within a Political Business Cycle. *Current Perspectives in Social Theory*, 6, 169–197.

Melossi, D. (1993). Gazette of Morality and Social Whip: Punishment, Hegemony and the Case of the US, 1970–1992. *Social & Legal Studies*, 2 (3), 259–279.

Melossi D (1994). The 'economy' of illegalities: normal crimes, elites, and social control in comparative analysis. In David N., ed., *The Futures of Criminology*. London: Sage, 202–219.

Melossi, D., ed. (1998). *The Sociology of Punishment*. Aldershot: Dartmouth.

Melossi, D. (2003). Introduction to the Transaction edition. The simple 'heuristic maxim' of an 'unusual human being'. *In*: Rusche, G. and Kirchheimer, O., *Punishment and Social Structure*. New Brunswick: Transaction.

Melossi, D. (2006). Penalità e 'governo delle popolazioni' tra Marx e Foucault. *Aut-Aut*, 332, 160–184.

Melossi, D. (2011). Neoliberalism's elective affinities: Penality, political economy and international relations. *In*: Melossi, D., Sozzo, M., Sparks, R., eds, *Travels of the Criminal Question. Cultural Embeddedness and Diffusion*. Oxford: Hart, 45–64.

Melossi, D. (2013). Punishment and migration between Europe and the USA: A transnational 'less eligibility'? *In*: Simon, J. and Sparks, R., eds, *The Sage Handbook of Punishment and Society*. London: Sage, 416–433.

Melossi, D. and Pavarini, M. ([1977] 1981). *The Prison and the Factory: Origins of the Penitentiary System*. London: Macmillan.

Petersilia, J. (2016). Realigning Corrections, California Style. *The Annals of the American Academy of Political and Social Science*, 664, 8–13.

Petersilia, J. and Cullen, F.T. (2015). Liberal but Not Stupid: Meeting the Promise of Downsizing Prisons. *Stanford Journal of Criminal Law and Policy*, 2, 1–43.

Platt, A. (1969). *The Child Savers: The Invention of Delinquency*. Chicago: Chicago University Press.

Reiner, R. (2006). Beyond risk: a lament for social democratic criminology. *In*: Newburn, T. and Rock, P., eds, *The Politics of Crime Control*. Oxford: Clarendon Press, 7–49.

Reiner, R. (2007). *Law and Order: An Honest Citizen's Guide to Crime and Control*. Cambridge: Polity Press.

Riesman Jr, D. (1940). Book Review: Punishment and Social Structure, by G. Rusche and O. Kirchheimer. *Columbia Law Review*, 40 (7), 1297–1301.

Rosenfeld, R. and Messner, S.F. (2013). *Crime and the Economy*. London: Sage.

Rusche, G. ([1930] 1978). Labor Market and Penal Sanction: Thoughts on the Sociology of Punishment. *Social Justice*, 10, 2–8.

Rusche, G. ([1933] 1980). Prisons Revolts or Social Policy: Lessons from America. *Social Justice*, 13, 41–44.

Rusche, G. and Kirchheimer, O. ([1939] 2003). *Punishment and Social Structure*. New Brunswick: Transaction.

Schoenfeld, H. (2016). A Research Agenda on Reform: Penal Policy and Politics across the States. *The Annals of the American Academy of Political and Social Science*, 664, 155–174.

Seeds, C. (2017). Bifurcation Nation: American Penal Policy in Late Mass Incarceration. *Punishment and Society* (forthcoming).

Sellin, T. (1937). *Research Memorandum on Crime in the Depression*. New York: Social Science Research Council.

Sellin, T. (1944). *Pioneering in Penology*. Philadelphia: University of Pennsylvania Press.

Simon, J. (2011). Editorial: Mass Incarceration on Trial. *Punishment and Society*, 13 (3), 251–255.

Simon, J. (2013). Punishment and the political technologies of the body. In Simon, J. and Sparks, R., eds, *The Sage Handbook of Punishment and Society*. London: Sage, 60–89.

Simon, J. (2014). *Mass Incarceration on Trial: A Remarkable Court Decision and the Future of Prisons in America*. New York: The New Press.

Simon, J., Haney-Lopez, I. and Frampton, M.L. (2008). Introduction. *In*: Frampton, M.L., Haney-Lopez, I. and Simon, J., eds, *After the War on Crime*. New York: New York University Press, 1–20.

Sutton, J.R. (2000). Imprisonment and Social Classification in Five Common Law Democracies, 1955–1985. *American Journal of Sociology*, 106 (2), 350–386.

Sutton, J.R. (2004). The Political Economy of Imprisonment in Affluent Western Democracies: 1960–1990. *American Sociological Review*, 69 (2), 170–189.

Taylor, I., Walton, P. and Young, J., eds (1975). *Critical Criminology*. London: Routledge and Kegan Paul.

Valverde, M. and O'Malley, P. (2014). Foucault, criminal law and the governmentalization of the state. *In*: Dubber, M., ed., *Foundational Texts on Modern Criminal Law*. Oxford: Oxford University Press, 317–333.

Van Dijk, J. (2014). It is not just the economy: Towards an alternative explanation of post-World War II crime trends in the Western world. *In*: Body-Gendrot, S., Hough, M., Kerezsi, K., Lévy, R. and Snacken, S., eds, *The Routledge Handbook of European Criminology*. Abingdon: Routledge, 109–124.

Wacquant, L. ([1999] 2009). *Prisons of Poverty*. Minneapolis: University of Minnesota Press.

Wacquant, L. (2005). The great penal leap backward. Incarceration in America from Nixon to Clinton. *In*: Pratt, J., Brown, D., Brown, M., Hallsworth, S. and Morrison, W., eds, *The New Punitiveness. Trends, Theories, Perspectives*. Cullompton: Willan, 3–36.

Wacquant, L. (2009). *Punishing the Poor: The Neoliberal Government of Social Insecurity*. Durham: Duke University Press.

Wacquant, L. (2013). Crafting the neoliberal state: workfare, prisonfare and social insecurity. *In*: Scott, D., ed., *Why Prison?* Cambridge: Cambridge University Press, 3–36.

Wallace, D. (1980). The Political Economy of Incarceration Trends in Late US Capitalism: 1971–1977. *The Insurgent Sociologist*, 11 (1), 59–66.

Weatherburn, D. (1992). Economic Adversity and Crime. *Trends and Issues in Criminal Justice*, 40, 1–9.

Western, B. and Beckett, K. (1999). How Unregulated is the US Labor Market? The Penal System and a Labor Market Institution. *American Journal of Sociology*, 104 (4), 1030–1060.

Zimring, F.E. (2007). *The Great American Crime Decline*. New York: Oxford University Press.

Chapter 1

Between struggles and discipline
Marx and Foucault on penality and the critique of political economy

Dario Melossi

What follows is a reconstruction of the conceptual genesis of *The Prison and the Factory*[1] and some of its aftermath. When, around 1974, Massimo Pavarini and I, our law degrees fresh in our pockets, decided to approach the issue of the origins of imprisonment, we seemed to have in front of us two possible venues of exploration. One we had found mentioned in Maurice Dobb's *Studies in the Development of Capitalism* (1946: pp. 23, 235) and we had then retrieved it in British libraries during a 'grand tour' of the British Critical Criminology scene: Georg Rusche and Otto Kirchheimer's *Punishment and Social Structure* ([1939] 2003).[2] However, as I later happened to suggest (Melossi 2003), I found Rusche's emphasis on the importance of the labour market a good example of 'economism' but not really of 'Marxism', as I will try to show in the remainder of this chapter. The other one was the one that we took (and, in my opinion, that Foucault took) and that was the importance of, and the emphasis on, the issue of *discipline*.

Political economy of punishment: class struggle and discipline

Much in accordance with the times that surrounded us and that we lived in, we located the site of class struggle in the factory, about the extraction of 'surplus value'. According to a view, essentially to be found in the first volume of *Capital*, at the end of the day, the value of production has to be greater than the cost of the various factors of production. This very simple and rather banal statement is at the heart of the idea of class struggle. The government of production is in fact in the hands of capital on one hand and of workers' resistance on the other. In terms of the history of imprisonment, one could not underestimate therefore the crucial importance of the institution of the 'workhouse' (Sellin 1944). The workhouse, which early seventeenth-century Dutch people called the *Rasphuis*, would in fact be central as a link with the future penitentiary, through William Penn and the Quakers especially.[3] Central also as prefiguration of the new prison institution, because of the fame and notoriety of the *Rasphuis*. Central, especially, in the relationship between penality and capitalism. What other institution could better represent in fact the Weberian 'elective affinity' (Howe 1978) of capitalism and the new form of penality? A new form of penality that could be taken to instantiate the 'spirit of capitalism' itself, a stand-in for the 'Protestant ethic' (Weber [1904–1905] 1958). Indeed, one could claim that the very 'invention' of capitalism took place in the invention of the workhouse. 'The penal question' has in fact always been close to social innovators' hearts, and both reformers and revolutionaries alike have been taken in a love-hate relationship with the prison, in which they found, perhaps, the Utopia of society they wanted, especially the Utopia of 'the new Man' they wanted to mould.

So, from the Workhouse to the Penitentiary. Then, about one century later, from the Penitentiary to the Panopticon, later celebrated in Foucault's pages. Jeremy Bentham wrote on the frontispiece of *The Panopticon* that 'The Panopticon ... [is an] ... inspection-house: containing the idea of a new principle of construction applicable to any sort of establishment, in which persons of any description are to be kept under inspection' ([1787] 1971, p. 40). He goes on to exemplify that the principle is therefore applicable to 'penitentiary-houses, prisons, houses of industry, work-houses, poor-houses, manufactories, mad-houses, lazarettos, hospitals and schools' (Ibid.). In *The Prison and the Factory* (Melossi [1977] 1981, pp. 42–46), I called this panoply of institutions 'ancillary' to 'the factory', in the sense that they were crucial to constituting, and reproducing the social discipline demanded by a capitalist mode of production.

According to Marx's reconstruction, in fact, once the labourer has entered the not so metaphoric gates of the sphere of production, it is within those gates that, like by miracle, the sale of his or her labour power eventually gives more, to the capitalist, than what the latter has anticipated for the various costs of production. This difference, which is at the basis of the capitalist's profit, can come into being, however, only if the 'freedom' of the sphere of circulation turns into the kind of (temporary) servitude of the 'sphere of production'. In fact, the capitalist will be a full-title capitalist only if, having bought the worker's labour power, he will be able, as every good proprietor, to use and enjoy his property as he likes, and therefore to impose that *discipline* of production that only warrants the difference which makes his profit. Because one has to note that, in a most 'unfortunate' manner, the labour power, which is the merchandise the capitalist has bought, comes with a human being attached, often behaving in ways that are different from those predicted and demanded by the capitalist. This struggle between a human being, the labourer, and the labourer as mere carrier of labour power, is the substance of 'class struggle'. This is the reason why it is silly to say, as it is often said, that Marx's theory is 'based on the economy'. Rather, it is, as the subtitle to *Capital* reads, a '*critique* of political economy' which locates the core of the matter in the conflict between capital and labour about exploitation. It is about a political/power struggle (which Marx called 'class struggle') over the management of human resources. The society that is ruled by capital is therefore organized around the constitution and maintenance of 'discipline', a discipline that permeates all the fundamental social institutions. It does not seem to be quite correct therefore to state that the 'Marxist theses' on penality 'do not depend upon specifically Marxist arguments such as the theory of surplus value' (Garland 1990, p. 130) because the concept of 'discipline' could not be more strictly linked to the concept of surplus value, which is indeed the core of Marxian theory. It is in fact only if the discipline 'in the sphere of production' warrants the extraction of surplus value that a capitalist system can indeed even exist as such. Whether or not one agrees with the general validity of such a view – and that is an altogether different question – there is however no doubt that the connection between 'ancillary' institutions, and the sphere of production, as institutions of reproduction of that *disciplined* labour power which is necessary to produce surplus value, is the very clear theoretical linkage between Marx, our work in *The Prison and the Factory*, and, I claim in the next section, Foucault's.[4]

The destructuration of authority: struggles

What happened since the 1970s was the destructuration of this system of authority – it was not by chance that many among the most successful movements in the late 1960s called themselves 'antiauthoritarian' – a system of authority that many misunderstood to be one and the same with 'capitalism' (what one could probably call the most consequential *quid pro quo* of my generation). Destructuration, in other words, not only of the centrality of discipline in the organization of a 'panoptic' society but, also, of a homogeneous, mass, organized, disciplined, working class. As Rosa Luxemburg had already quite incredibly divined in her invective against the 'discipline' of the factory *and* especially of the Russian social-democratic party under Lenin's guidance (Luxemburg [1904] 1961), such discipline had been bred within the factory (and in fact what happened in the Left after the 1960s and 1970s was *also* the destructuration of all that). In the 1970s, this set of social arrangements went into deep crisis, or at least appeared to go into crisis. Maybe we started 'seeing' the crisis of authority in the 'total institutions' exactly because the society that had fed them, and that had fed on them, entered into such a deep crisis.

The role of struggles in this work of material but also conceptual deconstruction can be hardly minimized. Struggles developed, at the same time, within factories, prisons and in all 'ancillary institutions' (mental hospitals being the most classical example (Goffman 1961, Basaglia 1968)). Suddenly, we realized that these institutions were not eternal, would not last forever, that, as they were born, they could go. The 'critique of institutions' – echoing perhaps what the German student leader Rudi Dutschke (Bergmann *et al.* 1968) had prophetically called 'the long march through the institutions' – could not have existed apart from such struggles. David Garland (2014) has reminded us that this was indeed the case about Michel Foucault's concept of a 'history of the present' in *Discipline and Punish*:

> That punishment in general and the prison in particular belong to a political technology of the body is a lesson that I have learnt not so much from

history as from the present. In recent years, prison revolts have occurred throughout the world. There was certainly something paradoxical about their aims, their slogans and the way they took place. They were revolts against an entire state of physical misery that is over a century old: against cold, suffocation and overcrowding, against decrepit walls, hunger, physical maltreatment. But they were also revolts against model prisons, tranquillizers, isolation, the medical or educational services [...]. In fact, they were revolts, at the level of the body, against the very body of the prison. What was at issue was not whether the prison environment was too harsh or too aseptic, too primitive or too efficient, but its very materiality as an instrument and vector of power it is this whole technology of power over the body that the technology of the 'soul' – that of the educationalists, psychologists and psychiatrists – fails either to conceal or to compensate, for the simple reason that it is one of its tools. I would like to write the history of this prison, with all the political investments of the body that it gathers together in its closed architecture. Why? Simply because I am interested in the past? No, if one means by that writing a history of the past in terms of the present. Yes, if one means writing the history of the present.

(Foucault [1975] 1977, pp. 30–31)

This long fragment, and especially its close, is very significant in order to understand the endeavour that Foucault had set for himself, by writing a book about the birth of the prison.[5] In such connection, one contribution by Foucault that seems particularly relevant, is an interview with John Simon, a professor of French and comparative literature at SUNY Buffalo, who had received Foucault in the United States and who helped him organize a visit to Attica a few months after the famous revolt. He then interviewed Foucault in April 1972 (then originally published in *Telos* (Foucault 1974)). The revolt at the Attica penitentiary in the State of New York, probably the (politically) most important prison revolt in the history of the United States, generated great impact for its media diffusion, but also for the level of violence in its resolution.[6] That interview is very interesting because Foucault gave his impressions after visiting Attica, noting also its 'modern' aspects, such as the uses of psychiatry, the various forms of therapy, the aseptic character, etc. In fact, there where Foucault writes of a revolt that was also 'against model prisons, tranquillizers, isolation, the medical or educational services' he seems to quote almost verbatim from the interview with Simon, which, after all, had taken place only a couple of years before.[7]

The destructuration of authority: Marx and Foucault

Foucault's relationship with the Marxist tradition and Marx more specifically is quite problematic. Some have claimed that in the 1972–1973 course of lectures at the *Collège de France* leading up to the writing of *Discipline and Punish*, and now collected in a volume called *The Punitive Society* (Foucault [1973] 2015), the influence of Marx over Foucault's analysis would show more clearly (Elden 2015, p. 161; Harcourt [2013] 2015, pp. 283–289). However, it seems to me that, to the one open to see it, *Discipline and Punish* would also lend itself to such an interpretation. In the crucial pages on 'Panopticism', closing the central section of the volume on 'Discipline', Foucault claimed that 'the two processes – the accumulation of men and the accumulation of capital – cannot be separated' (Foucault [1975] 1977, p. 221). Moreover, development of technology and development of disciplinary techniques were intimately related, according to this very passage. Foucault includes here in parenthesis one of his very rare citations to a classic text, Marx's discussion, in Chapter XIII of the first Volume of *Capital*, on 'Co-operation'. In this chapter, Marx makes the point – essential to the concept of surplus value – that, at this stage of development in the history of capitalism (i.e. before the introduction of complex machinery), labour, after being purchased and assembled together by the capitalist, was forcibly organized by the capitalist's very physical authority, who co-ordinated the production process with his eye, his voice and his command (Marx 1867, pp. 322–335; Melossi [1977] 1981, p. 43). In other words, at this time, discipline was constitutive of the organization of work and therefore also of the capitalist's profits.

In the next page, Foucault adds,

> Historically, the process by which the bourgeoisie became in the course of the eighteenth century the politically dominant class was masked by the establishment of an explicit, coded and formally egalitarian juridical framework, made possible by the organization of a parliamentary, representative regime. But the development and generalization of disciplinary mechanisms constituted the other, dark side of these processes [...]. The real, corporal disciplines constituted the foundation of the formal, juridical liberties. The contract may have been regarded as the ideal foundation of law and political power; panopticism constituted the technique, universally widespread, of coercion [...]. The 'Enlightenment', which discovered the liberties, also invented the disciplines.
>
> (Foucault [1975] 1977, p. 222)

It is hard for the reader not to see these lines as a gloss on Marx's quintessential opposition of a 'sphere of circulation' – which is 'a very Eden of the innate rights of man [where] alone rule Freedom, Equality, Property, and Bentham'[8] – and that 'sphere of production' marked on the contrary by servitude. Re-reading these pages now, it appears a bit clearer to me why we seemed to think that on this analytical path we had found the answer to the question of ideology – the conceptual starting point of our generation. However, ideology was now transformed from a matter of practical reason and morality to one of specific techniques of control over the body (Melossi [1977] 1981, p. 45). In this light, the secret that we were trying to unveil, indeed to unmask, the secret of capitalist hegemony, could be understood, with a little help from Weber, as the hegemony of a *mentalité*, of a mindset, of an ethos. Exactly as the good merchants of seventeenth-century Amsterdam believed, profit was the 'collateral advantage' of their good deeds!

It seems to me that, both in *Discipline and Punish* and – and perhaps even more so – in the pages of the lectures in *Punitive Society*, Foucault sounded a bit like a 'New Left' Marxist, critical at the same time of Social Democracy and Stalinism (both somehow embodied at the time in the French milieu by the French Communist Party (the PCF)). Perhaps also for such reason, Foucault's statements resonated, to our ears educated in the tradition of the New Left, with the 'Marxism' of the British historian E.P. Thompson and his collaborators[9] (Hay *et al.* 1975; Thompson 1975) but also, I would dare to add, with Harry Braverman's *Labour and Monopoly Capital* (1974) in the US.

Each season reads the classics in a way that suits it, and Marx is certainly not exception to this. On the contrary. The Marx that was popular, also in Italy but not only in Italy, during the years up to 1968 was a Marx read through the eyes of the Frankfurt School, where the critique of authority was paramount. The structures of authority that had been set up by the modern State – especially, in Continental Europe, the French/German State structures – seemed to find a deep affinity with that 'barrack discipline' exposed by Luxemburg, the discipline of the modern factory, as well as with a whole host of disciplinary institutions. Foucault's fascination – as well as our own in *The Prison and the Factory* – with Bentham's *Panopticon* finds here its roots, the fact that Bentham had already conceived the Panopticon as the patterned model of all institutional structures of authority. Foucault was therefore giving a sense of direction to what Rudi Dutschke had called a 'a long march through the institutions' (Bergman *et al.* 1968), or to the unperishing words with which Mario Savio, a few years before, speaking on the steps of Sproul Hall, on 2 December 1964, had incited the Berkeley students – and, with them, our whole generation – to 'stop the machine': '…you've got to put your bodies upon the gears and upon the wheels…upon the levers, upon all the apparatus, and you've got to make it stop!' (Rosenfeld 2012, p. 217).

Therefore, the disciplinary power mechanisms of Russian Stalinism or of Western 'Communist' Social Democracies, were part of the problem, not of the solution, were one and the same thing with 'the enemy'. This, it seems to me, was the kind of 'Marxism' that Foucault was criticising, and the reason why Garland or Harcourt may today portray Foucault as critical of Marx. This was also the origin of the affinity of Foucault – especially in *Discipline and Punish* – with the English historians such as E.P. Thompson, with Harry Braverman's reading of the relationship between the 'scientific-technical revolution' and the 'degradation of work', or even with aspects of Italian *operaismo*. In short, his penchant for a reading of Marx not as the author of the idea that economic structure 'determines', even if 'in the last instance', everything else (Marx [1859] 1977) – but Marx as the one who places at the centre of history and change, not the economy but class struggle. And what else if not class struggle is at the roots of Foucault's paean to 'illegalism and refusal to work' in *The Punitive Society* ([1973] 2015, pp. 186–190, but see the whole Lecture of 14 March 1973) or of Foucault's description of a dialectic between '*illégalismes*' and 'delinquency' which seems to border on a classic anarchist argument ([1973] 2015, pp. 139–151, and the lecture of 21 February 1973)? And what about Foucault's discussion of the relationship between wages and punishment in a way that is reminiscent of Evgeni Pashukanis' ([1924] 1980) in *The General Theory of Law and Marxism* (see the Lecture of 31 January 1973; see also Elden 2015, p. 154)?

Visions of social control

So, we thought, factories are now obsolete (after all, a 'bourgeois' sociologist, Daniel Bell, had already written, years before, of the advent of a 'post-industrial society' (Bell [1960] 2000)), therefore, if the origins of the prison were irremediably tied to the origins of the factory, then also the prison was to be on its way out. And we could see sure evidence of that: at the time, everywhere emphasis was placed on the importance of 'community', and the critique of 'total institutions' (Goffman 1961; Basaglia 1968) had ushered in the rhetoric of decarceration (Scull 1977). Much as it has been happening lately, the emergence of a 'fiscal crisis of the State' (O'Connor 1973), connected to problems of State legitimacy (Habermas [1973] 1975), had translated in what seemed to be the inevitable reduction if not disappearance of the old-fashioned and costly prison institutions. It was indeed a bad timing for such prognosis – especially in the US, very few years later would mark the start of the longest and most pronounced increase in the number of people committed and confined to prisons ever.[10]

In my own version, this meant that it was now the time to go 'beyond the Panopticon' (Melossi 1979, 1980b) and realize that ghettoes of all sorts had taken the place of total institutions (Kraushaar 1978): the new places of confinement had no walls any longer! In Stanley Cohen's version (1985) instead it was a story of 'net-widening' and 'warehousing' the now clearly increasing number of 'inmates'. For Malcolm Feeley and Jonathan Simon (1992, 1994), it was now the time of replacing 'actuarial' notions of 'risk' for the passé concepts of 'rehabilitation' and 'discipline'. When I look back to what happened between the 1970s and 2008, in the US, I have trouble with all these readings: the State of California for a good 30 years built a new prison every year, in the average, bringing the total number of inmates from 24,000 to 160,000 (without counting jail inmates), and the power elites of the state did not 'believe' in prisons, and in the essentially disciplinary function of prisons? But if the goal had been to contain an 'excess population' within walls in order to warehouse them and limit the risk they posed to free citizens outside, why bother about overcrowding? Why not set up enclosed 'camps' to detain men as cattle? After all, this had happened before! Instead, I believe prisons have kept performing their historical role as presiders to a kind of 'internal' colonization (and 'external' as well).[11]

Once again, I submit that there is a basic misunderstanding about the notion of 'discipline' (and, indirectly, about the reading of *The Prison and the Factory*). The point of 'discipline' is not really to teach actually useful skills to potential workers, in order to fit them in the historically given cycle of production – as a certain rhetoric of 'resocialization' or 'rehabilitation' would suggest. The point of discipline rather is to teach (at least programmatically) the lesson of what we could call 'subordinate inclusion', obedience, if you would rather like plain speaking. As we have seen, Marx never relented from noting that 'subordination' is indeed the main issue, because it is the necessary premise of 'discipline'. Where Marx describes the shift of analysis, and at the same time of the scene of action, from the 'sphere of circulation' to 'the sphere of production', he everlastingly describes the point I tried to make in *The Prison and the Factory* and that, I believe, Foucault was making – among others – in *Discipline and Punish*:

> On leaving this sphere of simple circulation or of exchange of commodities, which furnishes the 'Free-trader Vulgaris' with his views and ideas, and with the standard by which he judges a society based on capital and wages, we think we can perceive a change in the physiognomy of our *dramatis personae*. He, who before was the money-owner, now strides in front as capitalist; the possessor of labour-power follows as his labourer. The one with an air of importance, smirking, intent on business; the other, timid and holding back, like one who is bringing his own hide to market and has nothing to expect but – a hiding.
>
> (Marx 1867, p. 176)

The revanche of capital: discipline and subordinate inclusion

We could think of the prison therefore as a Utopian representation of order consisting in the subordinate inclusion of its guests, who are the *outsiders* by definition, the perennial outsiders perhaps. What makes them outsiders of course may change. As Zygmunt Bauman stated, 'all societies produce strangers; but each kind of society produces its own kind of strangers, and produces them in its own inimitable way' (Bauman 1995). And those strangers, those outsiders, so inimitably produced, are usually the guests of the prison, no matter when and where. Somewhere else, and trying to conjugate Marx with Rusche and Kirchheimer ([1939] 2003), I offered the idea that there is indeed a connection between the cycle of class struggles and the 'behaviour' of imprisonment rates (Melossi 2008, pp. 229–252), according to which, in periods of strength of the working class, for a number of reasons imprisonment rates would be at a minimum (and 'penal standards of life' at a maximum!). One of such periods was in the 1970s, when the political hegemony of work and labour was in fact accompanied by a minimum of imprisonment. In other words, the 'refusal to work' among the marginal strata of society reached a peak in the generalization of anti-institutional and anti-authoritarian struggles of the 1970s due to the increasing questioning of the Fordist factory, struggles described in neo-Marxists' writings as well as, indirectly, in the emergence of Foucault's very relevant concept of *illégalismes* in *Discipline and Punish*.

The problem therefore, from the perspective of capital, was the restoration of command discipline. Nowhere this was clearer – it seems to me – than in the United States, especially in relation to the issue of '*illégalismes*' and 'delinquency'. As Jonathan Simon reminds us (2014), the (generally very young) leaders of the Black Panthers in the 1960s and 1970s were, in a sense, second generation 'migrants', the children and grandchildren of the people who had moved northward and later westward from the South. So, for instance, in the LA area, a leader of his people as Bunchy Carter had contributed to the 'politicization' of the Blousons gang in the 1960s and it was only after the demise of the Black Panthers and the fall of leaders such as Carter himself and John Huggins[12] that the young poor Black people from LA were brought back to the reality once again of street gangs such as the Bloods and the Crips.[13] Hadn't it been after all C. Wright Mills who wrote about the necessity of turning 'private troubles' into 'public problems' (Mills 1959)?[14] After the fall of the various 1960s and 1970s movements, public problems – unemployment, the lack of collective rights, the repression of labour and political opposition – became again redefined as 'private troubles'. But, how much they were one or the other was of course a dependent variable of a power struggle defined in terms of 'class' and 'race'. In this sense, this period represented a textbook example of transformation of '*illégalismes*' into 'delinquency' in the way indicated in the last section of Foucault's *Discipline and Punish* ([1975] 1977, pp. 257–292). First, the repression of the political vanguard, then the processes of criminalization in the double meaning of the term, as helping to construct a criminal underworld[15] and as the construction and diffusion of mass imprisonment (see, on the connection between mass imprisonment and criminalization in the US, the work of Philippe Bourgois (1995), Victor Rios (2011) and Alice Goffman (2014)).

The nexus of discipline to the teaching of obedience to the goal of subordinate inclusion (whether there is a rhetoric of 'rehabilitation' at work or not) seems therefore to be the perennial (programmatic) *raison d'être* of the prison. This nexus always concerns, mainly, outsiders, marginal strata, even if these may be 'ethnic' in some places and 'migrant' in others. At the end of a study of the relationships of crime, punishment and migration in Europe, I came to the conclusion that, given that the new mass of immigrants went to replenish the ranks of the lowest strata of the working class, European societies recently have done nothing less but treat the immigrants as they were accustomed to treat the most disadvantaged among their own – something that had become hard to do after the workers' militancy of the 1960s and 1970s (Melossi 2015). We went therefore from the low levels of incarceration around 1970 (in spite of the cry of 'repression repression!') to those much higher later on. But even in the days of the Great Recession, the prisons, these literally[16] monumental gateways conducing from the abstract sphere of equality and rights to the concrete one of discipline and subordination, seem to stand as tall as ever, presiding to the social processing of outsiders of all qualities and stripes, in a sort of 'internal colonization'. Whether Black and Latino people in Los Angeles and New York, or Africans and Eastern Europeans in the 100 cities of Europe, whether Arabs in Israel or Asians in the Gulf States, whether peasants *sin tierra* in Colombia or Brazil or peasants without legal residence in Shenzhen or Shanghai, they seem to huddle in slums and crowd jails in ways not too dissimilar from those described by Frederick Engels ([1845] 1975) in 1844 Manchester. The process we described in *The Prison and the Factory* and that we deemed to have arrived at its final crisis when we were writing it, seems to have instead developed much beyond the borders of Europe and North America, accompanying the 'enlarged reproduction' of capital together with its geographic and military spread. Prisons have generally followed not far behind troops, and this also where very few factories have appeared on the scene. If capitalist society – whether characterized by private or by public capital – is essentially marked by class struggle, the idea of subordination seems to constitute its original and dominant principle, a necessary premise to the goal of (a profitable) production.

Notes

1 I reproduce here a sizable section of my Introduction to a new edition of *The Prison and the Factory*, a book that the late Massimo Pavarini and I published in Italian in 1977 (Melossi and Pavarini 1977) and then in English translation in 1981 (Melossi and Pavarini 1981). Macmillan Palgrave is reissuing a new edition now and I thank them for allowing us to reproduce part of the Introduction to this new edition. I would like to thank my good friends Maximo Sozzo and José A. Brandariz-Garcia for all the feedback and exchanges that took place when I presented the main ideas for what follows within Lectures given at the Winter School in Criminology of the Faculty of Legal and Social Sciences, Universidad Nacional del Litoral, Santa Fe, Argentina (July 2014) and at two International Conferences organized at the University of A Coruna, Spain, in September 2014 and September 2016 (I am particularly grateful to Maximo for his comments on a previous version of this chapter). I would also like to thank the Center for the Study of Law and Society of the University of California, Berkeley, for having provided me once more with the ideal physical and intellectual space during the completion of this work!

2 Later on, in my work on Georg Rusche's biography (Melossi 1980a, p. 57) I discovered that Maurice Dobb had also helped Rusche settle in London in the mid-1930s, writing letters of reference for him.

3 Also in the Lectures collected in *The Punitive Society* where, contrary to *Discipline and Punish*, Foucault ([1973] 2015) sees the importance of the role of Quakers, he does not see however the importance of the workhouse and its constituting a very important link towards the penitentiary, especially by the action of William Penn and the Quakers. Penn had very probably met what was at the time the very new institution of the Workhouse – of which the Amsterdam *Rasphuis* was the most famous example – during his travels to the Netherlands and Northern Germany in 1677 (Lewis [1922] 2005, p. 10, Seidensticker 1878). In his penal reform a few years later (1681), part of the broader Quaker 'holy experiment' of Pennsylvania, he established

the clearest and most explicit link between the workhouses and the modern penitentiaries when he decreed that, 'all Prisons shall be workhouses for felons, Thiefs, vagrants, and Loose, abusive, and Idle persons, whereof one shall be in every county' (Dumm 1987, p. 79).
4 In the 'ancillary institutions', rules an authoritarian style that is however geared to producing self-governing, and therefore 'free' Subjects. Subjects also able to govern themselves collectively in the historical trajectory from the social contract to the Republic to democracy. These Subjects – capable of self-government because capable of self-control – would soon become those individuals endowed with 'free will' by criminal and penal theorists of the Enlightenment. In the years of American independence, Benjamin Rush will call such Subjects, supposedly forged also by the newly discovered 'penitentiaries', 'republican machines' (Dumm 1987, pp. 87–112).
5 See Harcourt ([2013] 2015). Michael Welch (2010, 2011) has written in recent years on the relationship of Michel Foucault with the 'Groupe d'information sur les prisons' – an activist group in France, in the early years of the 1970s, in which Foucault participated, trying to expose what was happening inside prisons, and connect with the prisoners' movement. In answering a letter that I had written to him on 20 April 1974, asking, among other things, whether 'your group' had published on the prison, Foucault answered, on 2 May 1974, that '*we* have published a few pamphlets about the situation in French prisons' but adding right away that '*I* am going to complete a work on the history of prisons in a few months' (my translation from French).
6 On 9 September 1971, the prisoners had managed to take the prison, and held a group of prison guards hostage. And while the Governor of the State of New York, Nelson Rockefeller, gave to understand that it was possible to generate a negotiated solution, at the same time prepared an armed intervention of the National Guard, together with the prison guards who had escaped the hostage-taking situation, who eventually, on 13 September 1971, stormed the prison and produced something like 39 dead, 10 hostages and 29 prisoners. See the special issue of *Social Justice* of Fall 1991 dedicated to a commemoration of the events. See also, now, the reconstruction by historian Heather Ann Thompson (2016) according to whom both the prisoners and the hostages were killed by the indiscriminate shooting during the retake of the prison.
7 In the interview Foucault refers what he has seen in Attica and how Attica operates but nothing about the Attica rebellion. This is certainly quite bizarre, especially because in that very interview Foucault makes reference to the struggles of prisoners in France.
8 Marx 1867, p. 176 (quoted in Melossi [1977] 1981, p. 43).
9 Referenced more than once in the Lectures of *The Punitive Society* (see also Elden 2015, p. 160, Harcourt [2013] 2015, pp. 277–278). Cf. Jock Young (2013) in the new Introduction to *The New Criminology* on the importance of British social historians on the emergence of the new deviancy theorists.
10 The prognosis however was not entirely wrong: there was no Franco Basaglia in the US but drugs produced the same result as far as psychiatric institutions were concerned. Bernard Harcourt has shown that summing up psychiatric and criminal commitments there has indeed been an overall deinstitutionalization in the last half a century or so, even in the US (Harcourt 2010).
11 As Angela Davis claims in an interview on *Social Justice* commenting on the building of new prisons in Latin America, 'more prisons are being built to catch the lives disrupted by [...] movement of capital. People who cannot find a place for themselves in this new society governed by capital end up going to prison' (Davis 2014, p. 51).
12 Who were both gunned down by members of competing organizations on the campus of UCLA on 17 January 1969.

13 See the 2006 documentary film *Bastards of the Party*, produced by Antoine Fuqua and directed by former Bloods gang-member Cle Sloan. See also the interview with Ericka Huggins (2014), former Black Panther member and widow of John.
14 I believe we should distinguish between what Taylor, Walton and Young defined as 'romanticisation of crime' in *Critical Criminology* (1975) and what I would call a 'dialectic of crime and politics' here, that is the back and forth between a tradition of criminal behaviour of the lower classes wholly subordinated to the hegemony of power elites and the transformation instead of such behaviour into a political action able to challenge such hegemony. What looms in the background is of course the traditional debate, within the workers' movement, about so-called *lumpenproletariat*.
15 Once again specific to the LA area, see the story about the CIA carrying drugs to the LA African American community in order to finance its own dirty wars – a story 'discovered' by journalist Gary Webb with articles on the *San José Mercury Journal* in the 1990s and who was then perhaps too quickly later discredited as another 'conspiracy theorist' (see www.huffingtonpost.com/2014/10/10/gary-web-dark-alliance_n_5961748.html [accessed 29 October 2015]). Of course the 1990s were the years of the 'crack cocaine epidemic' (and related 'murder epidemic') in the US.
16 See Foucault's description of Attica's entrance, 'that kind of phony fortress *à la* Disneyland' (Foucault 1974, p. 26).

References

Basaglia, F., ed. (1968). *L'istituzione negata*. Torino: Einaudi.
Bauman, Z. (1995). Making and Unmaking of Strangers. *Thesis Eleven*, 43, 1–16.
Bell, D. ([1960] 2000). *The End of Ideology: On the Exhaustion of Political Ideas in the Fifties*. Cambridge: Harvard University Press.
Bentham, J. ([1787] 1971). Panopticon. In: J. Bentham, *The Works of Jeremy Bentham*. New York: Russell & Russell, 37–66.
Bergmann, U., Dutschke, R., Lefèvre, W. and Rabehl, B. (1968). *Die Rebellion der Studenten oder Die neue Opposition*. Berlin: Rowohlt.
Bourgois, P. (1995). *In Search of Respect: Selling Crack in El Barrio*. Cambridge: Cambridge University Press (see also the 'Preface to the 2003 Second Edition', pp. xvii–xxiii).
Braverman, H. (1974). *Labour and Monopoly Capital: The Degradation of Work in the Twentieth Century*. New York: Monthly Review Press.
Cohen, S. (1985). *Visions of Social Control*. Cambridge: Polity Press.
Davis, A. (2014). Interview with Angela Davis. *Social Justice*, 40 (1–2), 37–53.
Dobb, M. (1946). *Studies in the Development of Capitalism*. London: Routledge.
Dumm, T.L. (1987). *Democracy and Punishment: Disciplinary Origins of the United States*. Madison: The University of Wisconsin Press.
Elden, S. (2015). A More Marxist Foucault? Reading *La société punitive*. *Historical Materialism*, 23, 149–168.
Engels, F. ([1845] 1975). *The Condition of the Working Class in England in 1844*. New York: International.
Feeley, M.M. and Simon, J. (1992). The New Penology: Notes on the Emerging Strategy of Corrections and Its Implications. *Criminology*, 30, 449–474.
Feeley, M.M. and Simon, J. (1994). Actuarial justice: the emerging new criminal law. In: D. Nelken, ed., *The Futures of Criminology*. London: Sage, 173–201.

Foucault, M. ([1973] 2015). *The Punitive Society: Lectures at the Collège de France 1972–1973*. Basingstoke: Palgrave Macmillan.
Foucault, M. (1974). Michel Foucault on Attica: An Interview. *Telos*, 19, 154–161 (reprinted in *Social Justice*, 18 (3)).
Foucault, M. ([1975] 1977). *Discipline and Punish*. New York: Pantheon.
Garland, D. (1990). *Punishment and Modern Society: A Study in Social Theory*. Chicago: University of Chicago Press.
Garland, D. (2014). What is a 'History of the Present'? On Foucault's Genealogies and Their Critical Preconditions. *Punishment and Society*, 16, 365–384.
Goffman, A. (2014). *On the Run: Fugitive Life in an American City*. Chicago: University of Chicago Press.
Goffman, E. (1961). *Asylums: Essays on the Social Situation of Mental Patients and Other Inmates*. Garden City: Anchor Books.
Habermas, J. ([1973] 1975). *Legitimation Crisis*. Boston: Beacon.
Harcourt, B.E. (2010). Neoliberal Penality: A Brief Genealogy. *Theoretical Criminology*, 14, 74–92.
Harcourt, B.E. ([2013] 2015). Course context. *In*: M. Foucault, *The Punitive Society: Lectures at the Collège de France 1972–1973*. Basingstoke: Palgrave Macmillan, 265–310.
Hay, D., Linebaugh, P., Rule, J.G., Thompson, E.P. and Winslow, C. (1975). *Albion's Fatal Tree: Crime and Society in Eighteenth-Century England*. New York: Pantheon.
Howe, R.H. (1978). Max Weber's Elective Affinities: Sociology within the Bounds of Pure Reason. *American Journal of Sociology*, 84, 366–385.
Huggins, E. (2014). Two Interviews with Ericka Huggins. *Social Justice*, 40, 54–71.
Kraushaar, W., ed. (1978). *Autonomie oder Getto, Kontroversen über die Alternativbewegung*. Frankfurt: Neue Kritik.
Lewis, O.F. ([1922] 2005). *The Development of American Prisons and Prisons Customs 1776 to 1845*. Whitefish Kessinger.
Luxemburg, R. ([1904] 1961). Organizational questions of the Russian social democracy. *In*: R. Luxemburg, *The Russian Revolution and Leninism or Marxism?* Ann Arbor: University of Michigan Press.
Marx, K. ([1859] 1977). Preface to *A Contribution to the Critique of Political Economy*. Moscow: Progress Publishers.
Marx, K. (1867). *Capital: Volume I*. New York: International Publishers.
Melossi, D. ([1977] 1981). Prison and labour in Europe and Italy during the formation of the capitalist mode of production. *In*: D. Melossi and M. Pavarini, *The Prison and the Factory: Origins of the Penitentiary System*. London: Macmillan, 9–95.
Melossi, D. (1979). Institutions of social control and capitalist organization of work. *In*: B. Fine *et al.*, eds, *Capitalism and the Rule of Law: From Deviancy Theory to Marxism*. London: Hutchinson, 90–99.
Melossi, D. (1980a). Georg Rusche: A Biographical Essay. *Crime and Social Justice*, 14, 51–63.
Melossi, D. (1980b). Oltre il 'Panopticon'. Per uno studio delle strategie di controllo sociale nel capitalismo del ventesimo secolo. *La questione criminale*, VI (2–3), 277–361.
Melossi, D. (2003). The simple 'heuristic maxim' of an 'unusual human being'. *In*: G. Rusche and O. Kirchheimer, *Punishment and Social Structure*. New Brunswick: Transaction, ix–xlvi.

Melossi, D. (2008). *Controlling Crime, Controlling Society: Thinking about Crime in Europe and America*. Cambridge: Polity Press.

Melossi, D. (2015). *Crime, Punishment and Migration*. London: Sage.

Melossi, D. and Pavarini, M. (1977). *Carcere e fabbrica: alle origini del sistema penitenziario*. Bologna: Il mulino.

Melossi, D. and Pavarini, M. (1981). *The Prison and the Factory: Origins of the Penitentiary System*. London: Macmillan and Totowa: Barnes and Noble.

Mills, C.W. (1959). *The Sociological Imagination*. New York: Oxford University Press.

O'Connor, J. (1973). *The Fiscal Crisis of the State*. New York: St. Martin's Press.

Pashukanis, E. ([1924] 1980). The general theory of law and Marxism. *In*: P. Beirne and R. Sharlet, eds, *Pashukanis: Selected Writings on Marxism and Law*. London: Academic Press, 37–131.

Rios, V.M. (2011). *Punished: Policing the Lives of Black and Latino Boys*, New York: New York University Press.

Rosenfeld, S. (2012). *Subversives: The FBI's War on Student Radicals, and Reagan's Rise to Power*. New York: Farrar, Straus and Giroux.

Rusche, G. and Kirchheimer, O. ([1939] 2003). *Punishment and Social Structure*. New Brunswick: Transaction.

Scull, A.T. (1977). *Decarceration: Community Treatment and the Deviant – A Radical View*. Englewood Cliffs: Prentice-Hall.

Seidensticker, O. (1878). William Penn's Travels in Holland and Germany in 1677. *The Pennsylvania Magazine of History and Biography*, 2 (3), 237–282.

Sellin, T. (1944). *Pioneering in Penology*. Philadelphia: University of Pennsylvania Press.

Simon, J. (2014). A Radical Need for Criminology. *Social Justice*, 40 (1–2), 9–23.

Taylor, I., Walton, P. and Young, J., eds (1975). *Critical Criminology*. London: Routledge.

Thompson, E.P. (1975). *Whigs and Hunters: The Origin of the Black Act*. London: Penguin.

Thompson, H.A. (2016). *Blood in the Water: The Attica Prison Uprising of 1971 and its Legacy*. New York: Pantheon.

Weber, M. ([1904–1905] 1958). *The Protestant Ethic and the Spirit of Capitalism*. New York: Scribner's.

Welch, M. (2010). Pastoral Power as Penal Resistance: Foucault and the Groupe d'information sur les prisons. *Punishment and Society*, 12 (1), 47–63.

Welch, M. (2011). Counterveillance: How Foucault and the Groupe d'information sur les prisons Reversed the Optics. *Theoretical Criminology*, 15 (3), 301–313.

Young, J. (2013). Introduction to 40th anniversary edition. *In*: I. Taylor, P. Walton, and J. Young, *The New Criminology: For a Social Theory of Deviance. 40th anniversary edition*. London: Routledge, xi–li.

Chapter 2

The renaissance of the political economy of punishment from a comparative perspective

Máximo Sozzo

Introduction

Over the last decade, the exploration of the link between "political economy" and "punishment" has experienced a sort of renaissance within the field of the sociology of punishment, mainly in English-speaking countries.

One of the main perspectives in this renaissance is built around the transformation of capitalism within the process of globalization, usually defined as the transition between "Fordist" and "postFordist" capitalist regimes of production and accumulation. It argues that the economic, social and cultural consequences of that change have played a significant role in molding contemporary penal discourses, practices and outcomes. This approach reveals a strong link with the tradition of the "political economy of punishment" based on the pioneering work by Georg Rusche and Otto Kirchheimer (Rusche [1933] 1980; Rusche and Kirchheimer [1939] 2003; see on this point Melossi 1978, 1998, 2003; Garland 1990, pp. 83–110; De Giorgi 2006, pp. 3–9, 2013a, pp. 41–44). That body of research revisiting Rusche and Kirchheimer's seminal work has taken two different paths since the 1970s. On the one hand, the revisionist exploration of the history of the prison in the US and Europe—its birth in particular (Ignatieff 1978; Melossi and Pavarini 1981; see De Giorgi 2006, pp. 9–19, 44–46; Melossi, this volume). On the other hand, the largely quantitative sociological exploration of the nexus between the evolution of the economy—mainly the labor market, and taking unemployment rates as an indicator of its changes—and penality—taking incarceration rates as an indicator of its changes—in societies of advanced capitalism (Jankovic 1977; Box 1987; Chiricos and Delone 1992; Melossi 1993; see De Giorgi 2006, pp. 19–39). The contemporary approach above mentioned considers itself an update of the latter group of studies, departing from some criticisms about its limitations to understand our present, both in the economic and penal fields. It regards itself as global in extent and tends to emphasize similarities and convergences across national frontiers. It highlights the significance of the USA case and its "punitive" and "neoliberal" turns as a model for the global development of the link between "punishment" and "political economy." A highly relevant example of this approach is the recent work by De Giorgi (2006, 2013a, 2013b).

Nevertheless, there is another significant perspective involved in this renaissance. It is built through a comparative perspective that identifies variations in the current penal discourses, practices and outcomes of different national contexts, and tries to explain them in terms of diverse types of contemporary capitalist political economies. My aim in this work is to analyze the most significant approaches produced in this last direction. I will focus on the works by Michael Cavadino and James Dignan, and Nicola Lacey. To start with, I will try to identify whether they establish any connections, and that being the case, of what type, with the classic works of the "political economy of punishment" (PEofP) as an intellectual tradition. Second, I will try to identify how these studies define political economy and comparatively delimit its contemporary variants. Third, I will analyze how these theoretical alternatives establish the link between that level of reality defined as "political economy" and the penal field—particularly, if other factors are recognized as playing a role in that connection, and in that case, which they are and to what extent they are significant. Through this analysis I will try to highlight some contributions of this type of comparative perspective that are crucial for the exploration of the link between political economy and punishment today. However, I will also signal some of its limitations and some challenges in the future development of research in this area.

Comparative approach I: Cavadino and Dignan

In 2006, Michael Cavadino and James Dignan published an essay titled "Penal Policy and Political Economy" (2006a), which presents a synthesis of their broader work, *Penal Systems. A Comparative Approach* (2006b). More recently, they revisited this precedent work in two book chapters (Cavadino and Dignan 2011, 2014). Their work has been widely read and discussed within the contemporary sociology of punishment, especially among those researchers interested in developing comparative visions able to outdo the focalization of this intellectual production on few privileged national cases—the United States, and to a lesser extent, Great Britain (Lacey 2008, pp. 43–46; Nelken 2010a, pp. 59–66). The book is one of the most ambitious comparative studies in recent literature, working on twelve contemporary societies (from Sweden to Japan), in cooperation with researchers in each of these countries and departing from a general analytical scheme.

This scheme is based on a "typology of late modern capitalist societies" (2006b, p. 6), which in turn derives from the classification by Esping Andersen (1990). All throughout their book, this typology is alternatively presented as a classification of "political economies," "societies" or "states," an ambiguity that persistently pollutes their analytic scheme. This is probably due to the researchers' belief in a strict correspondence between state, society and economy. In any case, they reject the idea that this potential correspondence is based on a privileged position of the economy. In this regard, and reducing Marxism in a rather simplistic way to the deterministic metaphor of "structure" and "superstructure," they point out: "Whereas Marxism traditionally sees the economy as the 'base' of society that ultimately determines the 'superstructure' containing the realms of ideology, politics and law, we do not believe that any one realm is 'basic'" (Cavadino and Dignan 2006b, p. 12).[1]

It is worth mentioning that in their last works about these issues, the authors resolved this ambivalence by referring exclusively to types of "political economy." However, they sustained that political economy is a complex phenomenon, that includes "a constellation of national characteristics which is partly economic, partly political institutions and arrangements, partly political culture" (Cavadino and Dignan 2011, p. 207).

As it can be guessed from the above quotation about Marxism, and despite the importance these authors give to the expression "political economy," they present their approach as absolutely disconnected to the classic works of the PEofP tradition. This becomes evident as there are no substantial references in their book, chapters or articles to the main authors of that tradition.[2] Although Nelken points out that "they build on prior neo-Marxist analyses of the role of the prison in relation to the labor force" (2010a, p. 60, 2011b, p. 14)—see also De Giorgi (2013a, pp. 48, 51)—I have not found any element justifying such direct connection.

The main argument presented by Cavadino and Dignan is that these different types of capitalist political economies generate penal differences, particularly unequal levels of punitiveness—measured centrally through the incarceration rate (2006b, pp. 4–5).[3] They distinguish four types—or "family groupings"—(a) neoliberalism (NE, the archetypal example is the USA, but they also include England and Wales, Australia, New Zealand and South Africa); (b) conservative corporatism (CCE, archetypal example: Germany, but they also include France, Italy and the Netherlands); (c) social democratic corporatism (SDCE, archetypal example: Sweden, but they also include Finland); (d) oriental corporatism (OCE, archetypal example: Japan). They identified common characteristics in each type that are related to: (a) economic and social policy organization; (b) income differentials; (c) status differentials; (d) citizen-state relations; (e) social inclusivity/exclusivity; (f) political orientation (2006b, p. 15). They state that there are "clear dividing lines between the different types of political economy as regards imprisonment rates" (2006b, p. 21). NEs have higher incarceration rates than CCEs, which in turn have higher incarceration rates than SDCEs. The OCEs are thus the ones with the lowest incarceration rates.

As regards NE, the authors wonder about how to explain its association with "harsh punishment," which implies not leaving the analysis at the stage of identifying the co-existence of these two elements but trying to explain their nexus (Cavadino and Dignan, 2006b, p. 22). This does not mean that they are successful in doing so. The authors' interpretation becomes winding at this point. They present certain possibilities but, at the same time, they outline evidences that obstruct them (2006b, pp. 22–36). In their conclusion, they recognize:

> Some patterns give rise to puzzles. One which continues to trouble us is this. We think we have demonstrated that the position of a country within our typology of political economies has an important effect on the punishment level of that country. But why, exactly?
>
> (2006b, p. 339)

In their latest works, they specifically go back to this point. They define five hypotheses to explain the nexus between political economy and penality, no longer exclusively in relation with "NEs" but more generally. They include new arguments but still reaching cautious conclusions—which is evident in the heading of one of the chapters: "puzzling relations" (Cavadino and Dignan 2011, 2014).

In the book, they state that a possible explanation of the association between NEs and harsher punishment could be that the economic and social policies that characterize this type of economy are highly exclusive, which brings about criminogenic consequences—inequalities, relative deprivation, anomie, alienation—that create more crime and criminals to be caught and incarcerated. In addition to this, the informal mechanisms of social control associated to community life are wrecked due to the exacerbation of individualism, which would explain the recurring resort to penality as a formal mechanism of social control. In their more recent texts, they state that, according to this "crime-driven punishment hypothesis," the opposite would take place in CEs, where there would be a more developed welfare state and more equality, and informal social control would have greater weight. This would thus result in less crime and would lead to a less extended use of incarceration. In fact, they assert that the link between the type of political economy and the amount of crime has largely been empirically proved—especially as regards violent crime. But what makes this hypothesis fail is the absence of such empirical evidence on the subsequent step in the casual chain trying to demonstrate a strong statistical relationship between crime and incarceration (Cavadino and Dignan 2006b, pp. 22–23, 46, 2011, pp. 195–197, 2014, p. 9251).

In the book, they discuss another explanation linked to the diffusion of exclusionary "cultural attitudes" in relation to the deviant and marginalized who are "embodied (and embedded)" in the NE. A "highly individualistic social ethos" "leads a society to adopt a neoliberal economy in the first place, but conversely the existence of such economy in return fosters the social belief that individuals are solely responsible for looking after themselves, thus reproducing the individualistic culture" (Cavadino and Dignan 2006b, p. 23). It is worth highlighting that the authors are here establishing a dialectic relationship between economy and culture, as "mutually determining" (2014, p. 9544). This "social soil is fertile ground for a law and order ideology," which is reflected in the adoption of harsher penal policies (2006b, p. 24). CEs—particularly, SDCEs—are traditionally embodied and embedded in a different cultural attitude, a "communitarian ethos," which gives rise to more inclusionary social and economic policies, but which is shaped by such policies in return. This is typically—though not invariably—translated into the form of penal welfarism—with different degrees—diversely combined with the importance of informal social control (family, religious institutions)—higher in conservative and lower in social democratic CEs (2006b, pp. 24–26). In this hypothesis, "public sentiments form the link between political economy and penality" (2006b, p. 339). However, they present empirical data that discredit this possible link and state that the incarceration rate is not the simple reflection of "common sentiments of ordinary people." They add, taking into account Beckett's work (1997), that it is "politicians and the media who give the lead to the public in penal matters rather than the other way round" (2006b, p. 31, 339). Nevertheless, in their latest works they also point out that this "public-driven punishment hypothesis" sheds light on certain constraints and influences by the public opinion in liberal democracies, but that they cannot be thought as determinants, as penal policy and practice have a great deal of autonomy from it (2011, pp. 197–199, 2014, p. 9337).

In their latest works they present a third hypothesis in which the link between political economy and punishment is constructed through the media (Cavadino and Dignan 2011, pp. 200–201, 2014, p. 9344)—there were also some references to this in their book (2006b, pp. 31–32, 47). They state that in NEs the commodification of the media leads to a sensationalist way of producing information about crime that helps increase punitiveness, shaping the citizens' orientations, as well as those of politicians and criminal justice officials. On the other hand, in CEs, the commodification is more limited, there is public media, and there are more state regulations for those that are private, which results in less sensationalism and a more limited impact on the increase of punitiveness. However, they point out: "The evidence is thin to date. We would speculate that it has some validity, but it is only one component in a much larger picture" (2011, p. 201).

In the book, they introduce another element. They assert that punishment is a "political construct." That means that it is shaped by the "policy choices of politicians and state functionaries," the "penal elite" who "have particular power to determine a nation's penality." However they argue that these policy choices "are always conditioned by the type of society in which they occur" (2006b, p. 31). At other points, they state that the "policy choices" that more directly produce penal outcomes are those occurring within sentencing, rather than in the legislative field—even when its role also has to be recognized. And such elections are influenced, above all, by a "country's penal culture and ideology," "although this is of course by no means hermetically insulated from the general mood and temper of the times," "as expressed in political and media discourse about crime and punishment" (2006b, pp. 46, 338–339). This element has been revisited in their more recent texts. They affirm that it is not just about the culture of the "penal elite" but the "elite" in general: "It is the ideology of the powerful that is crucial" (2011, p. 201). They point out how in NEs there have been parallel mutations in "government ideologies" since the 1970s, as regards economy—toward neoliberalism—and punishment—toward penal toughening (2011, pp. 201–203). This was translated into concrete political and legal initiatives in this direction and in a climate that had a great impact on everyday decisions made by criminal justice officials (2011, p. 203).

They also state in their book—based on the work by Savelsberg (1999)—that in NEs these "policy choices" oriented toward penal toughening are in turn associated with some "institutional" conditions, like political parties that are weak in terms of platform and politicians that try to connect with the voters by reflecting and promoting populist issues. In some cases—like in many states in the US—this is strengthened by popular election or through "political (and sometimes heavily politicized) processes" of nomination and confirmation of criminal justice officials. The opposite would happen in CEs (Cavadino and Dignan 2006b, pp. 31–32). In their more recent texts, this reference to institutional conditions is presented as an alternative hypothesis, in critical dialog with Lacey's work (2008). They consider the effect of electoral systems, "first-past-the-post" (typical of NEs) or proportional representative (typical of CEs): the former would promote penal populism and the latter would block it. They discredit this factor, using the example—also analyzed by Lacey—of New Zealand, where the adoption of the PR electoral system coincided with the expansion of penal populism (2014, p. 9458). However, they stress the importance of other political arrangements, like the role and status of professional bureaucracy in the practice of government. But they point out that the ones that matter are at least to some extent seemingly independent of the type of political economy, so "the causative chain does not seem to run neatly all the way through" (2011, p. 209).

In their book, Cavadino and Dignan state that the outcomes in the penal field—higher or lower punitiveness—depend, in general terms, on the type of political economy. However, this dependence would be mediated by cultural attitudes that, at the same time, produce and are produced by political economy. Nevertheless, they are not enough to explain how such penal outcomes are produced, as it is necessary to account for the elections made by the "penal elites"—politicians but also judges and prosecutors. These in turn would be conditioned by certain institutional features—presumably associated with the types of political economies, though not so rigidly—and, essentially, by the predominant "penal culture and ideology"—influenced in turn by the "general mood and temper of the times." As we can see, the authors' arguments turn more and more cautious and complex. In their more recent texts, the authors point out that none of the hypotheses considered account for the relationship between political economy and punishment on their own, but "the link is surely there and something must be causing it." Given that political economy is a complex phenomenon, so is its relationship with the penal field. Consequently, in their view there is no need to fear "explanatory eclecticism" (2014, p. 9491, 2011, p. 210). They argue that the characteristics of public opinion and the media are relevant though not determinant, and that the role played by political institutions and culture, joined together, are much more significant (2011, p. 211, 2014, p. 9498). They clearly put here their emphasis on "the interaction between the political culture and the political and state institutions" (2014, p. 9498, 2011, p. 211): "The key to penality lies in the political realm, broadly defined within an area of contest and struggle whose outcome is not totally predetermined or entirely bounded by unchangeable social facts" (2011, p. 211).

Cavadino and Dignan close the first chapter of their book, where they summarize the results of their research, pointing out their approach is not a "reductionist one," so they cannot explain all variations in punishment by reference to the differences in political economies, since "there are other factors as well" (2006b, p. 36).[4] This opens the distinct possibility that there are processes producing penal outcomes independently rather than as mediators of the type of political economy—for example, some institutional conditions of politics. They also state there:

> However many factors we incorporate into our theory, it will still not give us the whole story. Individual nations can be just as quirky and esoteric as individual human beings. People sometimes talk about the "exceptionalism" of France or the USA; but it is not going too far to say that we have found all of the countries in this study to be exceptional in at least some respect.... Particularities of geography, history, and even highly specific political circumstances can all play their part.
>
> (2006b, p. 36)

This poses a very important methodological question about their own style of analysis. I will come back to both these topics in the last section of this chapter.

Comparative approach II: Lacey

Nicola Lacey's book, *The prisoners' dilemma. Political economy and punishment in contemporary democracies* (2008), later complemented with a series of articles and chapters of books (Lacey 2010a, 2010b, 2011a, 2011b, 2012, 2013; Lacey and Soskice 2015), is explicitly based on Cavadino and Dignan's work (Lacey 2008, pp. 43–46, 52–53).

Unlike those authors, Lacey (2008, pp. 47–50) recognizes the work by Rusche and Kirchheimer, and the literature that followed it, as significant precedents. She particularly praises De Giorgi (2006) for avoiding "the perils of economic reductionism" (2011a, p. 215). She affirms, "Marxian structuralism has many analytic strengths" and "I have a great deal of sympathy for key aspects of its approach—notably its recognition of the centrality of the political economy to an understanding of punishment" (2008, p. 50). However, she criticizes their little interest in carrying out "systematic comparisons," which makes them assume that the changes in the "production regimes" are similar and have the same effects everywhere. No significant variations are identified, which leads to predicting similar developments on a global scale—in both fields, political economy and penality (2008, pp. 50–51). In addition, she partially detaches herself from Marxism—like Cavadino and Dignan, by associating this tradition to some sort of "economic reductionism"—when she highlights the importance of institutional factors in her analysis:

> My analysis builds on structural theories inspired by Marxism, but argues that political-economic forces at the macro level are mediated not only by cultural filters, but also by economic, political and social institutions. I will argue, moreover, that it is this institutional stabilization and mediation of cultural and structural forces, and the impact which this has on the perceived interests of relevant groups of social actors, which produce the significant and persistent variation across systems at similar stages of capitalist development.
> (2008, p. 57; see also, 2011a, p. 217)

An essential starting point for Lacey is the work by Peter Hall and David Soskice (2001) on "varieties of capitalism," which distinguishes the "coordinated market economies" (CMEs) from the "liberal market economies" (LMEs) as two different types of political economies in current advanced capitalism. The former work primarily in terms of long-term relationships and stable structures of investment, and incorporates a wide range of social groups and institutions into a highly coordinated governmental structure. The latter are more individualistic and less interventionist in regulatory stance, and depend far less strongly on the sorts of coordinating institutions to sustain long-term economic and social relations, encouraging flexibility and innovation. In the CME there is a tendency to create incentives for a moderate and inclusionary penal policy. In the LME—especially under conditions of surplus unskilled labor (which LMEs are also more likely to produce)—there is a tendency to create incentives for a harsh and exclusionary penal policy. According to Lacey, this distinction can be used to read the penal variations identified by Cavadino and Dignan. Most of the NEs in their study would be examples of LMEs (USA, England and Wales, New Zealand, Australia), and most of the SDCEs and CCEs in their study would be examples of CME (Sweden, Finland, Netherlands, Germany).[5]

Lacey presents a model that, in her view, is not limited to a "diagnostic typology" of the kind offered by Cavadino and Dignan, but which tries to explain these penal differences among countries at similar levels of economic development. She tries to provide an answer to the "why" and "how" questions, employing a number of "interlinking variables" (Lacey 2008, p. 56, 2011a, p. 216, 2012, pp. 209–210). This model is complex and it does not only include elements of the "economy," defined in restrictive terms. Lacey admits that these different variables are intricately intertwined and are hence difficult to separate in an analytically satisfactory way (2008, p. 61). However, she proceeds to do an exercise that schematically identifies five spheres. A great deal of her work after the book was published was aimed at refining and deepening the analysis of these variables—as well as applying them to national cases. We will resume here their formalization in a more recent text—and the order in which she enunciates them, which is the most appropriate (2011a, pp. 222–235).

The first domain is the structure of the economy, referring to the general typology of advanced capitalist economies that is the basis of her analytical framework (Lacey 2008, pp. 77–84, 2011a, pp. 222–224). In the LME, the collapse of the Fordist production regime and increasing global economic competition, produced an upshot of structural economic insecurity that affects particularly the bottom third of the workforce that risks becoming a socially and economically excluded group, in a context of more flexible and service oriented economic activities and stronger disparities of wealth. By contrast, in CMEs another kind of economic culture has survived global changes, related to different variables: the incorporation of employers and unions in the management of the economy, the nature of the economic activities on which these countries have concentrated their efforts, the tradition of strong investment in education and training. These elements produced high-skill, more regulated, production regimes and lower disparities of wealth. These differences in the structure of the economy are translated into the weakness or strength of an "anti-degradation mentality and sensibility," respectively, in the LME and the CME, as a cultural result of their own dynamics. Thus, the different tendencies in penal policy: in the LME towards harsh and exclusionary penalty, in the CME toward moderate and inclusionary penality.

The second domain is the political system, where she identifies two essential variables (Lacey 2008, pp. 62–77, 2011a, pp. 224–228). First, electoral arrangements. She points out that different electoral models tend to reflect, to a greater or lesser degree, public attitudes toward punishment—regardless of how they have been previously created, "from above" or "from below"—into penal policies. The first-past-the-post, winner-takes-all electoral systems—often found in the LME[6]—tend to make politicians more sensitive toward public opinion as elections get closer. This, in turn, is associated with a general weakening of party affiliation and the growing dependence of politicians on a large number of floating median voters.[7] When these floating median voters present "tough-on crime" attitudes and opinions, within this electoral framework, they are often translated into penal decisions and outcomes, through politicians' discourses and practices. This dynamic would be limited in proportional representation systems—frequently found in the CME—because of the strong weight of negotiation among diverse groups incorporated into the governmental process, and the hard work of reaching consensus, which makes taking decisions less dependent on the perceived swings of public opinion.[8] Besides, according to Lacey, the well-organized single-issue pressure groups, notably those representing the interests of the victims of crime, tend to be stronger in majority systems than in proportional representation systems—contrary to what it might be initially assumed.

This is particularly the case when the issue these groups deal with appeals to floating median voters, as it has actually happened in the LME, especially in the USA.[9] On the other hand, in the proportional representation system, this influence is usually blocked in the negotiation process among the diverse actors incorporated to the governmental process.[10]

Second, the weight of professional bureaucracy. Lacey stresses the importance of a professional and expert bureaucracy whose role is significant in the decision-taking process around penal policy—made up by the civil service, but also by criminal justice officials. In her view, in the CME this presence tends to be stronger, and this is a major reason for the moderate and inclusionary penal policy, whereas in the LME—especially in the USA and the UK—this presence is weaker and helps to understand the opposite penal outcome. In these last contexts, this is associated with the growing dominance of political party leaders who prefer their own politically appointed advisers and ignore the advice of technically neutral civil servants, in the framework of the politicization of crime and punishment. Therefore, their decisions turn even less insulated from the flow of perceived public opinion.

The third domain is the welfare state (Lacey 2008, pp. 84–91, 2011a, pp. 228–231, 2013, p. 271). Following other precedents in the sociology of penality, she states that an essential variable is the type and extension of welfare policies in the different contemporary capitalist economies. She differentiates—as Cavadino and Dignan using Esping Andersen's work (1990)—between "liberal," "continental" and "social democratic" welfare regimes, in a decreasing scale in terms of generosity of provision and scope of coverage. Punitiveness would vary inversely in relation to this scale. Lacey asks explicitly how this connection is explained, trying to identify the "precise causal mechanisms." She points out that a way of doing it is through a culturalist argument: the wide scope and generosity of the welfare regime and the moderate and inclusionary penal policy are the result of the same diffused cultural attitudes. Without denying the role of cultural attitudes, Lacey highlights the "political-economic reasons" related to the structure of the economy and its needs in terms of comparative advantages in the global context that in last instance foster cultural attitudes.

Within the fourth sphere, constitutional structure, she identifies three crucial variables (Lacey 2008, pp. 91–110, 2011a, pp. 231–234). In the first place, the constitutional distribution of decision-making power among different actors. Lacey states that the distribution of veto points across the constitutional structure and the need for coordinating different decision-making actors, opens potential for checks and balances and helps to resist external pressures toward penal severity. This is something that can be seen in certain federal states—Germany or Canada—though not in all—US. The difference is that in the former examples key aspects of penal policy have to be centrally determined, so the need of coordination. Lacey's perspective in this point is more tentative, recognizing the need for "careful empirical analysis" (2008, p. 93). As the examples given show, the variable analyzed here—unlike the other three spheres in her model—does not correlate with the broader differentiation of political economy between LMEs and CMEs.

In the second place, the tenure and selection of the judiciary and prosecutors. Lacey indicates the relevance of the difference—already highlighted in the literature—between a system where judges and prosecutors are appointed through popular election—as in some US states—and a less politicized system, based on their professional credentials and which regard them as part of the civil service—as in European states. The former is clearly more vulnerable to external pressures toward penal severity. She also highlights the relationship between the judiciary and the government as an important aspect of this variable, distinguishing between systems like the UK, where the principle of independence encourages the absolute lack of coordination, and the German system, which does not impede communication and discussion of the penal policy. She states that, within contexts of politicization of crime and punishment like the ones in the UK and the US, the first alternative has boosted conflicts between governments and judges and the loss of prestige and authority of the latter, as well as the capacity to influence legal and policy decision-making processes, which they seem to preserve in the CME contexts. If for this second aspect Lacey seems to sustain a certain correlation with the types of political economy, it does not seem to be the case for the first aspect, in which the US appears to be an exceptional case.

In the third place is the impact of the constitutional framework on what may be criminalized. Lacey highlights the difference between the common law and the continental legal system, as the latter tends to establish stronger constitutional constraints—which have deep historical roots—to the processes of criminalization. For her, this is translated into the tendency in the former to treat certain incidents as crimes, whereas the latter would regard them as administrative infractions. Besides this would imply a more "robust attitude to the need for the state to justify its penal power" in continental legal systems that would have a moderating impact on penal policy (2008, p. 106). In this case, Lacey explicitly states—unlike with the other variables in this sphere—"there is an association between this variable and the liberal/coordinated market economies distinction" (2011a, p. 234).[11]

Finally, the fifth domain is the institutional capacity to include those regarded as "others" (Lacey 2008, pp. 106–109, 115–169, 2011a, pp. 234–235, 2013, p. 272).

> While the laissez-faire and individualistic culture typical of LME may well make it relatively easy to integrate geographical or "cultural" outsiders such as recent immigrants wherever they find access to the labor market, the more intensively group- and skill-based system of the coordinated market economies may well pose significant challenges in terms of integrating newcomers into the representative and decision making structures which have helped to sustain a relatively moderate criminal justice policy with relatively high institutional capacity for reintegration.
>
> (2008, pp. 107–108)

Within the context of the boom of migration experienced in Europe in recent years, this variable could then challenge the tendency of the CMEs toward a moderate and inclusive penal policy.

As we can see, it is a complex descriptive and explanatory model that establishes different variables linked to one another. The differentiation between types of political economies is articulated here with a series of other components—although in some cases the correlations are not completely clear, as we have already said—which are different but substantively inscribed at an institutional level.

Contributions, limitations and challenges

It is possible to build a balance about these contemporary approaches to the renaissance of the political economy of punishment in a comparative framework. This implies highlighting important contributions and simultaneously identifying certain limitations and dilemmas for the future development of this type of inquiry.

Penal differences

A very important contribution of these comparative approaches, in terms of description, has been stressing significant differences in penality in different national contexts. This involves confronting an alternative vision that has been widely diffused in the last years in the sociology of punishment—particularly in English-speaking countries. This vision emphasizes the existence and development of a growing penal homogenization and convergence, based on a simplistic reading of the globalization process. Perhaps one of its best-known expressions is the "neoliberal penality thesis" elaborated among others by Loïc Wacquant (2000, 2009).[12]

Table 2.1 Incarceration rates (countries included in Cavadino and Dignan (2006b))

	1992	2002/2003	2016
USA	501	756	694 (2014)
South Africa	285	402	291
New Zealand	119	155	208
England and Wales	90	141	145
Australia	89	115	162
Italy	83	100	91
Germany	71	98	76
The Netherlands	49	100	61 (2015)
France	84	93	101
Sweden	60	73	53
Finland	70	70	55
Japan	36	53	45

Source: World Prison Brief, Institute for Criminal Policy Research.

At the same time, it is also important that the authors developing these comparative approaches—each one in their own way—have acknowledged the existence of pressures in the more moderate penal contexts—related with types of CMEs or CEs—toward increasing punitiveness. These pressures are in turn associated to global economic changes (Cavadino and Dignan 2006b, pp. 32–35, 43–49; Lacey 2008, pp. 115–169). They link these pressures to the evolution of the levels of incarceration in recent years, which in some moderate contexts showed significant growth, with the paradigmatic example of the Netherlands. If we return to the data set in the book by Cavadino and Dignan (2006b, p. 22) on the years 2002 and 2003, and compare them with the incarceration rates in these countries a decade before, in 1992—using the same source of information—an increase is observed in all the CCEs, though with varying degrees: 104 percent in the Netherlands, 38 percent in Germany, 20 percent in Italy and 11 percent in France. There was also an increase in one of the two SDCEs included in the study: Sweden, 22 percent—while the other, Finland, presents an absolute stability. This increasing trend was observed even in Japan, the only case of OCE included in their study, with a significant growth of 47 percent, albeit departing from a very low base. Despite these trends, the authors maintained that notwithstanding the existing pressures toward increasing punitiveness, it was inappropriate and premature to indicate the existence of a process of both economic and penal homogenization, under the American "liberal" or "neoliberal" model—see also in the case of Lacey (2010b, pp. 781–782, 2011a, pp. 215–216, 2013, pp. 270–271). More than a decade later, penal differences—considered only on the basis of this indicator—are sustained and reinforced, since most of these countries have experienced declines in their incarceration rate. In some cases, these drops are quite strong: 39 percent in the Netherlands, 27 percent in Sweden, 22 percent in Germany and 21 percent in Finland. The only exception is France, where it took a further growth of 8 percent.[13]

Punitiveness and the incarceration rate

The recognition of penal differences in these narratives has been structured primarily using the quantitative indicator of the incarceration rate, pointing to a crucial dimension of punitiveness. Matthews (2005) has criticized the extensive use of this last notion in recent literature on the sociology of punishment for not being clearly defined. He highlights what are its normal connotations of excess, related to punishment beyond or above what is necessary or appropriate, and putting forward the logical problems about how to define those levels of necessity or adequacy (Matthews 2005, p. 179)—in a similar sense, see Pease (1994, p. 118) and Roche (2007, pp. 539–541). Although the authors that contributed to these comparative approaches have not stated this concept in a precise way, from their work it seems to be understood, in broad terms, as the levels of pain or suffering produced by the penal system (Christie, 1982). I think this is a simpler and more useful way to define this notion. (Sozzo 2011, pp. 43–45).[14]

The incarceration rate as an indicator of the degree of punitiveness is obviously incomplete—as it has been repeatedly pointed out (Pease 1994, p. 117; Kommer 2004, p. 9; Nelken 2005, pp. 220–221, 2010a, p. 36, 2010b, p. 332; Tonry 2007, pp. 7–9; Brodeur 2007, pp. 61–63). However, it is one of the few indicators that are easily available in many national contexts, and it at least allows approaching the crucial phenomenon of the extension of the penal system comparatively. An important remaining task for this type of inquiry—even about the national contexts that are addressed by the authors under examination—is to explore other quantitative indicators referred to the extension of the penal system—from the rate of prison admissions to the rate of persons on probation and parole. And crucially, it is also necessary to include quantitative indicators referred to the other dimension of punitiveness, i.e., the intensity or severity of the penal system—from the rate of the different types of sentences imposed (custodial and non-custodial, effective and suspended, etc.) to the rate of deaths in custody. Besides, on both dimensions, this exploration should not be restricted to the identification of quantitative indicators, but should include qualitative indicators as well. Cavadino and Dignan (2006b) have taken an interesting step in this direction by including the age of criminal responsibility as a complementary indicator in their analytical framework.[15] Clearly, the expansion of the empirical indicators used to describe these penal differences could reinforce the picture these approaches have produced but it could also make them more complex and difficult to interpret (Nelken 2010a, p. 36). It is one of the main challenges for this type of inquiry in the near future.

The questions of "why" and "how"

Another important contribution these comparative approaches have produced is the attempt to connect observed penal differences with different types of contemporary political economy, even with characterizations—as we have seen—that are not identical. Per se, I considered these attempts a positive antidote against the "culturalist turn" that has flooded the sociology of punishment since the late 1980s.

A major point raised by these attempts is the identification of a number of elements and dimensions that are crucial to understand the "why" and "how" (Nelken 2011a, p. 106) of the relationship between political economy and penality, beyond the assumption of a direct and simple link. As we have seen, in Cavadino and Dignan's book (2006b) this identification is more tentative and winding, but in their later work (2011, 2014) it has become clearer. This by no means implies that the authors are conclusive, as they keep a certain caution about diverse elements and dimensions. Particularly, the "political realm," configured both by "political culture" and "political institutions," appears to be crucial—although they recognized some influence of the media and public opinion. In their argument, these elements and dimensions are always plural and play as filters or mediations. They operate in a space of influence that is opened up by the type of political economy and have, therefore, relative autonomy. The characteristics of these dimensions and elements are shaped by political economy, and they, in turn, shape penality. However, as we have seen, they also acknowledge, briefly, the possibility that elements and dimensions—even some political arrangements, like the popular election of criminal justice officials—that are independent of the general type of political economy have also produced penal outcomes. Although they still argue that the type of political economy is extremely relevant and shape penality through various mediations, they also recognize that the complexity of the penal field is open to other types of significant influences that need to be taken into consideration (Cavadino and Dignan 2006b, pp. 36, 337, 2011, pp. 209–210).

At first, Lacey's approach seems to go in the same direction. We can remember a quote from her book we used above where she says that political-economic forces "are mediated not only by cultural filters, but also by economic, political and social institutions" (2008, p. 57; see De Giorgi 2009, p. 400). In more recent texts she emphasizes this notion of mediation (2010a, p. 104, 2011a, pp. 215, 217). Nelken criticized her approach because cultural influences are only included as a consequence of economic and institutional arrangements but are not treated as independent variables that "need to be explored in their own right" (2011a, p. 108).

However, Lacey also claims "these comparative differences are not just a question of economic organization: indeed, economic differences are themselves reinforced by *independently important* features of political structure and organization" (2010a, p. 105, 2013, p. 274, my emphasis). The author recognizes these elements as "independently important" but at the same time, indicates that their effects "reinforce" "economic differences." In this sense, it would seem that these other elements could not hinder the influences that come from the economic field, generating divergent penal outcomes. However, in fact, Lacey suggests precisely this in the few pages she devoted to the cases of Canada and the state of Victoria in Australia, which can be considered "anomalies" in the context of LME because of their moderate incarceration rates and, particularly, because of their stability during the last decades (2008, pp. 118, 181–183, 2010a, p. 105).[16] In addition, in the original presentation of her argument, as we have seen, she emphasized that it was a model of "interlinking variables," which could be interpreted as a definition that goes beyond the idea of filter or mediation. And in this model she includes some variables related to the constitutional structures that are not correlated with the LME and CME distinction.[17] This would imply recognizing—as Cavadino and Dignan seem to do it, though without developing the argument in detail—that other elements or dimensions can produce an influence regardless of the type of political economy.

The implications of this recognition are very important and require further discussion (Nelken 2010a, p. 63). I think it is crucial for the renewal of the debates around the PEofP tradition. From my perspective it implies moving in a positive direction: it does not mean arguing that these elements or dimensions always play a role independently from the type of political economy, but that they can do it in specific cases and that we have to be aware of them in order to understand our penal present.

This recognition is particularly important to account for the penal differences that exist—in some cases very marked differences, just think of the USA example—between countries sharing a type of political economy—I will return to this point later. In turn, if we do not recognize the independent role of certain dimensions or factors beyond the type of political economy, it is very difficult to understand the penal mutations that have occurred recently in certain national contexts. For example, the case of the Netherlands. In 1980, its extremely low incarceration rate (27/100,000) perfectly reflected what in these comparative approaches could be expected of a CME or CE. However, from then on the incarceration rate almost increased fivefold, to 125/100,000 in 2006—a higher level than that of the other national scenarios of these family groupings and identical to the one in Australia, one of the LMEs or NEs. This extraordinarily significant punitive turn could be read as a consequence of the neoliberalization of this economic scenario and its social, political and cultural effects. Nevertheless, in less than ten years the incarceration rate fell back to less than half, 61/100,000. It seems difficult to reconcile this volatility of the levels of punitiveness in such a brief period with an argument about changes in the type of political economy (Nelken 2010a, p. 62, 2011a, p. 107).[18]

The central role of politics

These comparative approaches give a central role to politics in the construction of this connection between penality and political economy. This important contribution feeds a strong tendency in the contemporary sociology of punishment to claim the place of politics as crucial to our understanding of the dynamics and mutations of the penal field. At the same time, since these authors believe politics operates within a framework given by the types of political economies—even though, as we have just seen, it is acknowledged that some of its elements may have an independent influence on the penal field—their approaches are also an antidote against those that fall into "voluntarist" positions, imagining that politics operates without restrictions (Garland 2004, p. 181; Barker 2009, p. 29, 33; Gottschalk 2013a, pp. 253–254; Goodman et al. 2014, p. 5). As Jock Young posed (2004, p. 554) in a more general and classic way—recalling Marx's words in *The Eighteenth Brumaire of Louis Bonaparte*: "We exist, as it is said, in a world not of our making, we make our history not just as we please but under circumstances not chosen by ourselves, but encountered and transmitted from the past." The type of political economy and its transformations become especially significant when assessing why and how politics produces penal outcomes.

Generally speaking, in the contemporary literature exploring the link between politics and penality, there are many different ways of thinking politics. Lacey highlights the "institutional" dimensions of political systems, which usually have a legal or constitutional translation (electoral systems, the characteristics of professional bureaucracy, mechanisms of selection and tenure of the judiciary and prosecutors, etc.). As we have seen, Cavadino and Dignan have also emphasized this dimension—particularly in their latest texts—in dialogue with her work. The exploration of these institutional dimensions is very interesting and fruitful. It connects with a whole literature that has been working in this direction (Savelsberg 1994, 1999, 2002, pp. 692–695, 2004; Barker 2006, 2009, 2013; Garland 2010, 2013; Gottschalk 2013a, 2013b). Nevertheless, I think it is incomplete.

The way in which Cavadino and Dignan think about politics involves other significant components beyond these institutional dimensions. Reference is made to the "culture," to the "ideologies" of the "elites" and, in particular, of the "penal elites," which influence policy, legislative and judicial choices. Undoubtedly, this is a crucial element to understand the link between politics and penality, and has been pointed out in parallel by several authors in this field of study using diverse theoretical keys (e.g., O'Malley 1999, 2004; Sparks and Loader 2004, 2016). However, it is also essential to link it with the exploration of the empirical processes of strategies, struggles and resistances of state actors—including penal agents—and non-state actors through which decisions and actions that produce penal outcomes are forged. This is essential for the development of a more "substantively political" account of penality (O'Malley 1999, p. 189; see also Beckett 1997) that, as Sparks and Loader put it: "… sees political combat as pivotal" (Sparks and Loader 2004, p. 16; see also O'Malley 2004, pp. 185, 188; Brown 2005, p. 42; Goodman et al. 2014, pp. 12–14). Aspects of these elements appear when Lacey analyzes certain specific cases, such as Scotland, New Zealand or the United States in detail. It does not seem casual that this happens when she tries to do this kind of exercise.

A taxonomical approach?

These comparative approaches have been defined by Mc Ara (2011, p. 96) as "taxonomical," since they are based on grouping the objects to be analyzed according to a pre-established classification scheme—types of political economy—assigning different consequences—degrees of punitiveness—to the diverse categories. I think this definition fits better the work of Cavadino and Dignan. Although they include specific chapters about different countries in collaboration with local experts (2006b, pp. 151–196), they do not play a central role in the construction of the general model (Nelken 2010a, p. 61, 2011a, p. 106). Nelken believes that something similar can be said of Lacey's approach (2011a, p. 106). In my opinion, this could be pointed out with regard to her book—although there are already symptoms of going beyond the taxonomy—but it is more difficult to assert that as regards her later work. As a style of comparative research, these taxonomies face a number of limitations.

One of the most significant limitations is the fact that there are national contexts not originally included in the classification but that share the general features of one category or "family grouping" that present different penal policies and outcomes than those expected considering the general model. I have already mentioned the case of Canada as an apparent "anomaly" in the family of LMEs or NEs, which is briefly addressed by Lacey (Downes 2011, pp. 115–116).[19] Understanding this "anomaly"—as Lacey recognizes—requires the development of a specific and detailed empirical case study. This study should produce a diachronic analysis, rather than a synchronic one, typical of taxonomies (Mc Ara 2011, p. 99). Its results might imply—and, as we said above, Lacey herself is oriented in this direction—the recognition that there are independent factors that can influence the penal field despite the type of political economy. The challenge would be to identify them, to explain why and how they exist and why and how they produce these effects.

In addition, these comparative approaches cannot account for the differences that exist between different national contexts that are included in the same family groupings (Garland 2013, p. 492). The case of the USA stands out here in the framework of the LMEs or NEs, given the extreme levels of punitiveness in comparison with the other national contexts that fall into this category. Again, it is necessary here to go beyond the task of model building and to produce a specific and detailed empirical study of a diachronic nature. In fact, Lacey has devoted sustained efforts to this, showing that the variables associated with the LME are present to an extreme degree in the US, but also identifying other dimensions and elements that help to explain their huge level of punitiveness (Lacey 2008, pp. 119–130, 2010a, 2011a, pp. 239–245, Lacey and Soskice 2015). The same type of limitation is evidenced when it comes to accounting for the differences that exist within these "family groupings" as regards the recent evolution of incarceration rates. As we have seen, in the last decade, the national contexts considered to be LMEs or NEs in these studies present divergent tendencies: decline (USA, but also South Africa if included, as in Cavadino and Dignan's work), stability (England and Wales) and rise (Australia and New Zealand).[20] The question about such differences also calls for a detailed empirical inquiry of a diachronic nature but with the complexity required for a plurality of national contexts.[21]

In any case, the taxonomic exercises that these comparative approaches present initially can be considered a starting point rather than an end point for the comparative inquiry. This has been recognized by Lacey, who advocates the need for "model building" or "theoretical generalization" to go hand in hand with "detailed empirical research" because "both are interdependent" (2011a, p. 219). She states: "Models, like maps, inevitably simplify the terrain which they chart. But without their orienting framework, we cannot interpret the local data which we are collecting. Nor are we well equipped to decide which data is worthy of our attention" (2011a, p. 246). Simultaneously, the model has to be revised and refined in light of further findings.[22] In this light, as we have seen, she has explored various cases in detail in the works that followed her book (Scotland, New Zealand and USA). In some explorations she has addressed a single national context and the comparative exercise has been carried out in relation to the theoretical model (Lacey 2008, pp. 119–130, 2010a; Lacey and Soskice 2015). But in others she has included two jurisdictions selected for their relevance to a specific theoretical argument (Lacey 2011a, 2012). These valuable exercises have reconstructed aspects of the empirical processes that help understand strategies, struggles and resistances of state and non-state actors around the power to punish and how they have generated penal outcomes over time in a more general framework given by the type of political economy. These explorations have begun to open the "black box" that taxonomic exercises leave untouched (Garland 2013, p. 491). But not all of its implications have been identified and formalized—as we have already suggested—in general theoretical propositions. A crucial challenge for the future of this type of comparative research on the relationship between political economy and penality is to promote this type of studies, in depth comparisons between a few jurisdictions using both qualitative and quantitative indicators—as Garland (2013, p. 489)[23] has recently encouraged it, in general, for the sociology of punishment.

Beyond the Global North

These approaches were designed to think comparatively about the Global North. It surprises, in this regard, the inclusion of South Africa in the work of Cavadino and Dignan (2006a, 2006b). Is it possible to think this national context through the parameters of the "advanced capitalism," "advanced economies" or some similar category? Is it possible to understand its political economy with the classification used by these authors and originally designed by Esping-Andersen (1990)? It does not seem to be the case. As we have seen, Lacey cautiously acknowledges the need to generate "adaptations" when thinking of Central and Southern Europe and Latin America. Going beyond what in the most general field of "comparative capitalisms research" has been defined as the "Triad"—the US, Japan and some Western European countries—(Ebeneau 2015, p. 46) is probably the most important challenge for the future of this type of comparative research on the relationship between political economy and penality.

The questions are multiple and complex. Let us consider briefly the example of Latin America as a region of the Global South. At present, many Latin American countries have incarceration rates that are equal to or even higher than those of the countries identified as NEs or LMEs—with the exception of USA—in the literature we have analyzed—as it can be seen in Table 2.2. This single empirical data, coupled with a set of evidences about the strong strategies of neoliberalization of the Latin American economies since the 1970s—although with different modalities, intensities and temporalities—could lead to a line of inquiry that tries to associate these national cases within the NEs or LMEs type and in this way describe and explain their high levels of punitiveness. Even the marked contrast between contemporary incarceration rates and those in many of these countries in the early 1990s could feed a reading of this evolution of punitiveness in terms of transition from one type of political economy to another using the same typologies designed for the Global North—from CEs or CMEs to NEs or LMEs.[24] However, it does not seem a convincing route.

In recent years studies on comparative capitalisms have been holding a major debate about Latin America in relation to the "varieties of capitalism" approach launched by Hall and Soskice (2001). The work of Schneider (2009, 2013; Schneider and Soskice 2009) can be highlighted. Starting also from a neoinstitutionalist vision, Schneider has tried to postulate a new ideal type that makes the original dichotomy between LME and CME more complex when applied to Latin American cases: the Hierarchical Market Economy (HME). It is characterized by a strong domination by transnational corporations and domestic business groups that is translated into weak innovative capacities, forced concentration on activities less likely to generate quality employment, low economic growth and high levels of inequality, despite reform efforts in both a neoliberal and a neodevelopmentalist direction. This exercise has received different criticisms. In the first place, it has been criticized for its inability to account for a singular type out of the wide diversity of Latin American capitalisms. Consequently, the authors of this criticism intend to advance in the direction of a specific typology that differentiates in the region between a "state model oriented towards internal markets" (Brazil, Argentina); an "outwardly oriented model with considerable degree of state regulation if not direct intervention" (Chile), and an a "model of positive international integration and non intervention" (Mexico) (Bizberg 2011, 2012). In the second place, it has been pointed out that the type of HME, with its underlying business-centered framework, has not taken into account the central role of the state in Latin American economies and the importance and effects of recent neodevelopmentalist policies in some national contexts (Boschi 2011; Gaitan and Boschi 2015). Finally, more radically, it has been questioned the

Table 2.2 Incarceration rates in Latin America

	1992	2016
Brazil	74	307 (2014)
Argentina	62	169 (2015)
Colombia	78	235
Chile	154	235
Venezuela	133	159 (2015)
Uruguay	100	291 (2015)
Peru	69	257
Ecuador	74	162 (2014)
Bolivia	78	130
Paraguay	51	180 (2015)

Source: World Prison Brief, Institute for Criminal Policy Research; Sozzo (2016, 2017).

methodological nationalism of the literature on "varieties" of capitalism and the need to recognize the centrality of the transnational influences and the weight of the historical differentiation between center and periphery in order to understand Latin America capitalism, rescuing theoretical elements of dependency, imperialism and postcolonial approaches (Fernandez and Alfaro 2011; Ebenau 2012, 2014, 2015; Fernandez and Bazz 2016). As it is evident, there is extremely fertile ground for understanding penal mutations in Latin America that would arise from the dialog with these debates about Latin American capitalisms, and that seems to go far beyond the concepts and arguments originally proposed by these comparative approaches on the relationship between political economy and penality for the Global North.[25]

To conclude, I consider that these comparative approaches on the relationship between political economy and penality generate very significant contributions and open up a series of questions and alternatives that are extremely important for the development of this line of research, in a "post-reductionist" direction— as it has recently been advocated by Alessandro de Giorgi (2013a, pp. 52–56, 2013b, pp. 40–43). This post-reductionist direction has to depart from a strong recognition of differences—both economic and penal—across the globe, and commit itself to understanding them comparatively in innovative ways—in this sense, see also De Giorgi (2013, pp. 51–52). A great deal of its possibilities depend on this kind of move.

Notes

1 The authors believe the results of this comparative research are compatible with what they define as "a radical pluralist theory of societies, which seeks to synthesize aspects of Marxist, Durkheimian and Weberian traditions of sociology" (Cavadino and Dignan 2006b, pp. 12–14; on this approach, Cavadino and Dignan 2002, pp. 76–79, 2011, p. 198).
2 In fact, key authors like Melossi, Ignatieff, Jankovic or Box did not even appear on the list of references of their book. In addition, Rusche and Kirchheimer—whose book is included on the list of references—are only quoted once in the foreword by David Downes (VIII).
3 They also include qualitative features, like the receptiveness to prison privatization, dominant penal ideologies or the model of youth justice—particularly, the age of criminal responsibility (Cavadino and Dignan 2006b, p. 15).
4 In the conclusion, they state that this association of the penal outcomes with the different types of political economy is not an "iron law of penality" (Cavadino and Dignan 2006b, p. 337, 2011, p. 210).
5 The exceptions are, on one side, France and "the countries of southern Europe"— among the ones included in Cavadino and Dignan's study there is only Italy—which for Hall and Soskice combine features of both coordinated and liberal market economies (Lacey 2008, p. 59, 2012, p. 210). On Italy, using elements of Lacey's approach see Gallo (this volume). South Africa is also excluded from Lacey's analysis because it is not included in the literature on "varieties of capitalism" (2008, p. 59) and because she deals with "advanced economies." She mentions the need to adapt this approach "in relation to other regions such as Latin America" (2010b, p. 789, 2011a, p. 219, 2012, p. 210).

6 Lacey recognizes the divergent case of New Zealand (2008, p. 64). She will go back to this example several times, emphasizing that the different penal outcomes in contexts with the same electoral arrangement is an evidence of the need to take into consideration a model of "interlinking variables." The weight of one single variable is not determinant. In the case of NZ, she points out that the PR arrangement has been introduced in 1996 in an already organized LME, without reflecting established class interests articulated with the production regime and embedded social identities represented in political parties (see also Lacey 2011a, pp. 236–239, 2011b, 2012, pp. 216–227, 2013, pp. 276–277). Mc Ara (2011, p. 98) also critically indicates the example of Scotland, after the devolution. Lacey has also recently addressed this case, trying to demonstrate the need to consider the "interlinking variables" in relation to the pre-existence of a multiparty system, the lack of single issue groups, and the weight of other themes in the public debate—as the question of independence (2012, pp. 227–234).

7 This can be regarded as a general phenomenon in contemporary liberal democracies, beyond the type of electoral arrangements and beyond "advanced economies." Lacey seems to confine it in her original analysis to the LME (see also, Lacey 2012, pp. 213–214). In one of her articles about the US case she highlights that this element is present in other contexts but in this national context it is older and more extreme (2010a, p. 109).

8 Lacey (2008, pp. 67–68) in turn connects this to the results borne out of empirical research in political science that the proportional representation systems show a tendency toward building left-of-center governments, which would be subsequently translated into the substance of social and economic policies.

9 Lacey points out that this has been strengthened in the USA due to two peculiar elements of its political system. In the first place, the weak levels of party discipline, which implies that the individual candidates build their own platforms in an attempt to connect with the floating median voters. Second, the extraordinarily decentralized nature of democracy in the US (see also Lacey 2010a, pp. 109–111). I wonder if the first of these two elements could not be considered a variable that is not confined to the US case or dependent on the electoral arrangements: strength/weakness of political parties, relationship with a program or platform, individual candidate's weight and intra-party dynamics. More recently, Lacey seems to be going in this direction (2011a, pp. 242–243, 2012, pp. 226, 232, 234).

10 With the important exception, again, of New Zealand (Lacey 2012, pp. 219, 222–223). I wonder if the uneven development of these well-organized, single-issue pressure groups representing the victims of crime cannot be considered an important element, regardless of the electoral arrangements.

11 Lacey also mentions the difference between unicameral and bicameral/multicameral legislatures, although—as with the federal/unitary divide—she highlights its divergent influence on the penal field in different national cases (2008, p. 92). She also refers to the scale or size of the political system—considering the work of Mc Ara (2005) on Scotland and Cavadino and Dignan (2006b) on the Netherlands—to stress again that in different scenarios, it produced opposite penal outcomes (2008, p. 93). More recently, she points out the availability of citizen-initiated referenda as an important variable in some cases (2012, p. 208). In any case, none of these other elements are correlated with the differentiation between LME and CME. One interesting point would be whether, beyond these variables, other kind of more general distinctions about the types of political systems could be useful for comparative purposes between LME and CME—but also beyond this distinction. For example, the differentiation between majoritarian and consensual democracies, which has also been used recently to compare penal policies (Green 2007, 2008; Tonry 2007). This was somewhat referred by Lacey's herself, but associating it to the different electoral systems she

identified (2008, p. 65, 2012, p. 213). Another important distinction would be between parliamentary and presidentialist regimes. Many political systems with a presidentialist regime have a PR electoral arrangement but operate in many respects in the form that Lacey attributes to winner-takes-all electoral arrangements. Finally, the distinction between two-party electoral competition and multi-party electoral competition that is not strictly correlated with the electoral arrangements and seems to be important—as Lacey states in relation to Scotland (2012, pp. 233–234).

12 It is not by chance that Lacey has recently made substantial efforts to discuss this thesis critically (2010b, 2013).
13 Interestingly there are national contexts considered NEs or LMEs that have also experienced a strong decrease in the incarceration rate. Notably, South Africa—included in Cavadino and Dignan's research but not in Lacey's study—with a 28 percent decrease. Also the US, though in a much more moderate way (8 percent). England and Wales remained stable. On the contrary, Australia and New Zealand continue to experience strong growths: 41 percent and 34 percent, respectively. In any case, this evolution introduces the problem of the existence of different trends in the same family grouping. I will go back to this point later on.
14 In this sense, it is practically a contradiction in its own terms to refer to "non-punitive sanctions" or "non-punitive societies." Sanctions always imply, from this point of view, a certain amount of pain or suffering and therefore, they are always "punitive," to a greater or lesser degree. Of course, this way of defining punitiveness also creates great difficulty for its empirical research—see Pease (1994); Kommer (1994, 2004); Frost (2006, 2008); Tonry (2007, pp. 7–13); Hamilton (2014, pp. 109–132).
15 A very interesting recent study that advances in this direction is Hamilton's comparison between Ireland, Scotland and New Zealand (2014).
16 In the case of Canada, Lacey mentions the influence of Francophone legal and political culture, the distinctive structure of federalism and its relation with decision-making processes in the penal field, a political culture oriented toward consensus and the cultural and political significance of differentiating Canada from the US (2008, p. 182, 2010a, p. 105). And in the case of Victoria she points to some liberal penal policies and the relatively low number of Aboriginal Australians in this state (2008, p. 182; see on this case, Tubex, this volume). She states: "Our understanding of these differences is as yet relatively shallow, and a thorough analysis would need to look closely at the circumstances and institutional features of particular countries which either buck, or lead, the general trend towards penal harshness" (2008, pp. 182–183). I will go back to this point later on.
17 In an article about "coalition politics" and its impact on penality, she asks explicitly if the institutional features of political systems operate as independent variables and in what measure (Lacey 2012, p. 216). However, her answer, after exploring two case studies, seems to be negative.
18 The Netherlands is not the only case that presents this degree of volatility in terms of punitiveness. We also mentioned before the recent decline of incarceration rates in South Africa—a country included in Cavadino and Dignan's study. Just to put an extreme example from the Global South, in Ecuador the prison rate of 2014 was 162/10,000, but in 2009 it was less than half, 73/100,000. In turn, in 2007, it had reached 130/100,000 and in 2000 it was 64/100,000. The last two strong penal turns have been produced during a period of national governments of a postneoliberal political alliance (Sozzo 2016, 2017).
19 Regarding the classification of Cavadino and Dignan, we can also mention the case of the Netherlands. At certain times over the last 40 years (such as the 1980s and early 1990s and, again, today), taking in consideration its rate of incarceration, this country could be included in the SDCEs family rather than in that of the CCEs—something that these authors explicitly recognized (2006b, p. 21).
20 The same could be said of France and its moderate increase as the exception to the generalized downward trend in all types CEs, using Cavadino and Dignan's

classification. Lacey made this point incidentally about the previous evolution of incarceration rate in the Netherlands, markedly different to the one of Germany (2011a, p. 236).
21. It could also be pointed out that it is difficult for an exclusively taxonomic perspective to account for the strong differences observed at the subnational level in many of the cases addressed by this comparative literature (Mc Ara 2011, pp. 97–98). I noted above the case of the state of Victoria in Australia. The case of the United States also stands out here. Again, in some later works, Lacey analyzes it by going beyond the dimensions and elements originally included in her theoretical model (2013, pp. 275–276).
22. Lacey appeals, in this sense, to avoid a tendency present in comparative studies of penality, "to become mesmerized by the fascinating details of local peculiarity" that ends up reducing it to a "study of the particular and in its less sophisticated forms, the 'exotic'" (2011a, p. 218).
23. Recalling the classic example of David Downes' (1988) study, to which studies that are more recent could be added, as Green (2007, 2008) and Hamilton (2014).
24. The punitive turn in Latin America has been recently interpreted using the notion of neoliberalism but as a transnational political project rather than a type of political economy (Iturralde 2010, 2012, 2014; Müller 2011).
25. For example, a crucial question in this context is which are the economic, social, political and cultural effects of the postneoliberal and neo-developmentalist policies that were launched in the last years in some countries of Latin America (Venezuela, Ecuador, Bolivia, Argentina, Brazil, etc.) and what impact, in turn, they produced in the penal field—see about some of these national scenarios, Sozzo (2016, 2017).

References

Barker, V. (2006). Politics of punishing: building a state governance theory of American imprisonment. *Punishment and Society*, 8 (1), 5–33.
Barker, V. (2009). *The politics of imprisonment. How the democratic process shapes the way America punishes offenders*. New York: Oxford University Press.
Barker, V. (2013). Prison and the public sphere. Towards a democratic theory of penal order. *In*: Scott, D., eds., *Why Prison?* Cambridge: Cambridge University Press, 5–33.
Beckett, K. (1997). *Making crime pay*. New York: Oxford University Press.
Bizberg, I. (2011). The global economic crises as disclosure of different types of capitalism in Latin America. *Swiss Journal of Sociology*, 37 (2), 321–339.
Bizberg, I. (2012). Types of capitalism in Latin America. *Interventions Economiques*, 49, 1–26.
Boschi, R.R., ed. (2011). *Variedades de Capitalismo, Politica e Desenvolvimento na America Latina*. Belo Horizonte: Editora UFMG.
Box, S. (1987). *Recession, crime and punishment*. London: Rowman & Littlefield.
Brodeur, J.P. (2007). Comparative penology in perspective. *In*: Tonry, M., eds., *Crime, punishment and politics in comparative perspective*. Chicago: The University of Chicago Press, 49–91.
Brown, D. (2005). Continuity, rupture of just more of the "volatile and contradictory"? Glimpses of the New South Wales penal practices behind and through the discursive. *In*: Pratt, J., Brown, D. and Brown, M, eds., *The new punitiveness. Trends, theories, perspectives*. Cullompton: Willan, 27–46.
Cavadino, M. and Dignan, L. (2002). *The penal system. An Introduction*. London: Sage.

Cavadino, M. and Dignan, J. (2006a). Penal policy and political economy. *Criminology and Criminal Justice*, 6 (4), 435–456.
Cavadino, M. and Dignan, J. (2006b). *Penal systems. A comparative approach.* London: Sage.
Cavadino, M. and Dignan, J. (2011). Penal comparison: puzzling relations. *In*: Crawford, A., ed., *International and comparative criminal justice and urban governance.* Cambridge: Cambridge University Press, 193–213.
Cavadino, M. and Dignan, J. (2014). Political economy and penal systems. *In*: Body-Gendrot, S., Hough, M., Kerezsi, K., Lévy, R. and Snacken, S., eds., *The Routledge handbook of European criminology.* Abingdon: Routledge (Kindle Edition).
Chiricos, T. and DeLone, M. (1992). Labor surplus and punishment: a review and assessment of theory and evidence. *Social Justice*, 39 (4), 421–446.
Christie, N. (1982). *Limits to pain.* London: Sage.
De Giorgi, A. (2006). *Re-rhinking the political economy of punishment. Perspectives on post-Fordism and penal policy.* Aldershot: Ashgate.
De Giorgi, A. (2009). Book review: Nicola Lacey: the prisoner's dilemma. Cambridge: Cambridge University Press, 2008. *Theoretical Criminology*, 13 (3), 398–402.
De Giorgi, A. (2013a). Punishment and political economy. *In*: Sparks, R. and Simon, J., eds., *The Sage Handbook of Punishment and Society.* London: Sage, 40–59.
De Giorgi, A. (2013b). Prisons and social structure in late-capitalist societies. *In*: Scott, D., eds., *Why Prison?* Cambridge: Cambridge University Press, 25–43.
Downes, D. (1988). *Contrasts in tolerance. Post war penal policies in the Netherlands and England and Wales.* Oxford: Clarendon.
Downes, D. (2011). Against penal inflation. Comment on Nicola Lacey's The prisoners' dilemma. *Punishment and Society*, 13 (1), 114–120.
Ebenau, M. (2012). Varieties of capitalism of dependency? A critique of VofC approach to Latin America. *Competition & Change*, 16 (3), 206–223.
Ebenau, M. (2014). Comparative capitalism and Latin American developmentalism: a critical political economy view. *Capital & Class*, 38 (1), 102–114.
Ebenau, M. (2015). Directions and debates in the globalization of comparative capitalisms research. *In*: Ebenau, M., Bruff, I. and May, C., eds., *New directions in comparative capitalisms research. Critical and global perspectives.* London: Palgrave Macmillan, 45–61.
Esping-Andersen, G. (1990). *The three worlds of welfare capitalism.* Cambridge: Polity Press.
Fernandez, V.R. and Alfaro, M.B. (2011). Ideas y políticas de desarrollo regional bajo variedades de capitalismo: contribuciones desde la periferia. *Revista Paranaense de Desenvolvimento*, 120, 57–99.
Fernandez, V.R. and Bazza, A. (2016). Repensando las variedades de capitalismo desde la periferia. *Desevolvimento em Questao*, 14 (35), 5–34.
Frost, N. (2006). *The punitive state. Crime, punishment and imprisonment across the United States.* New York: LBF Scholarly Publishing.
Frost, N. (2008). The mismeasure of punishment: alternative measures of punitiveness and their (substantial) consequences. *Punishment and Society*, 10 (3), 277–300.
Gaitan, F. and Boschi, R.R. (2015). State-business-labour relations and patterns of development in Latin America. *In*: Ebenau, M., Bruff, I. and May, C., eds., *New directions in comparative capitalisms research. Critical and global perspectives.* London: Palgrave Macmillan, 172–188.

Garland, D. (1990). *Punishment and modern society*. Chicago: The University of Chicago Press.
Garland, D. (2004). Beyond the culture of control. *Critical Review of International Social and Political Philosophy*, 7 (2), 160–189.
Garland, D. (2010). *Peculiar institution. American death penalty in an age of abolition*. Cambridge: Harvard University Press.
Garland, D. (2013). Penality and the penal state. *Criminology*, 51 (3), 475–515.
Goodman, P., Page, J. and Phelps, M. (2014). The long struggle: an agonistic perspective on penal development. *Theoretical Criminology*, 19 (3), 315–335.
Gottschalk, M. (2013a). The politics of the carceral state: yesterday, today and tomorrow. *In*: Scott, D., eds., *Why prison?* Cambridge: Cambridge University Press, 233–258.
Gottschalk, M. (2013b). The carceral state and the politics of punishment. *In*: Sparks, R. and Simon, J., eds., *The Sage Handbook of Punishment and Society*. London: Sage, 205–241.
Green, D. (2007). Comparing penal cultures. *In*: Tonry, M., ed., *Crime, punishment and politics in comparative perspective*. Chicago: The University of Chicago Press, 591–643.
Green, D. (2008). *When children kill children: penal populism and penal culture*. Oxford: Oxford University Press.
Hall, P.A. and Soskice, D., eds. (2001) *Varieties of capitalism*. Oxford: Oxford University Press.
Hamilton, C. (2014). *Reconceptualising penality. A comparative perspective on punitiveness in Ireland, Scotland and New Zealand*. Farnham: Ashgate.
Ignatieff, M. (1978). *A just measure of pain: the penitentiary in the Industrial Revolution, 1750–1850*. New York: Pantheon.
Iturralde, M. (2010). Democracies without citizenship: crime and punishment in Latin America. *New Criminal Law Review*, 13 (2), 309–322.
Iturralde, M. (2012). O governo neoliberal da insegurança social na América Latina: semelhanças e diferenças com o Norte Global. *In*: Malaguti, V., ed., *Loic Wacquant e a questao penal no capitalismo neoliberal*. Rio de Janeiro: Revan, 169–196.
Iturralde, M (2014). La revolución desde arriba. La sociología política del estado penal neoliberal y su relevancia para América Latina. Paper presented at the Latin American Studies Association Conference, Chicago, 2014.
Jankovic, I. (1977). Labor market and imprisonment. *Crime and Social Justice*, 8, 17–31.
Kommer, M. (1994). Punitiveness in Europe: a comparison. *European Journal of Criminal Policy and Research*, 2 (1), 29–43.
Kommer, M. (2004). Punitiveness in Europe revisited. *Criminology in Europe*, 3 (1), 8–12.
Lacey, N. (2008). *The prisoners' dilemma. Political economy and punishment in contemporary democracies*. Cambridge: Cambridge University Press.
Lacey, N. (2010a). American imprisonment in comparative perspective. *Daedalus*, 139 (3), 102–114.
Lacey, N. (2010b). Differentiating among penal states. *British Journal of Sociology*, 61 (4), 778–794.
Lacey, N. (2011a). Why globalization doesn't spell convergence: models of institutional variation and the comparative political economy of punishment. *In*: Crawford, A., eds., *International and comparative criminal justice and urban governance*. Cambridge: Cambridge University Press, 214–250.

Lacey, N. (2011b). The prisoner's dilemma and political systems: the impact of proportional representation on criminal justice in New Zealand. *Victoria University of Wellington Law Review*, 42 (2), 615–637.
Lacey, N. (2012). Political systems and criminal justice: the prisoners' dilemma after the coalition. *Current Legal Problems*, 65, 203–239.
Lacey, N. (2013). Punishment, (neo)liberalism and social democracy. *In*: Sparks, R. and Simon, J., eds., *The Sage Handbook of Punishment and Society*. London: Sage, 260–280.
Lacey, N. and Soskice, D. (2015). Crime, punishment and segregation in the United States: the paradox of local democracy. *Punishment and Society*, 17 (4), 454–481.
Loader, I. and Sparks, R. (2016). Ideologies and crime: political ideas and the dynamic of crime control. *Global Crime*, 17, 3–4.
Matthews, R. (2005). The myth of punitiveness. *Theoretical Criminology*, 9 (2), 175–201.
Mc Ara, L. (2005). Modelling penal transformations. *Punishment and Society*, 7 (3), 277–302.
Mc Ara, L. (2011). Global politics and local culture. A response to Nicola Lacey. *Punishment and Society*, 13 (1), 96–104.
Melossi, D. (1978). George Rusche and Otto Kirchheimer: punishment and social structure. *Social Justice*, 9, 73–85.
Melossi, D. (1993). Gazette of morality and social whip: punishment, hegemony and the case of the US, 1970–1992. *Social & Legal Studies*, 2, 259–279.
Melossi, D., ed. (1998). *The sociology of punishment*. Aldershot: Dartmouth.
Melossi, D. (2003). Introduction to the Transaction edition. The simple "heuristic maxim" of an "unusual human being." *In*: Rusche, G. and Kirchheimer, O., *Punishment and Social Structure*. New Brunswick: Transaction, ix–xlv.
Melossi, D. and Pavarini, M. (1981). *The prison and the factory. Origins of the penitentiary system*. London: Macmillan.
Müller, M.M. (2011). The rise of the penal state in Latin America. *Contemporary Justice Review*, 15 (1), 57–76.
Nelken, D. (2005). When a society is non-punitive? The Italian case. *In*: Pratt, J. et al., eds., *The new punitiveness. Trends, theories, perspectives*. Cullompton: Willan, 218–235.
Nelken, D. (2010a). *Comparative criminal justice*. London: Sage.
Nelken, D. (2010b). Denouncing the penal state. *Criminal Justice and Criminology*, 10 (4), 329–338.
Nelken, D. (2011a). Explaining differences in European prison rates: a comment on Lacey's the prisoner dilemma. *Punishment and Society*, 13 (1), 104–114.
Nelken, D. (2011b). Making sense of punitiveness. *In*: Nelken, D., ed., *Comparative criminal justice and globalization*. Farnham: Ashgate, 11–26.
O'Malley, P. (1999). Volatile and contradictory punishment. *Theoretical Criminology*, 3 (2), 175–196.
O'Malley, P. (2004). Penal policies and contemporary politics. *In*: Sumner, C., ed., *The Blackwell Companion to Criminology*. Oxford: Blackwell, 183–195.
Pease, K. (1994). Cross national imprisonment rates. Limitations of method and possible conclusions. *British Journal of Criminology*, 34 (Special Issue), 116–130.
Pratt, J. (2007). *Penal populism*. London: Routledge.
Roche, S. (2007). Criminal justice policy in France: illusions of severity. *In*: Tonry, M., ed., *Crime, punishment and politics in comparative perspective*. Chicago: The University of Chicago Press, 471–550.

Rusche, G. and Kirchheimer, O. ([1939] 2003). *Punishment and social structure*. New Brunswick: Transaction.
Savelsberg, J. (1994). Knowledge, domination and criminal punishment. *American Journal of Sociology*, 99 (4), 911–943.
Savelsberg, J. (1999). Knowledge, domination and criminal punishment revisited. Incorporating state socialism. *Punishment and Society*, 1 (1), 45–70.
Savelsberg, J. (2002). Cultures of Control in contemporary societies. *Law and Social Inquiry*, 27 (3), 685–710.
Savelsberg, J. (2004). Historical contingencies and institutional conditions of criminal punishment. *Law and Social Inquiry*, 29 (2), 373–401.
Schneider, B.R. (2009). Hierarchical market economies and varieties of capitalism in Latin America. *Journal of Latin American Studies*, 41 (3), 553–575.
Schneider, B.R. (2013). *Hierarchical capitalism in Latin America: business, labour and the challenge of equitable development*. Cambridge: Cambridge University Press.
Schneider, B.R. and Soskice, D. (2009). Inequality in developed countries and Latin America: coordinated, liberal and hierarchical systems. *Economy and Society*, 38 (1), 17–52.
Sozzo, M. (2011). *Transition to democracy and penal policy. The case of Argentina*. Straus Working Paper, March 2011.
Sozzo, M., ed. (2016). *Postneoliberalismo y penalidad en América del Sur*. Buenos Aires: CLACSO.
Sozzo, M. (2017). Mas allá de la "tesis de la penalidad neoliberal"? Giro punitivo y cambio político en América del Sur. *Revista Brasileira de Ciencias Criminais*, 25 (129), 321–348.
Sparks, R. and Loader, I. (2004). For an historical sociology of crime control policy in England and Wales. *Critical Review of International Social and Political Philosophy*, 7 (2), 5–32.
Tonry, M. (2007). Determinants of penal policy. *In*: Tonry, M., ed., *Crime, punishment and politics in comparative perspective*. Chicago: The University of Chicago Press, 1–48.
Wacquent, L. (2000). *Las prisiones de la miseria*. Buenos Aires: Manantial.
Wacquant, L. (2009). *Punishing the poor*. Durham: Duke University Press.
Wacquant, L. (2013). Crafting the neoliberal state: workfare, prisonfare and social insecurity. *In*: Scott, D., eds, *Why prison?* Cambridge: Cambridge University Press, 3–36.
Young, J. (2004). Crime and the dialectics of inclusion/exclusion. Some comments on Yar and Penna. *British Journal of Criminology*, 44 (4), 550–561.

Chapter 3

For and against the political economy of punishment

Thoughts on Bourdieu and punishment

Ignacio González-Sánchez[1]

This chapter offers up proposals in the hope of overcoming some of the limitations of the political economy of punishment. To that end, some of the main contributions this trend makes will be highlighted; their value acknowledged and recovered for future works. Next, the most recent criticisms will be reviewed. The third part will be devoted to proposing some solutions departing from the work of sociologist Pierre Bourdieu, who considered some of the limitations of Marxist approaches in his own work.

The political economy of punishment

The political economy of punishment is a branch of the study of punitive forms, of their articulation, functioning and functionality, which has a long and intermittent tradition. It is mainly based on Karl Marx's analysis of capitalism and of the relations and dynamics it generates and Pashukanis' analysis of Law. It became consolidated in the social sciences by Rusche's (and Kirchheimer) work. After its revival in critical criminology in the 1970s, over the last decades specific contributions have been made, some proposing theoretical renewal (Melossi 1985; De Giorgi, 2006), and others the accumulation and refinement of empirical support (for instance, Chiricos and Delone 1992; Jacobs and Carmichael 2001; Sutton 2004). Throughout, it has become one of the main perspectives for the study of punishment (see Garland 1990).

Probably, its major contribution was initiating *the empirical study of punishments*, against philosophical studies on punishment. In this respect, Rusche and Kirchheimer ([1939] 2004, p. 3) pointed out that 'Punishment as such does not exist; only concrete systems of punishment and specific criminal practices exist'. That is, necessitating the study of concrete forms of punishment in their historical specificity (Garland 1990, p. 90), making a materialistic and historical approach possible about specific times and places – and even acknowledging, within this same tradition, that categories of 'time' and 'space' are contingent (Spitzer 1995, p. 13).

Furthermore, its more characteristic contribution has to do with the importance given to modes of production in the form and intensity punishments take

(Rusche and Kirchheimer [1939] 2004, pp. 3, 5, 7; Melossi and Pavarini [1977] 1981, p. 7), and with how class struggles contribute to their transformation (Humphries and Greenberg 1981, p. 213). Given that this approach advocates for a historically and geographically situated study, and that its interest has been coupled with modern forms of punishment, when 'modes of production' is called upon, reference to capitalism is usually being made. *The relationship between productive and penal systems* has been described as being indirect and fundamentally mediated by understandings of time, value and penalties within a homogenizing contractual matrix (Melossi and Pavarini [1977] 1981, pp. 3, 185; Spitzer 1981, p. 215). In turn, the intensity of punishments, especially that of prison, is related to the principle of less eligibility, while its extension has more to do with the needs of labour and both aspects are not independent from each other (Melossi and Pavarini [1977] 1981, p. 51; Rusche and Kirchheimer [1939] 2004). In other words, what determines the extension and conditions of punishment is outside of punishment itself (the demand for labour and the living conditions to which the lower working class can have access to).

In addition, this approach contains interesting clues for *understanding penal institutions as disciplinary mechanisms destined to make subjects willing and ready to work under capitalist conditions* – that is, ready for exploitation (Foucault [1975] 1977, pp. 135–169;[2] Melossi and Pavarini [1977] 1981, p. 11, 21). By this logic, confinement institutions influence labour's economic value, not just by temporarily kidnapping the labour force (and thus manipulating supply), but also by removing people's freedom of movement and, after disciplining them reinserting them in the 'free' market (De Giorgi 2006, p. 13).

The condition of deprivation of liberty under which the body is disciplined is a result of the application of Law – 'bourgeois' Law, for this tradition. It does so by creating legal subjects who have rights, generally of an individual nature (Garland 1990, p. 112). Thus a form of punishment that takes the form of a deprivation of some of those rights when Laws are not observed can be seen to exist. In this approach, on the one hand, Law gathers and defends a set of rules that represent the interests of the ruling class – linked to conditions for being able to grow richer and to preserve the status quo. On the other hand, some necessary fictions are created so that people consent to living under the capitalist system; these include the existence of general interests, submission to exploitation as an act of free will between equal individuals, and so on (Garland 1990, p. 92). Thus, another important contribution relates to *understanding juridical forms as representations destined to conceal the reality of the conditions of exploitation* and, by these means, achieving consent and consolidating these social conditions.

As a consequence of the imperative of studying specific forms of punishment, the political economy of punishment has produced *a considerable amount of empirical evidence* (notwithstanding, see the considerations made in Lynch 1987). A good number of studies have provided, in this sense, strong correlations between the evolution of labour market and that of penality. Specifically, the most fruitful empirical contributions seem to have been those that study the relations between imprisonment rates and unemployment rates (see a good summary in De Giorgi 2006, pp. 20–32). Comparatively, there seems to be a more intense and stable relationship between these two indicators than that which exists between imprisonment and crime rates, questioning what Melossi (1989, p. 311) calls 'legal syllogism'.

To sum up, the political economy of punishment is a very fruitful branch of study that contributes a good deal of conceptual tools and empirical evidence for understanding the dynamics of punishment, and that not all the theoretical traditions are able to match. Notwithstanding, its reception has been rather ambivalent and is still marked by extra scientific features, such as the association of Marxist analysis with left-wing political positioning and the traditional American structural censorship of the use of Marx in social sciences. In fact, still nowadays, it is possible to find uses of the label 'Marxist' as a criticism itself, substituting an argued criticism. By comparison, it is difficult to find the same treatment with labels such as Durkheimian or Weberian, which are usually used in a more descriptive fashion.

Sharing Garland's idea of punishment as a complex social institution (1990, pp. 281–283), I think that the existence of influences running between penality and capitalism cannot be ignored. Moreover, it is fair to characterize most of contemporary societies as capitalist, while acknowledging the multiple varieties existing (Hall and Soskice 2001) and avoiding reductionism. It is not hard to see that we are part of many concrete capitalist relations, which generate, and are carried out within, markedly capitalist institutions, and that those relationships are maintained and changed thanks to these institutions. Thus I see no theoretical or empirical reasons to carry out studies on punishment without paying attention to the relation it has with the productive system[3] – unless it is thought that when the words 'capitalism' or 'productive system' are mentioned research stops being 'rigorous'.

I do not mean to suggest that the analytical proposals of the political economy of punishment are not problematic. The most recurrent criticism will be briefly reviewed for the purpose of elaborating a theoretical proposal that enables the remarkable contributions of this approach to be retained, while taking some of its limitations as a starting point.

Criticisms of the political economy of punishment

Before dealing with criticisms, some issues must be specified. First, Marxist literature is measureless: it consists of more than 100 years of writing in all imaginable areas of knowledge (this is of very varied quality and means that it is easy to find references for whatever idea that needs support and, dangerously, it is easy to exclude thinkers who disagree with whatever portrayal of Marxism is being put forward). For this reason, it may well be that some of the criticism of the political economy of punishment might have been solved in other areas where the political economy is applied, and that the division of disciplines make us try to solve issues which have already been overcome in other areas.

Therefore, this work is limited to authors who specifically work on punishment and it will mostly include criticisms that have already been made.[4]

Second, it is characteristic of this tradition that a good deal of criticism comes from authors whose work is influenced by Marxist thought. It is, in fact, a perspective that tends to be very critical with itself (due perhaps to the epistemological question of the approach itself, or the idiosyncratic competition among Marxists over who seems most critical). That is, criticisms *of* the political economy of punishment are to a great extent criticisms *from* the political economy of punishment. As a matter of fact, precisely due to much having been written and to this logic of internal differentiation, most criticisms are collected by the authors criticized. This poses the fundamental question of what criticisms are legitimate. Last, almost every criticism directed towards an approach in general runs a high risk of being unfair to specific authors or works. Even though specific pieces of work will be referenced, that risk is not avoided.

The most recurrent criticism relates to the main bid of this approach: that priority is given to the productive system over the other variables. This has been repeatedly qualified as 'economic determinism' (De Giorgi 2013, p. 47). Part of the discussion revolves around whether this influence fully determines or conditions punishment (Greenberg 1981, p. 241). Another part of the discussion centres on the omission of other important factors conditioning punishment (such as social policies or cultural values). It has also been pointed out that this approach does not pay enough attention to existing reciprocal influences operating between the productive, penal, political and cultural systems (see Garland 1990, p. 280).

Related to this criticism, there is the issue of these analyses prioritizing the material over the symbolic (Wacquant 2009, p. xvii). This point is abridged in the simplifying metaphor of an – economic – infrastructure that determines an – ideological – superstructure (for instance, Althusser [1970] 1974). In the way this account is interpreted in this type of criticism, furthermore, the material is real and the ideological is illusory (Garland 1990, p. 108). In its use for punishment, this formulation is to be clearly found in Pashukanis ([1929] 1989) and was openly criticized by Poulantzas ([1978] 2016), among others. Sometimes it is acknowledged that the issue of ideology is more complex, but this is seldom further developed. In any case, analytical primacy is given to the material over the symbolic (or 'ideological', in this tradition (for instance, De Giorgi 2006, pp. 4, 18)) like in the model criticized above.[5]

In this perspective the social seems to revolve around the economic, and to be at its service: thus, there is a tendency to employ a functionalist reading of the non-economic.[6] For reasons more or less evident, the analysis of the state, of its functioning and of its functions has attracted another part of the criticisms. Even though it is a particularly complicated issue, the usual view of the state in this approach tends to portray it as a supplementary entity of, if not submitted to, the market. The state is not usually an object of interest in itself, but because of the functions it fulfils; these are reduced to the regulation of the relations of economic exchange through the Law and its application by police and prisons, so as to ensure the workers are under conditions of exploitation for capitalists (see, for instance, Rusche and Kirchheimer, [1939] 2004, pp. 36–38).[7] In this sense, the state is understood as a body that ensures that capitalism can continue to operate through punishment.

Last, its emphasis on quantitative correlations using aggregate data has roused different critical comments. It has been noticed that 'the conditions of the system of production' of which Rusche and Kirchheimer speak should not be reduced to the conditions of the labour market, and that these cannot be reduced to unemployment rates – or even temporariness when analysing a post-fordist economy (De Giorgi 2006, pp. 23, 33, 62). Besides, these correlations are much more complicated when political, cultural or demographic variables are included, and theoretical propositions have been operationalized in a more direct and simple fashion than they could have been (Jacobs and Helms 1996; Sutton 2004, p. 172, Lappi-Seppälä 2008). Furthermore, confinement is not regulated by social class solely; the influence of nationality and race, alien to older versions of this approach, must be taken into account (Melossi 1989, p. 317; Western 2006). That is, it is necessary to nuance the empirical evidence provided by the political economy of punishment at a quantitative level, and to further develop the qualitative part, usually disregarded by an approach that has a tendency towards macrostructural views. Thus, beyond the theoretical framework's basic axioms a better understanding of the links which seem to exist between economy and punishment, and in the interpretation agents make of them, could be developed (Box and Hale 1985, p. 210; Garland 1990, p. 109). In fact, the development of case studies that can account for specific political-institutional arrangements is being called for, with the purpose of improving the comprehension of causal mechanisms (De Giorgi 2013, pp. 51–52; Lacey 2008, p. 56).

This brief presentation of criticisms will be further developed through the exploration of positive proposals, stressing the practical aspects of research that can present solutions to some of the problems mentioned. The discussion of Bourdieu's logic and concepts does not mean to preclude the use of other authors. Notwithstanding, I do advocate a wider and more systematic use of his work in the study of punishment.[8] Its pertinence or validity should be settled through empirical research, since every approach emphasizes specific aspects and fails to see others – or only partially glimpses them.[9] For the interests of the political economy of punishment, Pierre Bourdieu's work is an advance, but it is important to remember that Bourdieu is not the solution for every problem – even if the nature of his enterprise results in an approach that can be applied to different areas (building on their peculiarities through empirical research).

Beyond Marxism: Pierre Bourdieu and the theory of practices

Bourdieu's work is testimony to a constant struggle to overcome limitations found in Marx, Weber, and Durkheim when applied to empirical research (Bourdieu [1987] 1990, p. 34). As a result of these agreements and disagreements, he forged a broad conceptual apparatus, about which only some general observations can be made here (see further in Bourdieu [1980] 1990, [1997] 2000; Bourdieu and Wacquant 1992).[10] Features from authors who were traditionally considered to be incompatible were combined, the analytical advantages of one articulated to correct the blurred edges of another (for instance, Bourdieu and Passeron [1970] 1977, pp. 44–45). To quote a good synthesis of Bourdieau's framework, Bourdieu worked with Marx against Marx, with Durkheim against Durkheim, and with Weber against Weber (Bourdieu [1987] 1990, p. 49).

It has been pointed out that applying Marx's concepts to the study of punishment is problematic. This is largely due to the fact that his concepts were designed to analyse productive and economic relations, and not penal issues (Hirst 1975, p. 204). Similar issues are involved with invoking Bourdieusian concepts, since they have their origins in the analysis of colonialist relations in Algeria, in studies on the education system, arts, or the transmission of social positions, among other themes. What is presented here, therefore, is an invitation to think about punishment alongside Bourdieu. It ought to be read as a starting point, rather than a point of arrival.

Bringing together the materialist and symbolic analysis of punishment: symbolic power

To the aforementioned critique that the political economy of punishment gives considerably greater importance to the material than to the symbolic, another could be added. Particularly in macro-level approaches, a proper symbolic analysis of the institutions in charge of punishment is not usually carried out, and most of the time the analysis refers to discursive constructions stemming from outside of penal institutions – in the media or in political discourse.[11] It is true that other traditions, such as the labelling approach, have paid attention to this (mainly in relation to the transformation of identities), and that there have been some explicit efforts to reconcile these approaches with a materialistic approach (see Melossi 1985). However, a concept which would join both realities together and which would allow for understanding their functioning is missing.

Societies work through symbolic systems. These systems, following Durkheim ([1912] 2001), are forms of classification that fulfil a function in social order integration. These forms of classification are social and historical, that is to say, they are variable, become dated, and have their origin in relations. They tend to produce agreement on what the world is and how it works, since there is a tendency towards structural homology between social conditions and their symbolic representation – that usually results in a tendency towards the preservation of those social conditions. In this sense, mental structures can be understood as incarnations of social structures (Bourdieu and Wacquant 1992, pp. 12–14).

The importance of symbolic systems lies in that they shape and impose shared principles of vision and division, thus symbolic power acts on the level of (practical) knowledge (Bourdieu [1993] 1994, pp. 7–8, [1977] 1979, p. 79). The importance of paying attention to punishment as a system of signs and meanings, and to its symbolic and unifying strength – bigger than other social phenomena – has already been stressed (Garland 1983, p. 59). An approach such as the one presented here – that links forms of classification acquired within social contexts to the specific forms of collective conscience and social solidarity – can relate these processes to those of domination between groups.

The question the Durkheimian approach usually neglects, however, is the political implications of symbolic systems, especially affecting the legitimation of differences and hierarchies which are established between groups, as well as between their practices (Fernández 2005, pp. 11–12). The triple functionality of symbolic systems – knowledge, communication, and social differentiation – makes them instruments that communicate a determinate knowledge about the social. Through the consent they generate (due to the adjustment between mental and social structures), they naturalize (arbitrary and historically contingent) social relations, concealing the class struggles which underlie existing social order, and who benefits from them. This is where Bourdieu brings Marx in for understanding the reproduction of relations of domination (Bourdieu [1977] 1979, pp. 79–80).

For a better understanding of the genesis and dynamics of these struggles, the bureaucratic field and the orientation of actor's situated actions was introduced by Bourdieu employing Weber. This author is useful for questions of legitimacy, too. The misrecognition which facilitates the recognition[12] of the relations of domination legitimates them, and allows the contribution made by the dominated to their own domination to be analysed as more than an issue of mere ignorance or false consciousness (Bourdieu [1977] 1979, p. 80). This strengthens relations of domination like the ones the political economy of punishment analyse in capitalist societies.

The fundamental notion here is that of *symbolic power*: power exerted based on the naturalization that relations of domination undergo because of the homology between symbolic schemas and social structures. That is, the power of imposing categories as legitimate, without this imposition being perceived. Symbolic power is productive.

Consequently, despite sharing similarities with the concept of ideology, symbolic power enables capitalist relations of domination to not only conceal the nature of those relations, but also produce them. The symbolic system that makes them possible is not a mere addition to these relations: it is part of them. Using this conceptual framework, the effect of misrecognition is not elaborated by the ruling classes to deceive the dominated people, but the effect of people applying mental categories, which are the product of social structures, to the perception of those very same structures, that thus appear evident. This consistency generates a doxic relation with the world (a concept from Husserl's phenomenology), which is precisely where its strength comes from (Bourdieu and Wacquant 1992, pp. 167–169).

Despite this, such a domination is not the mechanical effect of objective conditions, but involves an active interpretation of the situation by actors. This interpretation is based on dispositions (habitus) and in specific social spaces (fields). Besides, Bourdieu argues that there are conflicts and struggles around symbolic processes of nomination and social categorization, since different social groups make efforts to define the world in a way that better fits their interests. Class struggle is also classification struggle (Bourdieu [1982] 1991, p. 105, [1977] 1979, p. 80; Bourdieu and Wacquant 1992, p. 14). Even if the homology between mental and social structures may make the existence of discrepancies or social change seem impossible, it is necessary to remember that symbolic frameworks are 'matrices' or 'schemas', in which not everything is determined, even though it is conditioned. Precisely habitus, as a practice generator schema, allows for the needed innovation when confronted with discrepancies between the different visions of the world that different positions in the field entail, thus helping to confront differences between expectations and concrete situations. It also means results are not necessary or prearranged. They are contingent, meaning they could have been different.

Bourdieu speaks of symbolic violence to refer to the type of violence exerted in this way, consisting in naturalizing matters that are the arbitrary result of relations of domination rooted in the unequal distributions of capitals throughout society. It is a form of violence not perceived as such, and this inability to account for its sources (a misrecognition) adds up to the relations of domination and constitutes a power in itself. It is the effect of symbolic power.

Nomination is important, especially the language employed, because 'By structuring the perception which social agents have of the social world, the act of naming helps to establish the structure of this world' (Bourdieu [1982] 1991, p. 105). But the question coming next is: who does nominate? Specifically, who does nominate legitimately? Bourdieu states that one of the conditions for locating the principle of a message's symbolic efficacy is 'the relationship between the properties of discourses, the properties of the person who pronounces them and the properties of the institution which authorizes him to pronounce them' (Bourdieu [1982] 1991, p. 111, [2001] 2004). If the message is sent with an appropriate discourse, by an authorized agent, and with sufficient symbolic backing, the message is considered legitimate, in a process in which delegation games are key. This does not mean it is automatically accepted, but its chances of acceptance increase. The answer he gives to the question, for our societies, is that it is 'the state' (the bureaucratic field) that has more chance to get nominations to be perceived as legitimate (Bourdieu [1993] 1994, p. 9, [2012] 2014, pp. 165–169; Bourdieu and Wacquant 1993, p. 39).

Therefore, punishment forms an institution of first importance in producing and differentiating social categories. On the one hand, since it comes from the state, the differentiation it produces is imposed with greater legitimacy. On the other hand, the fact that this differentiation comes from a state institution linked with the fight against crime displaces the political character of domination to the more aseptic terrain of egality. In consequence, its arbitrary nature is more thoroughly concealed, making it less recognizable and, therefore, more effective.

Nevertheless, this differentiation is not only symbolic: 'the prison symbolizes material divisions and materializes relations of symbolic power' (Wacquant 2009, p. xvi). It is not about separating the material and the symbolic aspects, but about understanding that both operate together, intertwined, supporting each other, and are often processes which can only be separated in analytical terms. The challenge is, in each process, to identify material and symbolic components and effects operating at the same time. Consequently, domination cannot be reduced to legitimation or nomination (as the use of police and prison clearly shows), but they are key for understanding how arbitrariness becomes naturalized (Vázquez García 2002, p. 91).

For instance, Loader (1997) points to the existence of dispositions orienting people to relate in a certain way with police, including the tendency to think of police as a good solution whenever there is a crime problem. The importance of visual symbols in the influence of people's perception is also acknowledged. Thus, there is way of studying the symbolic effects of punishment without needing to resort to non-punitive institutions. For example, and recognizing the important influence of media in the construction of migrants as dangerous subjects, the very effects of police action should be taken into account when they regularly conduct racist identity checks or stop-and-search practices (a material action not accompanied by discourse to the eyes of the beholder).

Following this line of argument, punishment should stop being seen as a dependent variable of the productive system. Studying reciprocal relations between both is necessary (not to imply that they are always equally reciprocal), and it may also be pertinent to look at other institutional frameworks that condition both (Sutton 2004, p. 172; Greenberg 1981, p. 242). So, here, like in the next section, Bourdieu's work is shown to permit a fruitful approach to the role of the state.

Bringing some autonomy to the state: the bureaucratic field

The state is of central importance for punishment. It is important to take the danger of over-simplification seriously where the state is mainly understood as a tool at the service of the ruling class. This implies taking (some of) the results of state action as its *raison d'être*, and disincentivizes analysing its inner dynamics, since it is only important as far as it contributes to the accumulation of capital. Hence specific institutional determiners of conditions (Lacey 2008, Barker 2009) and, at least equally importantly, the relations and struggles which determine the concrete influence of those institutional arrangements (Cavadino and Dignan 2011; Page 2013) are overlooked. Acknowledging that the state is fundamental for the unification and homogenization of a territory needed for the functioning of the market is important. But it must be taken into account that different institutional arrangements make for different forms and degrees of punishment, and that important state actions that are not directly related to capitalist processes do exist (including some aspects of penality). The notion of field helps studying how these different groups relate and the directions some policies take (Page 2011, p. 10).

A solid concept of the state is yet to be developed in punishment studies. This is odd because, due to the nature of penality in contemporary societies, it is practically impossible to study any aspect of it and not find the state (in the definition of crime, in the police, prisons, courts, etc.). It may well be that this struggle around the political nature of punishment is a symbolic effect of the state's own role.[13] Notwithstanding, it seems this tendency is changing (see Scheingold 1998; Cavadino and Dignan 2006; Lacey 2008; Barker 2009; Garland 2013).

Talking of the state, and giving it central importance in theory, does not mean saying that the state is the cause of everything. It does not mean using the state as an analytical shortcut instead of reconstructing causal chains, as some Marxist approaches tend to (Melossi 1989, p. 319). In order to understand the role of the state better, it is convenient to substitute it for the concept of 'bureaucratic field',[14] and to place it within the field of power, a metafield in which different dominant groups in their respective fields – due to their accumulation of different capitals – struggle to increase the value of their capitals. It is a space in which hierarchies and relations of domination in and between the different fields are disputed (Bourdieu [2012] 2014, pp. 197, 311; Bourdieu and Wacquant 1993, p. 42). In those fights, the bureaucratic field is of particular importance, since it has an enormous influence on the value of different types of capitals and on their conversion rates.

Using this notion has the advantage of avoiding a view of the state which interprets it as a power tool at the service of *the* ruling class, and facilitates an understanding of the state as a space of struggles in which different groups and logics try to impose themselves on each other to gain control of public capital and its associated power. They seek to, in turn, influence state action and the distribution of public resources in accordance with their material and symbolic interests. It is important to understand that conflicts exist between dominant groups based on imposing different forms of power (not all of them economic). They do not act as a block or in the same direction because they do not have the same specific interests, and therefore it is not appropriate to assume that these conflicts end up benefiting these different groups as a block.

The bureaucratic field is a structured space defined by objective positions, which are defined by the different capitals actors hold. It has been pointed out that two fundamental axis of struggle and alliance formation exist inside the bureaucratic field (Wacquant 2009, pp. 289–290). There is a division among the members of this field between bureaucrats linked to the civil service ('the low nobility of the state') and those more directly linked to elected political positions ('the high nobility of the state'). There is another division between the right hand and the left hand of the state, through a fundamental division of policies. At the same time, each of these blocks are crossed by inner struggles.

To put it differently, relations of domination resulting from state action are usually the indirect effect of a whole network of actions of individuals and groups that interact within the field. At the same time, the bureaucratic field, as a field, relates to other fields. This influences its functioning and its results. Fields are not impermeable to the influence of other spheres in society, and they are not fully dependent on them either (they filter and transform them). They have a relative autonomy (which implies a relative dependency) that varies over time. This is dependent, to a great extent, on the capacity of the field for generating a specific type of capital (Bourdieu 1986, p. 823; Lenoir 2004, p. 123).

Thus, it must be taken into account that the bureaucratic field is intersected by group and individual struggles aiming to gain state power and the struggles of people who are in the field and their interests, as well as by the field's own logic. This can be articulated in many ways, one example being the denial of particular interests in favour of universal interests, even if that is itself a 'strategy' through which particular interests are promoted (Bourdieu [2012] 2014, pp. 342–343). This influences the materiality of the struggles, but also their justification, representation and, therefore, the form struggles take. Here, besides Marx's conflictual perspective, Bourdieu ([1977] 1979. pp. 81–82) brings in Weber's work on the sociology of religion, and the orientation of agent's actions according to the sense they make. Thus trying to move away from a structural logic that reduces people to the reproduction of structures and Law to the reflection of ruling class' interests.[15]

The state, according to Bourdieu ([1993] 1994, pp. 41–42), ensues from a process of concentration of diverse capitals, resulting in the emergence of a juridical capital that allows the objectivation and codification of symbolic capital. Hence, turning back to Durkheim, a certain vision of the world can be imposed, as well as demarcations of social categories. To some extent, the state is a 'fiction', and exists only through the representation specialists make of it through juridical regulation, and as a result of the constitution of a bureaucratic field around the juridical capital (Bourdieu [2012] 2014, p. 25). Furthermore, and of special relevance for punishment, it allows the emergence of a system of justice administration which can employ physical violence, as well as symbolic violence (Bourdieu [1993] 1994, pp. 3–5, 8–11). That is, this approach enables an understanding of state action using two completely intertwined facets: the material and the symbolic. Official nominations – typical of the running of the penal system (see Garfinkel 1956) – have the capacity to act over people's cognitive order, exerting a symbolic effect that appears disconnected from struggles – *in* the state and *for* the state – which give rise to the legislations and modes of operation of the penal system. These nominations and their effects go beyond penality and have causal influences, for example, in the labour market.

In this way, attention can be paid to the internal complexity of the state and the different logics running through it. Methodologically, an inversion of the usual approach in the political economy of punishment is enabled: it goes from stressing the state's function and then discursively nuancing its complexity[16] to departing from the complexity of relations using the concept of field and, only later, affirming its diverse functions, referring them to specific episodes, conflicts, and policies. In addition, this approach makes more pressing claims for the empirical and historically specified study of state processes since its importance is more acknowledged than its functions.

For instance, in *Prisons of poverty* (Wacquant [1999] 2009), relations between different fields, and their autonomy, play a central role in the book's mode of analysis. In general, it is shown how, under neoliberalism, the economic field notably influences the other fields taken into account (the bureaucratic, the journalistic, the academic) acting as a gravitational axis. Specifically, the way in which certain agents of the academic field resort to the accumulation of a capital which is not specific to their field (like scientific capital) as a means of improving their position within the field (obtaining, for instance, symbolic capital awarded by their participation in the journalistic field – the media). How the studies carried out by these agents are used in bureaucratic fields in order to legitimate certain policies is just one among many examples in Wacquant's book.

Thus, a complex situation is presented in which the criminalization of poverty results, not only from multiple interactions within the academic field, but also from its interaction with other fields. Furthermore, the concrete implementation of penal and social policies belongs to different agents with different interests (since they occupy different positions in the field – more related to bureaucracy, or more related to middle classes), who are able to carry out diversions from the measures planned.

It has been claimed that the state should be abandoned as an explicative variable in the study of social control (Young 1983; Melossi 1985, p. 204, [1990] 1992, p. 231). Here the state is not understood to be the cause of anything, it is not a subject. The bureaucratic field is a space of struggles, an object of struggles, and a tool by which those struggles are regulated.[17] Along with the materialist approach, the symbolic analysis does not limit itself to discourse and imagery. The focus moves to embodied dispositions, onto bodies and categories of perception and thought. We mostly think and feel through the state, naturalizing its ways of working and the need for it (through official language, its measures, numbers, calendars, etc.) (Bourdieu 1986, pp. 837–840, [2012] 2014, pp. 156–161; Bourdieu and Wacquant 1993, pp. 40–41).

Last, the notion of 'bureaucratic field' is also useful for highlighting that decisions taken in the state (and in the field of power) are not the decision of a person. They are rather the result of thousands of decisions that are not guided by the rational calculus for maximizing capitals, but by practical choices (Bourdieu [1993] 1994, p. 100; Bourdieu and Wacquant 1993, p. 31).

These practical choices are guided by 'habitus'.

Bringing people with dispositions to the analysis: habitus

Within the political economy of punishment, in a problem shared by social sciences in general, a theory binding structuralist approaches to those which focus on agency has been called for, so as to be able to understand the processes by which the social is constituted, works and changes (Humphries and Greenberg 1981, pp. 212–213). Habitus is an important concept in Bourdieu's persistent effort for overcoming scholarly oppositions between structuralism and subjectivism, and between macro and micro analyses. At the same time, or precisely as a way of doing it, it gives clues about how social conditionings operate through actors' actions, and not as external factors that are imposed on them. So, it encourages scholars to stop seeing the opposition between agency and structure, and commits them to seeing both as manifestations of the social (which is, the relational that is historically formed). This duality of the social, manifested in both objective positions (fields) and in subjective dispositions (habitus), allows the levels of analysis to be linked (see Bourdieu [1997] 2000, pp. 128–173).

Habitus is formed by conditionings associated with certain conditions of existence ('conditioning' implies that it both makes possible and impossible, positively and negatively). They are 'structured structures predisposed to function as structuring structures, that is, as principles which generate and organize practices and representations' (Bourdieu [1980] 1990, p. 53). It is habitus from which we interpret and feel the world, and from which we develop corporal predispositions and lines of action, that we tend to see as reasonable (what 'makes sense' is conditioned by the social position occupied, not by a decontextualized reasoning). By intimately interlinking 'ways of acting, thinking, and feeling' (Durkheim) with social positions, also defined relationally and historically, actions are allowed to be made intelligible 'without explaining them from individual psychological motives nor deriving them from unconscious structural laws' (Vázquez García 2002, p 63).[18] The possibility of conscious, reflexive practices is not excluded, however it is remembered that this deliberation is not made in a vacuum, but inserted in social situations. It is also taken into account, besides, that most everyday doings are not explicitly reflective, and they work on a state previous to conscience, which is that of dispositions, generated in some specific social conditions.

Talking of habitus does not mean explaining all conducts according to social positions in what would be an automatic application of those schemes, as this would mean little more than pure social reproduction (Bourdieu [1997] 2000, p. 149). As a matter of fact, the concept is developed in Bourdieu's empirical work precisely for explaining change (Wacquant 2014b, p. 5). In addition, the relational logic of fields, and the constant negotiation of positions, force habitus to work from previous states of the field which do not necessarily correspond with the current one, creating a lag, in what it is known as 'hysteresis' (Bourdieu [1997] 2000, p. 160). This requires active interpretation, and constant invention of actions and interpretations. Now, of course, these do not come out of nowhere, or from actor's pure conscience. They tend to be made based on previous experiences in specific social situations, so that the role of habitus has more to do with making the perception of particular lines of action possible. Precisely because of this, habitus must be connected to fields, which determine social position through the distribution of capitals and their process of accumulation. Furthermore, habitus tend to get activated when they are appealed to by fields; they are stirred by existing interests in the fields' dynamics and rules, which is also where they get formed (Bourdieu [1997] 2000, p. 135). Bourdieu establishes in this way something like a reciprocal causality between social structures and the actions of individuals.

Thus, habitus works differently in different fields, since it is not rigid, but adaptable, and is modified over time. Besides, people usually have different habitus that overlap. Bourdieu used to distinguish between primary habitus – related to family origins, with a greater weight and a longer and more subtle formation over time – and secondary habitus – acquired later through specific and explicit training. He then gave way to a progressive coupling between different acquired habitus (Wacquant 2014b, p. 7). For example, a habitus developed in the juridical field through training and practice does not work the same in people coming from different backgrounds. This recalls the need for studying trajectories and the set of relations in which actors are located in order to understand how their relations and attitudes towards the penal system are built.

Placing perceptions, problematizations, solutions and actions in a specific context enables the peculiar nature of penality to be taken into account: as functioning through its agents, alongside its specific norms of functioning as a field. This calls for nuancing approaches like those that see judges as little more than a prolongation of the ruling class, sanctioning and ideologically reinforcing the interests of other class fractions. Putting the aforementioned characteristics of habitus into play, the functioning of penal systems can be presented in its complexity.

For instance, it can be seen that judges' interests do not respond to a conscious class interest, by understanding their behaviours in relation to the dispositions acquired throughout their professional socialization (an attitude towards Law, a perception strongly marked by the juridical frame) and in relation to their specific position within the juridical field (in relation to other positions in the field: judges belonging to opposite tendencies within the judiciary, judges willing to prove that they deserve higher posts, judges with a strong belief in the principles of Law, etc.).

In addition, habitus has a strong corporal dimension. It has to do with the way we sit down, walk, eat or wear a suit (the difference in how a suit suits an ex-prisoner and a lawyer cannot be reduced to economics). Body expression of social conditionings is important, and existing differentiations can be very upsetting for agents, and can be interpreted as personal, or even institutional, lacks of respect (i.e. bodily behaviour while waiting in a trial, and the spontaneity with which some develop it, and the real challenge, with important consequences, that it is for others). Knowing how to nod, how to be in a corporal disposition of listening is important for the interactions within the penal system, and taking this into account, therefore, is important for studying them.

This corporal dimension (sometimes taken as 'lack of respect' due to the effect of symbolic power) constitutes another difference regarding the concept of ideology, for which domination processes usually refer to processes of the conscience (Bourdieu [1997] 2000, p. 142). Bringing in the concept of *doxa* is fundamental for exploring relations of domination far beyond conscience and representations, since they often arise from just 'being in the world'. Otherwise, knowing what sexism is would be enough to stop being sexist, or repudiating capitalism to stop being capitalist.

The enormous contribution that has been made by studies working on specifying disciplinary techniques of the body cannot be neglected. Especially, investigations into the inculcation of ways of acting and thinking involved in these disciplinary techniques, like the production of the 'working class' and the production of bodies ready for exploitation (see Simon 2013). The difference here has to do with the concept of discipline presupposing an externality working over the body and the individual and producing it as such (despite the fact that, later, the subject develops it as a self-subjectivity). The concept of habitus, with its corporal dimension, puts the emphasis on the corporal dispositions arising from the individual's social position. The effect of 'auxiliary institutions' (Melossi [1990] 1992, p. 236) is not assumed, but a silent adaptation between positions and dispositions, more the fruit of symbolic violence than that of the physical violence of that explicit 'training' (Bourdieu and Wacquant 1993, p. 34). Talking of symbolic domination makes resistances more difficult.

This point, like others throughout the text, leaves the door open to the issue of theoretical preference for choosing concepts that, saying similar things, differ in nuances. Bourdieu's concepts did not stem from studying prisons, or the 'Big confinement', but from studying the education system and the cultural field. Thus, the possibility that both processes of body formation can exist and that in concrete historical episodes – for instance, the process of primitive accumulation described by Thompson (1975), or by Melossi and Pavarini ([1977] 1981) – disciplinary imposition from the outside can hardly be questioned. Where the focus is on wider social functionings, this is more problematic. Even, if one assumes with Durkheim ([1925] 1961) that punishment is mostly directed towards those not being punished, and that, despite mass imprisonment, people directly targeted by punitive institutions are still a large minority, other ways of enquiring into relations with the body in studies of punishment are open.

Using the concept of habitus could be a strategy for developing qualitative studies within the political economy of punishment, since it avoids presenting subjects as beings that choose freely outside of the structural conditions of capitalism, and outside relations of power or domination. At the same time, framing its development in a field of objective positions (that usually calls for a quantitative approach) can account for the capitalist dynamics revealed in their actions (also for the non-capitalist dynamics and their articulation with them). It can also point to how these dynamics influence the transformation or maintenance of actions and institutions (for example, with the maladjustment of rural habitus in factories and cities during the Industrial Revolution). This can explain how exploited classes adapt to the dynamics of capitalism without constant external disciplining or the ideologization of social relations (there is no wish to deny that this does exist – above all in concrete episodes.) Turning to symbolic power, homology between objective and subjective structures and their activation in specific contexts can help to better understand why people do what they do – and why an explanation based on a group transmitting ideas to people can result insufficient. This is true even in significantly more sophisticated theoretical developments that problematizes the existence of 'democratic' social (self) control exerted through images and vocabularies of motives which people identify as their own (see Melossi [1990] 1992, esp. pp. 235–253). Habitus is also useful for quantitative approaches, as it warns researchers against attributing reasons to individuals' actions according to correlations between variables.

Concluding remarks

The objective of this chapter was to outline a positive proposal for studying punishment: placing the contributions and limitations of the political economy of punishment into dialogue with some of the analytical tools forged by Pierre Bourdieu, but not attempting to catalogue the complex debates running through them.

Bourdieu is not easy; neither is applying his theories directly to punishment. Still, the concepts presented here facilitate thinking about the political economy of punishment (as well as other approaches) and sketching new guides for research.

Specifically, the idea of the productive system as a determining causal factor has been questioned. On the one hand, because signalling an adaptation of people's interests and actions and the 'necessities' of capitalism is insufficient and imprecise. On the other hand, the evident importance the economic field has over the rest of the fields is not a constant, but a variable that requires study (by looking at disputes existing in the metafield of power and placing them in specific times and places.) Besides, it does not seem to be a justified motive for prioritizing the material over the symbolic, fundamentally because the material is symbolic, and the symbolic is material. If, in addition, a structuralist approach is to be abandoned, paying attention to dispositions and social categorizations – naturalized by power relations that are symbolic – takes us to the issue of what to prioritize. This is particularly important if the aim is to conduct a social science in which people have some relevant role. Here, tools for not having to prioritize have been provided – even though analytically the objectivistic moment precedes the subjectivist one (Bourdieu and Wacquant 1992, p. 11). The concept of habitus allows for capturing and studying the incorporation and setting in motion of social processes. Last, given the huge importance of the state in the material execution of punishment, but also in the symbolic construction of social relations (and not as a mere epiphenomenon), the pertinence of studying the bureaucratic field, in all its complexity, has been introduced. Thus, existing unequal social positions, struggles generated around the distribution and valourization of capitals and fields, and their functioning through actions guided by habitus, can be taken into account.

Another positive element of Bourdieu's work is its integrative character, through some aspects of Marx, Durkheim and Weber (and some other notable influences that have not been incorporated). Methodologically, Bourdieu adopts a structuralist approach from Marx, in its relational sense (in that things are defined by a process of differentiation with others). At the same time, from Weber he adopts the imperative to consider the subjective meaning and the orientation of actions – which are defined, precisely, through relations and differentiations. In order to explain these actions, he adopts Durkheim's emphasis on their dispositional character, and incorporates the fact that dispositions are shaped within relations of domination (Marx), and he can thus study the processes of legitimation of these relationships (Weber). Due to these legitimations, these relations of domination become part of the moral order (Durkheim), they stop being perceived as violent and people develop them with a naturalness that makes them feel personal.

Coming back to punishment, this approach enables the researcher to observe: how certain expressions of moral indignation present in punitive processes are not dissociated from relations of domination; how these relations of domination (more varied than the purely economic) come to be perceived as something natural and legitimate, since they concur within dispositions shaped in a social space; how actions are oriented according to moral beliefs about what needs to be punished that are considered legitimate, and how all this has an impact on those relations of domination. Since actions are always grounded in ever changing contexts, and conflict is at the base of differentiations, values, as well as their legitimations, are always in dispute. Neither relations of domination, nor legitimations, nor moral orders are eternal or complete. Neither dispositions, nor actions, nor inequalities are static or closed. All of them are social processes always open to relations and history, and so is punishment.

Notes

1 I would like to thank Javier Rujas for his sharp and generous comments on the draft of this text. I would also like to thank the editors of the book for their help and patience. This work has benefited from research projects DER2015–64403-P and DER2014–52674-R, financed by the Spanish Ministry of Economy and Competitiveness.
2 For interesting considerations about the inclusion of Foucault in this approach, see Melossi and Sozzo 2008, p. 150; Simon 2013, p. 85.
3 At least in studies aiming to account for broad aspects of punishment. This is different from some aspects of penality in which it may not be relevant to pay attention to their relation with the productive system, since the degree of dependency is variable and this does not mean that it has a centrality in the process studied.
4 For this reason, the way the political economy of punishment is here portrayed is more closely related to classical approaches than to more recent heterodox approaches.
5 As an example of some of the points mentioned above, Humphries and Greenberg (1981, p. 242) say that 'Capitalism provides the class experience from which ideologies of control are developed', even if in the same page they acknowledge these

distinctions are complicated and that we should advocate for 'joint or reciprocal determination, rather than unidirectional causality' (it is not said how). Another example is Reiman's 'pyrrhic theory' ([1979] 2001), where he claims that he incorporates the ideological function of punishment though the works of Durkheim and Erikson. Nevertheless, he makes a functionalist reading that attributes a clear intentionality on the part of rich people, submitting the symbolic to the material as a means to ensure its stability and reproduction.

6 The differentiation between 'the social' and 'the economic' is a problematic issue and it exceeds the purposes of this chapter. A study on the constitution of the economic as a separate sphere from the social can be found in Polanyi (1944).
7 Despite acknowledging more nuanced views which point out Law does not reflect the interests of the ruling classes solely (for example, Greenberg 1981, p. 212).
8 Some remarkable examples of using Bourdieu for penal questions are Lenoir ([1993] 1999); Loader (1997); Wacquant ([1999] 2009, 2009, 2014a); Page (2011); Hathazy (2016). The intention here is insisting on this and showing, by a dialogue with the political economy of punishment, what advantages adopting Bourdieusian concepts can offer.
9 '"Theories" are research programs that call not for "theoretical debate" but for a practical utilization that either refutes or generalizes them or, better, specifies and differentiates their claim to generality' (Bourdieu and Wacquant 1992, p. 77).
10 A fair criticism of Bourdieu's approach can be found in Alonso et al. (2004); Calhoun et al. (1993); Corcuff ([2007] 2015, pp. 52–60).
11 The media and political discourse are, of course, part of penality, or punishment in its broader sense, but here the broader symbolic effects produced by institutions directly in charge of punishment is what is being referred to.
12 Bourdieu's writing is full of word games that are as useful and specific as they are hard to translate, especially into non-Romance languages. See the translator's note for Bourdieu and Passeron [1970] 1977, p. xxvi.
13 It is interesting to note the peripheral role the state plays in the translation of the classics of sociology into the sociology of punishment. Many times it gets lost inside 'processes of rationalization', 'civilizing processes', 'representations of the collective conscience', or the 'rise of the disciplines', when it could be read as the historical rise of the modern state and of its influences in the punitive forms (see, for instance, Garland 1990).
14 Bourdieu's attempts, always unfinished, of thinking about the state without the very categories that the state produces passes for trying not to use its vocabularies and representations, paying attention to Kelsen's warnings (Bourdieu [2012] 2014, p. 108). The use of 'bureaucratic field' is a proposal for being able to define the state sociologically (with a similar preoccupation, but within the tradition of the political economy of punishment, see Melossi [1990] 1992, pp. 16–20, 102–106).
15 Acknowledging the existence of struggles inside the state, or surrounding the state, is not alien to the Marxist tradition, with an important influence of Poulantzas' work (among others, Humphries and Greenberg 1981). Nevertheless, the differences in the approach are some: Bourdieu acknowledges the existence of conflictual axes beyond the economic ones; he does not consider the objective existence of groups determined by their position in the productive system, but group making requires a symbolic dimension which is in itself a matter of struggles; he highlights the existence of autonomy within the bureaucratic field, with genuine interests by the bureaucrats; and he contributes with an explanation of social functioning which brings people back – through the habitus – in opposition to more structuralist approaches. In this line, even if not applied directly to punishment, Jessop's approach is especially interesting. It combines Luhmann's idea of system, Poulantzas' balances of political powers and

Gramci's concept of hegemony. See Jessop (2002) and Boyer (2004). A proposal for its use in the study of punishment, precisely as a way for reformulating the political economy of punishment, can be seen in De Giorgi 2013, p. 53.

16 This is, probably, the main methodological criticism that can be levelled against Wacquant (2009) in his application of the Bourdieusian theoretical framework to the study of punishment. However, it must be borne in mind that his approach to punishment belongs to a wider research project, not just penality (see Wacquant 2014a). Hence its weaknesses, but also its strengths.

17 The bureaucratic field is explained here due to the peculiar relationships the political economy of punishment establishes between the economic and the penal fields. Notwithstanding, the penal fields (Page 2013) or the penitentiary (sub)field (Hathazy 2016) can be studied, depending on the approach and interests of the research.

18 Actions, by their insertion in the field – which is a space of struggles – can be understood as strategies. Strategies are actions carried out that, without being fully conscious, have a purpose, in keeping with perception schemas, that is not unconnected with social positions. Bourdieu here, again, tries to bring together the Weberian orientation and sense of actions with a Durkheimian dispositional model together with the Marxist teaching on the differentiated and unequal organization of societies.

References

Alonso, L.E., Martín Criado, E. and Moreno Pestaña, J.L., eds (2004). *Pierre Bourdieu, las herramientas del sociólogo*. Madrid: Fundamentos.

Althusser, L. ([1970] 1974). Ideology and ideological state apparatuses. In: Althusser, L., *Lenin and philosophy and other essays*. New York: Monthly Review Press, 127–186.

Barker, V. (2009). *The politics of imprisonment. How the democratic process shapes the way America punishes offenders*. Oxford: Oxford University Press.

Bourdieu, P. ([1977] 1979). Symbolic power. *Critique of Anthropology*, 4, 77–85.

Bourdieu, P. ([1980] 1990). *The logic of practice*. Stanford: Stanford University Press.

Bourdieu, P. ([1982] 1991). *Language and symbolic power*. Cambridge: Polity Press.

Bourdieu, P. (1986). The force of law: toward a sociology of the juridical field. *The Hastings Law Journal*, 38, 805–853.

Bourdieu, P. ([1987] 1990). *In other words. Essays towards a reflexive sociology*. Cambridge: Polity Press.

Bourdieu, P. ([1993] 1994). Rethinking the State: genesis and structure of the bureaucratic field. *Sociological Theory*, 12 (1), 1–18.

Bourdieu, P. ([1997] 2000). *Pascalian meditations*. Stanford: Stanford University Press.

Bourdieu, P. ([2001] 2004). The mystery of the ministry: from particular wills to the general will. *Constellations*, 11 (1), 37–43.

Bourdieu, P. ([2012] 2014). *On the State*, Cambridge: Polity Press.

Bourdieu, P. and Passeron, J.C. ([1970] 1977). *Reproduction in education, society and culture*. London: Sage.

Bourdieu, P. and Wacquant, L. (1992). *An invitation to reflexive sociology*. Cambridge: Polity Press.

Bourdieu, P. and Wacquant, L. (1993). From ruling class to the field of power. *Theory, Culture & Society*, 10 (3), 19–44.

Box, S. and Hale, C. (1985). Unemployment, imprisonment and prison overcrowding. *Contemporary Crises*, 9 (3), 209–228.

Boyer, R. (2003). L'anthropologie économique de Pierre Bourdieu. *Actes de la recherche en sciences sociales*, 150, 65–78.

Calhoun, C., LiPuma, E. and Postone, M., eds (1993). *Bourdieu: critical perspectives*. Chicago: The University of Chicago Press.

Cavadino, M. and Dignan, J. (2006). *Penal systems: a comparative approach*. London: Sage.

Cavadino, M. and Dignan, J. (2011). Penal comparisons: puzzling relations. *In*: Crawford, A., ed., *International and comparative criminal justice and urban governance*. Cambridge: Cambridge University Press, 193–213.

Chiricos, T. and Delone, M. (1992). Labour surplus and punishment: a review and assessment of theory and evidence. *Social Problems*, 39 (4), 421–446.

Corcuff, P. ([2007] 2015). *Las nuevas sociologías. Principales corrientes y debates, 1980–2010*. Buenos Aires: Siglo XXI.

De Giorgi, A. (2006). *Rethinking the political economy of punishment*, Aldershot: Ashgate.

De Giorgi, A. (2013). Punishment and political economy. *In*: Simon, J. and Sparks, R., eds, *The SAGE handbook of punishment and society*. London: Sage, 40–59.

Durkheim, É. ([1912] 2001). *The elementary forms of religious life*. Oxford: Oxford University Press.

Durkheim, É. ([1925] 1961). *Moral education: a study in the theory and application of the sociology of education*. New York: The Free Press.

Fernández, J.M. (2005). La noción de violencia simbólica en la obra de Pierre Bourdieu: una aproximación crítica. *Cuadernos de Trabajo Social*, 18, 7–31.

Foucault, M. ([1975] 1977). *Discipline and punish. The birth of the prison*. New York: Vintage Books.

Garfinkel, H. (1956). Conditions of successful degradation ceremonies. *American Journal of Sociology*, 61 (5), 420–424.

Garland, D. (1983). Durkheim's theory of punishment: a critique. *In*: Garland, D. and Young, P., eds, *The power to punish. Contemporary penality and social analysis*. London: Heinemann, 37–61.

Garland, D. (1990). *Punishment and modern society. A study in social theory*. Oxford: Clarendon Press.

Garland, D. (2013). Penality and the penal state. *Criminology*, 51 (3), 475–517.

Greenberg, D. (1981). *Crime & capitalism. Readings in Marxist criminology*. Palo Alto: Mayfield.

Hall, P. and Soskice, D. (2001). *Varieties of capitalism: the institutional foundations of comparative advantage*. Oxford: Oxford University Press.

Hathazy, P. (2016). Remaking the prisons of the market democracies: new experts, old guards and politics in carceral fields of Argentina and Chile. *Crime, law and social change*, 65 (3), 163–93.

Hirst, P. (1975). Marx and Engels on law, crime and morality. *In*: Taylor, I., Walton, P. and Young, J., eds, *Critical criminology*. Oxford: Routledge, 203–232.

Humphries, D. and Greenberg, D. (1981). The dialectics of crime control. In: Greenberg, D., ed., *Crime & capitalism. Readings in Marxist criminology*. Palo Alto: Mayfield, 209–254.

Jacobs, D. and Carmichael, J. (2001). The politics of punishment across time and space: a pooled time-series analysis of imprisonment rates. *Social Forces*, 80 (1), 61–89.

Jacobs, D. and Helms, R. (1996). Toward a political model of incarceration: a time-series examination of multiple explanation for prison admission rates. *American Journal of Sociology*, 102 (2), 323–357.

Jessop, B. (2002). *The future of the capitalist state*. Cambridge: Polity Press.
Lacey, N. (2008). *The prisoners' dilemma: political economy and punishment in contemporary democracies*. Cambridge: Cambridge University Press.
Lappi-Seppälä, T. (2008). Trust, welfare and political culture: explaining differences in national penal policies. *Crime and Justice*, 37 (1), 313–387.
Lenoir R. ([1993] 1999). Disorder among agents of order. In: Bourdieu, P., ed., *The weight of the world: social suffering in contemporary society*. Stanford: Stanford University Press, 227–254.
Lenoir, R. (2004). Pierre Bourdieu y el Derecho? In: Alonso, L.E., Martín Criado, E. and Moreno Pestaña, J.L., eds, *Pierre Bourdieu, las herramientas del sociólogo*. Madrid: Fundamentos, 115–130
Loader, I. (1997). Policing and the social: questions of symbolic power. *British Journal of Sociology*, 48 (1), 1–18.
Lynch, M. (1987). Quantitative analysis and Marxist criminology: some old answers to a dilemma in Marxist criminology. *Crime and Social Justice*, 29, 110–127.
Melossi, D. (1985). Overcoming the crisis in critical criminology: toward a grounded labeling theory. *Criminology*, 23 (2), 193–208.
Melossi, D. (1989). An introduction: fifty years later, *Punishment and social structure* in comparative analysis. *Contemporary Crises*, 13 (4), 311–326.
Melossi, D. ([1990] 1992). *El estado del control social*. México: Siglo XXI. [In English: *The state of social control*. New York: St, Martin's Press, 1990].
Melossi, D. and Pavarini, M. ([1977] 1981). *The prison and the factory. Origins of the penitentiary system*. London: Macmillan.
Melossi, D. and Sozzo, M. (2008). Entrevista con Dario Melossi. Por una criminología crítica. Trayectoria, debates, agenda (I). *Delito y Sociedad*, 25, 141–156.
Page, J. (2011). *The toughest beat. Politics, punishment, and the Prison Officers Union in California*. Oxford: Oxford University Press.
Page, J. (2013). Punishment and the penal field. In: Simon, J. and Sparks, R., eds, *The SAGE handbook of punishment and society*. London: Sage, 152–165.
Pashukanis, E. ([1929] 1989). *Law and Marxism. A general theory*. Pluto: London.
Polanyi, K. (1944). *The great transformation: economic and political origins of our time*. New York: Rineheart.
Poulantzas, N. ([1978] 2016). *State, power, socialism*. Verso: London.
Reiman, J. ([1979] 2001). *The rich get richer and the poor get poorer. Ideology, class, and criminal justice*. 6th ed. Needham Heights: Allyn & Bacon.
Rusche, G. and Kirchheimer, O. ([1939] 2004). *Pena y Estructura Social*. Bogotá: Temis. [In English: *Punishment and social structure*. New Brunswick: Transaction Publishers].
Scheingold, S. (1998). Constructing the new political criminology; power, authority, and the post-liberal state. *Law & Social Inquiry*, 23 (4), 857–895.
Simon, J. (2013). Punishment and the political technologies of the body. In: Simon, J. and Sparks, R., eds, *The SAGE handbook of punishment and society*. London: Sage, 60–89.
Spitzer, S. (1981). The political economy of policing. In: Greenberg, D., ed., *Crime & capitalism. Readings in Marxist criminology*. Palo Alto: Mayfield, 314–340.
Spitzer S. (1995). Directions for research on space, time, and social control. In: Melossi, D., ed., *Social control, political power, and the penal question: for a sociology of criminal law and punishment*. Oñati: Oñati IISL, 13–20.
Sutton, J. (2004). The political economy of imprisonment in affluent Western democracies, 1960–1990. *American Sociological Review*, 69 (2), 170–189.

Thompson, E.P. (1975). *Whigs and hunters: the origin of the Black Act*, London: Allen Lane.
Vázquez García, F. (2002). *Pierre Bourdieu: la sociología como crítica de la razón*. Barcelona: Montesinos.
Wacquant, L. ([1999] 2009). *Prisons of poverty*, Minneapolis: University of Minneapolis Press.
Wacquant, L. (2009). *Punishing the poor. The neoliberal government of social insecurity*. Durham: Duke University Press.
Wacquant, L. (2014a). Marginality, ethnicity and penality in the neoliberal city: an analytic cartography. *Ethnic & Racial Studies Review*, 37 (10), 1687–1711.
Wacquant, L. (2014b). *Homines in extremis*: what fighting scholars teach us about habitus. *Body & Society*, 20 (2), 3–17.
Western, B. (2006). *Punishment and inequality in America*, New York: Russell Sage Foundation.
Young, P. (1983). Sociology, the state and penal relations. *In*: Garland, D. and Young, P., eds, *The power to punish. Contemporary penality and social analysis*. London: Heinemann, 84–100.

Chapter 4

Do economic depressions reduce the use of fines?

Revisiting Rusche and Kirchheimer's *Punishment and Social Structure*

Patricia Faraldo Cabana

Introduction

'Money is probably the most frequently used means of punishing, deterring, compensating and regulating throughout the legal system' (O'Malley 2009: 1). Therefore, it is surprising how little Anglo-Saxon criminologists, sociologists and legal scholars write about the nature of monetary punishments and of their specific characteristics as legal sanctions. Indeed, until recently in the Anglophone academic world we have only been able to find no more than a handful of generally recognized attempts to think about fines in terms of socio-legal theory. One of these theorizations was Georg Rusche and Otto Kirchheimer's, whose brief analysis of the fine in terms of Marxist theory is found in *Punishment and Social Structure* (New York 1939, republished in 1968, here cited through the 2003 Transaction edition).[1]

Punishment and Social Structure established the sociological foundations of what would later become the political economy of punishment. The first half of the book analyses changes in punishment systems in use in Europe, including fines, from the Middle Ages until the early twentieth century. Its more influential part provides an explanation of the historical emergence, consolidation and transformation of the penitentiary system according to the logic of the principle of less eligibility, and ultimately of the dynamics of the labour market. Penal change is understood as a result of new socioeconomic conditions, not as the progressive implementation of the ideas of well-intentioned reformers in a linear advancement towards more human punishments. This part was originally written by Rusche in 1935, and based on a paper about the labour market and penal sanctions he published in German in the *Zeitschrift für Soziologie* in 1933 (Rusche 1933 [1978]). At the end of this historical analysis of the developments in criminal law since the Enlightenment, there is one chapter dedicated to the fine in penal practice. Kirchheimer was the only author of the chapter on fines (Weihofen 1939: 145; Bottoms 1983: 168; Melossi 2003: xviii). He also wrote the chapter on new trends in penal policy under Fascism and revised the chapters written by Rusche.

Kirchheimer was convinced that fines would only develop into a major sanction when poor people could afford to pay them, since the application of fines has its natural limits in the material conditions of the lower strata of the population (Rusche and Kirchheimer 1939 [2003]: 176). For him, the two elements that had the greatest influence on reinstating the fine in the catalogue of punishments were the decrease in poverty and the more widespread distribution of wealth in European societies at the end of the nineteenth century. Moreover, he argued that during periods of depression the fine becomes less feasible, and consequently short terms of imprisonment become more prevalent, with the number of defaults going up rapidly. He also hypothesized a further shift towards the replacement of imprisonment by fines in the future.[2]

Using Rusche and Kirchheimer's insightful work to establish a dialogue, my intent with this chapter is to discuss if the basic premise of the political economy of punishment is applicable to the fine. If the severity of punishment is correlated to the value of labour, do economic depressions really reduce the use of fines? A good way of confirming this thesis is to analyse what happened in Germany during the Great Depression of 1929 and in Spain during the Great Recession of 2008. Regarding Germany, not only was there good statistical data, but Germany was the example used by Kirchheimer to illustrate the inverse relationship between fines and imprisonment during periods of depression. The case of Spain, one of several Southern European countries hit hard by the financial crisis of 2008, offers an interesting counter example.

This study will analyse trends in prison and fine sentences, as well as in imprisonment for default to test the explanatory power of the Rusche-Kirchheimer hypothesis.[3] The next section will first of all outline the main thesis advanced by Rusche and Kirchheimer on the link between forms of society and forms of punishment with particular attention being paid to their explanation of the development of fines. The third section summarizes the German case followed by the fourth section, which presents the Spanish case. In the last section I will come to some conclusions.

This topic is definitely a timely one. The relationship between economic crises and imprisonment has been widely studied and criticized (Jankovic 1977; Wallace 1980; Galster and Scaturo 1985; Parker and Horwitz 1986; Inverarity and McCarthy 1988; Hale 1989a, 1989b; Michalowski and Carlson 2011, and many others). However, the one between economic crises and fines has been neglected in literature so far. This chapter aims to fill this gap.

The Rusche–Kirchheimer hypothesis

What has come to be known as the Rusche–Kirchheimer hypothesis holds that

> [e]very system of production tends to discover punishments which correspond to its productive relationships. It is thus necessary to investigate the origin and fate of penal systems, the use or avoidance of specific punishment, and the intensity of penal practices as they are determined by social forces, above all by economic and then fiscal forces.
>
> (Rusche and Kirchheimer 1939 [2003]: 5)

Regarding imprisonment, they defended the notion that labour market dynamics could explain the emergence of the prison system and the subsequent changes in penal severity throughout the nineteenth century both in Europe and in America, as well as the limits of modern prison reform (Rusche and Kirchheimer 1939 [2003]: 133–165). Following a historical approach, Rusche and Kirchheimer found a correlation between the severity of punishment and the value of labour, so that when labour is scarce, and its value high, the specific methods of punishment become relatively milder, while when labour is abundant, their severity increases.

This analysis, understood in terms of a narrow economic determinism, was heavily criticized in the first reviews of their work (Burgess 1940: 986; Hall 1940: 971–972; Marshall 1940: 126–127; Riesman 1940: 1299). Combined with the outbreak of World War II, and the subsequent hostility towards all kinds of Marxist approaches to social sciences, this critical assessment led to the complete disappearance of *Punishment and Social Structure* from criminological discussion. Its rediscovery in the late seventies would produce a considerable number of works over the next decades that successfully applied the Rusche-Kirchheimer hypothesis, in particular the part related to the impact of unemployment on levels of incarceration, to contemporary penal practices in the United States and the United Kingdom (Greenberg 1977; Jankovic 1977; Yeager 1979; Box and Hale 1982; Carroll and Doubet 1983; Inverarity and McCarthy 1988; Inverarity and Grattet 1989; Michalowski and Pearson 1990; McCullagh 1992; Hochstetler and Shover 1997; see also Melossi and Sozzo, this volume). However, the nineties would see another wave of criticism, since support for the hypothesized relationship between unemployment and imprisonment was not considered inconclusive (Jacobs and Helm 1996: 326) or overstated (D'Alessio and Stolzenberg 1995: 350), and even insufficient when used to explain variations in imprisonment within capitalist modes of production (Melossi 1989: 75).

A much less known part of the Rusche–Kirchheimer hypothesis looks at the development of fines. Kirchheimer continued Rusche's analysis of the first interwar period and opened up a new intellectual path. He paid great attention to trends in fascist Germany and Italy, explaining the shift towards harsher punishments in both countries as a consequence not only of the transformation of earlier forms of capitalism into the monopolistic capitalism characteristic of totalitarian states, but mainly of the economic crisis (Rusche and Kirchheimer 1939 [2003]: 185). He also considered the development of fines during the 1930s as particularly telling in this regard, because it indicated 'how the market [...] weakens and neutralizes penal tendencies moving in another direction' (Rusche and Kirchheimer 1939 [2003]: 187).

Kirchheimer supported the idea that during an economic crisis the number of fines levied decreases, while the number of defaults goes up rapidly. He explained that in a period of severe unemployment the possibilities of collecting the fine are reduced, and therefore the percentage of imprisonments for default rises. According to him (1939 [2003]: 171),

[t]he extent to which a fine system can be developed and the character of the offenses to which it is to be applied in any given country are not merely problems of legislation and judicial custom. They are decisively influenced by the whole social situation and by the conditions of the various social strata.

This observation closely stems from Ruche's proposition that a declining standard of living among the working class will lead to an increased use of imprisonment. Consequently, in a situation of economic crisis,

[w]e see an inverse proportion between imprisonment for nonpayment of fines and the number of fines levied. The latter decreases in a period of severe unemployment because of the reduced possibilities of collecting the fine, while the number of defaults goes up rapidly.

(Rusche and Kirchheimer 1939 [2003]: 171)

To corroborate his argument Kirchheimer used the following data from Germany, by that time hard hit by the Great Depression of 1929.

Germany during the Great Depression of 1929

Once World War I was over, 1920s Germany witnessed a period of dominance of the social-democrat party and preponderance of radical reformist tendencies. The dominant literature of that time fully took on board the nineteenth-century criticisms against short-term imprisonment (Bumke 1926 and 1928; Hellwig 1924; Schäfer 1924; Pitschel 1929). Preliminary drafts of the 1871 Imperial Penal Code were presented that were very favourable towards the fine. One example is a 1919 draft, which intended to broaden the scope of the fine by making a greater number of offences punishable by fine and by requiring courts

Table 4.1 Commitment to prison for non-payment of fines. German Empire: 1926–1931

Year	Total convictions	Total sentences to fines (percent of total convictions)	Fines paid in full	Per cent of fines levied	Imprisonment in default of fine	Per cent of fines levied
1926	598,460	65.6	316,022	72.2	40,186	9.2
1927	612,215	66.7	347,743	76.8	38,641	8.5
1928	588,492	69.8	353,530	77.6	37,360	8.1
1929	595,656	68.4	341,825	76.5	44,085	9.8
1930	596,127	66.2	316,463	71.9	53,027	12.5
1931	564,903	67.8	240,296	63.2	59,076	15.4

Source: compiled by Rusche and Kirchheimer ([1939] 2003: 171) from Reichskriminalstatistik (1933: 44–46).

to ensure whether the purpose of the punishment could be fulfilled by a fine in cases where the law provided for the fine and imprisonment as alternatives (Oetker 1922: 161ff.). A second example is a 1922 draft written by Radbruch – then Minister of Justice – which was described as 'by and large the zenith of the legislative reform work' beginning in the nineteenth century (Jescheck, quoted by Kubink 2002: 173), and as 'the most progressive ever submitted in the history of German criminal law' (Grünhut 1944: 27). This ground-breaking draft conceived the fine as the primary reaction against offences and placed it at the centre of the criminal justice system (Radbruch 1952: 55). It was never enacted.[4] The failure of the Penal Code reform projects led to laws being established for the fine that formed the basis of its recovery (Bumke 1928: 16–19, with statistical data; Reichskriminalstatistik 1930: 44ff.).

The four laws enacted between 1921 and 1924[5] established the following objectives:

- set a maximum amount of the fine, which did not exist until then;
- substitute imprisonment sentences of less than 3 months with a fine of up to 150,000 Marks, 'whenever the purpose of punishment can be achieved just as well by a fine'.

In order to avoid the vicious circle of an offender first being fined instead of being sent to prison, and then subsequently, however, being imprisoned because he was unable to pay the fine, the first law:

- obliged courts to take the financial circumstances of the offender into account in determining the amount of the fine;
- authorized courts to give the offender leave to pay the fine in instalments within a specified period of time if immediate payment of the total amount could not reasonably be expected; and
- provided for work (*freie Arbeit*) to be used as a way of dealing with fine defaulters, so that the offender could remain free and work off his or her fine.

The three other laws were centred in the problem of inflation. Law of 27 April 1923 adjusted fines to the increasing inflation – the maximum limit grew from 150,000 to ten million Marks, an amount that could be increased when it was not 'enough' (§27c of the 1871 German Imperial Penal Code). It had to be complemented only a few months later by the law of 23 October 1923 and the decree of 23 November 1923, both of which included new measures to fight the persistent problem of inflation (Alsberg 1924: 276–277).

These laws, particularly the first one, had the desired effect of increasing the percentage of fine sentences and reducing prison sentences, even if the possibility to allow the offender to work his or her fine off in liberty remained dead letter (Grünhut 1944: 14). In 1921 the percentage of prison sentences reached 56.9 per cent, but in 1922 it went down to 36.9 per cent. This decrease was also very significant regarding short-term imprisonment, which, over the same period, went down from 38.3 per cent in 1921 to 20.2 per cent of all penalties in 1922. During the same period the percentage of imposed fines grew from 39.3 per cent to 59.5 per cent of all penalties (according to Reichskriminalstatistik 1930: 44), with literature elaborating on a 'strong effect of the Acts on Fines' (Pitschel 1929: 10). These laws brought a significant change in the sanctioning practice, a fact that can only be described as 'a turning point of German penal policy' (Heinz 1981: 159; Stapenhorst 1993: 45).

The positive effects of the enacted laws were, nevertheless, not without their ups and downs. The inflationary process that the German economy of the 1920s went through had an adverse effect on the fine. In fact, it was a decisive factor, which rendered the fine ineffective despite the frequency with which it was imposed by the courts.[6] In essence, the constant depreciation of the value of money meant that the amount the judge set in the sentence bore little relation to the amount actually paid by the offender. If we also take into account that it was obligatory to grant an extension and instalment periods for payment in cases where the offender was unable to pay, the time that elapsed between the fine being set and it actually being paid made the real value of the fine have no connection whatsoever with the intention of the judge who originally imposed it (Kitzinger 1923: 599; Kronecker 1924: 578ff.). This led to a decrease in the use of the fine in 1924 and 1925, so that the percentages of 1913 and 1925 were practically the same (Pitschel 1929: 10). This break was quickly overcome, at least until the Great Depression unleashed its effects.

In fact, the assertion that economic depressions have an adverse effect on the propensity to fine seems to find a certain statistical correlation. Regarding the Great Depression of 1929, Germany was the European country 'in which the crisis was most severe, and in which wage cuts and unemployment created the sharpest decline in the living standard of broad sections of the population' (Rusche and Kirchheimer 1939 [2003]: 177–178). During the depression the

Table 4.2 Commitment to prison for non-payment of fines (total numbers and percentage). German Empire: 1925–1931

Year	Fines	Prison sentences for fine defaulters	% fines converted into imprisonment
1925	337,649	22,653	6.7
1926	437,325	40,186	9.1
1927	454,019	38,641	8.5
1928	461,718	37,360	8.1
1929	449,407	44,085	9.8
1930	440,140	53,027	12.0
1931	383,003	59,076	15.4

Source: Statistik des deutschen Reichs (1930, p. 44 ff., 51). All offences against the Reich and the federated states are included.

proportion of unpaid fines increased, as expected. As indicated by the *Reichskriminalstatistik* (1930: 45), if in 1928 77.7 per cent of fines were paid in full, the percentage fell to 62.7 per cent in 1931. That is to say that the number of fines levied decreased because of the reduced possibilities of collecting the fine (Rusche and Kirchheimer 1939 [2003]: 171; Albrecht 1978: 174). Consequently, the number of defaults went up rapidly, and so did imprisonment for defaulters: the percentage of fines that were left unpaid and converted into a prison sentence increased from 6.7 in 1925 to 8.1 per cent in 1928 and almost doubled to 15.4 per cent in 1931 (Albrecht 1978: 188; Janssen 1994: 12).

The proportion of sentences that *imposed* fines also declined, but clearly not as sharply as it should have according to Kirchheimer's thesis: from 58.1 per cent of all convictions in 1922 to 56.6 per cent in 1931. It only increased again after the Nazis came to power.[7]

O'Malley (2009: 39) observed that

> Rusche and Kirchheimer (1939: 169–172) put stress on the proportions of fines that are not paid in full and that therefore result in imprisonment. But the proportion of *sentences* that are fines does not decline as it should, given the severity of the depression. They dip by only three per cent throughout the period. In short, people may be unable to pay, but the courts are only marginally changing their sentencing behaviour. (emphasis in the original)

O'Malley relates this slight decline with the possibility that courts do not sentence as a reflex of the state of the economy, but are influenced far more by other considerations. He only takes into account the data up to 1931, while the strongest decrease of fine sentences until World War II can be seen in 1932, just before the Nazis came to power. By then, fines were only 56.2 per cent of all convictions, while prison sentences under three months increased to 26 per cent and prison sentences between three months and one year to 12.9 per cent (Rabl 1936: 8).

Table 4.3 Prison and fine sentences (percentages). German Empire: 1920–1932 (in 5-year periods, except 1930–1932)

Year	Prison					Fines
	Penal servitude (Zuchthaus)	Prison (total percentage)	Prison of 1 year or over	Prison from 3 months to 1 year	Prison under 3 months	
1920/1921	1.3	56.8	4.4	13.8	38.6	38.7
1922/1924	1.3	36.9	3.5	13.7	19.7	60.1
1925/1929	1.1	30.8	2.1	9.9	18.8	66.9
1930/1932	0.9	36.4	2.2	11.1	23.1	61.4

Source: adapted from Rabl (1936: 8). Only sentences for offences against the Reich are included.

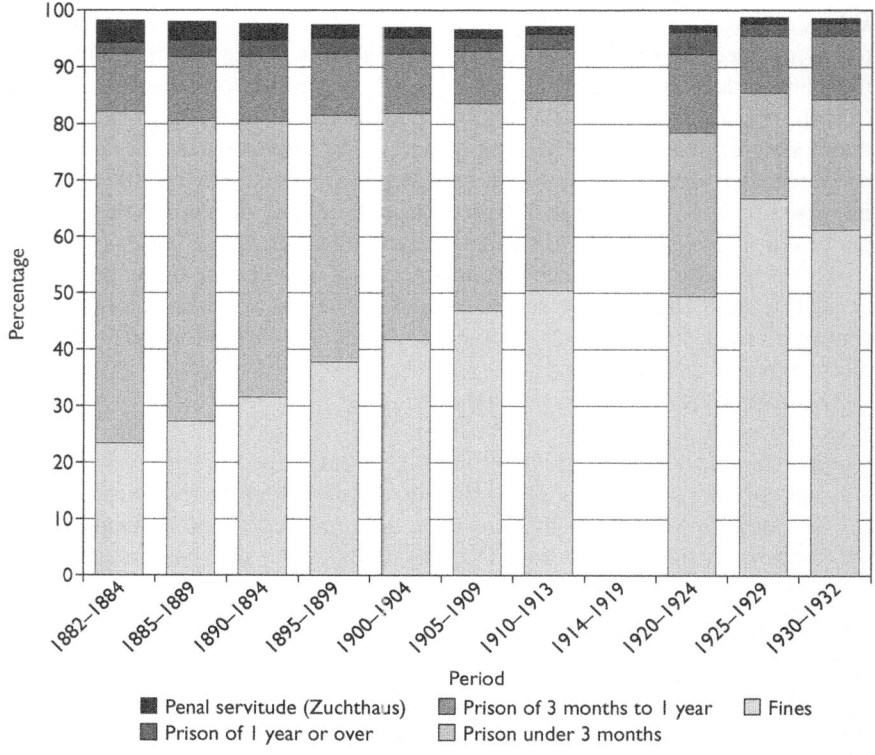

Figure 4.1 Prison and fine sentences (percentages). German Empire: 1882–1932.*
Source: adapted from Rabl (1936: 8). Only sentences for offences against the Reich are included.
Note
* There is no data for World War I.

On the contrary, German literature agreed that 1929 put a stop to the growth in the proportion of sentences that were fines (Exner 1932: 749; Stapenhorst 1993: 45). The explanation given was that because many offenders could not pay their fines, due to their dire financial situation, courts went back to imposing custodial sentences (Stapenhorst 1993: 45). This would mean that there was a change in the attitude of judges.

Conversely, the available statistical data show that throughout the reporting period the proportion of offenders sentenced to terms of over three months of imprisonment remained fairly stable, with only negligible growth. Fines were substituted only by the shortest periods of imprisonment. It is worth keeping in mind that imprisonment for defaulters was also a short-term prison sentence that increased the percentage of these prison sentences. The German legislation on fines in the years 1921, 1923 and 1924, which established work penalty without imprisonment

(*Arbeitsstrafe ohne Einsperrung*) as a substitute for an unpaid fine, failed in practice (Best 1932: 19; Grünhut 1944: 14; Grebing 1978: 151; Pfohl 1983: 29–30), just as the precedent regulation in the 1871 German Imperial Penal Code also did.[8]

In sum, this means that the courts were not changing their sentencing behaviour due to the growing percentage of unpaid fines, but only applying the statute that provided imprisonment in case of default, due to the lack of alternatives. The normative framework was too harsh. Imprisonment was always applicable in the case of non-payment, even if this was involuntary, without allowing the amount of a fine to be reduced if the offender's financial circumstances worsened after sentencing. This explains the higher levels of fines converted into imprisonment in a period of economic difficulties. Nevertheless, the available data also show that the percentage of sentences to fine remained almost intact, meaning that under conditions of poverty the fine can still operate as a mass sanction. The German experience illustrates that the fine could be applied according to the economic circumstances of the time as well as to the offender's financial situation and the seriousness of the offence.

Spain during the Great Recession of 2008

Spain adopted the day-fine system in 1995, with the enactment of the new Penal Code, which entered into force in May 1996. The so-called 'Penal Code of Democracy' did not expand the use of fines, quite the opposite: it maintained a fairly stable use of prison sentences while substantially increasing the number of non-custodial sentences other than fines (Díez Ripollés 2006: 15–16). As a result, the proportion of fines correspondingly decreased, since fines were substituted by other intermediate punishments, such as disqualifications, removal of professional status and other deprivations of rights, or community service. This means that the increase in alternatives to imprisonment did not come at the expense of prison sentences, as their designation would suggest, but at the expense of fines.

Table 4.4 Prison, fine and other intermediate sentences (percentages). Spain: 1994–2002

Year	Prison sentences	Fine sentences	Other non-custodial sentences
1994	57.7	40.9	0.4
1995	56.1	42.5	1.3
1996	55.8	41.0	2.2
1997	54.0	28.8	15.3
1998	60.6	18.7	19.7
1999	63.4	14.4	21.7
2000	63.4	12.9	23.1
2001	62.4	12.1	25.0
2002	61.8	13.9	23.4

Source: Spanish Statistical Office (Instituto Nacional de Estadística, INE).

The increase in punitiveness made possible by the 1995 Penal Code was reinforced by amendments passed in 2003, which included a significant toughening of prison penalty provisions and the re-establishment of short-term prison sentences between three and six months (Díez Ripollés 2007: 4–5). Penalty provisions included the option to incarcerate a person for up to 40 years and restrict prisoners' access to open prison regime, temporary leave or conditional release on parole. Regarding fines, while almost half of offenders got away with nothing more than a fine in 1995, only less than one-fourth could expect to do so three years later, when the Great Recession began. Did the economic crisis reinforce this tendency?

In 2008 Spain was badly affected by the global credit crisis. The Spanish real estate market collapsed leading to a deep recession that the country is still struggling to recover from. At the peak of the crisis, there were high levels of long-term structural unemployment – more than 20 per cent of the workforce, five million people – mass youth unemployment – over half of the Spanish population of under-25-year-olds – and over a million people lived in households with no monthly income at all.

Replicating almost exactly Kirchheimer's hypothesis, this historical period (2008–2015) witnessed:

1 a substantial increase in the percentage of imposed prison sentences from 20.5 per cent in 2008 to 25 per cent in 2015, mainly for sentences of less than two years; combined with
2 a decrease in the percentage of fine sentences from 23.1 per cent in 2008 to 19 per cent in 2011, during the worst years of the crisis, with a slow but steady increase afterwards, achieving 22.5 per cent in 2015.

Despite appearances, this does not mean that the severity of punishment rose. Two aspects do not correspond to what could be expected, according to Kirchheimer:

1 there was a sharp decline of the prison population, which decreased from 73,558 prisoners in 2008 to 61,614 in 2015, with a peak of 76,079 in 2009 (Ministerio del Interior 2016: 527); and
2 subsidiary penalties for defaulters, including imprisonment, home arrest and community service, did not increase but *decreased* during this period. They were 11.4 per cent of all imposed fines in 2008, 6.9 in 2009, 6.2 in 2010, and a slightly higher 6.8 per cent in 2011. The percentage for 2012 is not reliable. It is probable that by then subsidiary penalties were already being added to the penalty finally imposed, as it was established in 2013.

This development is particularly clear if we look at the percentages. It seems obvious that at least substantial numbers of fines were substituted by the shortest prison sentences, the ones of less than two years.

Table 4.5 Prison and fine sentences (total numbers). Spain: 2007–2015

Year	Total prison sentences	Of which, prison sentences below 2 years	Of which, prison sentences of 2 years and more*	Fines	Subsidiary penalties for defaulters**
2007	121,217	–	–	96,717	11,796
2008	129,890	–	–	145,819	16,734
2009	139,663	–	–	158,250	11,023
2010	141,849	126,513	15,336	126,199	7,873
2011	135,713	122,416	13,297	104,783	7,202
2012	142,444	130,116	12,328	108,373	1,667
2013	153,950	141,083	12,867	121,971	41
2014	156,799	144,825	11,974	125,223	–
2015	152,937	141,749	11,188	138,927	–

Source: Spanish Statistical Office.

Notes
* Before 2010 there are no data available about the duration of prison sentences.
** The sharp drop between 2012 and 2013 reflects a change to the classification of subsidiary penalties for fine defaulters, which from 2013 are included in one of the three other categories of: prison, community service, or house arrest (Blay and Larrauri 2016: 196).

Contrary to what could be expected, the tendency to increasingly resort to imprisonment is not linked to the number of individuals in prison. The decrease of the Spanish prison population and incarceration rate follows a pattern found in other European countries (Austria, Finland, Germany, Italy, Sweden, The Netherlands) and in the United States (according both to the 11th edition of the World Prison Population List and to the Council of Europe Annual Penal Statistics 2014; see also Gottschalk 2012: 343–344). This means that although this reduction can be partly seen as the result of national strategies consciously directed at the emptying of prisons – e.g. in the Spanish case, the astonishing growth of criminal law-related deportations of foreign criminals (Brandariz García 2016) – smaller prison populations must also be considered as a consequence of other forces connected with the crisis, such as the lower number of foreign criminals and suspects and the corresponding decrease in pre-trial prisoners (for Spain, Brandariz García 2014, 2015) or the downscaling of sentences against drug trafficking (for Spain, Rodríguez and Larrauri 2012: 10–13; for the United States, King 2009). Nevertheless, the most surprising fact is that imprisonment for defaulters did not increase but *decreased* during this period, from 11.4 per cent of all imposed fines in 2008 to 6.8 per cent in 2011. This drop opposes Kirchheimer's thesis.

Discussion

Overall, the results laid out in this chapter lend some support to the proposition that the Rusche-Kirchheimer hypothesis regarding the use of fines during

Table 4.6 Prison and fine sentences (percentages). Spain: 2007–2015

Year	Prison sentences (percentage of total convictions)	Of which prison sentences below 2 years (percentage of prison sentences)	Of which prison sentences of 2 years and more (percentage of prison sentences)	Fines (percentage of total convictions)	Subsidiary penalties for defaulters (percentage of imposed fines)
2007	27.3	–	–	21.8	12.1
2008	20.5	–	–	23.1	11.4
2009	22.2	–	–	25.2	6.9
2010	22.7	89.1	10.8	20.2	6.2
2011	24.6	90.2	9.8	19.0	6.8
2012	25.5	91.3	8.6	19.4	1.5
2013	25.2	91.6	8.3	20.0	0.0
2014	25.5	92.3	7.6	20.3	0.0
2015	25.0	92.6	7.3	22.5	0.0

Source: Spanish Statistical Office.

economic crises can help predict shifts in the use of prison and fine sentences. However, the relationship between economic crises and imprisonment for defaulters seems weaker.

In my opinion, the proportion of unpaid fines and default imprisonment has less to do with economic crises and more to do with both the kind of fine system applied in a certain country – whether a fixed-fine system, a day-fine system, or a mixed one – and the techniques used to avoid imprisonment for fine defaulters. Measures such as limiting the possibility of converting the fine into imprisonment to cases in which the offender does not pay the fine wilfully, giving time to pay in instalments or paying off the fine by working outside the prison can help offenders pay their fines and thus avoid prison. The proportion of unpaid fines may depend not only on the designed system, but also on proper implementation. The German and Spanish experiences during severe depressions are a good example.

With the German fixed-fine system, the law obliged courts to take the financial circumstances of the offender into account in determining the amount of the fine and authorized them to give the offender leave to pay the fine in instalments within a specified period of time if immediate payment of the total amount could not be reasonably expected. Nevertheless, there were no practical alternatives to imprisonment in the case of default, due to the fiasco of community service. And if the offender's economic circumstances changed after receiving the sentence, the fine amount could not be accordingly altered. Moreover, no alternatives were available for those no longer able to pay after being granted time to do it.

In Spain is there a day-fine system in which the amount of the fine imposed is based on the seriousness of the offence as well as on the offender's ability to pay. This is only theoretical, because in practice the courts do not investigate the offender's wealth (Morillas *et al.* 2013: 325–328). Only in 10 per cent of the cases there is a previous research of the offender's financial situation, while in the remaining 90 per cent courts simply impose the lowest fine (Cid and Larrauri 2002: 27), thereby depriving fines of much of their potential deterrent and retributive effect. This practice undermines the equality principle, but is beneficial for poor offenders. Moreover, there are functioning alternatives to imprisonment for defaulters, with the main one being the conditional suspension of prison sentences imposed to replace unpaid fines, used in 40.5 per cent of the cases (Cid and Larrauri 2002: 88). House arrest and community service are scarcely used alternatives, with percentages of 2 per cent and 1 per cent respectively. Using all these alternatives equates to only 56.5 per cent of unpaid fines being converted into non-suspended prison sentences. Additionally, it is considered inappropriate to impose imprisonment for fine default on prisoners who are already sentenced to long-term custodial sentences. Last, if offender's circumstances change after receiving the sentence, the fine amount must be accordingly altered. This provision is particularly interesting in light of both the debt burden imposed by Spain's mortgage crisis on many individuals and the creditor-friendly foreclosure system that pushed many middle-class families into social exclusion.

Conclusion

The main disadvantage of the penal fine in modern times is its unequal impact on poor and rich offenders (Faraldo Cabana 2014, 2015). The only way to address it is 'the precise calculation of the fine according to the conditions of the delinquent and the amount of damaged caused by his crime' (Rusche and Kirchheimer 1939 [2003]: 169). Germany could do it in the late 1920s and early 1930s, but when the rate of unpaid fines began to grow due to the economic crisis, he was not able to implement a viable alternative to imprisonment for defaulters. The growing rate of imprisonment for defaulters was linked to a rigorous regulation that only stipulated imprisonment in the case of non-payment, even if this was involuntary, without viable alternatives and without allowing the amount of a fine to be reduced if the offender's financial circumstances worsened after sentencing. On the contrary, fine amounts in Spain are so low that they only pose an insurmountable burden for the very poor. Moreover, they can be adapted to the offender's economic situation even after sentencing and there are functioning alternatives to imprisonment, namely conditional suspension. In sum, differences in the levels of imprisonment for defaulters are principally due to disparate statutory requirements governing conversion of unpaid fines. Differences in the proportion of unpaid fines probably depend on different factors, some related to the criminal justice system and some not. On the one hand, the fact that the fine in Germany was calculated according to the offender's financial circumstances and in Spain it was not. On the other hand, although in both countries the effects of spiralling unemployment were devastating, Spain has a functioning system of state welfare and an informal economy that helped sustain the majority of poor families. The situation in Germany was different.

All in all, although it has been said that the section on fines is 'less convincing than the first part of the book' (De Giorgi 2013: 44), being the result of Kirchheimer's later reworking of Rusche's original manuscript, the truth is that many insights regarding the use of fines in periods of economic hardship can be found. It seems clear that there is an inverse relationship between imprisonment and fines, so that fines are less used and prison sentences more so, but the increased use of prison sentences does not mean increased punitiveness since this depends on other factors.

While the foregoing analysis lends some support to the Rusche-Kirchheimer hypothesis – namely, the inverse relationship between the proportion of imposed prison and fine sentences in periods of depression – I must offer at least one caution regarding the interpretation of the findings. My research is based on the same data used by Kirchheimer to formulate his hypothesis. Further analysis may identify additional factors, or reveal that the factors on which I have focused are less significant than I suggest.[9] Nevertheless, given the lack of attention paid to fines in general, it is my hope that these preliminary findings of historical veracity in the relationship Kirchheimer hypothesized between economic crises and fines will encourage others to join me in developing a better understanding of the impact of economic crises on other forms of punishment besides imprisonment.

Notes

1 Co-authorship does not mean that both authors worked together. They did not. On the difficult process of writing and re-writing of *Punishment and Social Structure* until its final publication in 1939, see Melossi (2003).
2 Kirchheimer recognized the rise of the consumer society as a factor that was giving force to the use of fines. For him, '[t]he increasing emphasis on material goods provided an argument for the extended application of fines in place of short-term imprisonment' (Rusche and Kirchheimer 1939 [2003]: 168). He linked it with the changing meaning of money as an explanatory factor of the expansion of fines:

> Money had become the measure of all things, and it was only right that the state, which extends positive privileges in the form of monetary grants, should also introduce the negative privilege of taking wealth away in punishment for delinquency.
> (Rusche and Kirchheimer 1939 [2003] 168)

3 Unemployment and inequality increased sharply during the crisis of 1929 in Germany and of 2008 in Spain. The structure of crimes showed continuity, without major changes that could influence the use of punishments. However, we can find divergent developments related to crime rates. In Germany, the rate of property crimes considerably increased during the onset of the crisis (Franzmann 2016), but the general crime rate dropped – it had been very high during the previous crisis of the 1920s. In Spain, the rate of property crimes dropped perceptibly, and the same happened with the general crime rate (Ministerio del Interior 2014: 148, 2016: 153). Theft tended to rise in Germany (Stapenhorst 1993: 55) and recede in Spain, a phenomenon that can have many explanations. These aspects will not be explored here because Rusche and Kirchheimer did not approach them either.
4 The general structure of the 1922 draft remained the basis for the first official draft of 1925 which, after many parliamentary deliberations, came 'to a fatal stand-still' in 1931, when the right-wing parties refused to continue their cooperation with the legislative efforts of the Weimar Republic (Grünhut 1944: 28).
5 Law on the extension of the application field of the fine and the restriction of short-term imprisonment (*Gesetz zur Erweiterung des Anwendungsgebiets der Geldstrafe und zur Einschränkung der kurzen Freiheitsstrafen*) of 21 December 1921; Law on fines (*Geldstrafengesetz*) of 27 April 1923; Law on monetary penalties and fines (*Gesetz über Vermögensstrafen und Bußen*) of 13 October 1923; Decree on monetary penalties and fines (*Verordnung über Vermögensstrafen und Bußen*) of 6 February 1924.
6 It is interesting to point out that the percentage of fines actually paid was higher during this period when the fine imposed was lower. Data from 1926, contained in the annex of the 1927 penal code reform project, p. 46, show that 80.1 per cent of fines of less than 20 Reichsmarks were paid in full, 68.1 per cent of fines between 20 and 100 RM, 56.4 per cent of fines between 100 and 300 RM, 39.2 per cent of fines between 300 and 1,000 RM, 22.7 per cent of fines between 1,000 and 10,000 RM and only 6.3 per cent of fines of over 10,000 RM.
7 Penal fines were considered undesirable under the Nazi regime due to ideological reasons (Rusche and Kirchheimer 1939 [2003]: 186). In the words of a member of the Criminal Law Commission, which was appointed by the Nazi government and tasked with a complete renewal of the penal law, the fine was 'an unpleasant and unworthy means of punishment' associated with a capitalist and decadent society (Rietzsch 1934: 100–101). The rise in the use of fines during the Weimar Republic was seen as an unfortunate development that had to be halted. In spite of this ideological aversion, the use of fines experienced an increase between 1933 and 1939. In 1933, the prison sentence was used in

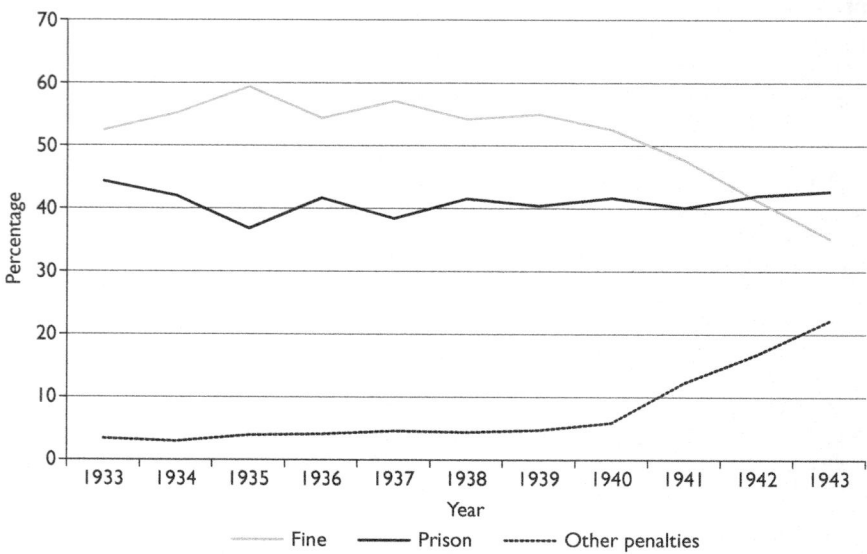

Figure 4.2 Convictions to prison, fine and other penalties (percentages). German Empire: 1933–first semester 1943.*

Source: adapted from Stapenhorst (1993: 66).

44.3 per cent of total convictions, while for the fine it was 52.3 per cent. In 1939, the ratio was 40.4 to 54.8 per cent. The situation only changed during the war. The rates of prison sentences remained steady, with an average of 41.3 percent, while the use of fines declined by 17 percent (Stapenhorst 1993: 66; Sevdiren 2011: 131).

8 This failure was due largely to the negligence of the authorities, which did not draft the provisions for enforcement prescribed by law, with the only exception of the Free State of Thuringia (Heinitz 1953: 41). In turn, this lack of interest stemmed from the economic and social situation prevailing over the interwar Germany, shaken by a severe recession, which, in a context of increasing unemployment, made the possibility of offering the alternative of community service unrealistic.

9 For example, the different level of welfare in Germany and Spain. In his 1933 paper, Rusche explained that unemployment assistance and, in more general terms, welfare benefits allowed wages and workers' standard of living not sink as low as they would have in the aftermaths of the Great Depression. Criminality did not rise to its pre-war level, but slightly declined. Therefore, humanitarian penal reforms that began before World War I were not given up, 'but were partially continued, given the favourable political climate…' (Rusche 1933 [1978]: 7). He considered this development as not contradictory with 'the simple heuristic maxim to which we evidently owe so many correct results'. It would be interesting to contrast this with the Spanish situation.

References

Albrecht HJ (1978) 'Statistische Angaben über die Geldstrafe in der Bundesrepublik Deutschland'. In: Jescheck HH and G Grebing (eds) *Die Geldstrafe im deutschen und ausländischen Recht*. Baden-Baden: Nomos, 165–191.

Alsberg M (1924) 'Geldentwertung und Strafrechtspflege'. *Juristische Wochenschrift* 10(5): 276–277.

Best E (1932) *Studien über die Anwendung der fakultativ angedrohten Geldstrafen im Deutschen Reiche*. Gießen: Univ. Diss.

Blay E and Larrauri E (2016) 'Community punishments in Spain: A tale of two administrations'. In: Robinson G and F McNeill (eds) *Community Punishments. European Perspectives*. London: Routledge, 191–208.

Bottoms AE (1983) 'Some neglected features of contemporary penal systems'. In: Garland D and Young P (eds) *The Power to Punish*. London: Heinemann, 166–202.

Box S and Hale C (1982) 'Economic crisis and the rising prisoner population in England and Wales'. *Crime and Social Justice* 17(Summer): 20–35.

Brandariz García JA (2014) 'La evolución de la penalidad en el contexto de la Gran Recesión: La contracción del sistema penitenciario español'. *Revista de Derecho Penal y Criminología* 12: 309–342.

Brandariz García JA (2015) 'La evolución del sistema penitenciario español, 1995–2014: Transformaciones de la penalidad y modificación de la realidad'. *Crítica penal y poder* (9): 1–31.

Brandariz García JA (2016) 'Crimmigration policies and the Great Recession: Analysis of the Spanish case'. In: Guia MJ, R Koulish and V Mitsilegas (eds) *Immigration Detention, Risk and Human Rights*. New York: Springer, 185–197.

Bumke E (1926) 'Wandlung der Strafen'. *Monatsschrift für Kriminalpsychologie und Strafrechtsreform* 17: 359–365.

Bumke E (1928) 'Die Freiheitsstrafe als Problem der Gesetzgebung'. In: Bumke E (ed) *Deutsches Gefängniswesen. Ein Handbuch*. Berlin: Verlag von Franz Vahlen, 16–32.

Burgess EW (1940) 'Book review: Punishment and social structure, by G. Rusche and O. Kirchheimer'. *The Yale Law Journal* 49(5): 986.

Carroll L and Doubet MB (1983) 'U.S. social structure and imprisonment'. *Criminology* 21(3): 449–456.

Cid Moliné J and Larrauri Pijoan E (eds) (2002) *Jueces penales y penas en España (Aplicación de las penas alternativas a la privación de libertad en los juzgados de lo penal)*. Valencia: Tirant lo Blanch.

D'Alessio SJ and Stolzenberg L (1995) 'Unemployment and the incarceration of pre-trial defendants'. *American Sociological Review* 60 (3): 350–359.

De Giorgi A (2013) 'Punishment and political economy'. In: Simon J and R Sparks (eds) *The Sage Handbook of Punishment and Society*. London: Sage, 40–59.

Deutsches Reich (1930) *Kriminalstatistik*. Berlin: P Schmidt.

Díez Ripollés JL (2006) 'La evolución del sistema de penas en España: 1975–2003'. *Revista Electrónica de Ciencia Penal y Criminología* 8: 1–25.

Díez Ripollés JL (2007) 'The "law and order" approach in Spanish criminal justice policy'. *Electronic Review of the International Association of Penal Law*: 1–9.

Exner F (1932) 'Kurze Mitteilungen. Die Reichskriminalstatistk für die Jahre 1928 und 1929'. *Monatsschrift für Kriminalpsychologie und Strafrechtsreform* 23: 747ff.

Faraldo Cabana P (2014) 'Towards equalisation of the impact of the penal fine: Why the wealth of the offender was taken into account'. *International Journal for Crime, Justice and Social Democracy* 3(1): 3–15. Available at www.crimejusticejournal.com/article/view/143/pdf [accessed 1 June 2017].

Faraldo Cabana P (2015) 'A certain sense of fairness? Why fines were made affordable'. *European Journal of Criminology* 12(5): 616–631.

Franzmann G (2016) *Die Entwicklung der Kriminalität im Deutschen Reich zwischen 1882 und 1936. Abgeurteilte nach Deliktarten, Häufigkeit einzelner Straftaten, verhängte Strafen*. Köln: GESIS Datenarchiv.

Galster G and Scaturo L (1985) 'The US criminal justice system: Unemployment and the severity of punishment'. *Journal of Research in Crime and Delinquency* 22(2): 163–189.

Gottschalk M (2012) 'The Great Recession and the Great Confinement: The economic crisis and the future of penal reform'. In: Rosenfeld R, K Quinet and C Garcia (eds) *Contemporary Issues in Criminological Theory and Research: The Role of Social Institutions*. Belmont: Wadsworth, 343–370.

Grebing G (1978) 'Die Geldstrafe im deutschen Recht nach Einführung des Tagessatzsystems'. In: Jescheck HH and G Grebing (eds) *Die Geldstrafe im deutschen und ausländischen Recht*. Baden-Baden: Nomos, 1–184.

Greenberg D (1977) 'The dynamics of oscillatory punishment processes'. *Journal of Criminal Law and Criminology* 68(4): 643–651.

Grünhut M (1944) *The Development of the German Penal System 1920–1932*. Toronto: The Canadian Bar Association.

Hale C (1989a) 'Unemployment, imprisonment, and the stability of punishment hypothesis: Some results using cointegration and error correction models'. *Journal of Quantitative Criminology* 5(2): 169–186.

Hale C (1989b) 'Economy, punishment and imprisonment'. *Contemporary Crises* (13): 327–349.

Hall J (1940) 'Book review: Punishment and social structure, by G. Rusche and O. Kirchheimer'. *Journal of Criminal Law and Criminology* 30(6): 971–973.

Heinitz E (1953) 'Der Ausbau des Strafensystems'. *Zeitschrift für die gesamte Strafrechtswissenschaften* 65: 26–52.

Heinz W (1981) 'Entwicklung, Stand und Struktur der Strafzumessungspraxis. Eine Übersicht über die nach allgemeinem Strafrecht verhängten Hauptstrafen von 1882–1979'. *Monatsschrift für Kriminologie und Strafrechtsreform* 64: 148–173.

Hellwig A (1924) *Das Geldstrafengesetz. Die Verordnung über Vermögensstrafen und Bussen vom 6. Februar 1924 mit der Begründung und den Ausführungsbestimmungen*. 3rd ed. München und Berlin: Müller.

Hochstetler AL and Shover N (1997) 'Street crime, labor surplus and criminal punishment'. *Social Problems* 44 (3): 358–369.

Instituto Nacional de Estadística (1994–2002) *Estadística de condenados*. INE: Madrid.

Inverarity J and McCarthy D (1988) 'Punishment and social structure revisited: Unemployment and imprisonment in the United States, 1948–1984'. *The Sociological Quarterly* 29(2): 263–279.

Inverarity J and Grattet R (1989) 'Institutional responses to unemployment: A comparison of U.S. trends, 1948–1985'. *Contemporary Crises* 13: 351–370.

Jacobs D and Helm RE (1996) 'Toward a political model of incarceration: A time-series examination of multiple explanations for prison admission rates'. *American Journal of Sociology* 102 (2): 323–357.

Jankovic I (1977) 'Labor market and imprisonment'. *Crime and Social Justice* 8: 17–31.

Janssen H (1994) *Die Praxis der Geldstrafenvollstreckung*. Frankfurt aM: Peter Lang.

King R (2009) *The State of Sentencing 2008: Developments in Policy and Practice*. Washington, DC: The Sentencing Project.

Kitzinger F (1923) 'Wertbeständige Geldstrafen!'. *Deutsche Juristen-Zeitung* 28: 599–602.

Kronecker (1924) 'Neuere Bestimmungen über Geldstrafen'. *Zeitschrift für die gesamte Strafrechtswissenschaft* 44: 578–647.

Kubink M (2002) *Strafen und ihre Alternativen im zeitlichen Wandel*. Berlin: Duncker & Humblot.
Leonard EB (2015) *Crime, Inequality, and Power*. New York and London: Routledge.
Marshall TH (1940) 'Book review: Punishment and social structure, by G. Rusche and O. Kirchheimer'. *The Economic Journal* 50(197): 126–127.
McCullagh C (1992) 'Crime, punishment and unemployment'. *Irish Journal of Sociology* 2 (1): 1–19.
Melossi D (1989) 'An introduction: Fifty years later, punishment and social structure in contemporary analysis'. *Contemporary Crises* 13 (4): 311–326.
Melossi D (2003) 'Introduction to the Transaction edition: The simple "heuristic maxim" of an "unusual human being". In: Rusche G and O Kirchheimer *Punishment and Social Structure*. New Brunswick: Transaction Publishers, ix–xlv.
Michalowski RJ and Carlson SM (2011) 'Unemployment, imprisonment, and social structures of accumulation: Historical contingency in the Rusche-Kirchheimer Hypothesis'. In: Lynch MJ and PB Stretesky (eds) *Radical and Marxist Theories of Crime*. Farnham: Ashgate, 393–425.
Michalowski RJ and Pearson MA (1990) 'Punishment and social structure at the state level: A cross-sectional comparison of 1970 and 1980'. *Journal of Research in Crime and Delinquency* 27 (1): 53–78.
Ministerio del Interior (2014) *Anuario Estadístico del Ministerio del Interior 2013*. Bilbao: Ministerio del Interior.
Ministerio del Interior (2016) *Anuario Estadístico del Ministerio del Interior 2015*. Bilbao: Ministerio del Interior.
Morillas Cueva L, Barquín Sanz J, Macías Espejo B and Olmedo Cardenete M (2013) *La aplicación de las alternativas a la pena de prisión en España*. Madrid: Defensor del Pueblo.
Oetker F (1922) 'Die Geldstrafe nach dem Strafgesetzentwurf von 1919'. *Der Gerichtssaal* 88: 161–268.
O'Malley P (2009) *The Currency of Justice. Fines and Damages in Consumer Societies*. New York: Routledge-Cavendish.
Parker RN and Horwitz AV (1986) 'Unemployment, crime, and imprisonment: A panel approach'. *Criminology* 24 (4): 751–773.
Pfohl M (1983) *Gemeinnützige Arbeit als strafrechtliche Sanktion*. Berlin: Duncker & Humblot.
Pitschel W (1929) *Die Praxis in der Wahl der Geldstrafe*. Leipzig: Wiegandt.
Rabl R (1936) *Strafzumessungspraxis und Kriminalitätsbewegung*. Leipzig: Dr. Ernst Wiegandt.
Radbruch G (1952) *Entwurf eines allgemeinen deutschen Strafgesetzbuches (1922)*. Tübingen: JCB Mohr (Paul Siebeck).
Reichskriminalstatistik (1933) *Statistik des deutschen Reichs. Kriminalstatistik für das Jahr 1930*. Berlin: Hobbing.
Riesman Jr. D (1940) 'Book review: Punishment and social structure, by G. Rusche and O. Kirchheimer'. *Columbia Law Review* 40(7): 1297–1301.
Rietzsch O (1934) 'Strafsystem'. In: Gürtner F (ed) *Das kommende deutsche Strafrecht*. Berlin: Vahlen, 85–105.
Rodríguez J and Larrauri E (2012) 'Economic crisis, crime, and prison in Spain'. *Criminology in Europe* (2): 10–13.
Rusche G (1933 [1978]) 'Labor market and penal sanction: Thoughts on the sociology of criminal justice'. *Crime and Social Justice* 10 (Fall–Winter): 2–8.

Rusche G and Kirchheimer O (1939 [2003]) *Punishment and Social Structure*. New Brunswick: Transaction Publishers.

Schäfer L (1934) 'Strafbemessung'. In: Gürtner F (ed) *Das kommende deutsche Strafrecht*. Berlin: Vahlen, 106–116.

Sevdiren O (2011) *Alternatives to Imprisonment in England and Wales, Germany and Turkey*. Berlin-Heidelberg: Springer.

Stapenhorst H (1993) *Die Entwicklung des Verhältnisses von Geldstrafe zu Freiheitsstrafe seit 1882*. Berlin: Duncker & Humblot.

Yeager MG (1979) 'Unemployment and imprisonment'. *The Journal of Criminal Law and Criminology* 70(4): 586–588.

Wallace D (1980) 'The political economy of incarceration trends in late US capitalism: 1971–1977'. *The Insurgent Sociologist* 11(1): 59–66.

Weihofen H (1939) 'Review of *"Punishment and Social Structure,"* by George Rusche and Otto Kirchheimer'. *Washington University Law Review* 25(1): 144–146.

Chapter 5

From one recession to another

The lessons of a long-term political economy of punishment. The example of Belgium (1830–2014)

Charlotte Vanneste

Introduction

The work discussed in this chapter finds its long-ago origin in the hypothesis formulated by Rusche and Kirchheimer in the 1930s (Rusche and Kirchheimer [1939] 1969), which laid the basis for a ground-breaking economic theory on criminal punishment. Although their writings are now well known, one less visible facet of their ideas is worth highlighting for it shows that their theory already heralded work emerging from recent analyses in terms of the political economy of punishment that emphasize the political, institutional and social dimensions.

The key notion of their work can be summarized as follows: 'Every system of production tends to discover punishments which correspond productive relations.' In their historical context of a Fordist industrial economy in full deployment, the determining category for understanding this relation was the labour market. As the heart of their reasoning the authors called on the principle of 'less eligibility' originally developed by nineteenth-century social philosophers – according to which all reform to the system of punishments found its upper limit in the condition reserved for the 'lowest proletarian classes'. According to a Marxist interpretation, however, in an innovative manner they articulated this notion with the labour market category. This principle referred to the classical postulate that the basic function of punishment was deterrence.

In the context of the 1930s, however, Rusche[1] was not seeking to strengthen the principle of less eligibility, but to find an alternative to it. Although the shortage or surplus of manpower was placed at the heart of the discussion, the weight of political interventions was equally stressed: the punishment regime would then have different roles depending on whether or not a social policy was applied. The title of one of Rusche's article of the 1930s (Rusche [1930] 1980) is thus thoroughly evocative: 'Prison Revolts or Social Policy'. It clearly poses the question in terms of an alternative.

Several empirical studies inspired by Rusche, developed in the 1970s and 1980s, conducted statistical verifications on the relation between economic change and penal repression that were almost exclusively based on unemployment indicators, with hypotheses that were later criticized for their overly mechanistic and instrumental nature. A careful reading of Rusche shows that it nonetheless contained an embryo of contemporary ideas put forward in recent analyses of the political economy of punishment. In addition to economic variables and their interrelation, they stress the importance of political, institutional and social variables.

This chapter is divided into three phases.

I shall first present a long-term analysis of Belgian data, with particular focus on a study of the past four decades. The interpretive schema for this analysis spanning almost two centuries illustrates two key components and two closely related explanatory links.

I shall then distinguish the two types of theses found in the political economy of punishment in relation with those observed in the field of economy (globalization thesis vs. varieties of capitalism thesis). At this point, through an analysis from a time-series perspective, we will be able to situate Belgium's specific position in relation with broader studies adopting more cross-cutting comparisons.

Last the wide angle adopted for our temporal perspective allows us to place in perspective two crucial moments of economic history – the two financial crises followed by the severe recessions of 1930 and 2008 – and to discuss prospects for the future in terms of punishment, obviously with a much shorter hindsight for the second crisis.

Economy and punishment: a long-term analysis of Belgian history

General presentation of the long-term analysis

The analysis made for Belgium (Vanneste 2001, 2013) is particular in that it covers the longest period studied to date. To a certain extent, this forced me to move beyond the narrow framework of economic indicators limited to unemployment figures in the first empirical studies. The time period envisaged also led me to place the analysis in reference to Kondratiev's ([1935] 1979) theory of long economic cycles, a theory developed by observing regularly alternating periods of 20 to 30 years of sustained growth followed by periods of recession equally long. When I included indicators relating to phases of the criminal justice system's activities I was also able to analyse the relation between economy and punishment taking penal dynamics into account.

The study thus pooled different types of indicators over some 180 years of Belgian history: statistics on prisons, in other words the evolution of the detainee population, and various statistics on the activity of criminal justice in its different phases but also – and especially – significant data on social and economic evolution.

When we visualize statistics on the prisoner population in Belgium[2] (Figure 5.1) the long-term perspective first highlights the strong variations

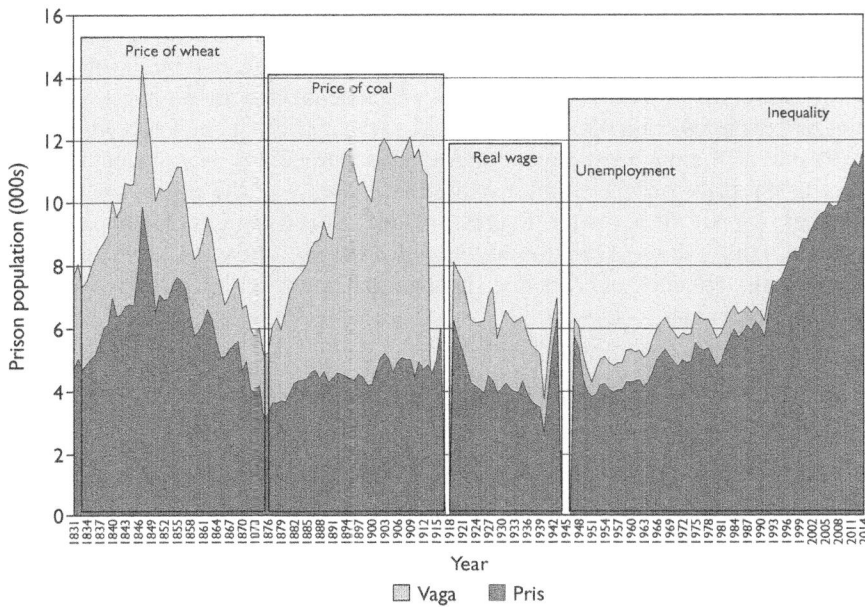

Figure 5.1 Prison population and significant indicators in successive periods (Belgium 1831–2014).

throughout this lengthy period. When they are compared to the economic cycle theory it is surprising to see that until the early 1900s at least, these cycles almost perfectly correspond with the evolution curves of the detention rate: the 'lows' of economic recession correspond to the 'peaks' of the prison population, and vice versa. This is especially clear in the serious economic crisis of 1848.

Over such a long period we cannot a priori hold just one economic variable as pertinent. And the Kondratiev cycles, however, are primarily based on the sole indicators of national wealth (such as Gross Domestic Product per capita, GDP). Consequently a study of the country's socio-economic history was needed in order to elucidate particularly significant indicators in the successive contexts.

From 1830 to 1873: the penal system is a reverse image of the economic context

This first period covers two phases of long economic cycles. A recession phase until around 1848, the peak of the economic crisis which in Belgium arose from a combination of three factors that provoked a great famine: the potato blight, a bad grain harvest and a structural crisis in the linen industry. This was followed by a phase of economic recovery and prosperity culminating about 1872.

In a society that was largely agricultural and not yet endowed with mechanisms for social regulation, the best measure of economic security was variations in the *wheat price*. Rises in the price of wheat directly affected the level of economic insecurity, in both the owner class which controlled the economy and politics and the population directly impacted by wheat prices in their everyday diet.

Result of the analysis shows a correlation particularly significant between rises in the price of wheat and increases in the level of the prison population, whether or not these latter figures include establishments specifically for vagrants. Thus we see a relationship in which the use of the prison is the direct and opposite effect of an economic situation that is not yet affected by any form of social regulation.

From 1873 to 1914: showing an extension of the penal field of action

The second period covers two successive phases: a first period of recession until 1896, followed by economic expansion until the First World War. Belgium's industrial economy reached new heights, the policy of importing grains strongly affected the price of wheat, and industrial production became the trade currency for imports. Coal mining was at the heart of Belgium's industrial economy. It led the game and henceforth the *price of coal* was a more pertinent measure of economic tensions.

Statistical analysis shows a particularly significant relationship between variations in coal prices and variations in the overall population of detainees. Although the economy-penal correlation is confirmed, the analysis reveals another type of interplay between the economy and the penal system, in which the repression of vagrancy played an important role. This gives us a target population that is clearly identifiable and can be defined. Indeed, as economic uncertainty grew, the population more intensely targeted were people categorized as vagabonds, 'drifters' and 'tramps', and among this group primarily those deemed to be responsible for their situation, who were locked up in workhouses instead of the less repressive shelters.

This focus on vagrancy is certainly not trivial in an analysis inspired to the Marxist reading of punishment. Melossi (2013) also recalls how the reference to migratory movements was crucial to understanding the historical formation of the working class. In the nineteenth-century vagrancy was an original form of migration, taking place within national borders. In Volume 1 of Marx's *Capital*, chapter XXVII on the expropriation of the rural population clearly refers to the way peasants chased from their land were turned into homeless proletarians, thus becoming the designated target for the process of 'primitive accumulation' to which they provided 'living capital', in other words, the workforce: 'They (the idyllic methods of primitive accumulation) conquered the field for capitalistic agriculture, made the soil part and parcel of capital, and created for the town industries the necessary supply of a "free" and outlawed proletariat' (Marx 1867).

During this period of history, calls for a redistribution of resources became more organized and exploded violently in the events of 1886. Everything happened as if the answer in terms of penality were recomposed more subtly, taking the road of moralization. The question of poverty and vagrancy was shifted from the economic register to the moral register, before becoming a favourite target of criminal punishment.

The inter-war period: punishment recedes, echoing a wider redistribution of economic security

The First World War overturned previously established social equilibriums. The right to vote, given in 1919 to all men over the age of 21, opened an innovative period through expanded participation in the exercise of power. Against the backdrop of a considerable growth in the trade union movement,[3] social gains swiftly accumulated. The link between salaries and the cost of living, introduced in 1920, led to a net improvement in the standard of living. Even if a coordinated set of social security measures only took shape after the Second World War, Belgium gradually began to introduce the main systems covering serious risks (old age insurance, child benefits) as early as the 1920s–1930s.[4]

These changes were firmly anchored in the economic concepts that Keynes had recently formulated. The shift from the iron law of wages and its Malthusian application to Keynesian logic was a complete break that introduced a hitherto totally ignored dimension. Workers were also consumers, thus it was of economic interest to further not only their capacity to work but also to consume. This logic led to a completely new and considerably broader sharing of the economic security.

Variations of the real wage, following introduction of indexation as an initial form of resource redistribution, constitute for this period the most pertinent indicator of significant economic tensions. A particularly significant correlation can be observed between the fluctuations of real salaries and fluctuations in the detention rate: an increase in the real wage corresponds directly to a proportional decrease in prison population.

The economy-penal relation becomes more complex. The 'economic resources' component is no longer the determining factor. Starting from an initial capital that had diminished during this long period of recession, economic security paradoxically grew thanks to a larger and more balanced redistribution. In Belgium, it was indeed the launching of a social policy that, as Rusche had hoped to see theoretically, fostered the tendency for a lower prison population.

After the Second World War, in two periods

The period following the Second World War opened with the full deployment of the consumer society and the *Welfare State*. After this first phase of economic expansion, a turning point arrived in 1973. With the first oil crisis the

Belgian economy, like those of most countries of the West, entered into a long phase of recession.

In a society that had become massively wage earning, the evolution of economic security and insecurity initially was best measured in relation to the part of the population that was progressively excluded from it. The strategic indicator became the unemployment rate. Joblessness began to soar in the mid-1970s and peaked in the mid-1980s, ranging from 10 per cent to 14 per cent, denoting an unemployment that had become structural.

With structural unemployment becoming entrenched, alongside the work force's growing flexibility and mobility, it became harder to evoke unemployment as the only valid indicator to measure the reality of an overall economic situation. One indicator at first seen as complimentary emerges as the most pertinent gauge of economic tensions: the measure of inequality in the distribution of income which, since the 1980s, has shown an increasing trend, both in Belgium and in a large part of Western society.

The correlation between the unemployment rate and the detention rate is significant for the whole period (1954–2014) ($r=0.70$), but since the 1980s it has been supplemented by a particularly significant correlation with indicators of inequality in income distribution.

Observation of this latter correlation has opened the door to a political dimension and the analysis reveals a particularly telling correlation between the detention rate and the proportion of votes for Right-wing parties. These two associations will be analysed more closely in the following discussion focusing on the last decades.

The relationship between economy and punishment over the last decades: the inequality indicator and the rise in votes on the Right

The inequality indicator

As shown by two prominent Organisation for Economic Co-operation and Development (OECD) reports (2008, 2011) on the rise in inequality, income gaps in the 30 OECD member countries have been growing since the 1980s. Later we shall see how the level and evolution of inequalities are closely linked to the socio-economic models adopted by the national economies and the role played by the institutions.

To assess the evolution specific to Belgium, we first needed to fill the lack of a single and same indicator over the long term. The Gini indicator,[5] generally used to measure income inequalities, especially in international comparisons, is not directly available for Belgium for a sufficient number of years.[6] However, thanks to publications on fiscal statistics, available since 1973, we were able to use – or calculate – different indicators on income distribution over the past four decades.[7] In order to have an image of how inequality evolved prior to the 1970s we used the disparity indicator[8] elaborated by Franzece (2002) for 25 OECD countries, which Koulinsky (2005) has shown to be a good approximation for the Gini index traditionally used to measure income inequalities, at least over the long term.

This indicator, available from 1948 to 1995, shows an evolution where we can trace the observations highlighted in the literature on the subject: the 1980s was a cut-off point when the income gap in most of the industrialized countries ceased to narrow. Study of the indicators collected in the fiscal statistics for 1973 to 2014 then confirm the growth of inequalities that became even sharper, especially between 2000 and 2007, followed by a relative stabilization until 2014 (Figures 5.2, 5.3, 5.4 and 5.5).

However, we cannot hide an open debate about the inconsistent results of different types of income inequality indicators available for Belgium between the mid-1980s and the late 2000s. While the fiscal data (pre- and post-tax) show a steady increase, the data based on sample surveys tend to show a relative stability. Thus the OECD reports (2008, 2011) based only on survey results cite Belgium as one of a few exceptions with regard to the global increasing trend. The literature does not give any definitive answer but points out the limits of the two types of sources.

The OECD indicators are actually based on three separate Belgian surveys[9] that apply different designs and income measurements. Trends over time therefore should be interpreted with caution (Horemans et al. 2001). Furthermore, a more recent report expresses doubts for some countries, and in particular for Belgium, about the consistency of the coding of the sample design variables, concluding that the power of Belgian SILC[10] data is not sufficient for closely monitoring the situation of relatively small vulnerable groups, especially at the regional level (Goedemé 2013). And last, even when researchers accept the 'stability conclusion', they still find evidence of a thick background of growing inequalities: regional differences between Flemish, Walloon and Brussels regions, high educational inequalities and immigration-linked inequalities are keys challenges in Belgium (Van Rie and Marx 2013).

On the other hand, the fiscal data could be partly skewed primarily because of the sociodemographic trend towards more single-person households. Unfortunately, Belgian tax data have not yet been carefully studied, as is the case for many countries listed in the 'World Wealth and Income Database' (Alvaredo et al. (n.d.). But if we refer to the analysis of the Danish data for example (Atkinson et al. 2011; Atkinson and Sogaard 2013), the researchers show that although the change in the definition from family to individual taxation certainly has effects, it does not fundamentally affect the increasing trend. A limited Belgian study (Rademaeckers and Vuchelen 1999) confirms this conclusion about a short period: when the evolution of Belgian wealth inequality (including real estate, financial assets, movable material property) is estimated between 1984 and 1994, based on a variety of sources (fiscal data and budget surveys), it indeed appears that wealth distribution became more unequal over time.

With some reservations, tax data can thus be used to analyse comparatively the changes in imprisonment and in inequalities. The analysis based on the fiscal indicators, available for 42 consecutive years, for each indicator shows clearly significant statistical correlations with the evolution of the prison population. The analysis was repeated, successively using the years 1973, 1981 and 1991 as the starting point for periods under consideration. We can see that the correlations are stronger as we move forward in time (Table 5.1). The strongest associations with highly significant coefficients are seen in the last period, between 1991 and 2014.

The results are most striking for the inequality indicators that are more sensitive to the effects of extreme values (as the ratio between average and median income) (Figure 5.3). This observation is confirmed by the negative correlation seen between the evolution of the portion of income for the poorest 10 per cent of the population and the evolution of the detainee population: the more this segment of the population slips into poverty, especially from 1991, the more the prison population increases (Figure 5.5). On the other end, the increase in the share of income for the richest 10 per cent corresponds to a rise in the prison population (Figure 5.4). The observation of the two indicators also confirms that the gap between the highest and the lowest incomes is due both to a rise in the former and a drop in the latter.

Another indicator coming from a different type of institutional data gives support to the observed relation between detention rate and inequality indicators.

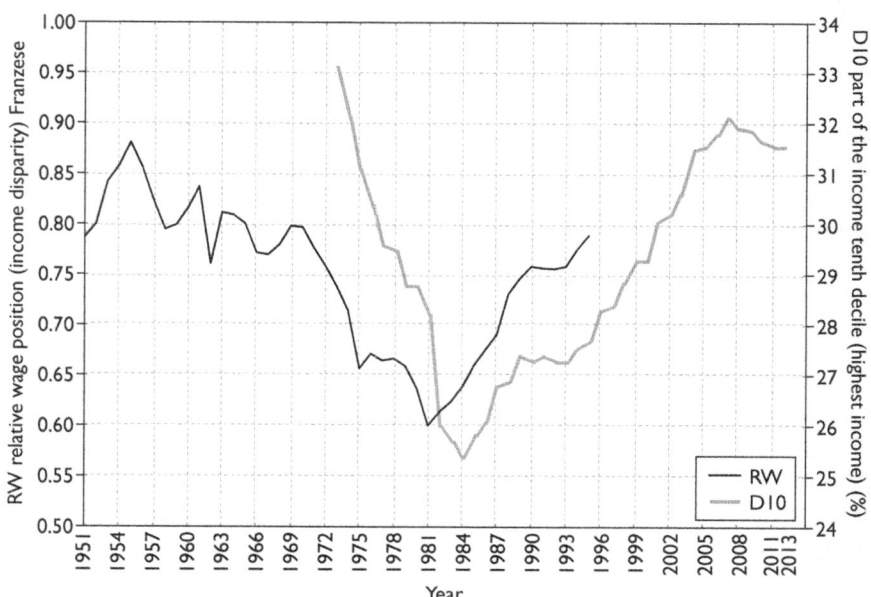

Figure 5.2 Indicators of inequality (Belgium 1951–2013).

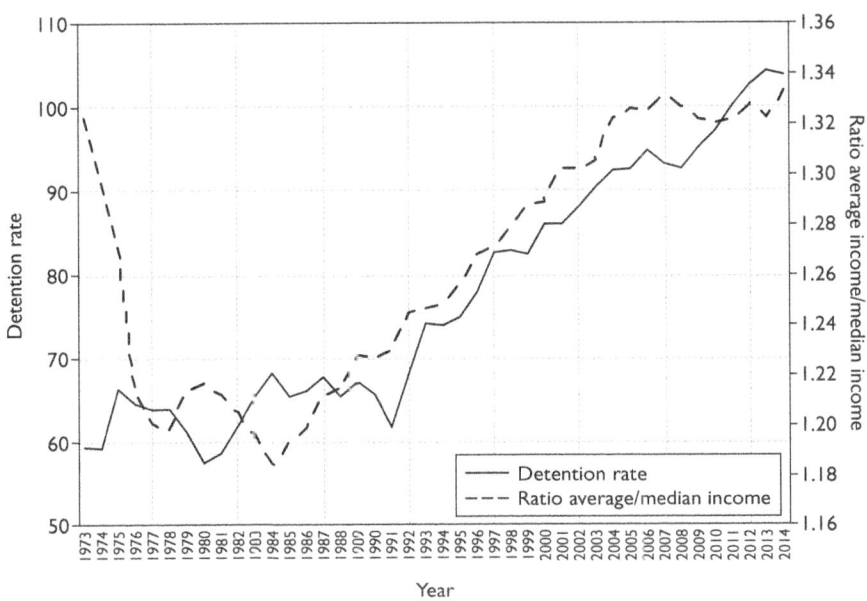

Figure 5.3 Detention rate and ratio average/median income (Belgium 1973–2014).

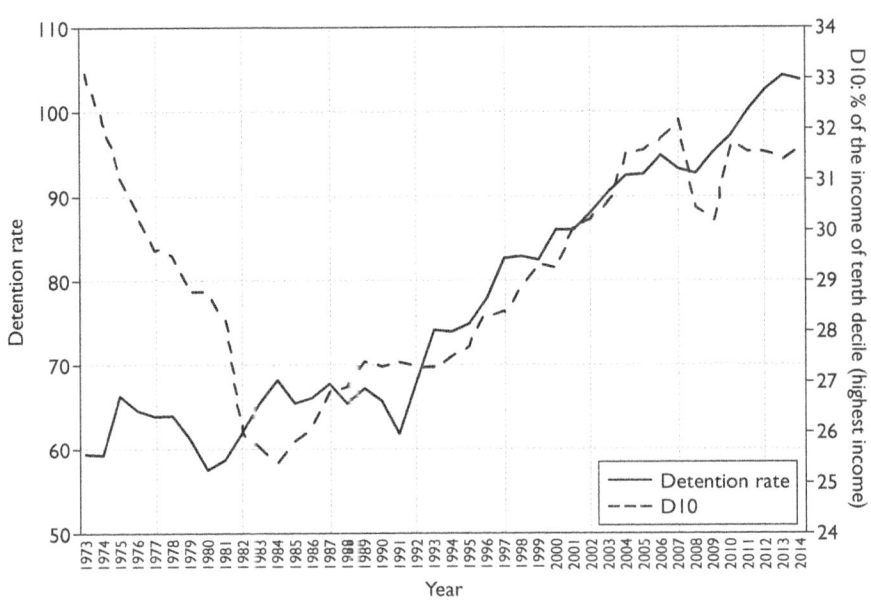

Figure 5.4 Detention rate and part of the income of tenth decile (Belgium 1973–2014).

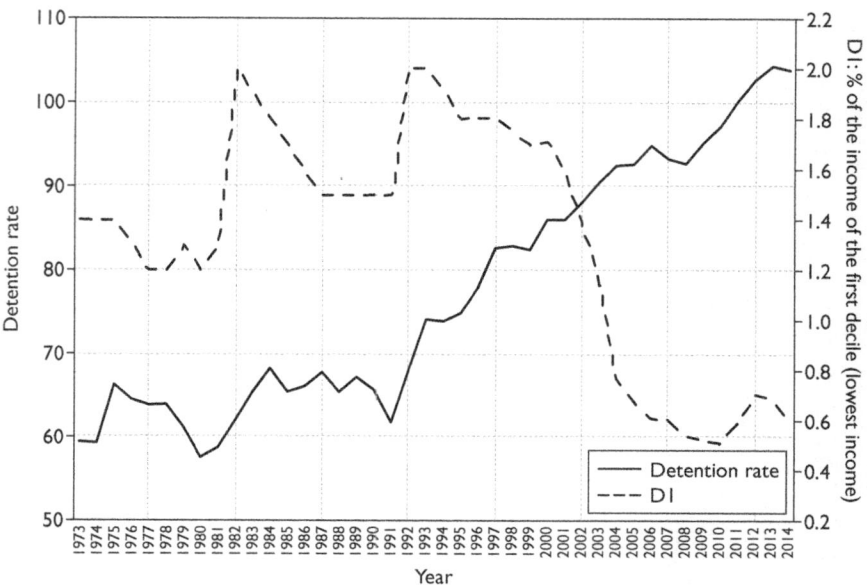

Figure 5.5 Detention rate and part of the income of first decile (Belgium 1973–2014).

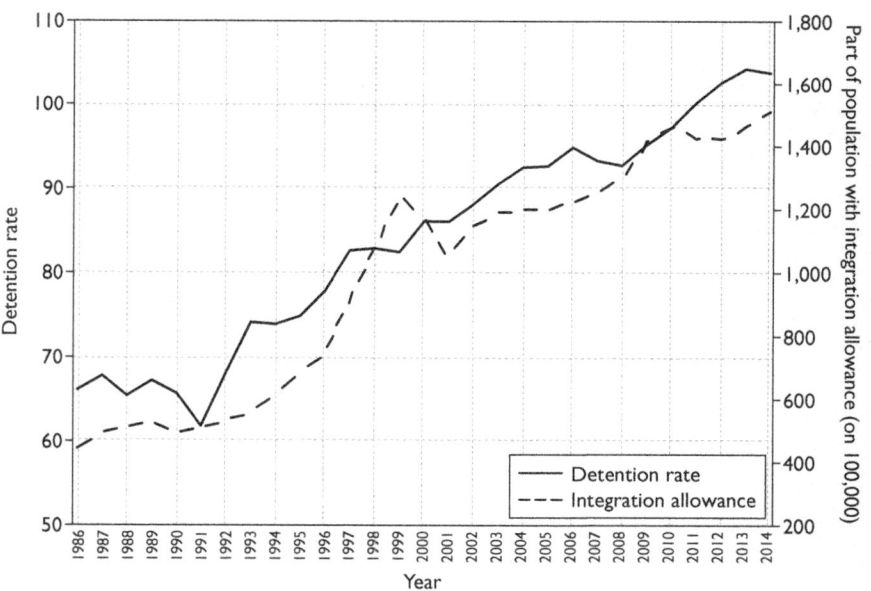

Figure 5.6 Detention rate and part of population with living allowance (Belgium 1986–2014).

Table 5.1 Correlations between detention rate and inequality indicators (1973–2014)

Correlations detention rate/inequality	1973–2014			1981–2014			1991–2014		
	R	R2	p	R	R2	p	R	R2	p
Interquartile coefficient	0.66	0.44	0.000003	0.83	0.69	0.000000	0.90	0.81	0.000000
Ratio average/median income	0.87	0.75	0.000000	0.95	0.90	0.000000	0.95	0.90	0.000000
Ratio S80/S20	0.60	0.36	0.000059	0.84	0.70	0.000000	0.86	0.74	0.000000
Ratio S90/S10	0.77	0.60	0.000000	0.82	0.67	0.000000	0.81	0.66	0.000003
% D1	−0.68	0.47	0.000002	−0.79	0.62	0.000000	−0.84	0.71	0.000000
% D10	0.67	0.45	0.000003	0.92	0.85	0.000000	0.92	0.84	0.000000
							1990–2008		
Gini before taxation	—	—	—	—	—	—	0.92	0.84	0.000000
Gini after taxation	—	—	—	—	—	—	0.88	0.78	0.000000

Indeed, during the period 1986–2014 we can also observe a strong correlation ($r=0.97$) (Figure 5.6), between the evolution of the detention rate and the increasing trend of the part of the population without income and excluded from unemployment insurance coverage, who receive a living allowance (called 'integration allowance').

This conclusive exercise warrants attributing a strategic role to the variable on income inequality in the link between the economy and punishment over the last decades. It also reinforces the hypothesis verified earlier which, from the immediate aftermath of the First World War, underlines the importance of resource redistribution in the significant relationship between economic indicators and indicators on the prison population.

Detention rate and political dominance

Noting the highly significant relationship between inequality and use of imprisonment allows us to introduce a directly political dimension to the analysis. In his book *Left and Right. The significance of a political distinction*, Bobbio ([1994] 1996) conceived the attitude towards equality as one of the two determining criteria of the political divide between Left and Right, the other being the tension between commitment to freedom and relation to the authority. Equality is thus viewed as the 'pole star' of the Left while the Right's is inequality (Bobbio [1994] 1996, p. 80). In the same perspective, several studies show a strong relation between a high level of tolerance to inequality and voting for the Right, while voting for the Left is highly associated with the objective to reduce social inequalities (Galland and Forsé 2011). If we can consider that votes in a democracy reflect a population's level of tolerance about inequalities – that voters accord more importance to one or another facet of the tension inherent to capitalism between freedom and equality – it thus makes sense to include in our analysis a political representation variable.

To conduct this analysis, we referred to figures in the political database of the *Comparative Welfare States Data Set*[11] in which the political parties were categorized as Left, Right or centre based on their position on social policy. Over time the same party can appear in one or another group depending on strong shifts in its position.[12] Several indicators are thus created: share of votes cast for parties classified in each category in the most recent election, share of seats in parliament won by each group, share of seats in parliament held by each group and share of seats won as a percentage of seats needed for a parliamentary majority.

Throughout the whole post-war period (1951–2011), let us look first to the evolution of votes on the Right, the Left and at the centre (Figure 5.7). The figures show an increasing trend of votes on the Right, and a decreasing trend of the votes at the centre. Votes on the Left decrease until the beginning of the 1990s and rise then again but far under the level reached in the fifties and sixties.

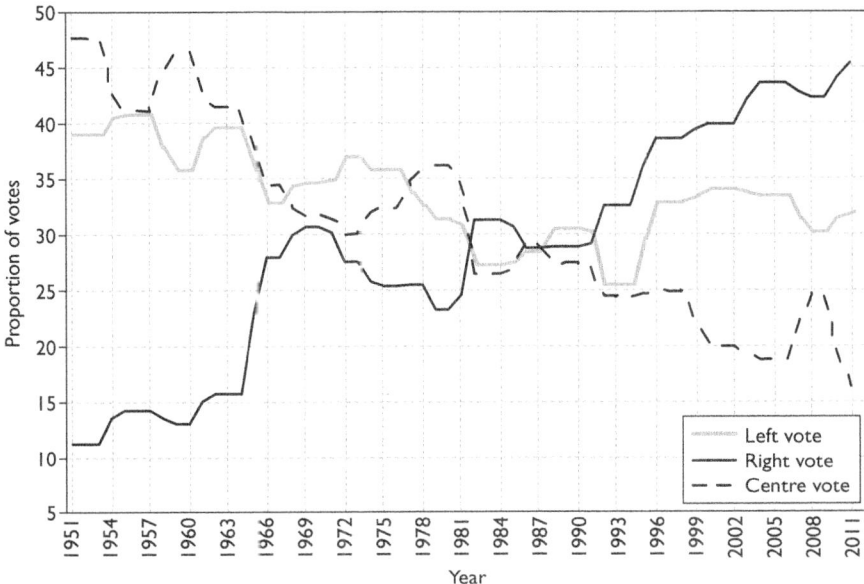

Figure 5.7 Proportion of votes in Belgium: Right, centre and Left (1951–2011).

We see then that the evolution of detention rates throughout the whole post-war period is inversely associated, significantly but weakly ($r=-0.32$) with the evolution (tending downward) of votes on the Left. It is much more significant when correlated to the downward trend of votes at the centre ($r=-0.77$) and its variations ($r=-0.36$). Last it is quite significantly correlated to the rising proportion of votes on the Right ($r=0.83$). This last (long-term) correlation is confirmed by an important correlation between short-term variations throughout the period ($r=0.48$).

An analysis split into different significant periods then shows that the period 1980–2011 yields the most significant results. The correlation between the detention rate and the proportion of votes on the Right is thus exceptional (Figure 5.8) ($r=0.97$), and confirmed by the still significant correlation in short-term variations ($r=0.48$). The inverse correlation with votes in the centre is also more significant than prior to 1980 (Figure 5.9) ($r=-0.86$) and in variations ($r=0.40$).

The analysis also reveals a correlation between inequality indicators and the evolution of votes on the Right, which is mainly significant after the year 1980, the year that inequality first began to rise ($r=0.53$ from 1973 to 2011 and $r=0.85$ from 1981 to 2011). In parallel we can also observe an inverse correlation with votes in the centre ($r=-0.69$). These correlations between inequality and political indicators are not a surprise. In his well-known *Capital in the Twenty-First Century*, Piketty ([2013] 2014) notes

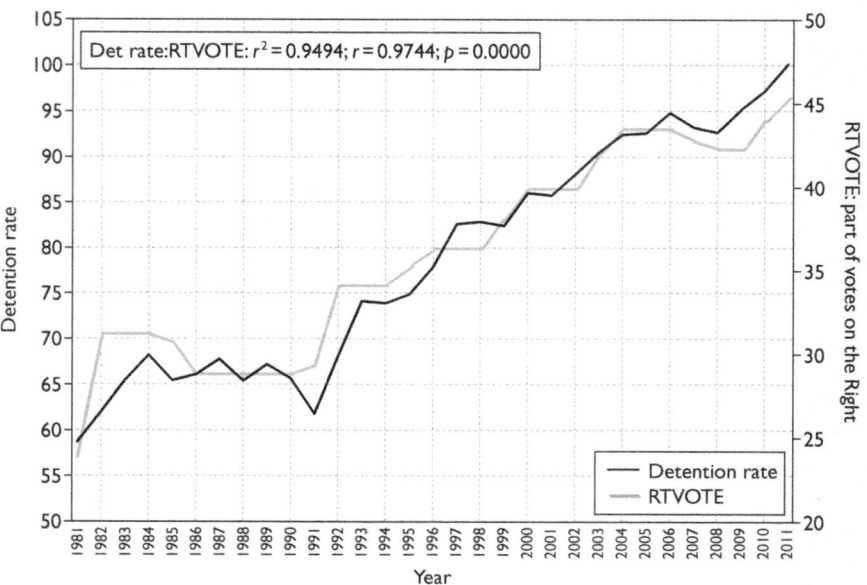

Figure 5.8 Detention rate and part of votes on the Right (Belgium 1981–2011).

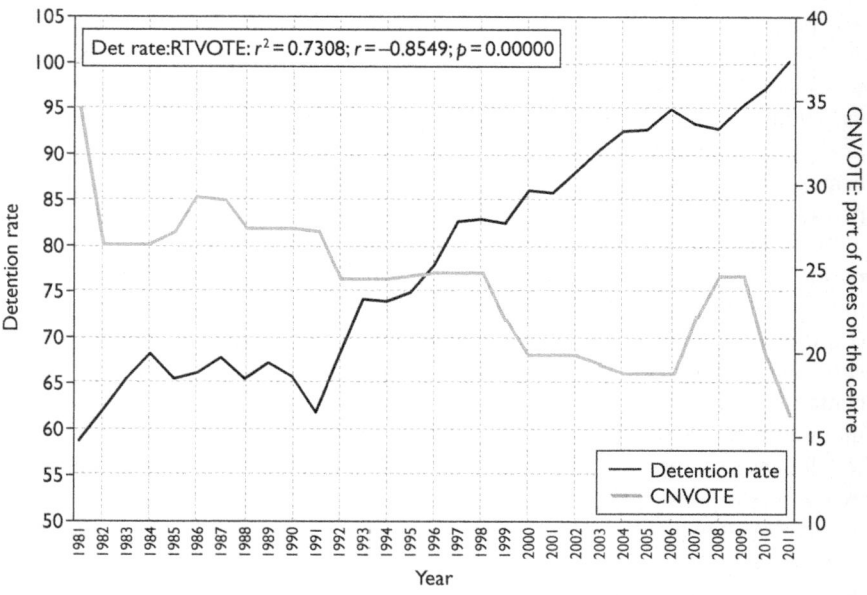

Figure 5.9 Detention rate and part of votes on the centre (Belgium 1981–2011).

> The history of the distribution of wealth has always been deeply political, and it cannot be reduced to purely economic mechanisms [...]. The history of inequality is shaped by the way economic, social, and political actors view what is just and what is not, as well as by the relative power of those actors and the collective choices that result. It is the joint product of all relevant actors combined.
>
> ([2013] 2014, p. 47)

Study of the data thus confirms beyond expectation the important role of the political component in the evolution of punishment. The respective weight of significant associations in relation to the detention rate, confirmed by a multiple regression, underlines the determining role of the political variable, i.e. the proportion of votes on the Right, compared to indicators on income inequality.

Interpreting the results

By adopting a wide historical angle, our hypothesis was that the indicators defined for each period would one by one be able to evaluate variations in the level of economic security in a given society and that this level of economic security should be understood as the result of two completely separate components: the evolution of the global mass of available economic resources ('the size of the cake') but also, starting from the inter-war period, the way these resources were redistributed ('cutting the cake'). The 'social policy component' became crucial from this inter-war period on.

For the past few decades, epidemiological research confirms the significant association between growing social inequality and the increase in anxiety and insecurity observed in the population, in particular insofar as these inequalities are related to social stratification and experienced as threats for social identity (Dickerson and Kemeny 2004).

The analysis of the whole set of indicators showed particularly significant correlations between these different strategic socio-economic indicators and indicators of the prison population. It all comes about as if throughout history the penal volume echoed a particular socio-economic logic. Everything happens as if the intensity of punishment were a direct and inverse function of the economic security generated by a given society.

In order to explain this undeniable relation, a crucial intermediary is needed: the term 'insecurity'. Economic insecurity and fear of crime maintain close ties, as evidenced in so many studies. Research on the fear of crime underlines its diffused nature, anchored in various spheres of individual and collective experience, of which the economic aspect is a fundamental dimension. Conceived as a general notion, insecurity about crime thus builds on multiple social dysfunctions before it becomes embodied in specific fears (Lagrange 1995) and led, in some periods, to a 'culture of control' (Garland 2001), or to 'governing through crime' (Simon 2007). In this process, criminality is a privileged convergence point. The equally close association between fear of crime and punitiveness thus makes it possible to understand the logic of the link initially observed. The two links, economic insecurity – fear of crime, and fear of crime – punitiveness, are able to explain the relation between economic insecurity and punishment. Recent empirical studies provide updated confirmations by demonstrating the positive effect of economic insecurity including the degree of economic inequality on fear of crime (Britto 2013; Vieno *et al.* 2013) and on individual punitive attitudes (Costelloe *et al.* 2009).

In the face of disparate unsettling elements, the process, as it were, sets things in order. Punishment achieves its function as one of the most important symbolic rituals in society. As Sumner so aptly explained: 'Power thus recharges its moral batteries. This ritual defeat of the Forces of Evil by the forces of good must stand as criminal law's most important ideological function, in comforting and reassuring the population' (Sumner 1990, p. 47). Melossi, in turn, highlighted the role of language, discursive chains and vocabularies of punitive motivation (Melossi 1985) that become increasingly severe in rough economic periods ('... the image of crime is blown up when this malaise reigns' (Melossi 1995, p. 93)).

This process also seems to hold several advantages: by pointing to a phenomenon in which a guilty party can be designated it is possible to divert attention from the incapacity to manage the more deep-seated and complex sources of the fear of crime. As management of economic and social dimensions can no longer provide the necessary legitimation, it is quite convenient to fill the void by resorting to punishment.

Recently, the association between economic insecurity – more precisely the extent of social inequalities – and the need for legitimation was once again verified: the correlation is definitely significant between indicators of inequality and those of political legitimacy, as measured in reference to the *World Values Survey*. The works of Andersen, cited among others (Van de Werhorst and Salverda 2012), also shows that the higher the degree of inequality in a society, the weaker its political legitimacy (Andersen 2012).

Two essential links thus seem to work together towards a growing punitive climate: the component related to the *fear of crime* and the component relating to the need for *political legitimacy* which is seen to be closely tied to the effective distribution of resources.

Theses in the field of economy and in the sphere of political economy of punishment

In the economic field, two types of theses can be confronted to situate the evolution of the Global North economic systems over the past few decades, in particularly during the era of globalization. It is important to make a distinction between them, one reason being because they reflect an observable divergence in the theses developed on the political economy of punishment (Sutton 2013).

In the field of economy: globalization versus heterogeneity

The first thesis from an economic angle is the *globalization thesis* sustained by Garrett, who predicted a growing international integration of markets that he describes as an irresistible force (Garrett 1998, 2000). The literature on globalization also identifies economic and political mechanisms linking this growing internationalization to a convergence in the retreat of social policies and the atrophy of democratic political institutions. While Garrett recognizes the existence of diversity – 'countries with left-wing governments and powerful trade unions tend to be more closed' – he clearly deems they are 'unlikely to have major effects' on the process (Garrett 2000, p. 978).

This globalization thesis can be placed in the perspective of what Atkinson (1999), called the *'transatlantic consensus'* leading him to consider that, since 1970 there has been just one viable economic model, the neoliberal model personified by the American economy (Koulinsky 2008). To begin with, there is a consensus that the structure of the labour force demand has changed to the detriment of the least qualified workers. The second consensus notes a dilemma between the employment objective and that of income equality, which is imputed to the fact that social welfare and public wealth redistribution institutions are sources of rigidity fostering involuntary or voluntary unemployment. The transatlantic consensus holds that the most flexible economies, thus theoretically the least equal, adapt quickly and thus can check the rise in their country's unemployment, but at the cost of growing income gaps that impact on the lower wage categories. In the most rigid economies, thus the more equal, the opposite occurs: with the aim of curbing the growth of income inequalities by strictly regulating the job market and attempting to redistribute resources, the rise in mass unemployment cannot be contained.

In contrast, the second thesis, that of the *varieties of capitalism*, stresses the importance of national institutional structures leading to varied arrangements and adjustments to the economy. This approach suggests that, although national economies are subject to the same cross-cutting destabilizing forces, they each have their own solutions which differ from those promoted by the neoliberal thesis. The monolithic dynamics traditionally associated with globalization is thus called into question.

The main precursors of this second approach, Hall and Solkice (2001), thus distinguish between national economies based on the way their companies solve coordination problems in five areas: industrial relations (including negotiations on wages, work conditions, social partners and other employers), professional training, company governance, inter-company relations (sharing information on technologies) and relations with their employees. They make a distinction between two types of economies: liberal market economies and coordinated market economies. The former rely on the market to coordinate their activities, the latter have high level coordination institutions that are outside the market. These institutions can be considered as vectors serving to mitigate the uncertainty of each party regarding the behaviour of the others, making it possible to negotiate trustworthy commitments among the stakeholders. Differences as regards the institutional framework of the economy give rise to systematic differences in company strategies between the liberal market and coordinated economies.[13]

Along the same order of ideas, Amable (2005) proposes a typology based on various features he qualifies as 'social systems for innovation and production', described as special modes of interaction among six sub-systems: science, technology, industry, education and training, labour market and finance. The interrelations among the different institutional forms describe the coherence of the different varieties of capitalism. The result is a set of clearly distinct models of capitalism. This goes far beyond the dichotomy suggested by Hall and Soskice (2001). In addition to the models based on market and social democratic capitalism, both partially related to those described by Hall and Soskice, Amable adds three specific models: the European continental model, the Mediterranean model and the Asiatic model.

The author points out that, starting from different premises, his typology is relatively compatible with other typologies found in the literature, such as the one proposed by Esping-Andersen (1990) in the area of social welfare where three models emerge: neoliberal, conservative corporatist and social democratic corporatist. Drawing from this first proposal, later analyses also distinguish the 'oriental corporatist model' and one that covers the Mediterranean countries. These models differ in the method of State involvement (welfare policy model that is more, or less, generous), the degree of equality in income,[14] level of social integration or exclusion,[15] and last the predominant political orientation.

Amable thus notes that partisan politics is significantly associated with certain facets of the diversity of capitalism (Amable 2005, pp. 236, 241). The closer a country resembles the liberal market model, the less voters choose parties on the Left ($r=0.56$). Votes on the Left express a wish for certain institutional particularities, such as welfare, redistribution policies and public investments, in other words policies that are definitely not the strong points of the liberal market model. Inversely, similarity with the social democratic model is associated with a higher percentage of votes on the Left.

Compared to the heterogeneity thesis, Amable's results lead him to a more nuanced position: he notes that, from 1980 until the late 1990s, the different 'systems' maintained their own particularities – thus contrasting with the convergence thesis – yet they did not remain static over time. On the contrary, the analysis provides indications of an infiltration of some market mechanisms in most economies, which is realized through a gradual, rather than radical, transformation of the systems (Amable 2005, p. 122).

Theses in the sphere of political economy of punishment

These two types of theses, convergence or variety, correspond to two interpretation schemes that can also be observed among the theses on the political economy of punishment.

One association (among others) that we can make with the first economic approach, convergence, is the analysis by Wacquant. He stresses indeed the existence of a transnational tendency to intensify penal repression that can be explained by the generalized success of neoliberalism. He posits that the advanced societies of Western Europe generate phenomena that are similar – although less sudden and pronounced – to those occurring in the United States insofar as increasingly they are adopting a neoliberal form of punishment and a punitive management model for inequality and marginality (Wacquant 2006). Wacquant thus transposes to the European situation a theory developed on the American situation, that of an ethno-racialization of the prison. This articulates quite logically with the hypothesis of a shift from a welfare state – or rather semi-welfare in the case of the US – to a penal state. His approach is of major interest, but his demonstration does not take into account the striking particularities of the various economic models, as we have just mentioned them here.

The second type of approach, the heterogeneity thesis, corresponds to analyses in the political economy of punishment, based on international comparative research, which stresses the varieties in the forms and extent of punishment in the light of specific national economic and social models. These theories refer to the varieties of capitalism as products of specific economic, institutional and political models and they highlight the association of these varieties with specific levels of penality (Figure 5.10).

We can refer to the works of Cavadino and Dignan (2006), Sutton (2004), Lacey (2007) or Lappi-Seppälä (2008, 2011a, 2011b, 2014). Their research

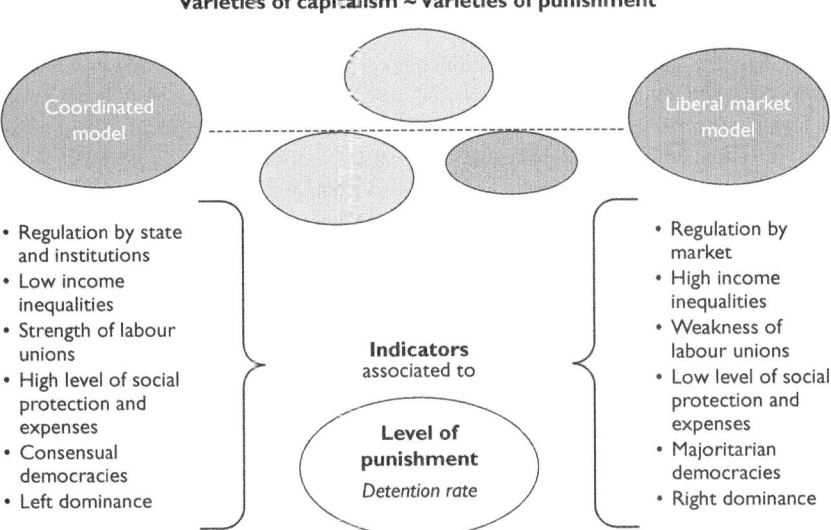

Figure 5.10 Varieties of capitalism and varieties of punishment.

shows respectively a set of significant correlations between detention rates on the one hand, and on the other, types of welfare systems and democratic systems, the degree of corporatism, inequality indicators and last the political dominance.

In 2006, Cavadino and Dignan (2006) demonstrated the correspondence between the distribution of countries under the Esping-Andersen social model typology and categories established on the basis of detention rates and penal culture. High detention rates are associated with the neoliberal model, average rates with corporatist conservatism, and low rates with social democratic corporatism and oriental corporatism. The key factor explaining the association is the degree of inclusion vs. exclusion linked to each type of model.[16]

Sutton (2004, p. 175), and later Lacey (2007, p. 110) added the Hall and Soskice typology (liberal market vs. coordinated economies) to this association and the role of a wider range of institutional specificities emerges. The relation between punishment and the democratic systems associated with these economic models has also been studied following the typology proposed by Lijphart (1999). In line with Lacey, Lappi-Seppälä (2008, 2011a, 2011b, 2014) on the basis of a vast comparative study also shows that consensual democracies are significantly associated with a punitivity that is lower compared to majoritarian democracies[17] which, due to the nature of their system, are more vulnerable to penal populism (Lacey 2007, p. 76). The same can be said for the degree of corporatism: among others, the integrating index (based on wage–bargaining processes, the role of unions and the degree of centralization in interest-group participation), is significantly correlated to detention rates recorded in 2001–2003 ($R2=0.467$) (Lappi-Seppälä 2011a, p. 59). Lijphart's general index (measuring the extent of power sharing, interest participation and the degree of corporatism) also shows a significant correlation ($R2=0.53$ in 2001–2003 (Lappi-Seppälä 2011a, p. 59) and $R2=0.64$ in 2007 (Lappi-Seppälä 2011b, p. 319, 2016, p. 323)). Lappi-Seppälä also successfully examined an inverse relation between levels of repression and indicators of trust in justice as illustrated by indicators used in the European Social Survey (ESS 2005),[18] thus providing another confirmation of the correlation between the punitivity level measured by detention rates and a State's need for legitimacy.

Last, the analyses of both Sutton and Lappi-Seppälä bring out a particularly significant correlation between detention rates and inequality. Sutton's demonstration is especially interesting, for his methodology integrates both the crosscutting dimension of international comparison and the vertical dimension of temporal analysis. Starting from a temporal series of detention rates in 15 countries over the period of 1960–1990, Sutton (2004) first tested Rusche's original model, the link between incarceration and labour force surplus, measured by the unemployment rate. Although this first model is certainly significant the association is somewhat weak. Sutton then introduced into the model an indicator measuring income inequality, as well as indicators of policies tending to have redistributive effects, i.e. the inflation rate and data on unemployment benefits, which much increased the explanatory power of the model. These results suggested that Rusche's hypothesis needs to be integrated not only by unemployment indicators but also by those about inequality and policies aiming to narrow the gap. In a third step, Sutton added indicators relating to the political and institutional configuration of the various countries, in other words the relative importance of trade unions, Leftist political parties and the degree of corporatism. This third model revealed the strong influence of political power: the correlations indicate that strong unions on one side and strong Leftist parties on the other both contribute independently to lower detention rates. The results suggested that these political variables were the most determining factors in the model, and that the relations observed between detention rates and unemployment, or else inequality indicators, arose from strong associations with the distribution of political power or with the institutional negotiating structures in the labour market.

Lappi-Seppälä's analysis (2008, p. 354) also revealed a strong positive correlation between the inequality (Gini) indicator and detention rates both recorded for the year 2000. The correlation was stronger when the analysis was restricted to Western European countries ($R2=0.7$). The author also verified the changes over time of these relationships by comparing associations for the year 1987 to those of 2000. The exercise, covering 15 countries, suggests that the association between income inequality and incarceration grew stronger over time, but that the hypothesis was verified differently from one country to another. A more detailed study of national specificities is thus particularly useful.[19]

Although the relationship between inequality and criminal punishment is now receiving greater attention in the literature on the political economy of punishment, the correlation was noted quite long ago. Although taking the inequality variable into account in empirical studies is certainly a more recent approach than for variables on unemployment, the inequality indicator already appeared in the 1980s. In 1986, Killias undertook an empirical study that incorporated an inequality indicator in the framework of an international comparative approach on variations in penal severity (Killias, 1986). The perspective adopted at that time moved from a strict economic interpretation to integrate a strong political component from the very start. Killias used the income gap as an indicator of concentration of power, and this with the aim to find a high correlation between wealth and power in Western capitalist societies. His hypothesis was that all power requires legitimation and that this becomes ever harder to attain as the gap widens between those who hold power and thus who are subject to it. The probability of crises in legitimation thus grows in proportion to the degree of inequality and concentration of power. Furthermore the legitimacy deficit leads to heavier recourse to criminal punishment. Among the independent variables retained (covering the 1970s), the Gini index shows the highest correlation coefficients with detention rates ($r=0.46$, 39 countries).

Shortly after Killias's analysis, Pease (1991) conducted an ambitious comparative study, this time to verify the hypothesis of a mirror image between social tolerance for a wider income gap and tolerance for inequality in the severity of sentences, thus towards increased severity. Using indicators, from 1980 World Bank figures, on the portion of the national income held by the richest 5 per cent of the population, and that held by the poorest 20 per cent, Pease verified a significantly important correlation ($r = 0.81$) between variations in the proportion of income earned by the top 5 per cent and variations in the average length of detention, an indicator voluntarily chosen as significant and negative to the prison admissions variable.

All these associations underline a strong relation between models of capitalism and levels of punishment: the closer a country resembles the liberal market model (low degree of corporatism, high inequality, and dominance on the Right) the higher are the detention rates. Inversely, the social democratic coordinated model is correlated with lower detention rates.

Taking account of the crucial role of the institutional and political components, we are here quite far from the 'economism' – and the determinist perspective it can involve – such as it has been criticized about early research based on the work of Rusche and Kirchheimer.[20]

Belgium's specific position

The results obtained from a long-term analysis in Belgium to determine strongly significant relation between growing inequalities, a rise in votes on the Right and increasing use of incarceration converge, as we have seen, with the empirical results obtained in international comparative studies.

When we refer to the second economic approach, that of the varieties of capitalism, which corresponds to a diversity of punishment modes and levels, it is possible to more clearly situate Belgium in both dimensions.

According to the Hall and Soskice dichotomy typology, Belgium can be found in the group of coordinated market economies. In Amable's more detailed typology, in the category of European continental capitalism. In Esping-Andersen's categorization of social welfare systems, Belgium fits in the conservative-corporatist model. And finally under Lijphart's approach, it is in the category of consensual democracies.

An analysis of Belgian industrial relations in the context of globalization points out that the country remains characterized by a high level of institutionalization, a high degree of internal coordination and a significant rate of union affiliation (Léonard and Dion 2003). From an international perspective, the redistributive effect of the Belgian welfare state is large and has played an important role in the observed levels of income inequalities (Van Rie and Marx 2013).

Considering the countries of Western Europe, these institutional contexts explain the average levels generally displayed for all the parameters considered: social expenditure, income gaps, neo-corporatism, trust in the legal system and so on, which correspond to the average level presented for the detention rate, higher than that of the Scandinavian countries and lower than in the United Kingdom and some Mediterranean countries like Spain and Portugal.

From a comparative perspective, the detention level found in Belgium compared to other European countries thus assumes its full meaning when it is analysed in reference to the varieties of capitalism.

However, when analysed from an historical angle focusing solely on Belgium, the most noticeable feature illustrating the indicator data we analysed is the progressive transformation of the economic system through the infiltration of market mechanisms. This can be seen more clearly both in the change in income distribution through the rise in inequalities and on the political side through the increase in votes on the Right.

Likewise, regarding punishment, Belgium's detention rate may appear as moderate compared to other rates in Europe and thus reflect a certain resistance to increased punitivity. Yet, when the Belgian situation is viewed on its own, we can observe an increasingly marked prison inflation, significantly correlated to political and economic indicators clearly related to a gradual penetration of characteristics of the neoliberal model.

From one crisis to another

The history of the twentieth and twenty-first centuries is punctuated by two major financial crises that preceded the Depression of the 1930s and the Great Recession that began in 2008. Economists have established several parallels between these two historical periods and the long-term analysis made for Belgium provides an opportunity to examine their respective impacts in terms of criminal punishment.

The 1929 crisis in Belgium came – as explained above – in a climate of recession, yet also against the backdrop of a rapid accumulation of social benefits initiated in 1920 when wage indexing was introduced under the impetus of the labour movement and the first government with Socialist participation. From 1926 real salaries made great gains, already opening the door to a new economic model centred on the sudden expansion of the domestic market (Cassiers 1989). In 1929 the country was hit hard: profits disappeared, employment plummeted and the rising trend of salaries and consumption for a time ground to a halt. A series of strikes followed, especially in 1932 and 1934.

As the crisis was identified as one of the 'overproduction of unsalable goods', solving it called for opening a new market. And a few years later it was the domestic market, that of mass consumption, to which politicians and economists turned, with the support of the workforce.

The turning point came in 1935. The new government affirmed loud and clear: economic expansion meant developing a domestic market and improving the purchasing power of the masses. Amid the catastrophe, the country turned to the State. Public contracts multiplied to build hospitals, schools, social housing and communications networks, thus offering a tangible response to the problem of unemployment.

The economic policy formulated by this new government appeared as arising both from pressures to implement a social policy and from the need to build a domestic market. And it was indeed this conjunction of interests that ushered in this new social contract anchored in the Keynes' recent economic concepts. As for punishment, the tendency was a strong downward trend. And as we have seen, a rise in real salaries, the prime indicator for the start of a social policy is significantly correlated to a decrease in the detainee population.

And what can be said for the 2008 crisis? Although our hindsight is certainly short, we can nevertheless refer to remarks by informed economists that will enable us to resituate and understand the most recent evolutions in punishment.

Amable (2012) again is a particularly interesting source. Referring to the French context, which closely reflects that of Belgium, he proposes an analysis of the crisis and its aftermath. The prevailing discourse before the onset of the Great Recession was the need for the 'developed economies to adjust their institutions in order to adapt to the requirements of modern capitalism', assimilated to the neoliberal model. Merely stepping up competition was expected to foster innovation. Job stability took a back seat and the leitmotiv was flexibility. It was up to the individual worker to manage his human capital to find new job opportunities. All forms of regulation that hindered a rapid adjustment between the companies' demand and the workforce offer had to disappear.

The crisis of 2008 and the Great Recession, Amable points out, were immediately perceived as the crisis of a special form of capitalism: the Anglo-American version, in other words the very model that had been held up as the ideal over the previous decade. The crisis revealed indeed the contradictions of this particular model of capitalism: it had promised that less regulated markets would bring greater economic stability, but the reality became greater instability due to the deregulation undertaken in the previous decades.

The crisis also turned out to be the consequence of the weaknesses of the neoliberal model. The serious rise in inequalities generated a macro-economic problem: how to support consumption when a large part of the population had seen their income decline, and how to ensure the middle class' continued political support of the neoliberal model? The only solution was to increase possibilities for credit. And it was the development of a regime based on credit that intensified vulnerable aspects of the financial market with the well-known result: the explosion of the financial bubble and the inevitable crisis. We should not forget, however, right up to when the crisis first occurred and also at times during the crisis, these instable economic mechanisms bring profit to some actors such as the financial sector, lenders and owners of bubble assets who get richer easily. Wisman (2013) identifies three dynamics through which wage stagnation and heightened inequality made the economy vulnerable to systemic dysfunction: besides greater indebtedness and speculation, the third dynamic is the rich taking larger shares of income and wealth; they gained more command over ideology, hence politics. The result was tax cuts for the rich, reduced welfare for the poor and deregulation (Stockhammer 2015).

After the 2008 crisis, radical changes in discourse could be heard, reflecting a large movement of public opinion calling for the end of neoliberal capitalism as a model. In Belgium we also saw how the politicians expressed a will to change. In his declaration of 14 October 2008 on general policy, and after stressing the heavy repercussions of the crisis, Prime Minister Leterme stated that 'considerable reforms must be adopted to repair the weaknesses of the financial markets and regulation measures'.

So did the effects of the crisis sound the death knell for the neoliberal model? As Amable expresses it, if we believe in the 'power of ideas' the answer is yes. But if we are more sceptical about the power of ideas alone, the answer is much less affirmative. The neoliberal reforms, in fact, were implemented not only in neoliberal markets but also in more regulated economies where certain social forces were powerful enough to impose them. And it is not easy to reverse the trend: the neoliberal reforms on the one hand have created a vast and powerful financial sector and on the other have weakened those actors who would be placed to exert pressure for more fair distribution. Furthermore, the actual responses to the crisis have focused on its consequences rather than on one of the main causes: growing inequality. All developed countries deployed austerity plans, topped by cuts in public expenditures and consumer taxes. And, like in other countries, the Belgian State first took measures to save the banks (Kickert 2012), which were relatively costly and unpopular.

Events after the crisis of 2008 thus seem to point to a situation exactly opposite to that following the crisis of 1930. The context of the 1930 crisis, and after a short hiatus, the post-crisis period in Belgium witnessed the arrival and rapid deployment of a Keynesian policy that generated a much broader distribution of resources and an increase in most salaries to meet the needs of consumption.

The tendency observed at the socio-economic level, some years now after 2008, is stagnating salaries and consumption for a majority of the population. Inequalities are still at the level reached in 2007, but they have not significantly grown since then. Perhaps could this be the sign of a possible reversal of the tendency? In parallel, detention rates continue their exponential growth, with no signs of a change to this tendency, unlike the inter-war period that had launched the Keynesian revolution.

Far be it from me to predict future prospects in terms of the use of criminal punishment. We are probably at a threshold. What transpires will depend on the balance that will be achieved over the next years among the different 'ingredients' discussed above.

However, what does seem to figure clearly is that, first of all, this outcome will be closely tied to economic and social evolutions. And second, that prospects both for the socio-economic realm and for punishment, far from being the result of a deterministic process, will emerge from political choices, or more generally from societal choices relating to the nation's wealth and its distribution.

Notes

1 The mention of only one of the two authors refers to the first articles of Rusche where the baselines of his views were already formulated. Furthermore, as carefully described by Melossi (1978) and later by René Lévy and Hartwig Zander in the introduction of the French version of the book (Rusche and Kirchheimer [1939] 1994), the fundamental ideas and the initial version of *Punishment and social structure* are clearly due to Rusche. The disappearance of Rusche during a certain period, in unclear circumstances, explains the revision work of Kirchheimer and the co-signing of the book (as result of a contentious process).
2 Including the population detained in specific establishments for vagabonds and beggars, which was quite high in the nineteenth century.
3 The Socialist trade union (General Federation of Belgian Labour) was the main beneficiary, growing from some 125,000 members in 1914 to 577,000 in 1919 and 688,000 in 1920.
4 Pension funds became obligatory in 1924, family allowances in 1930 and a 1927 law greatly expanded the applicability of illness compensation.
5 The Gini index measures the extent to which the distribution of income among individuals or households deviates from a perfectly equal distribution. A Gini index of 0 represents perfect equality, while an index of 1 implies perfect inequality.
6 The Gini indicator based on fiscal data is published only for the period 1990–2008.
7 Inter-quartile coefficient, part of the income of the first decile (lowest income) and the tenth decile (highest income), ratios part of the income of the 20 per cent highest income/20 per cent lowest income (S80/S20), and part of the income of the 20 per cent highest income/20 per cent lowest income (S90/S10), ratio average and median income.
8 The disparity indicator elaborated by Franceze is based on the primary incomes (in the manufacturing sector). It is the ratio of the average income and the median income, that gives an index of the skewness of the distribution.
9 SEP (1985–1997), ECHP (1993–2000) and EU-SILC (annual since 2003).
10 EU-SILC is the abbreviation of EU statistics on income and living conditions.
11 Comparative Welfare States Data Set (2014), compiled by David Brady, Evelyne Huber, and John D. Stephens, provides an array of country-level welfare state, economic, institutional, political, policy and demographic indicators. The CWS includes information on 22 rich democracies from 1960–2011 and is published by LIS (Cross-national data center – Luxembourg; www.lisdatacenter.org/; accessed 20 July 2014). Some longer series are available, notably for Belgium. Figures for the years 1951–1959 have been obtained after direct contact with the CWS team.
12 For example in Belgium, the French-speaking Ecolo Party was considered as being in the centre from 1981 to 1991, and after that on the Left. The assignment of each party in each group is re-assessed regularly.
13 To cite just one example: in coordinated market economies, the financial system ensures an access for companies to financing that is not solely based on public financial information on the annual accounts. Access to this capital enables companies to maintain their qualified workforce despite economic slowdowns and invest in projects that will generate profit only in the long-term. Another example: liberal market economy companies will be more tempted to move their activities to another country in search of cheap labour, while those in coordinated market economies often pursue strategies underpinned by high levels of qualification and an institutional structure that is hard to achieve elsewhere. Accordingly some comparative institutional advantages tend to make companies less mobile than suggested by theories that do not take this factor into account.

14 Amable observes a strong correlation between income inequality in a country and the distance of this country to the socio-democratic model ($r=0.70$) (Amable 2005, p. 229).
15 Minimalist or residual welfare state in neoliberalism model, status-related and moderately generous welfare in conservative corporatism, universalistic and generous welfare state in social democratic corporatism, private sector-based and paternalistic in oriental corporatism.
16 In a more recent publication, and in the light of the exceptions observed to this general picture, Cavadino and Dignan (2014), take a more nuanced view. They consider that the 'political economy is by no means the sole factor determining a country's penal practices and ideology' (2014, p 283). Nevertheless, 'the general picture seems clear enough. Neo-liberal political economies at least *tend* to have lower imprisonment rates than conservative corporatist countries, whose rates in turn *tend* to be lower than those found in social democracies' (italics in original) (2014, p. 284).
17 The majority principle means that the winner takes all, consensus means that as many views as possible are taken into account.
18 www.europeansocialsurvey.org/.
19 In Lappi-Seppälä (2014, p. 314), the correlation ($R2=0.52$) is verified, in the mid-2000s, on 28 countries joined together in six groups (Nordic, Central, Eastern, Anglo, Southern and Baltic).
20 Sutton (2004) for example identifies three weaknesses in Rusche-Kirchheimer research tradition. The

> second weakness is that the RK research is based on an impoverished notion of the economy. This is partly a problem of model specification: following Rusche and Kirchheimer's emphasis on labor surplus, most studies rely on a single predictor of imprisonment rates, usually unemployment [...]. But it points to a deeper theoretical problem: RK research implicitly assumes that all capitalist economies are the same and that business cycles are wholly exogenous to other kinds of social processes.
>
> (p. 171)

Furthermore a long time ago, regarding Rusche and Kirchheimer's book itself, Melossi (1978) had pointed out that

> Where there is shown to be 'economism' in *Punishment and Social Structure*, it is not produced by a lack of consideration for ideological issues that – as a bourgeois critic might maintain – should be eclectically juxtaposed to the economic driving forces. The 'economism' is produced however, by flaws in the analysis of the structural roots of our object, which emanate from the incomplete inscription of punishment into the scientific categories of Marxism.
>
> (1978, p. 77)

References

Alvaredo, F., Atkinson, A.B., Piketty, T., Saez, E. and Zucman, G. (n.d.) *The World Wealth and Income Database*. Available from www.wid.world [accessed 26 May 2016].

Amable, B. (2005). *Les cinq capitalismes. Diversité des systèmes économiques et sociaux dans la mondialisation*. Paris: Editions du Seuil.

Amable, B. (2012). The crisis an opportunity for the neo-liberal model of capitalism. *In*: H.-G. Soeffner, ed., *Transnationale Vergesellschaftungen.Verhandlungen des 35 Kongresses der Deutschen Gesellschaft für Soziologie in Frankfurt am Main 2010*. Wiesbaden: Springer, 1173–1181.

Andersen, R. (2012). Support for Democracy in Cross-national Perspective: The Detrimental Effect of Economic Inequality. *Research in Social Stratification and Mobility*, 30 (4), 389–402.

Atkinson, A.B. (1999). Is Rising Income Inequality Inevitable? A Critique of the Transatlantic Consensus. *The United Nations University. Wider Annual Lectures*, 3 (24), 433–452.

Atkinson, A.B., Piketty, T. and Saez, E. (2011). Top Incomes in the Long Run of History. *Journal of Economic Literature*, 48 (1), 3–71.

Atkinson, A.B. and Sogaard, J.E. (2013). The long-run history of income inequality in Denmark: Top incomes from 1870 to 2010. *EPRU Working Paper series*, Economic Policy Research Unit, University of Copenhagen. Available from http://web.econ.ku.dk/eprn_epru/Workings_Papers/WP-13-01.pdf [accessed 26 May 2016].

Bobbio, N. ([1994] 1996). *Left and Right: The Significance of a Political Distinction.* Chicago: The University of Chicago Press.

Britto, S. (2013). 'Diffuse Anxiety': The Role of Economic Insecurity in Predicting Fear of Crime. *Journal of Crime and Justice*, 36 (1), 18–34.

Cassiers, I. (1989). *Croissance, crise et régulation en économie ouverte: la Belgique d'entre les deux guerres.* Bruxelles: De Boeck.

Cavadino, M. and Dignan, J. (2006). *Penal Systems: A Comparative Approach.* London: Sage.

Cavadino, M. and Dignan, J. (2014). Political economy and penal systems. *In*: Body-Gendrot, S., Hough, M., Kerezsi, K., Lévy, R. and Snacken, S., eds, *The Routledge Handbook of European Criminology.* London: Routledge, 280–294.

Costelloe, M.T., Chiricos, T. and Gertz, M. (2009). Punitive Attitudes toward Criminals. Exploring the Relevance of Crime Salience and Economic Security. *Punishment and Society*, 11 (1), 25–49.

Dickerson, S.S. and Kemeny, M.E. (2004). Acute Stressors and Cortisol Responses: A Theoretical Integration and Synthesis of Laboratory Research. *Psychological bulletin*, 130 (3), 395–391.

Esping-Andersen, G. (1990). *The Three Worlds of Welfare Capitalism.* Princeton: Princeton University Press.

Franzece, R. (2002). *Macroeconomic Policies of Developed Democracies.* Cambridge: Cambridge University Press.

Galland, O. and Forsé, M. (2011). *Les français face aux inégalités et à la justice sociale.* Paris: Armand Colin.

Garland, D. (2001). *The Culture of Control: Crime and Social Order in Contemporary Society.* Chicago: The University of Chicago Press.

Garrett, G. (1998). *Partisan Politics in the Global Economy.* New York: Cambridge University Press.

Garrett, G. (2000). The Causes of Globalization. *Comparative Political Studies*, 33 (6/7), 941–991.

Goedemé, T. (2013). *Measuring Change with the Belgian Survey on Income and Living Conditions (SILC): Taking Account of the Sampling Variances.* Antwerpen: University of Antwerpen.

Hall, P.A. and Soskice, D., eds (2001). *Varieties of Capitalism: The Institutional Foundations of Comparative Advantage.* Oxford: Oxford University Press.

Horemans, J., Pintelon, O. and Vandenbroucke, P. (2011). Inkomens en inkomensverdeling op basis van Belgische enquêtegegevens: 1985–2007. *CSB-berichten/UA*, Centrum voor Sociaal Beleid Herman Deleeck, University of Antwerpen.

Kickert, W. (2012). State Responses to the Fiscal Crisis: Belgium. *Public Money & Management*, 32 (4), 303–310.
Killias, M. (1986). Power Concentration, Legitimation Crisis and Penal Severity: A Comparative Perspective. *International Annals of Criminology*, 24 (1–2), 181–211.
Kondratiev, N.D. ([1935] 1979). The Long Waves in Economic Life. *The Review of Economic Statistics*, 17 (6), 105–115
Koulinsky, A. (2005). *L'étude de la montée des inégalités à partir d'un indicateur de disparité des revenus primaires: apports analytiques et méthodologiques*. Paper presented at the 54th AFSE Conference, Paris.
Koulinsky, A. (2008). Y a-t-il un fatalisme néolibéral? Le dilemme emploi-égalité des revenus revisité/Neoliberalism fatalism? A Fresh Look at the Employment Income Equality Trade-off. *Revue économique*, 59 (1), 149–166.
Lacey, N. (2007). *The Prisoners' Dilemma: Political Economy and Punishment in Contemporary Democracies*. Cambridge: Cambridge University Press.
Lagrange, H. (1995). *La civilité à l'épreuve. Crime et sentiment d'insécurité*. Paris: PUF.
Lappi-Seppälä, T. (2008). Trust, welfare, and political culture: Explaining differences in national penal policies *In*: Tonry, M., ed., *Crime and Justice: A Review of Research*, 37, 313–387.
Lappi-Seppälä, T. (2011a). Explaining national differences in the use of imprisonment. *In*: Snacken, S. and Dumortier, E., eds, *Resisting Punitiveness in Europe? Welfare, Human Rights and Democracy*. London: Routledge, 35–72.
Lappi-Seppälä, T. (2011b). Explaining Imprisonment in Europe. *European Journal of Criminology*, 8 (4), 303–328.
Lappi-Seppälä, T. (2014). Imprisonment and penal demands. Exploring the dimensions and drivers of systemic and attitudinal punitivity. *In*: Body-Gendrot, S., Hough, M., Kerezsi, K., Lévy, R. and Snacken, S., eds, *The Routledge Handbook of European Criminology*. London: Routledge, 295–336.
Léonard, E. and Dion, D. (2003). Globalisation versus relations industrielles 'à la belge'?. *Reflets et perspectives de la vie économique*, 4 (17), 59–69.
Lijphart, A. (1999). *Patterns of Democracy: Government Forms and Performance in Thirty-six Countries*. New Haven: Yale University Press.
Marx, K. (1867), *Capital. Volume One. Part VII: Primitive accumulation, Chapter XXVII: Expropriation of the Agricultural Population from the Land* (English edition 1887).
Melossi, D. (1978). Georg Rusche and Otto Kirchheimer: Punishment and Social Structure, Book Review. *Crime and Social Justice*, 9 Spring–Summer, 73–85.
Melossi, D. (1985). Punishment and Social Action: Changing Vocabularies of Punitive Motive within Political Business Cycle. *Current Perspectives in Social Theory*, (6), 169–197.
Melossi, D. (1995). The effect of economic circumstances on the criminal justice. *In*: European Committee on Crime problems, ed., *Crime and economy: proceedings: reports presented to the 11th Criminological Colloquium*. Strasbourg: Council of Europe, 73–96.
Melossi, D. (2013). People on the move: From the Countryside to the Factory/Prison. *In*: Franko Aas, K. and Bosworth, M., eds, *The Borders of Punishment. Migration, Citizenship, and Social Exclusion*. Oxford: Oxford University Press, 273–290.
OECD (2008). *Growing Unequal? Income Distribution and Poverty in OECD Countries*. Available from www.oecd.org/social/socialpoliciesanddata/growingunequalincomedistributionandpovertyinoecdcountries.htm (accessed 26 May 2016).

OECD (2011). *Divided We Stand. Why Inequality Keeps Rising.* Available from www.oecd.org/els/soc/dividedwestandwhyinequalitykeepsrising.htm (accessed 26 May 2016).

Pease, K. (1991). Punishment demand and punishment numbers. *In*: Gottfredson, D.M. and Clarke, R.V., eds, *Policy and Theory in Criminal Justice*. Aldershot: Gower, 113–127.

Piketty, T. ([2013] 2014). *Capital in the Twenty-First Century*. Cambridge: Harvard University Press.

Rademaeckers, K. and Vuchelen, J. (1999). De verdeling van het Belgische gezins vermogen. *Cahiers économiques de Bruxelles*, (164), 375–429.

Rusche, G. ([1930] 1980). Prison Revolts or Social Policy: Lessons from America. *Crime and Social Justice*, (13), 41–44.

Rusche, G. and Kirchheimer, O. ([1939] 1969). *Punishment and Social Structure*. New York: Russell & Russell.

Rusche, G. and Kirchheimer, O. ([1939] 1994). *Peine et structure sociale. Histoire et 'théorie critique' du régime pénal, texte présenté par René Lévy et Hartwig Zander.* Paris, Les Editions du Cerf.

Simon, J. (2007). *Governing through Crime: How the War on Crime Transformed American Democracy and Created Culture of Fear*. New York: Oxford University Press.

Stockhammer, E. (2015). Rising Inequality as a Cause of the Present Crisis. *Cambridge Journal of Economics*, (39), 935–958.

Sumner, C. (1990). *Censure, Politics and Criminal Justice*. Philadelphia: Open University Press.

Sutton, J.R. (2004). The Political Economy of Imprisonment in Affluent Western Democracies: 1960–1990. *American Sociological Review*, 69 (2), 170–189.

Sutton, J.R. (2013). The Transformation of Prison Regimes in Late Capitalist Societies. *American Journal of Sociology*, 119 (3), 715–756.

Van de Werhorst, H. and Salverda, W. (2012). Consequences of Economic Inequality: Introduction to a special issue. *Research in Social Stratification and Mobility*, 30 (4), 377–387.

Vanneste, C. (2001). *Les chiffres des prisons. Des logiques économiques à leur traduction pénale*. Paris: L'Harmattan.

Vanneste, C. (2013). Pénalité et inégalité: nouvelle actualité des rapports entre pénalité et économie. L'exemple de la Belgique. *In*: Kuhn, A., Margot, P., Aebi, M., Schwarzenegger, C. and Donatsch, D., eds, *Criminologie, politique criminelle et droit pénal dans une perspective internationale*. Bern: Stämpfi, 689–711.

Van Rie, T. and Marx, I. (2013). *GINI Growing Inequalities' Impacts. GINI Country Report: Belgium*. Available from www.gini-research.org [accessed 26 May 2016].

Vieno, A., Roccato, M. and Russo, S. (2013). Is Fear of Crime Mainly Social and Economic Insecurity in Disguise? A Multilevel Multinational Analysis. *Journal of Community & Applied Social Psychology*, 23(6), 519–535.

Wacquant, L. (2006). Penalization, depolitization, racialization: on the over-incarceration of immigrants in the European Union. *In*: Armstrong, S. and Mac Ara, L., eds, *Perspectives on Punishment: The Contours of Control*. Oxford: Oxford University Press, 83–100.

Wisman, J.D. (2013). Wage Stagnation, Rising Inequality and the Financial Crisis of 2008. *Cambridge Journal of Economics*, 37 (4), 921–945.

Chapter 6

Political economy of punishment in Australia*

Hilde Tubex

Introduction

From a macro perspective, Australia shares many of the characteristics of other Anglo-Saxon countries that are associated with increased punitiveness, as measured by the imprisonment rate (number of prisoners out of 100,000 adult inhabitants). From a political economy perspective, it is a neoliberal political economy as described by Cavadino and Dignan (2006), or, in the words of Lacey (2008), a liberal market economy. Since the 1980s, neoliberalism overtook Australia's socio-democratic traditions and, despite these roots having moderated the neoliberal model as described by Wacquant (2009) for the US, penal policies progressively abandoned a rehabilitative approach to proscribed behaviours and substituted it with an increasing punitive approach, resulting in rising imprisonment rates (IR), most significantly reflected in the overrepresentation of Indigenous people in the prison.

However, on closer examination, significant differences between the IR of the eight jurisdictions within the Australian borders are revealed. The aim of this study is to investigate and explain the differences in the IR of the Australian jurisdictions over the last 25 years in six Australian jurisdictions which are representative of the country's penal diversity (New South Wales (NSW), Victoria, Queensland, South Australia, Western Australia and the Northern Territory).[1]

In Figure 6.1, I have taken the Northern Territory out, as the high IR in the Territory obscures the differences between the other states under investigation. Australian IR vary from the all-time high IR of the Northern Territory (885/100,000 in 2015), followed by Western Australia (278) always in second position, NSW mainly having the third highest IR (200), but recently being overtaken by South Australia (204), Queensland presenting the most volatile climbing pattern (198) and Victoria (134) being traditionally the state with the lowest IR. In another paper (Tubex *et al.* 2015), we discussed the trend being the same for all these jurisdictions, as their IR all increase since the 1980s, but maintaining their relative distinctiveness, demonstrating characteristic patterns of punishment and punitiveness.[2]

Besides the overall increasing trend, of particular concern are certain recent developments with regard to some of these jurisdictions. A first concern is the strong increase over the last five years of the IR in the Northern Territory (+34 per cent), South Australia (+32 per cent), and Victoria (+25 per cent), followed by Queensland (+19 per cent). Of even more concern is the fact that this growth is mainly due to the increase of the Indigenous IR in these jurisdictions: a 39 per cent increase in Victoria, 35 per cent in the Northern Territory, 20 per cent in South Australia, and 18 per cent in Queensland. Another alarming trend is the increase in the female prison population: they now account for 8 per cent of the prison population, while this was 5.5 per cent in 1990. In the past five years, the female IR has seen a dramatic upsurge in the Northern Territory (+183 per cent), while it increased with 44 per cent in Queensland and 23 per cent in Victoria. The Indigenous female IR is and remains the highest in Western Australia (ABS 2016). Finally, the remand rate is growing between 32.5 per cent (South Australia) and 89 per cent (Northern Territory) over the last five years (ABS 2016).

In this contribution, I look at the developments over the last 25 years from the perspective of political economy and investigate to what extent a model of political economy can explain the interstate differences in IR in Australia.

Methodology

To do so, I conduct a descriptive and statistical analysis, relying on information provided by the Australian Bureau of Statistics (ABS), as they collect data on crime and punishment in all Australian jurisdictions, setting a high standard of comparability and reliability, but refrain from any further interpretation or contextualisation of their data. For reasons of comparability, I use rates, as the size of the population in Australian states and territories differs considerably. With the methodological challenges of comparative criminology in mind (see Tubex 2013a), I try to address the criticism and use learnings of earlier work in this field.

A first hurdle to take is the use of IR as a measure of punitiveness, which has been discussed extensively in comparative criminology literature (see, e.g. Tonry 2007; Lappi-Seppälä 2008). In short, my position is that, being aware of the limitations and possible distortions using this concept, for reasons of availability of data and the consistency in how they are collected, and by lack of a better parameter, it is a valuable and satisfactory proxy measure for punitiveness (for a more extensive discussion, see Tubex 2013a). Further, as explained by Nelken (2010), to make sense of societies for comparing purposes, there are only certain strategies to do that in a reliable way: being 'virtually there', 'researching there' and 'living there'. The interpretation I provide is based on my expertise; having a European background but working and living in Australia for the last ten years, studying the data and literature on the penal culture in Australian jurisdictions and doing fieldwork in each of the states and territory discussed in this contribution, interviewing experts from academia, government and non-government organisations. Therefore, I have set out to develop a perspective that Nelken (2010) describes as 'living there'; being an observing participant and enjoying the status of 'insider-outsider', which is, according to him, 'the best – perhaps the only reliable – way to get a sense of what is salient' (Nelken 2010, p. 96). A final methodological issue will be discussed in more detail below, as it is of particular interest in my aim to compare differences between the IR in Australian jurisdictions.

Are we comparing apples with apples?

One of the criticisms of the analysis by Cavadino and Dignan (2006) is that they start from the assumption that crime is the same in all the countries they compare, while this is most probably not the case (Nelken 2010). For that reason, the first issue I am trying to resolve in this analysis is the question as to whether I am comparing apples with apples when looking at crime and victimisation patterns in the states and territory under investigation, and what their relationship is with the local IR.

Victimisation rates

Crime sources available on Australian jurisdictions are the crime victimisation data as published by the ABS (4530), which is, according to them, the best source for interstate comparison. The data are based on annual surveys that collect information through personal interviews about people's experiences of crime victimisation for a selected range of personal and household crimes. For this analysis, only personal crimes are considered. The first survey dates from 2008/2009, currently seven surveys have been conducted, and the last one dates from 2014/2015.

These data show that victimisation rates, as in most other developed countries, have been going down over the seven surveys in each of the selected jurisdictions. This decrease is significant in NSW, Western Australia and the Northern Territory ($p<0.05$).[3] The decrease is not significant in the other jurisdictions and there is a slight increase in the most recent survey in South Australia (+1.4 per cent), Victoria (+0.8 per cent) and Queensland (+0.6 per cent). From a comparative perspective, the obvious outcast is the Northern Territory, where the victimisation rate started very high in the first survey (16.5 per cent), but went down considerably over the following years, reaching a similar level as the other jurisdictions in 2014/2015 (8 per cent). The victimisation rate is also statistically different between the selected jurisdictions ($F(5)=13.75$, $p<0.001$). Despite the decline, the average victimisation rate in the Northern Territory (Mean = 12.8 per cent) across the years is still statistically higher than in the other jurisdictions. The second-highest victimisation rate is noted for Western Australia (Mean = 9.01 per cent), which is significantly higher than NSW (Mean = 6.43 per cent). The other states are not significantly different from each other. More importantly, for none of these jurisdictions there is a significant positive correlation between the victimisation rate and the IR over the time period victimisation surveys are available.

Looking at the recorded individual offences (physical assault, (non) face-to-face threatened assault, robbery and sexual assault), all categories, other than sexual assault – which rate is very low and fluctuating – have decreased. Sexual offences are known to have a high dark number and variations might be subject to changes in reporting. Reporting data are fragmented, but where they are available, they are the lowest for sexual assault. Again, one victimisation pattern stands out, which is the high level of physical assault in the Northern Territory, albeit decreasing over time.

Offender rates

A second source from which to measure crime is the recorded crime – offenders data series (ABS 4519). This collection provides statistics related to the number and characteristics of alleged offenders aged ten years and over who have been proceeded against by police during the 12-month reference period. Data are available since 2007/2008 and the last data refer to 2014/2015.

The overall offender rates are rather stable in the selected jurisdictions over the series, however, they went up in South Australia (+19 per cent) and down considerably in Western Australia (–35 per cent). There are significant differences between offender rates among the states ($F(5) = 197.92$, $p < 0.001$). The average offender rate in the Northern Territory is the highest, which is about 5,483 cases per year (Mean = 5,483) over the time period. The second and third states are South Australia (Mean = 2,930) and Queensland (Mean = 2,325). The other states are not significantly different from each other, but they are significantly lower than the first three. Again, there is no statistically significant correlation between the offender rate and the IR.

Looking at the four most frequent offences (theft, acts intended to cause injury, public order offences, illicit drugs) and homicide over time, illicit drug offender rates have gone up in all jurisdictions except for Western Australia, and homicide rates have gone down except for the Northern Territory.

When it comes to the crime pattern for these offences in the selected jurisdictions, it is different in a sense that the offender rate for theft is rather high in NSW (this is due to the fact that 70 per cent of the theft offenders in NSW had a principal offence of public transport fare evasion, which in most other jurisdictions is not a police responsibility), followed by South Australia. Illicit drug offences are extremely high in South Australia. The Northern Territory has an aberrant pattern, as the public order offences rates are astronomically high, and the rates for acts intended to cause injury and homicide rates are also considerably higher than in other jurisdictions, while their theft rate is a lot lower. In Western Australia, all offender rates are going down consistently, except for a recent spike in illicit drug offences.

The fact that the offender rate remains stable while the victimisation rate is going down can be explained by the fact that, over time, both the reporting rate and the police proceeding rate is going up.

Female offenders

Given the concerning increase of female prisoners, I looked a bit closer at the female offender rate. The female offender rate is rather stable in most jurisdictions, in the Northern Territory it is going up, and in Western Australia it is going down, reflecting the overall trend in offender rates in this jurisdiction, so it is most likely that other drivers than increased female offending are at stake. In 2014/2015, female offenders make up 28 per cent of all offenders in the Northern Territory, 24 per cent in Western Australia and Queensland, 21 per cent in NSW, 20 per cent in Victoria and 18 per cent in South Australia.

Conclusion

To answer the question if I am comparing apples with apples looking at the available crime data in the selected jurisdictions, there are some significant differences. The Northern Territory has a statistically significant higher crime rate than the other jurisdictions, measured by both their victimisation and offender rates. It also has a different crime pattern, with high victimisation rates for physical assault, and high offender rates for public order offences, acts intended to cause injury and homicide. However, their victimisation rate is decreasing substantially over time, and their offender rate remains stable. Victimisation rates are significantly higher in Western Australia, but going down over time, a trend that is even more pronounced in their offender rate. Offender rates are significantly higher in South Australia and Queensland than in the other states, except for the Northern Territory. South Australia has a distinctively high pattern of illicit drugs rates.

However, what is most important is the fact that no correlation could be found between the victimisation/offender rates and the IR in these jurisdictions. This means that the development of the IR is independent from changes in the crime rates. This conclusion has been reached or claimed by many other criminologists, and can now be shown to hold for the Australian situation. Therefore, while crime levels and patterns might be different in these states and territory, they do not provide us with a satisfactory explanation for the differences in their IR.

Political economy as a theoretical framework

I now turn to the investigation of political economy as a valid explanation for developments and differences in Australian IR. I start from the theoretical framework as provided in the analysis of Cavadino and Dignan (2006) Lacey (2008).

I will summarise their approach and findings, and will test them in this study. In the subsequent section, I will discuss the overrepresentation of Indigenous people in the Australian criminal justice system, and set that against the neoliberalism and racialisation claim as made by Wacquant (2009).

Penal systems: a comparative approach

Cavadino and Dignan (2006) base their model on three welfare regimes as developed by Esping-Andersen in his *Three Worlds of Welfare Capitalism* (1990). He distinguishes the 'liberal' welfare states, the 'conservative corporatist' welfare states, and the 'social democratic' welfare states. We find a slightly different categorisation in the work of Cavadino and Dignan (2006), in the wording, as well as the selected countries: neoliberal welfare states (United States (US), England and Wales, Australia, New Zealand and South Africa), conservative corporatism (Germany, France, Italy, Netherlands), social democratic corporatism (Sweden, Finland), and they add oriental corporatism (Japan).[4] Their claim is that these different models of welfare create 'families of countries' with similar IR as an expression of punitiveness. They link high IR to a neoliberal socio-economic policy that is exclusionary towards deviant and marginalised subgroups in that society. This is because the principles of the free market social and economic policies may disrupt informal social control and increase the demand for and use of punishment – particularly imprisonment – as a form of formal control. It is not that neoliberalism is criminogenic as such; it is mainly the individualistic ethos that leads to the adoption of neoliberalism in the first place, which conceptualises criminal behaviour in terms of individual responsibility. Conservative corporatist countries (continental European countries) and even more so social democracies (Scandinavian countries) are more inclusionary and have a lower IR. Their study confirms the earlier findings of Beckett and Western (2001) and Downes and Hansen (2006) that countries or states with a relatively high welfare spending as part of their Gross Domestic Product (GDP) tend to have lower IR. Further, they support the general assumption that the greater the economic inequality, the higher the overall level of punishment, while a more egalitarian society is more inclusive. They also find public attitudes towards crime and punitiveness being different between these family groups, and related to the IR. Public attitudes in neoliberal societies are more likely to be shaped by privately owned and market-oriented media, and by populist politicians. Finally, they conclude that

> punishment levels are relatively stable in the majority of conservative corporatist countries (with the notable exception of the Netherlands); relatively upwardly volatile in countries with marked neo-liberal tendencies; and usually much less likely to increase rapidly in the social democracies.
>
> (Cavadino and Dignan 2006, pp. 32, 35)

According to Cavadino and Dignan (2006), Australia is a member of the neoliberal family. They describe how Australia moved from being a social democracy in the late 1970s to becoming neoliberalist, according to them because the then generous welfare system was not powerfully embedded in corporatist institutional arrangements. Introduced by the Labor Government (under premier Hawke) in the 1980s, and taken up and expanded by subsequent governments, the neoliberal approach wound back the welfare state at a federal and state level and brought in 'authoritarian populism', and a consequential increased punitiveness. However, according to them, the sociodemocratic roots before the 1980s explain why punitiveness scores in Australia – according to the International Crime Victim Surveys – are lower than would be expected for neoliberal family group members. O'Malley (2002) emphasises more strongly the different nature of Australian neoliberalism. In contrast to the authoritarian conservative neoliberalism as we see it in the US, Australia developed a more socio-democratic neoliberalism which aim was not to dismantle the welfare model, but to make it more responsible and accountable. This did not result in the exclusion of the 'underclass' but in more inclusive corrective initiatives, including bipartisan attempts for reconciliation with the Indigenous population.

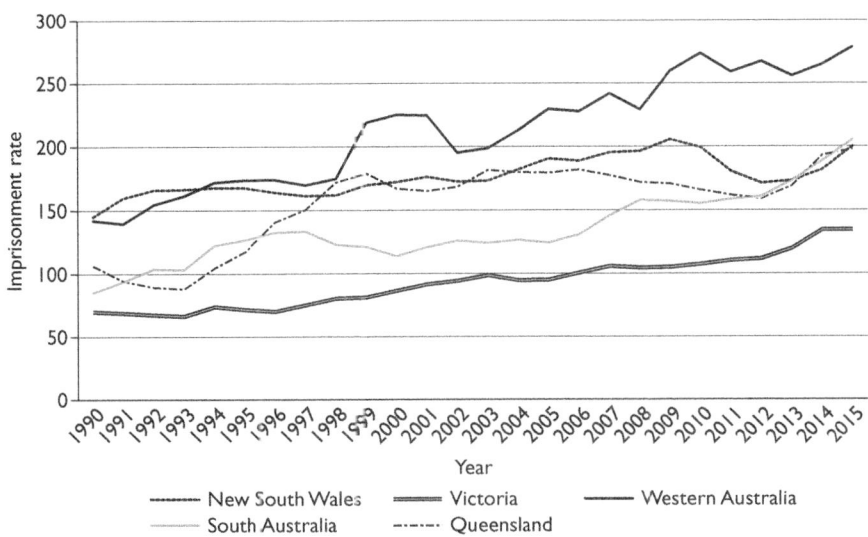

Figure 6.1 Australian imprisonment rates.*

Source: ABS 4517: Prisoners n Australia, snapshot on the 30 June of each year.

Note
* According to the latest data from the ABS 4517 in 2016, this trend continues with increased IR in all Australian jurisdictions, bringing the national IR to 208/100,000, an increase with 6 per cent from the previous year.

At this stage, I will only test the stability over time thesis, as the other factors that Cavadino and Dignan (2006) describe: exclusion and inequality, public opinion and media, are further developed in the second model I discuss, as described by Lacey (2008).

Family groups over time

Cavadino and Dignan (2006) worked with snapshot data of IR in 1986, 1990, 1995, 1997 and 2003. I tested if the trend that was identified over that period holds afterwards (2000–2015), based on the IR data on these countries which were kindly provided to me by Roy Walmsley, based on his World Prison Statistics Archive.

As the figure above demonstrates, the IR is still outstandingly high in the US, however showing a decrease since 2008 (from 755 to 693) and it is very high, although considerably reducing in South Africa over the period 2000–2015 (from 394 to 292). Looking at the other neoliberal countries, the IR has increased with between 20 and 30 per cent over the time period. The neoliberal countries are at the top end of all family groups with an IR that is consistently above a 100/100,000.

IRs in conservative corporatist countries look a bit more volatile than they are in the neoliberal countries. There is the substantial upward trend in the Netherlands, moving into the neoliberal family level for a while, followed by a considerable and ongoing decline, bringing the Netherlands to the bottom of the conservative corporatist family level. The exceptional pattern of the Dutch IR has been matter of much debate already, which I discussed elsewhere (see Tubex

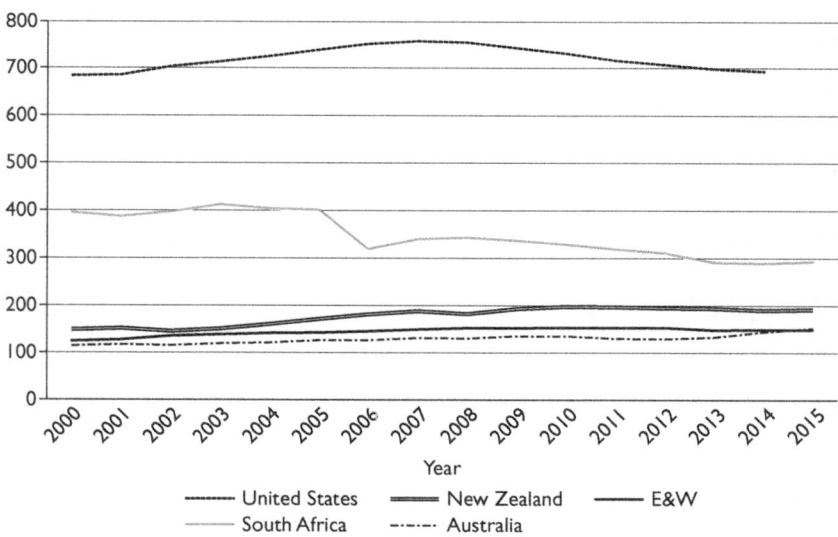

Figure 6.2 Neoliberal countries.
Source: World Prison Statistics Archive.

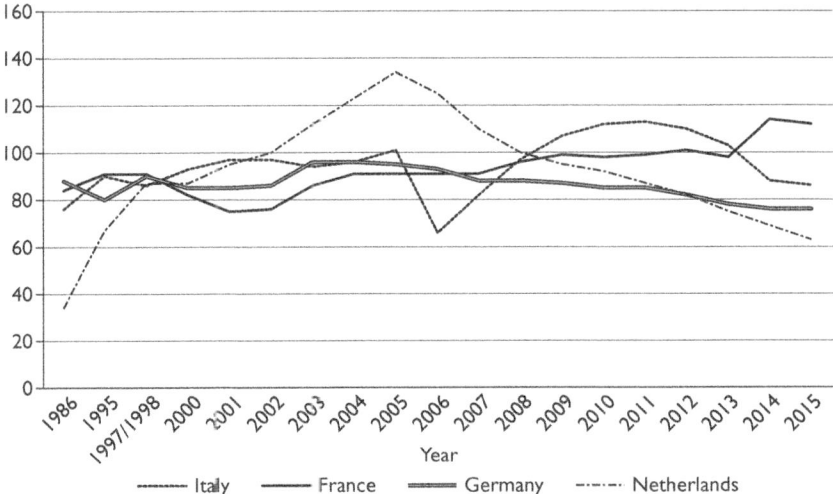

Figure 6.3 Conservative corporatist countries.

Source: World Prison Statistics Archive with the addition of the IR in France in 2012 from the European Prison Observatory and the IR in the Netherlands in 2015 from the Dienst Justitiele Inrichtingen.

2013b). Further, there is Italy going below the level of the Scandinavian countries in 2006, followed by a distinctive curb upwards. The sudden decrease in Italy was due to an *indulto* (or collective pardon), in August 2006 that led to the release of over a third of the prisoners (Nelken 2009). German IR slowly decrease over time, while France presents a growing pattern.

Social democratic countries remain at the lowest level, with the IR hovering between 60 and 80/100,000, and demonstrating a downward trend over the last decade.

Conclusion

Going back to the description of Cavadino and Dignan (2006), it is a fact that IR in the neoliberal countries after 2003 remain higher than in the other family groups, but they decline in two of these countries, including the prototype of the US. They increase in the other three, but not in a way that can be called 'volatile'. That adjective is much more appropriate for the pattern I see in the conservative corporatist countries, where Cavadino and Dignan (2006) expected them to be relatively stable. They reflect local penal policy changes that are either ad hoc (Italy), or more longstanding (increasing in France and decreasing in Germany and the Netherlands). The low pattern in the social democracies is confirmed over time, but it is actually decreasing, which is stronger than the expected 'unlikeliness of increasing rapidly'. Looking at the three pictures, one

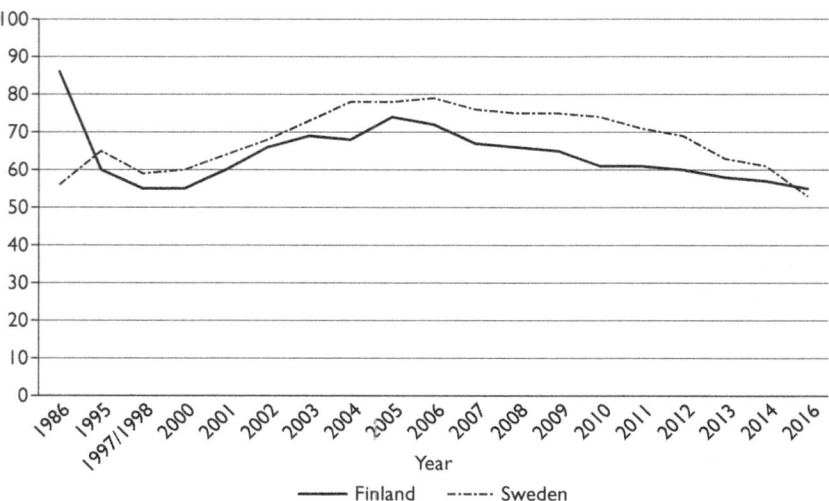

Figure 6.4 Social democratic corporatist countries.

Source: World Prison Statistics Archive with the addition of the IR in 2016 from the International Centre for Prison Studies.

could ask to what extent the neoliberal countries form a 'family group' as measured by their IR, as the level of their IR is so different and recent trends contradictory. This would even be more the case if Canada would have been included in the analysis – which is a somewhat surprising omission – and assuming that they would be categorised alongside the Anglo-Saxon neoliberal countries, while their IR is actually closer to that of the conservative corporatist countries (Webster and Doob 2011). I will leave that argument for now, as the focus of this contribution is on the IR in Australian jurisdictions and not on the neoliberal family group as such.

The IR in the Northern Territory is currently well above the US level, and the other Australian states fall within the neoliberal family: IR in Western Australia are the highest, approaching the South African level, South Australia, NSW and Queensland mainly move up and recently overtake New Zealand, while Victoria increases from a conservative corporatist level and is coming close to England and Wales. So one could say that the Australian states are well and truly members of the neoliberal family when it comes to punitiveness as reflected in their IR. If this is a matter of their political economy is subject to the rest of the analysis.

The prisoners' dilemma

Lacey's (2008) main claim is that the rise of penal populism is not inevitable and that not all 'late modern' democracies are punitive as there are a cluster of factors related to particular political and economic systems which impact on the capacity for penal tolerance. She analyses these factors on an institutional level and within the broader constitutional structure of a country.

Liberal market economies and co-ordinated market economies

Lacey (2008) investigates the institutional preconditions to achieve penal reform and to create inclusionary practices. To do so, she builds on Hall and Soskice's (2001) distinction between liberal market economies (LME or neoliberal countries in Cavadino and Dignan's classification) vs. co-ordinated market economies (CME or both social democratic and corporatist countries). The latter economic model invests in long-term relationships and stable structures, and is therefore more likely to generate an inclusionary criminal justice system, while the LME are more individualistic and require a flexible and innovative workforce, which results in a more exclusionary criminal justice system. From the perspective of the LME model, there is less gain in providing for generous welfare provisions for the temporarily unemployed and investments in education and training. CME on the contrary, are characterised by lower disparities in wealth and higher literacy rates.

In Australia, most welfare expenditures are a federal responsibility, and therefore not a valid measure for interjurisdictional comparison. Therefore, I used alternative measures to assess levels of inequality between Australian jurisdictions and their respective relationship with the IR in that jurisdiction, being the Gini index, unemployment rate, education level, and income inequity.

I first tested if the Gini index (measuring levels of inequality)[5] is different between the jurisdictions in this study for the period this information is available (1994–2014) (ABS 6523). It turns out that there are significant differences among the jurisdictions ($F(5)=13.70$, $p<0.001$). The Gini coefficient in NSW is the highest (Gini = 0.32) over the period, which is not significantly different from Western Australia. The next group includes Victoria, Queensland and South Australia. The Gini index in the Northern Territory is the lowest (Gini = 0.27). I then tested if a high Gini index correlates with higher IR, but this hypothesis was only partly supported in this study. In the following three states, the higher the Gini index – or level of inequality – the higher the IR: NSW ($r_{ln}=0.72$, $p<0.05$), Victoria ($r_{ln}=0.77$, $p<0.05$) and Western Australia ($r_{ln}=0.71$, $p<0.05$). Variables were logged to e when testing relationships to reduce the skewness and to achieve the multivariate normality of the time-series data (Jacobs and Carmichael 2001).[6] The hypothesis was not supported for Queensland, South Australia and the Northern Territory.

A second factor I tested was the unemployment rate in each jurisdiction (ABS 6202). Again, there are significant differences among the jurisdictions in terms of their unemployment rate over the period studied (1986–2016) ($F(5)=27.19$, $p<0.001$). The unemployment rate was calculated by unemployment amount/ (employed amount + unemployed amount) from the data set. The state with the highest unemployment rate is South Australia (Mean=7.58 per cent), which is not significantly different with Queensland (Mean=6.97 per cent). The following states are Victoria, Western Australia and NSW, who are not significantly different from each other. The state with the lowest unemployment rate is the Northern Territory (Mean=4.20 per cent). I subsequently tested if the unemployment rate was positively correlated with the IR and again, the hypothesis was only supported in three jurisdictions. In NSW ($r_{ln}=0.63$, $p<0.05$), Victoria ($r_{ln}=0.47$, $p<0.05$), and South Australia ($r_{ln}=0.45$, $p<0.05$), the higher the unemployment rate, the higher the IR. The hypothesis was not supported for Queensland, Western Australia and the Northern Territory.

The third factor I tested was the education level in the selected jurisdictions over the time period this information is available (2005–2015) (ABS 6227). The measure used was non-school trainings; this means above high school or another sort of training. There are significant differences among the states, in terms of their residents' education level index as generated in this study ($F(5)=4.28$, $p<0.05$). The average proportion of non-school training at NSW is the highest (Mean=63 per cent), which is not significantly different with Victoria, Western Australia and the Northern Territory. The education levels of NSW and Victoria (Mean=61 per cent) are significantly higher than Queensland (Mean=59 per cent) and South Australia (Mean=57 per cent). However, the hypothesis that the education level would correlate with the IR was not supported.

The last factor I checked for was the income inequity over the period these data are available (1994–2014) (ABS 6523). Inequity was measured by top 10 per cent income/bottom 10 per cent income. Also on this aspect the selected jurisdictions are significantly different ($F(5)=34.11$, $p<0.001$). The income inequity level in the Northern Territory is the highest (Mean=10.94), which is significantly higher than all the other states. This means that, on average over the 20 years, the income of the top 10 per cent earners is about 10.94 times of the bottom 10 per cent earners. Due to the fact that the level in the Northern Territory is so much higher than the other states, a second round of one-way ANOVA was conducted taking the Northern Territory data out to examine the differences among the other states. The test was still significant ($F(4)=4.06$, $p<0.05$). The income inequity of Western Australia (Mean=4.01) is significantly higher than the lowest income inequity state, being NSW (Mean=2.58). For the test if this income inequity was related to the IR, Western Australia is the only state which showed a supportive link as the higher the income inequity is, the higher the IR ($r_{ln}=0.76$, $p<0.01$).

Concluding, one could say that the (in)equality level is statistically different in the jurisdictions studied, but that there is no consequent pattern, as they perform differently according to the measure used. Inequality as measured by the Gini index is high in NSW and Western Australia, the unemployment rate is high in South Australia and Queensland, the education level is low in Queensland and South Australia, and income inequity is high in the Northern Territory and to a lesser extent in Western Australia. One could assume that the low levels of education in Queensland and South Australia are related to the high unemployment rate, and that the low unemployment rate in the Northern Territory and the high income inequity in the Northern Territory and Western Australia are related to the mining industry, providing employment with high salaries being paid to people working in and around mining business, while both are jurisdictions characterised by their vastness, with regional and remote communities where there is not much industry. In the case of the Northern Territory, these regions are mainly populated with Indigenous people, with hardly any access to the skilled workforce that is required these days.

However, for the purposes of this study, the more important finding is that there is no consistent correlation between these parameters and the IR. There is a positive correlation between the Gini index and IR in NSW, Victoria and Western Australia, there is a positive correlation between the unemployment rate and IR in NSW, Victoria and South Australia, there is no correlation between the education level and IR, and the correlation between income inequity and IR only holds in Western Australia. Therefore, from this analysis, there is no conclusive evidence that the neoliberal socio-economic situation, as measured by the Gini index, unemployment, education and household income, is correlated with the IR in these jurisdictions over the time tested.

Political and constitutional/electoral structures

According to Lacey (2008), there is an association between the LME and CME models and their political and constitutional and electoral structures. CME mainly have proportionally representative electoral systems, while LME tend to have first-past-the-post systems. Majoritarian/first-past-the-post-electoral systems might be more vulnerable to a politicisation of criminal justice and the impact of penal populism to win the votes of the 'floating' median voters who regard crime as a threat to their well-being.

Australia is a majoritarian system, however, according to Lijphart (1999), with signs of a consensual democracy as the first-past-the-post system has been replaced, both at the federal and state level, with a combination of a proportional representation in the upper house (called the Senate at the federal level and Legislative Council at state/territory level) and a preferential voting system in the lower house (called the House of Representative at the federal level and Legislative Assembly at the state/territory level). It is therefore not a full Westminster model, and there are some voting variants between the jurisdictions, but they all remain within the majoritarian model. Therefore, I investigated to what extent Australian jurisdictions are subject to politicisation.

As a first step I looked at the left/right division over the period under study (1990–2015). At the federal level there is a balance between Labor and Conservative governments, with a slight dominance of the latter. Looking at the state level, in most jurisdictions there has been a dominance of Labor governments, except for Western Australia and the Northern Territory. To see if there is any impact of left/right wing governments on the IR, I brought the political situation in these jurisdictions into the statistical analysis. I tested the assumption that the IR would increase under a Liberal (Conservative) government, and decrease under Labor, but this hypothesis was not supported, both using both raw data and logged data. This result is however not surprising, as earlier qualitative analysis already demonstrated that, while punitive initiatives are often introduced by a Liberal government, they are subsequently taken over by Labor, claiming the 'tough on crime approach' as a batch of honour in a bet for electoral success. Examples of this can be seen in all jurisdictions with the introduction of 'truth in sentencing' legislation, punitive initiatives towards high profile or sensitive offenders and offences, often taken in the suit of highly mediatised incidents (Tubex *et al.* 2015). The latter brings us to the role of the media in the politicisation of crime and punishment. Most Australian jurisdictions are dominated by the Murdoch Press, with popular and sometimes single newspapers providing the information. From our qualitative analysis we know that in all selected jurisdictions there are examples of headline grabbing incidents that lead to overnight decisions towards a more punitive approach (Tubex *et al.* 2015). Interestingly, Roberts *et al.* (2011) tested to what extent punitiveness scores of the public are different between Australian jurisdictions. They found that there are differences; punitiveness scores are significantly higher in Western Australia than in Victoria, NSW and South Australia. However, the size of the effect is too small (<2 points) to explain the differences in IR. In other words, punitive political decisions are not a reflection of a different level of punitive public opinion in that jurisdiction. Therefore, one can conclude that the Australian majoritarian democracy is driven by populist initiatives, but that, in the words of Beckett (1997), politics rather steer public opinion (political initiative) than that the presumed public opinion would lead their choices (democracy at work).

Further, Lacey (2008) discusses the embedding of criminal justice policy within the constitutional structure of a country, according to the distribution of decision-making power, and the structure of legal institutions – particularly the tenure and selection of the judiciary.

Australia is a federation, but, as in the US, criminal justice policy is mainly developed at the local level as the criminal law is predominantly a state responsibility with little federal intervention. The judiciary in Australia is not elected, but, as Lacey (2008) describes for the UK, the rise of penal populism has destabilised the relationship between government and judiciary, the latter being subject to public criticism as 'being out of touch with the reality'. Freiberg (2016) describes how, over time, Australian legislature has intervened in the discretionary power of the courts out of dissatisfaction with what they perceive as undue leniency and sentencing disparity. Examples of this are the introduction of mandatory sentences (Tubex 2016) and presumptive sentences. However, he describes how the judiciary has reacted to this interference, defending their discretion to enable a very individualistic sentencing approach (Freiberg 2016). Similar interventions have taken place regarding the operation of the parole boards, introducing standard non-parole periods (cf. NSW), restricting parole boards' ability to release offenders (cf. Victoria), changing the release policy, (cf. Western Australia) or enlarging parole board and police powers to revoke or terminate release (cf. South Australia and Victoria) (Bartels 2013; Tubex et al. 2015). The limited public confidence in the courts' discretion has been demonstrated in earlier research (Indermaur and Roberts 2009), but is also abundantly illustrated in the latest bail review in NSW, where the interventions of some shock-jocks led to a punitive revision of a recent and thoughtfully prepared reform of the system (Quilter and Brown 2014).

Finally, Lacey (2008) discusses the institutional capacity of both systems to integrate 'outsiders'. In that respect, the individualistic LME might have it relatively easy to integrate 'outsiders', such as immigrants if they find a place on the labour market, while the more group and skills-based CME's might have greater difficulties integrating migrants into the structures that helped them to maintain a moderate criminal justice policy. This assumption seems to be almost clairvoyant in the light of current developments in Europe, particularly in Scandinavian countries such as Sweden, as recently described by Pratt (2015) and Barker (2017).

In the analysis, I checked if the proportion of overseas migration over the period studied (1986–2015) is different from one jurisdiction to another (ABS 3101). The results show that there are significant migration rate differences among the states ($F(5)=9.96$, $p<0.001$). Western Australia is the state with the highest overseas migration rate (Mean=2.55‰). The following states are NSW (Mean=1.89‰) and Victoria (Mean=1.84‰), who are significantly higher than Queensland (Mean=1.56‰), the Northern Territory (Mean=1.33‰) and South Australia (Mean=1.12‰). The correlation test with the IR is rather surprising, as in each of the states, the higher the overseas migration rate, the higher the IR ($p<0.05$). Given Australia's immigration policy being highly selective, mainly allowing for skilled migration, one would expect that migrants are easily integrated into the labour markets, and are not impacting on the punitiveness scale as measured by the IR.

Conclusion

For now, I conclude from the above that Australia shares a lot of the characteristics of an LME, as described by Lacey (2008). Crime and justice are politicised, being high on the electoral agenda of both left and right parties, presenting a strong 'law and order' approach throughout the 1980s and 1990s, with a remarkable time lapse for Victoria, where that political discourse only kicks in in the 2010 elections (Tubex et al. 2015). This led to increasing IR regardless to the party in office, and this seems mainly a political choice, as there is no evidence that the public in these jurisdictions would be more or less punitive as reflected in their IR. Legislative interventions in judicial practices increased over time, again in a punitive direction, however, as Freiberg (2016) states, times might be changing, with the 'law and order' government in Victoria losing office in 2014, and the same happening in Queensland in 2015. From a political economy perspective though, there is no consistent evidence that this political embracement of punitivism is coupled with different socio-economic conditions in these jurisdictions. (In)equality levels are different as measured by our parameters, but their statistical correlation with the IR in that jurisdiction is inconsistent.

Neoliberalism vs colonialism: Indigenous overrepresentation

In this last section, I focus on the overrepresentation of Indigenous people in the Australian prison population. According to the last census data from 2011, 2.5 per cent of the Australian population identified as Indigenous.[7] The percentage of Indigenous people in the general population amounts to 26.8 per cent in the Northern Territory, while their proportion is minimal in the other selected jurisdictions: Queensland leads the pack with 3.6 per cent, followed by Western Australia (3.1 per cent), NSW (2.5 per cent) and South Australia (1.9 per cent), the proportion of Indigenous people being the lowest in Victoria (0.7 per cent) (ABS 2012). In big contrast to that is the percentage of the prison population that identifies as Indigenous: it is 84 per cent in the Northern Territory, 38 per cent in Western Australia, 32 per cent in Queensland, 24 per cent in NSW, 23 per cent in South Australia and 8 per cent in Victoria (ABS 2015).

The percentage of Indigenous people in the total population somewhat distorts the reality of the absolute numbers. Both the Northern Territory and Western Australia are states that are, regardless their vastness, only scarcely populated. 26.8 per cent of the overall population means that there are 57,000 Indigenous people living in the Northern Territory, while 3.1 per cent of the Western Australia population means about 70,000 Indigenous people. In comparison, in Queensland the 3.6 per cent stands for 156,000 Indigenous people and the 2.5 per cent in NSW means about 173,000 Indigenous people (ABS 2012). Another difference is the urbanisation of Indigenous people. In the Northern Territory, Queensland, NSW and Western Australia, most of them live outside of the capital area (respectively 80 per cent, 72 per cent, 68 per cent and 60 per cent), with problems of service delivery in regional and remote communities, while in South Australia and Victoria, Indigenous people are far more urbanised, with about half of them living in the capital area (ABS 2012).

Neoliberalism and racialisation

The link between neoliberalism and the overrepresentation of minorities in the prison has been explored by Wacquant (2009), discussing the situation of the black Americans. According to Wacquant, after the walls of the ghettos started to collapse in the 1970s, another institution had to arise to contain this stigmatised population, and that was the prison. He calls it one of the extra-penological functions of the prison, to become the regulator of poverty, race, and class inside of race, as it is the lower class of black Americans which is most affected. Wacquant links this development to a growing neoliberalism, being the main driver of increased punitiveness. This claim has been challenged by Brown (2011), who states that increasing punitiveness might have more to do with race and colonialism/post-colonialism than with neoliberalism, as most neoliberal political economies are also former colonial or post-colonial countries. Indeed, while the IR of these settler societies is not necessarily high per se (cf. Canada), they all suffer from an overrepresentation of Indigenous people in their criminal justice system.

Looking at the overrepresentation of Indigenous people in Australian prisons, a parallel can be drawn with the collapse of the black ghettos in the US. Until the 1960s, Indigenous people in Australia used to be segregated in reserves, missions and stations for their 'protection' (cf. The Aborigines Protection Act 1909). Despite their administrative nature, these places were just another form of 'total institutions', with a similar disciplinary regime and punitive character. When these institutions started to be closed down in the 1950s and 1960s for economic and other reasons, Indigenous people were forced to move to the cities where they were exposed to a white racist society, and ended up in marginalisation. While systematic data on ethnicity for this period are lacking – Indigenous people are only included in the national ABS census since 1971 – this stage has been identified as the start of the upsurge of Indigenous people in the prison population (Purdy 1996, Finnane and McGuire 2001, Hogg 2001).

In Australian criminology, there are two main streams of arguments explaining the overrepresentation of Indigenous people in the criminal justice system: a greater involvement in crime, related to multiple areas of social and economic deprivation, and a racial bias throughout the criminal justice system. As I discussed these arguments extensively elsewhere (see Tubex 2013b), I here summarise the findings from both perspectives.

Indigenous involvement in crime

Going back to the ABS recorded crime – offender data (ABS 4519), I looked at the division between Indigenous and non-Indigenous offender rates for the jurisdictions where this information is available (NSW, Queensland, South Australia and the Northern Territory).[8] The Indigenous offender rate in 2014/2015 is the highest in South Australia (11,623), followed by Queensland (11,077), the Northern Territory (8,762) and NSW (4,301). The non-Indigenous offender rate is the highest in Queensland (1,814), followed by South Australia (1,213), it is about the same in the Northern Territory (1,000) and NSW (964). These data seem to confirm the argument that there is a higher involvement of Indigenous people in crime, as is claimed in the writings from Weatherburn and his colleagues, because of the higher exposure to criminogenic risk factors (cf. Weatherburn 2014). On the contrary, it has been argued that this can also be related to criminalisation processes and race-related practices at the early stages of the criminal justice process, such as criminalisation of behaviour that is more frequent with Indigenous people, police presence and practices in Indigenous communities, and a higher visibility of Indigenous offending as it occurs more frequently in a public space (Blagg, 2016). Remarkable is that in three states the Indigenous offender rate is going down over time (2008–2015), which is most outspoken in NSW (−39 per cent), South Australia (−12 per cent) and the Northern Territory (−7 per cent), and in Queensland it remains stable (−1 per cent). Given the fact that their IR went up in these jurisdictions over the same time period, other factors must be at play.

Institutional racism

Information about the trajectory of Indigenous offenders throughout the criminal justice system over time are only fragmentally available in ABS statistics, and need to be controlled for other variables that might impact on the decision-making process, again to make sure we are comparing apples with apples. Therefore, I rely on other studies that have tested the institutional racism thesis (for an overview, see Tubex 2013b). The conclusion of these studies is that, at the sentencing level, results vary according to the state and between higher/lower courts, but based on the findings so far there is insufficient evidence to claim a systemic bias in the sentencing of Indigenous people.

Indigenous imprisonment rates

Finally, I looked at the Indigenous IR, based on available data and supplementary data I requested from the ABS. The Indigenous IR is high in all the selected jurisdictions, but there are significant differences: in 2015 it is the highest in Western Australia (3,621 per 100,000 Aboriginal and Torres Strait Islander adult population), followed by the Northern Territory (2,886), South Australia (2,563), NSW (2,138), Queensland (1,851) and it is the lowest in Victoria (1,541) (ABS 2016). These rates are increasing in every state and territory over time, resulting in 2015 in an overrepresentation rate of 18 in Western Australia, 15 in the Northern Territory, 12 in South Australia and 11 in the other states.

The variation in Indigenous IR is statistically different ($F(5)=56.73$, $p<0.001$). The average Indigenous IR rate in Western Australia (Mean = 2,757) is significantly higher than in the other states across the data period (1990–2015). South Australia is the second-highest state (Mean = 1,728), which is not significantly different from the Northern Territory (Mean = 1,683). They are followed by NSW (Mean = 1,474) and Queensland (Mean = 1,283), which are not significantly different from each other. The state with the lowest Indigenous IR rate is Victoria (Mean = 881), which is significantly lower than all the other states.

Given the fact that the IR of Indigenous offenders is so high, there is an evident correlation with the overall IR in these jurisdictions. Both the IR of Indigenous offenders and non-Indigenous offenders increase with the overall IR in the selected jurisdictions. To further explore the driving factor behind the increase of the overall IR, I tested if the increasing rate of Indigenous prisoners correlated with the increasing overall IR, and this is the case for all jurisdictions. From this finding one can conclude that it is mainly the increasing Indigenous IR that drives the increase of the overall IR in each jurisdiction.

The high Indigenous IR is linked to a high Indigenous recidivism rate. In 2015, 80 per cent of all sentenced Indigenous prisoners had a known prior imprisonment, against 52 per cent of the non-Indigenous sentenced prisoners (ABS 2015). Research has demonstrated that Indigenous offenders are readmitted to prison sooner and more frequently than non-Indigenous offenders (Allard 2010), they are nearly twice as likely to be readmitted to prison within two years and more than twice as likely to return to prison for assault, and half of them remained in prison until the expiry of their sentences (Willis and Moore 2008). A recent report demonstrated that Indigenous prisoners have limited access to culturally appropriate rehabilitation programmes, and this is particularly the case if they serve short sentences, which is often the case for Indigenous offenders. Of even more concern is the fact that this study could not rely on primary sources because of a lack of data on the availability of treatment programmes for Indigenous offenders, as well as evaluations on the effectiveness of these programmes, and a lack of support from the Corrective Services Administrators' Council for the researchers to approach correctional jurisdictions to obtain these data (Jones and Guthrie 2016).

Conclusion

Looking at the overrepresentation of Indigenous offenders in Australian prisons, I described similar extra-penological functions of the prison as set out by Wacquant (2009), as the increase started at the moment Indigenous offenders were no longer segregated in other administrative 'total institutions'. However, from the analysis in the earlier sections of this chapter, there is no evidence that this extra-penological function is driven by an increasing neoliberalism. Indigenous people are more involved in offending behaviour, and more affected by the criminal justice system, probably by a combination of their specific kind of offending and the institutional reaction to that. However, the Indigenous offender rate is going down/stable in the jurisdictions where this information available, while their IR is going up. Most importantly, it is the increase of the Indigenous IR that drives the increase of the overall IR and I am inclined to interpret that phenomenon as an expression of the consequences of, and an ongoing (post)colonialist attitude towards Indigenous people and their culture.

Discussion and conclusion

We previously referred to Australia as a 'penal laboratory' presenting the unique situation of separate jurisdictions within one federal unit (Tubex *et al.* 2015).

While there is a strong and pervasive federal government, regulating most economic powers and welfare, the criminal justice world is exclusively state based. It provides, therefore, as close as we get to an empirical 'ideal type' of independent penal cultures within a country, and therefore a particular challenge for a single explanatory model, such as the political economy being related to punitiveness as expressed in IR.

From the statistical and descriptive analysis I conducted, one can say that Australia sits well and truly in the neoliberal Anglo-Saxon community and has in general been following the trend towards increased punitiveness across that community. The Australian jurisdictions I investigated fit in the neoliberal family group that are more punitive as measured by their IR, it is only Victoria that used to stay below that level, but recently it seems to catch up with the overall trend. However, as explained by O'Malley (2002) Australia has its own neoliberal model, with roots in the more socio-democratic tradition of the 1970s that prevented it from the more outspoken and conservative neoliberalism as expressed in the US. Though, O'Malley might have been somewhat overoptimistic about the inclusiveness of our society, particularly when it comes to Indigenous people, as is demonstrated in their overrepresentation in the prison population. The Australian jurisdictions do present LME characteristics in the politicisation of crime and punishment and interventions to curtail judicial discretionary power, often under the pressure of a populist media that propagandise high-profile incidents, which in turn have led to punitive legislative and policy changes.

However, within this overall trend, levels of punitiveness vary substantially between the six jurisdictions under research and the aim of this contribution was to hold them against a political economy perspective. Available data about a variety of social/political/economic indicators do not show reliable correlations between any of the variables considered and the IR in these jurisdictions: there are some intrastate correlations between time series of some relevant data but these are dispersed. In no area are there consistent correlations displayed.

I demonstrated that trends described for the family groups over the period that Cavadino and Dignan (2006) covered (1986–2003) did not necessarily hold afterwards. This shows the importance of local changes impacting on punitiveness, resulting in a deviation from earlier pathways. Looking at the evolution of the IR in the family groups from the current perspective, the theory of a shared political economy falls short in explaining what has happened since the analysis of Cavadino and Dignan. The theoretical model of Lacey (2008) is valid for the overall trend in the Australian jurisdictions in this analysis, as features of an LME model can be found in all of them, but it does not explain the differences between the IR of these jurisdictions, and their relative stable level over time. Further, it has widely been acknowledged that attitudes in the early settlement of Australia have impacted on Indigenous offending and their relationship with the criminal justice system, but I think that the current situation is better captured in terms of (post)colonialism than racism or neoliberalism, as claimed by Wacquant

(2009). To further investigate how this interaction works requires the analysis of more detailed data on Indigenous offending behaviour and their treatment throughout the criminal justice system – which are now simply not available. This should be a national priority, as one can only conclude that the deplorable outcome of this relationship is that Indigenous IR are driving the overall IR. But again, this is an overall feature of our penal situation, and does not explain the differences between the IR in our jurisdictions. To explain the different levels of punitiveness as expressed in Australian IR, other forms of data are required to understand the emergence of different local penal cultures. To explain the glocalisation in Australian jurisdictions; being the persistence of national and even regional autonomy in the face of global pressures (Meyer and O'Malley 2005), it is my hypothesis that this kind of information might be sought in different historical developments of early settlement, leading to different punishment traditions and penal cultures nowadays.

Notes

* A/Prof Tubex is a recipient of an Australian Research Council Future Fellowship (Project number FT 100100627). I would like to acknowledge Dr. Shasha Wang who did the data analysis and statistical interpretation for this research. Dr. Wang is a lecturer at the Marketing Department of the Business School at the University of Western Australia.
1 For practical and financial reasons, the Australian Capital Territory and Tasmania are not included in this study.
2 Queensland and the Northern Territory were not included in that discussion.
3 This was calculated comparing the rate in the last survey to the average rate over the five previous surveys.
4 In this contribution, I will only work with the first three categories.
5 The Gini coefficient is a single statistical indicator of the degree of inequality. It equals zero when all people have the same level of income and equals one when one person receives all the income. In general, the smaller the Gini coefficient, the more equal the distribution of income or wealth (ABS 6523).
6 That is why 'r_{ln}' was used in the Pearson correlation test, instead of 'r'.
7 This means they self-identify as being from Aboriginal and/or Torres Strait Islander origin.
8 Based on an ABS assessment, Indigenous Status data for the other states are not of sufficient quality and/or do not meet ABS standards for self-identification for national reporting.

References

Allard, T. (2010). Understanding and preventing Indigenous offending. *Brief 9*, Indigenous justice clearing house.
Australian Bureau of Statistics (2012). 2075.0 – *Census of Population and Housing – Counts of Aboriginal and Torres Strait Islander Australians, 2011*. Available at www.abs.gov.au/ausstats/abs@.nsf/mf/2075.0 [accessed 20 October 2016].
Australian Bureau of Statistics (2015). *Prisoners in Australia* 4517.0. Available at www.abs.gov.au/ausstats/abs@.nsf/mf/4517.0 [accessed 20 October 2016].
Australian Bureau of Statistics (2015). *Customised report*.

Australian Bureau of Statistics, *Australian Demographic Statistics* 3101.0 – Available at www.abs.gov.au/ausstats/abs@.nsf/mf/3101.0 [accessed 20 October 2016].
Australian Bureau of Statistics, *Crime Victimisation* 4530.0 – Available at www.abs.gov.au/ausstats/abs@.nsf/mf/4530.0 [accessed 20 October 2016].
Australian Bureau of Statistics, *Education and Work* 6227.0 – Available at www.abs.gov.au/AUSSTATS/abs@.nsf/mf/6227.0/ [accessed 20 October 2016].
Australian Bureau of Statistics, *Household Income and wealth* 6523.0 – Available at: www.abs.gov.au/ausstats/abs@.nsf/mf/6523.0 [accessed 20 October 2016].
Australian Bureau of Statistics, *Labour Force* 6202.0 – Available at www.abs.gov.au/ausstats/abs@.nsf/mf/6202.0 [accessed 20 October 2016].
Australian Bureau of Statistics, *Recorded Crime – Offenders* 4519. Available at www.abs.gov.au/ausstats/abs@.nsf/mf/4519.0 [accessed 20 October 2016].
Barker, V. (2017). Nordic Vagabonds: The Roma and the Logic of Benevolent Violence in the Swedish Welfare State. *European Journal of Criminology*, 14 (1), 120–139.
Bartels, L. (2013). Parole and Parole Authorities in Australia: A System in Crisis? *Criminal Law Journal*, 37 (6), 357–376.
Beckett, K. (1997). *Making Crime Pay: Law and Order in Contemporary American Politics*. New York: Oxford University Press.
Beckett, K. and Western, B. (2001). Governing Social Marginality: Welfare, Incarceration, and the Transformation of State Policy. *Punishment and Society*, 3 (1), 43–59.
Blagg, H. (2016). *Crime, Aboriginality and the Decolonisation of Justice*. 2nd ed. Annandale: The Federation Press.
Brown, D. (2011). Neoliberalism as a Criminological Subject. *Australian & New Zealand Journal of Criminology*, 44 (1), 129–142.
Cavadino, M. and Dignan, J. (2006). *Penal Systems: A Comparative Approach*. London: Sage.
Downes, D. and Hansen, K. (2006). Welfare and Punishment in Comparative Perspective. *In*: Armstrong, S. and Mc Ara, L., eds, *Perspectives on Punishment: The Contours of Control*. Oxford: Oxford University Press, 133–154.
Esping-Andersen, G. (1990). *The Three Worlds of Welfare Capitalism*. Cambridge: Polity Press.
Finnane, M. and McGuire, J. (2001). The Uses of Punishment and Exile: Aborigines in Colonial Australia. *Punishment and Society*, 3 (2), 279–298.
Freiberg, A. (2016). The Road Well Travelled in Australia: Ignoring the Past, Condemning the Future. *Crime and Justice*, 45 (1). Available at www.journals.uchicago.edu.ezproxy.library.uwa.edu.au/doi/pdfplus/10.1086/685537 [accessed 8 February 2017].
Hall, P. and Soskice, D. (2001). An Introduction to the Varieties of Capitalism. *In*: Hall, P. and Soskice, D., eds, *Varieties of Capitalism*. Oxford: Oxford University Press, 1–68.
Hogg, R. (2001). Penality and Modes of Regulating Indigenous Peoples in Australia. *Punishment and Society*, 3 (3), 355–379.
Indermaur, D. and Roberts, L. (2009). Confidence in the Criminal Justice System. *Trends & Issues*, 387 (1), 1–6.
Jacobs, D. and Carmichael, J.T. (2001). The Politics of Punishment across Time and Space: A Pooled Time-Series Analysis of Imprisonment Rates. *Social Forces*, 80, 61–89.
Jones, C. and Guthrie, J. (2016). *Efficacy, Accessibility and Adequacy of Prison Rehabilitation Programs for Indigenous Offenders across Australia*. Melbourne: The Australian Institute of Judicial Administration Incorporated.
Lacey, N. (2008). *The Prisoners' Dilemma: Political Economy and Punishment in Contemporary Democracies*. Cambridge: Cambridge University Press.

Lappi-Seppälä, T. (2008) Trust, Welfare, and Political Culture: Explaining Differences in National Penal Policies. *Crime and Justice, A Review of Research*, 37 (1), 313–387.

Lijphart, A. (1999). Australian Democracy: Modifying Majoritarianism? *Australian Journal of Political Science*, 34 (3), 313–326.

Meyer, J. and O'Malley, P. (2005). Missing the Punitive Turn? Canadian Criminal Justice, 'Balance' and Penal Modernism. *In*: Pratt, J., Brown, D. and Brown, M., eds, *The New Punitiveness: Trends, Theories, Perspectives*. Cullompton: Willan, 201–217.

Nelken, D. (2009). Comparative Criminal Justice: Beyond Ethnocentrism and Relativism. *European Journal of Criminology*, 6 (4), 291–311.

Nelken, D. (2010). *Comparative Criminal Justice: Making Sense of Difference*. London: Sage.

O'Malley, P. (2002). Globalizing Risk? Distinguishing Styles of 'Neo-liberal' Criminal Justice in Australia and the USA. *Criminology and Criminal Justice*, 2 (2), 205–222.

Pratt, J. (2015). Inspector Wallander's Angst, Social Change and the Reconfiguration of Swedish Exceptionalism. *Punishment and Society*, 17 (3), 322–344.

Purdy, J. (1996). Postcolonialism: The Emperor's New Clothes? *Social & Legal Studies*, 5 (3), 405–426.

Quilter, J. and Brown, D. (2014). Speaking Too Soon: The Sabotage of Bail Reform in New South Wales. *International Journal of Crime, Justice and Social Democracy*, 3 (3), 73–97.

Roberts, L.D., Spiranovic, C.A. and Indermaur, D.W. (2011). A Country Not Divided: A Comparison of Public Punitiveness and Confidence in Sentencing across Australia. *Australian & New Zealand Journal of Criminology*, 44 (3), 370–386.

Tonry, M. (2007). Determinants of Penal Policies. *Crime and Justice, A Review of Research*, 36 (1), 1–48.

Tubex, H. (2013a). Pitfalls of Comparative (Penological) Research and How to Overcome Them. *In*: Beyens, K., Christiaens, J, Claes, B, De Ridder, S, Tournel, H & Tubex, H, eds, *The Pains of Doing Criminological Research*. Brussels: VUBPress, 195–215.

Tubex, H. (2013b). The Revival of Comparative Criminology in a Globalised World: Local Variances and Indigenous Over-representation. *International Journal for Crime, Justice and Social Democracy*, 2 (3), 55–68. Available at www.crimejusticejournal.com/article/view/110 [accessed 20 October 2016].

Tubex, H. (2016). Mandatory Sentencing Leads to Unjust, Unfair Outcomes – it Doesn't Make Us Safe. *The Conversation*. Available at https://theconversation.com/mandatory-sentencing-leads-to-unjust-unfair-outcomes-it-doesnt-make-us-safe-52086 [accessed 20 October 2016].

Tubex, H. et al. (2015). Penal Diversity within Australia. *Punishment and Society*, 17 (3), 345–373.

Wacquant, L. (2009). *Punishing the Poor: The Neoliberal Government of Social Insecurity*. Durham: Duke University Press.

Weatherburn, D. (2014). *Arresting Incarceration. Pathways out of Indigenous Imprisonment*. Canberra: Aboriginal Studies Press.

Webster, C.M. and Doob, A.N. (2011). Explaining Canada's Imprisonment Rate: The Inadequacy of Simple Explanations. *In*: Crawford, A., ed., *International and Comparative Criminal Justice and Urban Governance*. Cambridge: Cambridge University Press, 304–330.

Willis, M. and Moore, J.P. (2008). Reintegration of Indigenous Prisoners. *Research and Public policy Series n. 90*, Australian institute of Criminology.

Chapter 7

Punishment in a hybrid political economy

The Italian case (1970–2010)

Zelia A. Gallo

Introduction

In this chapter I investigate the relationship between punishment and the political economy in contemporary Italy. The chapter contributes to the debate on contemporary Western 'punitiveness' and its preconditions. 'Punitiveness' here refers to an increase in imprisonment rates, as experienced since the 1970s by (some) Western nations – most notably the United States (De Giorgi 2006; Garland 2001; Wacquant 2009b). It also refers to a *qualitative* shift in punishment, reflected in increased prison rates: punishment has grown harsher over time, tending at best towards retributivism laced with incapacitation (Hudson 2003, p. 36, 54) and at worst tending towards a certain vindictiveness vis-à-vis offenders (for a particularly vivid illustration see Smith 2013). The context for this chapter is the subset of literature that has tried to account for contemporary 'punitiveness' by reference to political economic evolution across Western polities. This body of work has linked punishment levels to changes and variations in modes of production (De Giorgi 2006; Lacey 2008; Lacey 2011, 2013; Melossi and Pavarini 1977; Rusche and Kirchheimer 1939; Wacquant 2009b, 2009a), as well as the retraction or persistence of welfare protection (Cavadino and Dignan 2006; Lacey 2008, 2011).

While engaging with this literature, in the pages that follow I will argue that, relevant as the political economy may be to punishment in Italy, it nonetheless cannot be our primary explanatory variable in accounting for Italian penality. The reason for this is that the Italian political economy is fundamentally a hybrid (Gallo 2015, pp. 613–614), with a high level of internal diversity. As such, Italy tends to challenge theories of punishment that rest on political economic models that presume systemic coherence. My primary referents here are Alessandro De Giorgi (2006, 2010) and his analysis of contemporary Western punishment as the penality of post-Fordism; and Nicola Lacey (2008, 2011, 2013), whose work focuses on the penal *divergence* visible across different 'varieties of capitalism' (VoC) (Hall and Soskice 2001). As I will show below, the Italian case can neither be subsumed in narratives of 'post-Fordist punishment', nor can it be classified as either of the two main VoC and their split between the poles of punitiveness and moderation.

In this chapter I argue that we can, however, factor the political economy into a systematic analysis of Italian penality – that is to say an analysis that is not just limited to describing Italy's particularities – if we look more explicitly to political variables (Gallo 2015). By focusing on politics as our key explanatory variable, we can then *return* to the political economy, using politics as a conceptual bridge to connect the political economy to punishment. The term *politics*, as I use it in this chapter, refers to the following three dimensions:

1 *Political institutions*: the Italian institutional set-up, with its varying veto points and opportunities for different political actors to influence decision-making.
2 *Political culture*, in particular post-war ideologies such as Catholicism and Communism. This second dimension relates to institutions insofar as political culture surrounds and imbues political institutions, but is also sustained and changed by their functioning. It also affects the way that institutions are reformed.
3 *Political dynamics*: the historical evolution of both political institutions and culture over time. My analysis is primarily concerned with the period 1970 to 2010, starting from the purported onset of 'post-Fordism' (De Giorgi, 2006: 91) but stopping just short of the Euro zone crisis. Though I do advance some brief observations on Italy since 2010, the Euro zone crisis and its penal and political implications are largely beyond the remit of this contribution.

In writing this chapter I have a number of aims: first, I aim to explain *why* the couplet 'political economy-punishment' cannot yield a systematic explanation for Italian penality. Second, I aim to illustrate how politics is in fact a better organising principle where we seek such a systematisation. Third, I aim to show how the political economy is *nonetheless* relevant to our understanding of Italian penal policy, and that it can be tied to the latter via an analysis of Italian politics. Looking beyond Italy, and to the literature on the political economy of punishment, my broader hope is that this analysis will restore some sense of agency to the debates on contemporary penality. A focus on politics – institutions, decisions, agents – helps us to resist the idea that the onset of punitiveness is inexorable (see also Zedner, 2002). If nothing else, a more explicit discussion of politics complicates the materialist picture by pointing out that penal outcomes can differ, even in the face of economic convergence, where political variables stand between the economy and punishment, catalysing and mediating economic developments.

The chapter is structured as follows: in the first section I detail the shape of Italian penality. Subsequently, I lay out the theoretical framework against which I am comparing Italian penality. Having set the scene for my analysis, I continue by giving an account of the Italian political economy with its hybrid and internally diverse nature. I then undertake a direct comparison between my theoretical framework and my hybrid case study. This analysis is followed by an account of the penal incentives produced by the Italian political system, an account that links Italy's fragmentation and permeability to the shape of Italian punishment. Finally, I illustrate this link by analysing the Italian welfare state, both its susceptibility to political dynamics, and its influence on Italian punishment.

Setting the scene: Italian punishment

Any explanation of Italian penality requires first a characterisation of contemporary Italian penal trends. The political economic theories from which this chapter takes its cue have been concerned with explaining contemporary 'punitiveness' (De Giorgi 2006), or with explaining penal divergence and the persistence of 'penal moderation' (as in Nicola Lacey's characterisation of Germany: 2008). In both cases, as in much of the contemporary penal literature, 'punitiveness' and 'moderation' are measured via the proxy of imprisonment rates, in part because of the 'accessibility of relevant comparative data' on imprisonment (Loader 2010, p. 358).[1]

Using the same proxy for Italy, we note that the nation presents neither unequivocal moderation nor unequivocal punitiveness. Rather, imprisonment rates between 1970 and the present day, progress in a series of peaks and troughs that point to an alternation of repression and leniency (Gallo 2015, p. 601). The troughs are given by repeat clemency provisions – amnesties and pardons that, if nothing else, reflect a willingness to be lenient in practice if not in principle (Gallo 2015, pp. 607–608).[2] Elsewhere I have argued that this alternation, so visible in data on incarceration, is not limited to imprisonment rates but can in fact be seen across Italian penal policy and penal history (Gallo 2015, p. 602). Italian penality as a whole is therefore characterised by a duality, and is marked by the co-existence and alternation of punitiveness and moderation (Gallo 2015, p. 602).[3] Italian punishment is differentially distributed across subjects, falling most heavily on migrants from outside the European Union (non-EU migrants). The differentiation also reflects Italy's informal social controls that have long acted as a counter-point to formal penal censure (Gallo 2015, p. 608; Melossi 2003, pp. 380–381).

In sum: Italian penality displays neither unequivocal moderation nor unequivocal punitiveness. It displays an alternation, and co-existence, of repression and leniency, which any theory of Italian penality should be able to account for.

Setting the scene: punishment and the political economy

Having characterised Italian penality, the next step is to lay down the theoretical framework against which I compare my case study. I focus here on Alessandro De Giorgi's and Nicola Lacey's arguments, as laid out in *Re-Thinking the*

Political Economy of Punishment (De Giorgi 2006) and *The Prisoners' Dilemma* (Lacey 2008).[4] De Giorgi's work provides an *explicitly* political economic analysis of contemporary punishment. Lacey's work then offers a systematic explanation for comparative penal divergence, and for the fact that some nations have remained 'moderate' even in the face of apparently irresistible pressures towards penal escalation. The emphasis here is on the provision of an *explanation* for penal difference (Lacey 2013, p. 261) with a view to identifying those features that act as buffers to the spread of 'punitive law and order ideology' (Cavadino and Dignan 2006, p. 4), and to reflecting on the possibility of replicating these features across contexts.[5]

Post-Fordism and punishment

Alessandro De Giorgi builds on Rusche and Kirchheimer's sociological account of punishment, in *Punishment and Social Structure* (1939), and their key claim that punishment varies with varying modes of production. Each mode of production possesses corresponding methods of punishment (Rusche and Kirchheimer 1939, p. 5), and in order to understand the distribution of punishment we need to look to the availability of labour. In particular we need to ask whether labour is in *surplus* or is *scarce*, given that punishment will be harsh or lenient depending upon this surplus or scarcity. When labour is in surplus, punishment is more reckless with human life, but when labour is scarce, punishment is more careful with human life and tends towards a reintegration of deviants into society and the economy. Where penal severity is then measured in terms of prison – the primary penal mode in capitalist societies – this relationship translates as follows: periods of labour surplus are marked by higher levels of incarceration, whereas periods of labour scarcity are marked by a decreasing use of incarceration (see De Giorgi 2006, pp. 1–40).

De Giorgi's account asks how this theory plays out in the contemporary scenario: how has punishment changed since 1970 and the shift from 'Fordist' capitalism to 'post-Fordist' capitalism? The term *Fordism* indicates capitalism between the end of World War II and 1970, with the expansion of mass industrial production dependent 'on high levels of relatively low-skilled labour' (Lacey 2008, p. 25 n. 46), labour market stability, and limited unemployment levels. Fordist capitalism was also marked by the expansion of the welfare state, and a conception of 'citizenship [...] as a complex of social rights' (De Giorgi 2006, p. 29). Social inclusion was then also the guiding principle for existing institutions of social control (De Giorgi 2006; see also Garland 2001, p. 46).

Contemporary 'post-Fordism' is harder to define (De Giorgi 2006, p. 39). For the purposes of this chapter we can focus on the global transformations seen at the levels 'of work and production' (De Giorgi 2006, p. 42). We witness a decline of the industrial model: factories are replaced by flexible and decentralised labour, performed either in the 'hyper-technological' factory, or in the 'sweatshops' where 'residual material labour' is carried out (De Giorgi 2006,

p. 44). The labour force itself has changed, and it is now fragmented and often involved in informal activities. Post-Fordism, De Giorgi argues, is characterised by 'total work-flexibility imposed by the de-regulation of markets in a neo-liberal economy' (De Giorgi 2006, p. 45). This is a mode of production marked by a *surplus* that, De Giorgi explains, is now both productive and social. It is a *productive surplus* because labour is informatised and automated, though sustained by residual material activity (De Giorgi 2006, p. 44). It is a *social surplus* because productive activity no longer carries with it 'stability [...] legal guarantees [and] social rights' (De Giorgi 2006, p. 51; see also Garland 2001, pp. 93–94; Wacquant 2009b). This leaves a surplus of poor, marginalised and insecure individuals (De Giorgi 2006, pp. 41–60). Contemporary punishment is the government of this productive and social surplus, with prison as the primary means of its containment (De Giorgi 2006, p. 76).

What is the scope of this analysis? De Giorgi's penal theory is a *macroscopic* one: his exploration of punishment relies on 'global level' political economic changes (De Giorgi 2006, pp. 41–66). This implies that the penal reverberations of such changes will themselves be experienced 'globally'.[6] Though the shift into post-Fordism and its mode of punishment may be more visible in the US (Garland 2001, p. 7), this is indeed a matter of visibility rather than of difference. The logical corollary is that Western democracies are converging around punitiveness: thus, though in his later work he qualifies his position (2013, pp. 51–52),[7] in his early analysis De Giorgi predicts a gloomy penal future for Western democracies. But is this analysis *in fact* equally valid across contexts? Here Lacey's account steps in to cast some doubts upon this tale of convergence.

Varieties of capitalism and varieties of punishment

Lacey's analysis begins from the observation that not all nations punish equally (Lacey 2008, p. xvi, 138–142; Loader 2010, p. 359), and not all nations are 'punitive'. In Europe, for example, some nations have displayed penal stability over time, and have maintained a re-integrative approach to punishment (Lacey 2008, 2013). They are therefore better characterised as penally 'moderate'. What is more, Lacey argues, these differences in punishment can be reconnected to systematic differences in 'social, political and economic organisation' (Lacey 2008, p. xvi), which 'favour or inhibit' penal harshness. In particular, Lacey urges us to look at the way in which different 'institutional factors' vary across contexts, a variation that seems to have persisted in the face of 'global' economic changes.[8]

Lacey here builds upon Peter Hall and David Soskice's VoC literature (2001) and the distinction it draws between liberal market economies (LMEs) and co-ordinated market economies (CMEs). In Europe these two models are represented by the UK as the paradigmatic LME, and Germany as the paradigmatic CME. LMEs and CMEs differ in terms of their 'comparative institutional advantage' and their 'capacity for co-ordination' (Lacey 2008, p. 56). Simplifying greatly, the idea of 'comparative institutional advantage' indicates that what is advantageous in a liberal market economy is not necessarily advantageous in a co-ordinated market economy. This further implies that LMEs and CMEs will *not* react in the same manner when placed under external pressures. So, in the face of globalisation (a term that I use as a short-hand for the type of political economic changes described by De Giorgi), LMEs and CMEs will evolve differently, in accordance with the incentives created by their institutional organisation. In particular, it appears that the institutional organisation in CMEs affords them a certain level of resilience to liberalisation (on different levels of vulnerability to the collapse of Fordism see Lacey 2013, p. 271).

LMEs and CMEs also differ in the extent to which their institutions are co-ordinated. Thus in CMEs we find governmental structures that incorporate a 'wide range of social groups and institutions' (Lacey 2008, p. 58), which are thereby rendered interdependent, and which form a 'co-operative whole'. Moreover, CMEs tend to function in terms of 'long-term relations and stable structures of investment' (Lacey 2008, p. 58).[9] The latter produce labour *scarcity*. LMEs differ insofar as their institutional structure is premised on 'flexibility and innovation' and a dislike for state regulation; furthermore, LMEs are premised on individualist, fast-changing interrelations (Lacey 2008, p. 59). Overall such systems are more likely to produce conditions of labour *surplus*.

How do these differences translate in terms of punishment? LMEs and CMEs can be seen as *producing different penal incentives*. With their labour surplus, LMEs tend to have harsher criminal justice systems, as the 'cost' of exclusionary criminal justice is relatively low given their institutional organisation. By contrast, CMEs produce labour scarcity, therefore the institutionally advantageous thing to do is to *re-integrate* deviants into the economy and society. Moreover, the institutional interdependence found in CMEs tends to produce and sustain informal social controls and moderate attitudes to punishment, and to reduce reliance on formal social control (Lacey 2008, p. 61).

In sum: CMEs' institutional organisation produces incentives towards penal leniency, whereas LMEs' institutional organisation produces incentives towards penal severity. This distinction is well illustrated by incarceration rates in England and Wales – on the increase since the 1970s – and in Germany – relatively stable over the same period (Lacey 2008, p. 139, figure 13; International Centre for Prison Studies, last accessed 9 November 2011).

The Italian political economy: hybridity and differentiation

The Italian political economy is not easy to slot into this framework. As I will show in this section, the contemporary Italian political economy is characterised by a hybridity that sets it outside models premised on system coherence. It is therefore difficult to rationalise Italy as ever having been unequivocally 'Fordist', or as having transitioned into a, similarly unequivocal, 'post-Fordism'.

Even from the comparative vantage point of the VoC literature, the Italian political economy defies easy classification, with analytical implications where penal changes are tethered to coherent political economic models.

The Italian political economy displays high internal diversity, '[*embodying*] no single model' but containing 'several [...] *within it*' (Crouch 2005, p. 47). The typical characterisation of these models is the one developed by Arnaldo Bagnasco in 1977, according to which there are three Italies (Bagnasco 1977): the northwest or *First Italy*, marked by the highest level of large-scale industrialisation; the *Third Italy*, made up of the north eastern and central Italian regions, with their small-scale kinship based firms; and the *South*, once rural, still possessing a few large-scale industries 'dependent on state subsidies' (Crouch 2005, p. 47), and now the source of a large numbers of tertiary sector workers (Cassese 1993, pp. 322–324; Colombo and Regini 2016, p. 10). This territorial diversity extends also to Italy's industries (Trento 2012, p. 440) and its welfare regime (Colombo and Regini 2016, p. 7).

In recent decades the First and Third Italy have drawn closer together as the industries of the First Italy have decentralised part of their labour to small concerns (Salvati 2000, p. 20), more flexible given their lower – indeed often informal – regulation (De Cecco 2009, p. 110).[10] This process has produced 'locally rooted networks of [...] firms' (Trigilia and Burroni 2009, p. 644), which partially mimic the Third Italy with its small and medium-sized industries (SMEs). In SMEs production is decentralised, but premised on high levels of collaboration (Trigilia and Burroni 2009, p. 638), and regulation tends to be 'micro-social' regulation (Reyneri 1987, p. 158), relying heavily on personal trust, community ties and – certainly during the era of the Italian mass parties (1946 to 1990 ca.) – on ideological belonging (Reyneri 1987).

Since the 1970s, the Italian economy has – unsurprisingly – changed. De Cecco describes Italy's industrial transformation as the transformation from a nation 'oriented towards large scale enterprise' to one whose industrial sector sports 'many very small producers, some medium-sized ones, and a few large ones' (2009, p. 110). Large-scale industrial manufacturing has contracted overall, with the percentage of those employed in industry falling from 38.4 per cent (of all employed individuals) in 1977 to 28.5 per cent in 2010 (Prospero 2015, note 34, 281–282; ISTAT 2013, p. 3). Large-scale industries have also reorganised (Ginsborg 2001, p. 13) and new forms of labour have been introduced, such as part-time work and, as of the 1990s, novel ('atypical') contractual forms including fixed-term contracts (Colombo and Regini, 2016; Molina and Rhodes 2007, p. 244).[11]

Contemporaneously, the service sector has grown, with the percentage of those employed in the service sector increasing from 50.6 per cent in 1977 to 67.6 per cent by 2010 (Ginsborg 2001, p. 17; ISTAT 2013, p. 3). Over this period the contraction of industrial labour has been more marked in the Northern regions (47.6 per cent to 33.2 per cent: ISTAT 2013, p. 3), while employment in the tertiary sector has increased across *all* regions (to reach peaks of 71.5 per cent in central Italy: ISTAT 2013, pp. 3–4). Italy has therefore experienced a reduction of industrial labour. However, at least until the late 2000s this reduction has not necessarily implied unemployment. Other mechanisms have been found that reconcile the need to reduce labour and the need to support the workforce in the face of this reduction (for a comparison with Germany see Hassell 2014). In the 1980s, for example, large-scale industries shed their workforce by means of early retirement (De Cecco 2009, p. 112) rather than simply consigning their workers to unemployment.

How does this political economy compare with other VoC? According to Molina and Rhodes (2007), Italy is a 'mixed-market economy' (MME) situated between the LME and CME models, and possessing elements of both. Italy also possesses elements that are best analysed in terms of 'Southern European' countries (Ferrera 1996). Examples include reliance on the family as welfare surrogate (on which see also Cavadino and Dignan 2006, p. 131) and clientelism, whereby employment and income transfers are exchanged, from patron to client, with political support, from client to patron (Ferrera 1996, p. 28). According to Molina and Rhodes Italy is '[...] more fragmented than either LMEs or CMEs by large/small firm, public-private and territorial divides' (2007, p. 225). Italy is also characterised by 'organizational fragmentation, [a] politicization of interest associations and [a significant role for] the state as a regulator and producer of goods' (p. 228). Italy is 'mixed' in the VoC classification because it presents a 'high degree of institutional incoherence' (p. 228) and thus falls outside a single political economic model with a single form of 'comparative advantage'.

Over the course of the last three decades – stopping just before the Euro-crisis – reforms have been passed that might have made Italy (more or less explicitly) a CME or an LME. However, no single market model has emerged from these reforms (Molina and Rhodes 2007, p. 241).[12] Reforms have been shaped by political conflict and exchange. No one interest group has emerged victorious from this conflict: neither the employers – beset by differences between different size firms (Molina and Rhodes 2007) – nor the trade unions – with their internal divisions (Colombo and Regini 2016, p. 6; Molina and Rhodes 2007; Trento 2012, p. 444,). Note, however, that trade unions remain 'rather strong and deeply rooted in the workplace' and are therefore 'still an important component of the Italian social model' (Colombo and Regini 2016, p. 7).[13] Though trade union strength and membership has declined over the years, membership was still set at 35 per cent in 2010, in comparison to Germany's 19 per cent and the UK's 27 per cent (Colombo and Regini 2016, OECD: last accessed 5 November 2016).[14] This suggests, at the very least, that we cannot assume an automatic (neo) liberalisation of the Italian economy, but must be able to account for the persisting influence of social partners on labour reform.

In Italy, political economic changes have been negotiated, though in a manner that reflects the fragmentation of the Italian context, and the relative interdependence of its socio-economic actors. As a result of this negotiation, novel forms of 'co-ordination' have developed. Examples include new mechanisms of concertation – negotiation between social partners – that evolved at the firm level rather than at the national level. Since 1990, Italy has also seen 'the spread of decentralized levels of negotiation of public policies, especially [...] regarding employment and economic development' (Colombo and Regini 2016, p. 12). Local negotiation has been further stimulated by the increasing devolution of decision-making powers to Italian political regions.[15]

Fragmentation and interdependence also explain why political economic change has been slower and less drastic in Italy than in other nations, including other 'Mediterranean MMEs' such as Spain (Molina and Rhodes 2007, p. 236). In Italy market flexibility has not yet become the rule (though see below on the effects of the Euro zone crisis). Even market deregulation 'seems to apply mainly to new labour-market entrants' and has, by and large, been negotiated with trade unions (Colombo and Regini 2016, p. 7). Though this 'differentiation' of deregulation does raise interesting questions about new and existing fracture lines within the Italian political economy – here new entrants and old employees – it still militates against reducing the latter's evolution to simple 'liberalisation' (and again see here the parallels with Hassel's account of the 'dualisation' of the German labour market: 2014).

The Italian political economy has in fact seen a mix of adaptive changes and continuity, which has produced what Molina and Rhodes define as 'a series of puzzles': reforms that might have been expected to make Italy more 'liberal', have not in fact seen the nation transition to full fledged liberal 'post-Fordism'.[16] Italy has also retained its territorial segmentation across the years, with a particularly sharpening divide between Southern and Northern regions (Colombo and Regini 2016).

Arguably, the period since 2011 and Mario Monti's technical executive, has seen reforms that bear the hallmark of a (neo) liberalisation of the economy, with a relative reduction in labour protection (Prospero 2015, p. 280). Thus, though the majority of changes in labour flexibility have tended to concern labour market entry (Colombo and Regini 2016, p. 7), Italy *has* witnessed the dilution and eventual abolition of unfair dismissal rules that had applied to firms with 15 or more employees (law 183/2014; Fana *et al.* 2016). Similarly, in 2012 the Italian pension system was reformed 'by extending to all workers the contribution-based system' (Colombo and Regini 2016, p. 5), in line with other European pension systems likewise changed under pressure from the European Union (see Dawson and De Witte 2013, p. 825). The economic effect of these reforms is yet to be determined, both in terms of their lasting impact, and the potential differentiation of such an impact across territories.

In sum: The Italian political economy is internally diversified, and displays marked territorial differentiation (whether across three or more 'regions': Trigilia and Burroni 2009). In the VoC literature, Italy features as a 'mixed' market economy, and labour market and welfare reform have, over the years, failed to align Italy with either LME or CME models. Where the Italian political economy *has* been reformed in response to the 'crisis of Fordism', such changes have yielded a, sometimes contradictory, balance of more 'market' oriented reforms (e.g. increased labour flexibility) and new forms of co-ordination (e.g. local concertation). Forms of co-ordination in Italy should, however, be distinguished from the type of co-ordination presumed in the CME model, i.e. integration into a system that functions according to positive feedback mechanisms and coherence (Molina and Rhodes 2007, p. 226; Trigilia and Burroni 2009, p. 63). The Italian system is comparatively chaotic, such that changes *are* constrained, but in a way that reflects fragmentation and interdependence between its institutional actors. A question mark remains over reforms passed during the Euro zone crisis, as the most recent changes in matters of labour and pensions have *not* been negotiated (Colombo and Regini 2016, p. 7; Prospero 2015, p. 282). This raises interesting questions on the relationship between politics and political economy at the present historical moment, and its potential impact on punishment levels. These questions are, however, beyond the scope of this chapter.

The Italian political economy and the political economy of punishment

My argument in this chapter is that Italian penality cannot be systematised by reference to the political economy. In this section I explore this claim by relating De Giorgi's and Lacey's accounts of the economy-punishment link, to the Italian political economy.

De Giorgi's argument is premised on the shift from Fordism to post-Fordism: post-Fordism, with its increase in labour flexibility and labour market deregulation (De Giorgi 2006, p. 45), produces a surplus contained through (increasing) imprisonment. At the most basic level, for this theory to apply to Italy, the nation would have had to be 'Fordist' and then 'post-Fordist'. I argue that this is problematic. First, Italy *as a whole* cannot be described as ever having been Fordist. We have seen that the Italian political economy is territorially segmented. Authors such as Trigilia and Burroni have emphasised that 'mass industrial production' premised on 'relatively low-skilled labour' – characteristics of 'Fordism' – developed only in certain portions of Italy. Though these industries may have been seen as 'hypothetically valid for the entire nation', and become 'the implicit framework in debates on [economic] policies' (Reyneri [1989] 2010, p. 133), they did not in fact represent the whole Italian political economy: our 'Fordist' starting point therefore begins to waver.

If we then look at the political economic changes that have occurred in Italy, between 1970 and 2010, we face similar difficulties in classifying the nation as 'post-Fordist'. Admittedly some of the innovations detailed above do mirror characteristics associated with (narratives of) post-Fordist change: increased labour flexibility, decreased industrial production, increased reliance on the service sector. However, we have seen that such shifts were not unequivocal: they were contained and locally varied. To the extent that containment and variation were the result of negotiation, they also evidence the availability of veto points through which social and economic actors have influenced decision-making, steering Italy away from the 'post-Fordist' paradigm.

The resulting political economic scenario is difficult to classify: Italy remains 'mixed', with differences persisting across its fracture lines (territorial, but also between large firms and small firms, and increasingly between generations of workers). I therefore argue that the political economic restructuring experienced by Italy cannot be seen as a transition into De Giorgi's 'post-Fordism'. The upshot of this is that Italian penality cannot itself be explained by a shift into 'post-Fordism'.[17]

This is where comparative approaches to punishment provide greater flexibility in accounting for contemporary penality. They allow for variations in the political economy, and for variations in the shape of punishment itself: recall that Italy has not been unequivocally 'punitive' across the years. Italy does share some similarities with Lacey's CMEs, insofar as elements of the Italian economic system and welfare state have cumulatively created incentives for the reintegration of deviants into the economy and society. This has occurred, for example, where the co-negotiation of labour policy resulted in unemployment provisions such as the *Cassa Integrazione Guadagni* (CIG) – 'a special state redundancy fund that covers salaries of laid off workers' (Reyneri [1989] 2010, p. 137). This was campaigned for, and achieved, by the Italian trade unions during the 1970s, and still exists today (albeit with some modifications). Cumulatively, union policy concerned with employment protection has thus acted as a protective barrier for workers, halting or limiting their exclusion from the labour market, and protecting workers from the penal consequences thought to follow from economic exclusion.

In Italy we also find that family ties have continued to act as buffers against the worst effects of economic changes. Family ties provide de facto welfare support (see below), and enhanced employment opportunities, with the family also informing employment structures (Ginsborg 2001, p. 11; Mingione 1994; Mingione and Morlicchio 1993).[18] The Italian political economy thus sustains mechanisms of reintegration such as formal unemployment provision, but also the support provided by families to their members. The informal collaborative relations present within sectors of the Italian political economy also sustain re-integrative mechanisms. Thus, in the more deregulated areas of the 'Third Italy', reintegration can result from reliance on the kinship structure and personal relations on which small and medium-sized enterprises are premised. SMEs and their productive structures often require informal collaboration to function and flourish, and are thus likely to be ruptured by resort to penal law in the face of social conflict. Penal interventions sit poorly within informal trust networks, which can therefore be seen to act as a disincentive for resort to formal punishment. Such trust networks consequently act as an incentive for a (de facto) moderate approach to punishment, and are also likely to act as a means of *informal social control* – pre-empting deviance – particularly where the enterprises rest on family or family-like ties (Gallo 2015; Garland 2001, pp. 89–90; Nelken 2014, p. 282).

It therefore appears that the Italian political economy *does* produce incentives towards reintegration, where local political economies are so structured that the exclusion of deviants disrupts their socio-political and economic balance. These local political economies can be said to sustain scarcity. This suggests that structural factors in Italy have persisted, that stand in the way of the exclusionary penality thought to accompany a free, 'liberal' economic system.

Clearly, here I am adopting Lacey's approach of identifying the penal incentives that follow from different political economic setups. However, given the diversity of the Italian economy, I argue that a focus on the political economy alone, still fails us where we wish to *systematise* Italian penality. We lack, that is, an organising principle with which to explain Italy's fluctuation between repression and leniency, and with which to produce an account that neither crowbars Italy into existing materialist frameworks, nor reduces it merely to its irreducibly 'Italian' features.

The problem here is at heart a methodological one: a hybrid economy does not lend itself to the construction of analytical frameworks that correlate 'the' political economy to punishment (Gallo 2015, pp. 17–18). In arguing this, I am *not* arguing that political economic dynamics do not affect Italian punishment. We have seen that the distribution of political economic incentives for reintegration of the workforce, *do* influence the highs and lows of Italian punishment. At is most basic, Italy can also be described in terms of the axiom of economic analyses of punishment (as articulated for example by Loïc Wacquant 2009a, 2009b), according to which punishment and poverty are closely correlated. This correlation is apparent, for example, in the incarceration of immigrants in Italy, with non-EU migrants overrepresented in Italian prisons (Melossi 2015, p. 67; also De Giorgi 2006, pp. 111–138, 2010).

Following Lacey, we nonetheless need to differentiate here between 'insiders' and 'outsiders': I argue that the overrepresentation of non-EU migrants in Italian prisons reflects their exclusion from those structures that provide natives (insiders) with a relative insulation from the formal criminal justice system. Note that this exclusion from re-integrative structures may persist even where non-EU migrants are in fact included within the Italian labour market. Well-rooted families are examples of such structures (see Mingione 1994, p. 28), capable of acting as informal means of social control, or of providing surrogate welfare support (Mingione 2009, p. 232). Patron-client relations are another example – that does not necessarily follow strict economic 'logic' – where income transfers occur from patron to client, acting as a surrogate for welfare provision, and (particularly where patronage relationships skirt illegality) also acting as an incentive for informal resolution of conflict (Gallo 2015, p. 603; see also Della Porta and Vannucci 2012). The mechanisms attendant on patronage are not available to non-EU migrants given that they lack the characteristic necessary to being a political client, namely voting rights (on which see Zincone 2006, p. 355). Note how exclusion from this particular 'locus' of reintegration does not follow exclusion from the labour market, but rather follows formal exclusion from the political community.[19]

Here Italy displays additional similarities to CMEs, which also 'reserve' their punitiveness to outsiders. Yet in Italy, this outsider status bears a particularly *political* flavour (Gallo 2015; on the importance of political contacts within the Italian political economy, see Trento 2012, p. 444) as migrants' exclusions is not necessarily, or not merely, exclusion from productive activity. Significantly, it is also exclusion from those broad political institutions – families, informal trust networks, patronage relations – that allow Italians to stave off economic marginality, *but also* catalyse penal diversion for their members (Gallo 2015, pp. 608–609, 611).

In sum: though punishment and the political economy *are* linked in Italy, the Italian political economy is too much of a hybrid to act as the key organising principle in an explanation of Italian penality. It is here that political variables provide us with a better framework with which to understand Italian punishment. As I will show in the following sections, political dynamics become the bridge that connects punishment to the political economy.

Fragmentation, permeability and penal incentives

We recall that Italian penality is characterised simultaneously by both punitiveness and moderation. This penal 'dualism' extends throughout the Italian penal system (Gallo 2015, pp. 600–605) and reflects, *inter alia*, Italy's reliance on informal social controls alongside formal penal censure. If, as I argue, politics are a key organising principle for Italian penality, how are we to understand the impact that politics have on punishment? Here I argue that political variables affect penality at a number of levels, post-war politics having constrained the evolution of the Italian political economy (Salvati 2000) and subsequently its penal effects.

In order to fully understand just how politics have affected Italian punishment, we need to look at the Italian institutional structure (for this method see Lacey 2008, 2011; Savelsberg 1994, 1999) and at how direct and visible the link can be between political arrangements – for example party dynamics – and policy evolution. This includes both criminal justice and political economic policy. In this respect it is significant that the Italian institutional structure can be said to have *incorporated* political conflict, magnifying rather than containing its effect on the functioning of the Italian polity (Ginsborg 2001, xi). It is also important that Italy can be conceived of as organised around constant political conflict (Bickerton and Invernizzi Accetti 2014, p. 23; Gallo 2015, p. 611; Lazar 2013, p. 321; Pavarini 1994, p. 52). The nation is composed of different political groupings that exist at various levels (for example parties but also kinship networks or political clienteles) all of which compete for power, resource distribution, and influence over decision-making. The visibility of such political conflict in post-war Italy can be explained as a function of the *fragmentation* of interests, and of the high *permeability* of decision-making to such interests (Lange and Regini [1989] 2010, pp. 22, 255; Rebuffa 1996, p. 156). Permeability follows from the high number of veto points present in the Italian institutional structure (Bull and Rhodes 2009, p. 3; Gallo 2015, pp. 611–612). Interests capable of exploiting this permeability include political parties but also what Alessandro Pizzorno refers to as the 'intermediate stratum' of the political class: '[party] currents, groups, clans, clienteles, single individuals and their personal following' (Pizzorno 1997, p. 340, my translation). I would also add social partners such as trade unions to this list – the latter having been engaged in policy negotiations across the decades – and other broadly speaking political groups such as well-rooted families. Political conflict should then be understood as the competition between these different interests.

This combination of fragmentation, conflict and permeability has led to policy decisions in Italy being influenced by the numerous pressures present within the system, so that policy does not in fact respond to any single agenda (Lange and Regini 2010; Salvati 2000, p. 112). Here we find the roots of Italy's political economic hybridity: Italy is a system in which 'a myriad of particular interests crystallise [...] seeking mutual protection [and] recognition' (Lange and Regini [1989] 2010, p. 267; Rebuffa 2007, p. 14). This produces 'a crazy quilt of sometimes contradictory, sometimes complementary modes and institutions for regulating the production and allocation of resources' which tend not to 'reflect the [aims] of any single actor or coalition' (Lange and Regini [1989] 2010, p. 267). In this sense Italy should be understood as a system that incorporates, but does not broker, stable compromises between the divided interests that it encounters. The Italian setup is therefore one marked more by reluctant interdependence than the harmonious co-operation associated with archetypal CMEs.

To further explain Italy's fragmentation and conflict, we can then look to the post-war Italian party system. Italy has been described as a 'republic of parties' (particularly between 1945 and 1990), i.e. a system within which political parties are the primary players, 'occupying' the state at national and local levels (Cotta and Verzichelli 2007, pp. 35–66; Pasquino 1995a, 2002; for a critical appraisal of the term, see Urbinati and Ragazzoni 2016). Pizzorno, for example, describes how the post-war governing parties – in particular the Christian Democracy – and their various constitutive groups (internal factions and affiliated interest groups) possessed a 'quota' of power that they used to veto legislative initiatives, or to broker political deals (1997, p. 319). Political parties were also involved in so-called *lottizzazione*: 'the subdivision of jobs and public posts, within public bodies and institutions, according to political rather than professional criteria' (Treccani 2010; also Schmidt and Gualmini 2013). Through this process, state institutions and resources have been divided up among and within parties (Pasquino 1995, pp. 347–348). This process was facilitated by the initial presence of a high level of party influence over job allocation and over economic resources (Pasquino 2002, p. 24). Over time the process has changed – after the 1990s (and again in recent years) Italian parties have been modified (Bickerton and Invernizzi Accetti 2014; Cotta and Verzichelli 2007, pp. 35–66; Pasquino 2002), as has their control over state resources. After the combined effect of the 1992 political corruption scandal known as *Tangentopoli* (on which see Nelken 1996), and after the end of the cold war, the post-war mass parties dissolved, and were replaced by new parties with new names and identities (Cotta and Verzichelli

2007, p. 55). These new parties were smaller; less capillary; less overtly ideological (Cotta and Verzichelli 2007, p. 54; Pasquino 2002, pp. 157–158; on the penal implications of this ideological change see Gallo 2015, p. 612). However, it can be argued that the practice of state occupation by particular interests has persisted (Pasquino 1995, p. 353), not least because belligerence and wrangling have continued, between and within parties and coalitions (Rebuffa 2007, p. 18).

It is this continuing 'carving up' of Italian institutions along political lines that has incorporated political conflict into the workings of the Italian system. Italy can therefore be seen as a nation in which political contrasts have not been reconciled within a 'collective project' that would have directed the Italian political economy towards one model, be it liberal or co-ordinated (Salvati 2000, p. 112). The absence of a collective project has also made it more difficult to create (national) collective goods (Della Porta 1996; Molina and Rhodes 2007, p. 231; Regini 1997, p. 107). This difficulty has important implications for the purchase of formal state law, including the criminal law: where the law appears as responsive to particular interests, rather than geared to serving the entire collectivity, it tends to lose purchase among its citizens. This in turn suggests a structurally incentivised willingness for citizens to rely on informal, rather than formal, legal norms (Gallo 2015). The particularisation of the law, and its compromised purchase, stimulate what has been referred to as Italy's 'widespread illegality': 'traditional practices of moderate but pervasive violations of the law' (Melossi 2003, p. 382; Nelken 2014, p. 282; Pavarini 1994, p. 50; also Gallo 2015, p. 608).

We have here a political system that is at one permeable and fragmented, and that has incorporated political conflict but failed to broker a stable compromise between its different 'factions'. What are the implications of this setup for Italian penality and its alternation between punitiveness and moderation? I argue that this political setup can be reconnected to penality insofar as *each level of political conflict can be seen as producing different penal pressures, in favour of penal exclusion or penal moderation*. Political conflict produces these contrasting pressures by affecting policies that directly or indirectly influence penality: this includes criminal justice policy, but also economic and social reforms. The conflict is diffuse – negotiation and renegotiation between fragmented political interests – and therefore produces *variable* penal pressures, which are then reflected in Italian penality's oscillation between punitiveness and moderation. It is in the effect of diffuse political conflict on economic and social reforms, that the link between the political economy and punishment is most visible, with politics – permeable institutions, conflicting players, puzzling policy agendas – acting as the bridge between a hybrid political economy and a dual penality.

From politics to punishment: the welfare state, political constraints and penal incentives

In this section I use the Italian welfare state to illustrate how Italian penality can be explained by reference to politics, while also accommodating the political economy into our understanding of punishment. Note that by looking at the couplet 'welfare-punishment' I am building on, and implicitly accepting, the starting point of literature that has correlated the two phenomena (see Beckett and Western 2001). At its most basic, this line of literature argues that the greater the welfare coverage, the lesser the likelihood of penal expansion; conversely, the lesser the welfare coverage, the greater the likelihood of penal expansion.

Italy can be said to possess a state-driven, 'social transfer-oriented welfare state' (Hancké et al. 2007, p. 26) limited by sector and territory (Mingione 1995). The divisions of the Italian political economy are mirrored in its welfare state, which is at one corporatist *and* fragmented (Ferrera 1996, p. 19), and maps imperfectly on to the 'standard liberal versus social democratic/[...] continental division' (Molina and Rhodes 2007, p. 225). Italy provides welfare entitlements to some (Ferrera 1996, p. 19), but excludes others from its provisions, and does so along definite fracture lines. Like the corporatist nations alongside which Esping-Andersen classifies it – Austria, France and Germany – Italy distributes social rights on the basis of status differentials, particularly individuals' position within the labour market (Cavadino and Dignan 2006, p. 17; Esping-Andersen 1990, pp. 26–32; Paci 2009, p. 298). Like other 'southern European' welfare systems, Italy then also favours employment protection over social protection (Ferrera 1996; Molina and Rhodes 2007, p. 226). Further divisions across which welfare is distributed include those between large and small firms, with labour regulation and welfare entitlements concentrated in large firms.[20] As mentioned, there are also regional divisions in welfare provisions, which reflect the territorial distribution of different economic activities (Colombo and Regini 2016, pp. 4–7), and the distribution of different sized firms across the nation.

According to Maurizio Ferrera, the most visible differentiation in Italian welfare is between a 'core sector of the labour market force located within the [...] regular market' and those located in irregular or less regulated sectors. The latter are entitled to 'weak subsidization' (Ferrera 1996, p. 19). Here, where formal entitlements are 'weak', additional support structures such as the family act to supplement welfare deficits (Ferrera 1996, p. 21). The family typically allows a sharing of protection, which moves from one member 'anchored' in the core labour sectors, to the remaining members (Ferrera 1996, p. 25). This sharing of welfare responsibilities is not exclusive to Italy, but is a feature of the corporatist welfare model in which state support is complemented by support from more traditional institutions such as the Church and the family (Cavadino and Dignan 2006, p. 18; Esping-Andersen 1990, p. 27). Perhaps more particular to Italy is the fact that political clientelism has also provided a measure of de facto redistribution of welfare, where 'the emergence of a "clientelistic market"' ensured 'state transfers to supplement inadequate work income [in exchange for] party support' (Ferrera 1996, p. 25). The centrality of income transfers – rather than service provisions – as measures of social support (Ascoli 1984; Paci 1987, 2009; Saraceno, 1994) may have facilitated this 'clientelistic' redistribution of entitlements. Income transfers are easier to distribute in a particularistic manner, and are also more susceptible to being used as 'currency' within a clientelistic exchange (Paci 2009, p. 276).

The Italian welfare system thus emerges as a mixed system where corporatist features co-exist with more universal welfare provisions,[21] and where the 'formal resemblance' to 'universalistic welfare states' combines with a 'particularistic' division of resources (Ferrera 1996, p. 25). The 'ethos' of such a welfare state is to some extent 'communitarian' and, in keeping with the 'overall philosophy […] of conservative corporatism', is premised on the integration of 'all citizens within the nation' (Cavadino and Dignan 2006, pp. 17–18). However, integration occurs via individuals' membership of interest groups and other social groupings (such as labour categories) that act as a link between the individual and the state (Cavadino and Dignan 2006, p. 17). This membership of intermediate interest groups is in fact a crucial characteristic of Italian welfare, and indeed of the Italian polity as a whole (Gallo 2015), though it may not have bound Italians so much to the nation as to their specific interest groups. Here again we find echoes of Italy's particularism and fragmentation.

The Italian welfare state has a number of effects on penal incentives. First, the 'corporatist' and occasional 'universalistic' features in Italian welfare offer some protection against what Cavadino and Dignan call the 'vicissitudes of unfettered market forces' (2006, p. 24). Economic exclusion is kept at bay with methods of support built into the Italian welfare state, whether support is through the provision of (some) services, or the provision of income. Support is likely to reduce exposure to formal penal sanction, where the latter is precipitated by economic marginality (Rusche [1933] 1978, p. 4; De Giorgi 2010, p. 149 on 'crimes of desperation'). However, the support provided by Italian welfare is fragmented, because divided by occupational status, by regional divergences in welfare provision (Saraceno 1994, p. 77) and across the large firm/small firm divide.

Where state-provided welfare support is not sufficient, we find increased reliance on 'private' forms of support. This interplay produces a dualism between public and private welfare in Italy – enhanced by clientelistic use of welfare entitlements – which further suggests that the Italian welfare state *does* create incentives to social and economic inclusion, but that these incentives are *stratified* and *conditional*. They may not be conditional on market forces, as in the more 'unfettered' (neo) liberal systems, but they do rest upon *qualifying* for support: through direct anchorage via the labour market, through indirect anchorage via a family member, through membership of a patron-client relation. These conditions for inclusion simultaneously provide a potential for the *exclusion* of those who do not 'qualify', as non-EU migrants might not.

A corollary of this dynamic is that, where welfare support passes through 'intermediate' bodies such as the family, or intermediate 'private' uses of the public realm such as clientelistic redistribution, this reinforces citizens' intermediate loyalties (Gallo 2015, p. 603). Should these loyalties develop in contrast to formal state norms, for example where a supposedly universalistic provision is carved up along politicised lines, then this dynamic will impact upon allegiance to state law.

I argue that here we find incentives for citizens not to rely on formal state censure in the resolution of social conflict. We also find incentives to respond to social conflict at the level of the intermediate loyalties and their normative dynamics (Cavadino and Dignan 2006, p. 25; Gallo 2015, p. 603; Nelken 1994, p. 234). The Italian welfare state can thus be reconnected to Italy's de facto penal moderation, which is stratified (as are the more formal incentives to penal re-inclusion) by membership of intermediate orders (Gallo 2015, p. 610).

Stratified is also the exposure to penal exclusion that comes from economic marginality: it falls most intensely on those who do not qualify for formal or informal support – *political*, as well as economic, outsiders who lack integration into the mechanisms that catalyse penal diversion. Here Italy again shares some features with CMEs and, as in CMEs, 'outsiders' tend to be non-EU migrants (Lacey 2008, pp. 106–109).

Where, in this welfare setup, do we see politics, such that politics operate as an organising principle with which to systematise Italian penality? Politics are relevant to the particular form taken by the Italian welfare state. The parties that dominated the post-war Italian political scene, in particular the Christian Democracy (DC) and the Communist Party (PCI), were both forces that stimulated a form of (broadly speaking) 'communitarian' welfare state (Cavadino and Dignan 2006, p. 140). Both, in their different ways and for different reasons, stood in the way of Italy becoming a liberal market economy, and stood in the way of the 'rolling back' of the welfare state that we have come to associate with 'late modernity', 'post-Fordism', 'neo-liberalism' or indeed LMEs (Lacey 2011, p. 229).

Politics are then relevant to the conflict between these two parties and their attendant ideologies: from the end of the Second World War to the early 1990s, Italian politics were formally organised around the broad division between the DC and the PCI, between Catholicism and Communism. We have seen that Salvati (2000) has pointed to this formal enmity as one of the reasons why the Italian political economy, and within it the welfare state, developed in a 'hybrid' fashion rather than becoming obviously liberal or obviously social democratic. Political conflict, within a system permeable to such conflict, subjected the evolution of Italian welfare to competing forces and competing visions.

Moving to more general features of the Italian political system, we then see another example of politics influencing welfare. Ugo Ascoli (1984) has observed that short-term political objectives have played an important role in the evolution of Italian welfare. In his account of the history of Italian welfare, Ascoli repeatedly mentions the 'use of social legislation' as a means to manufacture political consensus, and to increase the legitimacy of those in power (1984, esp. 43). This was a featured carried through from fascism, into the Italian Republic, and is thought to have brought about 'clientelistic dependency' among Italians (Saraceno 1994, p. 63), where welfare is used within a clientelistic exchange (see Della Porta 1992, p. 235). It is in this political use of welfare that we find a reason for the particularism of social provisions in Italy. Similarly, fragmentation of welfare support is rooted in the political use of 'social legislation' that aimed to attain the consensus of the social interests that multiplied after the Second World War (Ascoli 1984, p. 30).[22] Here Ascoli (echoed by Paci) describes the growth of Italian welfare as an 'incremental process': responding to 'specific pressures and problems' and interests, rather than a more unitary plan (Ascoli 1984, pp. 31, 38). This 'incremental' growth is significant because it represents the general tendency within the Italian system for reform to be likewise incremental, and responsive to short-term political pressures, creating *penal* incentives that are variable because they too are influenced by the tensions of a conflictual politics.

The dynamics that I have described – where welfare is carved up along political lines, or supplemented by surrogate support, leading its beneficiaries to develop intermediate loyalties that do not necessarily overlap with loyalty to the state – are themselves eminently political. They reflect the internal fragmentation of the Italian state, and its citizens' divided allegiances. Both these features reconnect to the existence of, and reliance on, the informal social controls that in part account for Italy's moderation (Gallo 2015, pp. 607–609). The informal social controls follow from citizens' belonging and allegiance to intermediate orders, orders that possess their own intermediate norms that may or may not overlap with state laws (Gallo 2015, p. 611). To the extent that a 'particularisation' of general norms, and a reliance on informal social controls, connects to Italy's diffuse illegality (Baldissera 2006, p. 69; Melossi 2003, p. 382; Nelken 2014, p. 282; Pavarini 1994, p. 50) it simultaneously creates the potential for heightened punitiveness. Indeed, as I have argued elsewhere (Gallo 2015), this punitiveness represents the state's attempt to impose its authority in the face of a conflictual, and internally divided, polity. Punishment and the criminal law are deployed in an attempt to counter diffuse illegality, and to paste over the fracture lines of a fragmented polity. Here, then, we have both punitiveness and moderation, both of which are sustained by political economic structures that incentivise differential reintegration, and that are hybrid because they reflect political contingency in a permeable institutional context.

Conclusions

In this chapter I have set up a conversation between existing materialist analyses of punishment and the Italian case. I have argued that Italian penality, with its alternation of punitiveness and moderation, cannot be systematically explained by reference to its political economy. Contrary to the assumptions contained in more macroscopic accounts of 'post-Fordist' penality, but also in the comparative penal literature premised on the VoC models, Italy presents us with a fundamentally hybrid political economy. The latter has, over the years, been shaped by the multiplicity of, broadly speaking, political groups that the nation is composed of. The Italian political economy thus expresses the polity's fragmentation and its institutional permeability.

I have argued that we can nonetheless factor the political economy into our understanding of Italian penality, if we focus on *politics*: in particular political institutions with their multiple veto points, and political culture, both of which (institutions and culture) have shaped Italian economic policy. Politics here act as the bridge between a hybrid political economy and a dual penality, between an 'incoherent' economic model and a penality characterised by both punitiveness and by moderation

I have used the Italian welfare state to illustrate my analytical conclusions. Political conflict, as well as short-term political pressures, have influenced the Italian welfare state, such that the welfare state provides some, but uneven, protection. To the extent that welfare protection correlates with punishment, we can say that, at the penal level, the incentives created by Italian welfare are reintegrative *but only in part*. Incentives for reintegration operate primarily for citizens who belong, where belonging is to be understood as something more than inclusion into the labour market. It also touches upon belonging to broader political structures that protect against economic marginality *and* incentivise informal resolution of social conflict.

What are the broader implications of these findings? I argue that the Italian case study casts further doubt on the inevitability of the political economy-punishment couplet. The political economy is responsive to politics – its agents and their cultural and institutional contexts. This responsiveness is particularly visible in Italy; but arguably it exists even where the role of politics is masked by coherent, national, economic models. The Italian example suggests that we need to be more attentive to the particular political contingencies that allow for seeming economic and penal convergence, particularly where convergence is towards greater inequality and greater punitiveness. Closer attention to the political processes and reforms that stand between one economic model and another, and between a polity's economy and its penality, may help us, if not replicate virtuous reforms across contexts, then at least stave off those changes that correlate with a growth in punitiveness. By problematising the linearity of materialist analyses of punishment, Italy's hybrid model may sharpen our eye to the political conditions of penal harshness and penal moderation.

Notes

1 See Loader (2010) for the need to transcend incarceration as the only measure of 'punitiveness'.
2 These planned deflations of the prison population produce moderation within the Italian system, even when they are motivated primarily by pragmatic reasons (Gallo 2015, p. 608). In a similar vein see here Michael Tonry in his discussion of the implausibility of amnesties in the Anglo-American context (2007, p. 37). On amnesties and pardons see also Levy (2007) and see Loader (2010) on complicating the notion of penal 'moderation'.
3 On conceptualising punitiveness and moderation as points on a spectrum rather than mutually exclusive see Nelken (2005). In this chapter punitiveness is being gauged primarily by reference to imprisonment rates: where high and increasing imprisonment rates are an indication of punitiveness, and a symptom of qualitative changes in punishment (see above). The implication is that moderation can also be understood in

terms of incarceration, and in particular in terms of a parsimonious use of imprisonment. On the numerous meanings of moderation again see Loader (2010), and Gallo (2015).
4 Notable examples of authors who have also addressed this link include Loïc Wacquant (2009a, 2009b), Robert Reiner (2007), and David Garland (2001).
5 Note that I am not presuming that it will indeed be possible to replicate such features across contexts, nor am I eschewing this possibility outright.
6 See also Wacquant (2009a) on the 'spread' of a neo-liberal common sense, including the neo-liberal recipes for economy, welfare and punishment.
7 In his later work, De Giorgi (2013) engages more explicitly with Lacey's comparative account.
8 For a critical perspective on the resistance to this 'divergence' see Wolfgang Streeck's analysis of German capitalism (2008).
9 Such as education, and training in company/sector specific skills.
10 The statute that set out workers' rights, applied only to firms with 15 or more workers: Legge 20 Maggio 1970, n. 300.
11 The expansion of fixed-term contracts culminated in 2003 (Colombo and Regini 2016, p. 7, referencing law 30/2003).
12 On the problem with having a framework in which only two models exist see Crouch (2005); on the limits of considering change only in terms of convergence and divergence from the liberal model see Streeck (2008).
13 By 'social model' Colombo and Regini mean a relatively generous welfare regime; labour market regulation which seeks to balance flexibility and high employment/ income protection; institutionalised industrial relations based on 'coordinated collective bargaining and [...] participation of the social partners in economic and social policy-making' (2016, p. 4).
14 Union density data for 1980 set Italy at 48 per cent, Germany at 35 per cent and the UK at 51 per cent (Gumbrell-McCormick and Hyman 2013, p. 5). Collective bargaining coverage for 2010 was 80 per cent for Italy, 33 per cent for the UK and 62 per cent for Germany. These data measure 'the extent to which the terms of workers' employment are influenced by collective negotiation' and is calculated on the number of employees covered by the collective agreements, divided by the total number of wage and salary earners (OECD glossary of statistical terms, https://stats.oecd.org/glossary/detail.asp?ID=3554. accessed 3 November 2016).
15 In 2001 the Italian constitution was modified and regions' competencies increased. See Menichelli (2015, p. 267).
16 That these should be 'puzzles' may well be the result of the expectations inherent in the VoC models, which have been critiqued both for having a bipartite model of political economies – LME and CME – and for assuming limited (as well as 'economically rational') patterns of change in such economies (Crouch 2005).
17 It might, of course, be possible to try and verify whether there are any 'regions' of Italy that have become post-Fordist, having started out as Fordist during the 1950s and 1960s, and to investigate whether or not punishment in such regions can be understood as the containment of the contemporary surplus. However I argue that to do so would be, in a sense, to distort De Giorgi's account: his analysis does not set itself out as having merely regional purchase.
18 Note also Trento's definition of contemporary Italian capitalism as still 'personal and familial' (2012, p. 442 my translation).
19 On the link between membership and punishment and its importance for non-EU migrants see, *inter alia*, Barker (2013).
20 For a historical overview of Italian economic divisions see Ginsborg (2001, pp. 13–29).

21 Notable examples of Italy's more 'typically' corporatist measures are work pensions and unemployment benefits, where the extent of coverage varies on the basis of individuals' occupational status (Saraceno 1994, p. 64). Examples of universalistic measures include the introduction of mandatory schooling (1962) and of a national health service (1978). These measures are universalistic in principle but have, since their introduction, not necessarily been universalistic in practice. Thus there are some health tasks, such as laboratory analyses, delegated to private clinics or labs, but paid for via public social contributions (Granaglia 1987, pp. 302–303, Paci 2009, p. 289).

22 The 1950s and 1960s, for example, saw reforms geared to satisfy the growing middle classes, and in particular Italy's self-employed workers (Ascoli 1984, p. 20).

Bibliography

Ascoli, U. (1984). Il Sistema Italiano di Welfare. *In*: Ascoli, U., ed., *Welfare State all'Italiana*. Roma: Editori Laterza, 5–52.

Bagnasco, A. (1977). *Tre Italie: la problematica territoriale dello sviluppo Italiano*. Bologna: Il Mulino.

Baldissera, A. (2006). L'illegalità diffusa in Italia: un'interpretazione sociologica. *Quaderni di Sociologia*, 50, 65–83.

Barker, V. (2013). Democracy and Deportation: Why Membership Matters Most. *In*: Aas, K.F. and Bosworth, M., eds, *The Borders of Punishment. Migration, Citizenship, and Social Exclusion*. Oxford: Oxford University Press, 237–254.

Beckett, K. and Western, B. (2001). Welfare, Incarceration, and the Transformation of State Policy. *In*: Garland, D., ed., *Mass Imprisonment*. London: Sage, 35–50.

Bickerton, C. and Invernizzi Accetti, C. (2014). Democracy Without Parties? Italy after Berlusconi. *The Political Quarterly*, 85, 23–28.

Bull, M. and Rhodes, M. (2009). Introduction – Italy a Contested Polity. *In*: Bull, M. and Rhodes, M., eds, *Italy – A Contested Polity*. Abingdon: Routledge, 1–14.

Cassese, S. (1993). Hypotheses on the Italian Administrative System. *West European Politics*, 16, 316–328.

Cavadino, M. and Dignan, J. (2006). *Penal Systems. A Comparative Approach*. London: Sage.

Colombo, S. and Regini, M. (2016). Territorial Differences in the Italian 'Social Model'. *Regional Studies*, 50, 20–34.

Cotta, M. and Verzichelli, L. (2007). *Political Institutions in Italy*. Oxford: Oxford University Press.

Crouch, C. (2005). *Capitalist Diversity and Change*. Oxford: Oxford University Press.

Dawson, M. and De Witte, F. (2013). Constitutional Balance in the EU after the Eurocrisis. *Modern Law Review*, 76, 817–844.

De Cecco, M. (2009). Italy's Dysfunctional Political Economy. *In*: Bull, M. and Rhodes, M., eds, *Italy – A Contested Polity*. Abingdon: Routledge, 107–127.

De Giorgi, A. (2006). *Re-Thinking the Political Economy of Punishment*. Aldershot: Ashgate.

De Giorgi, A. (2010). Immigration Control, Post-Fordism and Less Eligibility: A Materialist Critique of the Criminalization of Immigration across Europe. *Punishment and Society*, 12, 147–167.

De Giorgi, A. (2013). Punishment and Political Economy. *In*: Simon, J. and Sparks, R., eds, *The SAGE Handbook of Punishment and Society*. London: Sage, 40–59.

Della Porta, D. (1992). *Lo Scambio Occulto*, Bologna: il Mulino.
Della Porta, D. (1996). I circoli viziosi tra corruzione, clientelismo e cattiva amministrazione. *In*: Scamuzzi, S., ed., *Italia Illegale*. Torino: Rosenberg & Sellier, 95–116.
Della Porta, D. and Vannucci, A. (2012). *The Hidden Order of Corruption*. Aldershot: Ashgate.
Esping-Andersen, G. (1990). *The Three Worlds of Welfare Capitalism*. Cambridge: Polity Press.
Fana, M., Guarascio, D. and Cirillo, V. (2016). Did Italy Need More Labour Flexibility? *Intereconomics*, 51, 79–86.
Ferrera, M. (1996). The 'Southern Model' of Welfare in Social Europe. *Journal of European Social Policy*, 6, 17–37.
Gallo, Z. (2015). Punishment, Authority, and Political Economy: Italian Challenges to Western Punitiveness. *Punishment and Society*, 17, 598–523.
Garland, D. (2001). *The Culture of Control*. Oxford: Oxford University Press.
Ginsborg, P. (2001). *Italy and Its Discontents 1980–2001*. London: Penguin Books.
Granaglia, E. (1987). Intervento pubblico e politica sanitaria: un'analisi delle tendenze in atto. *In*: Lange, P. and Regini, M., eds, *Stato e Regolazione Sociale*. Bologna: il Mulino, 295–313.
Gumbrell-McCormick, R. and Hyman, R. (2013). *Trade Unions in Western Europe: Hard Times, Hard Choices*. Oxford: Oxford University Press.
Hall, P. and Soskice, D. (2001). *Varieties of Capitalism*. Oxford: Oxford University Press.
Hancké, B., Rhodes, M. and Thatcher, M. (2007). Introduction: Beyond Varieties of Capitalism. *In*: Hancké, B., Rhodes, M. and Thatcher, M., eds, *Beyond Varieties of Capitalism*. Oxford: Oxford University Press, 3–38.
Hassell, A. (2014). The Paradox of Liberalisation – Understanding Dualism and the Recovery of the German Political Economy. *British Journal of Industrial Relations*, 52, 57–81.
Hudson, B. (2003). *Understanding Justice*. Maidenhead: Open University Press.
International Centre for Prison Studies (last accessed 9 November 2011). *World Prison Brief*. London: ICPS.
ISTAT (2013). *Occupati e disoccupati dati ricostruiti dal 1977*. Roma: ISTAT.
Lacey, N. (2008). *The Prisoners' Dilemma*. Cambridge: Cambridge University Press.
Lacey, N. (2011). Why Globalisation Doesn't Spell Convergence: Models of Institutional Variation and the Comparative Political Economy of Punishment. *In*: Crawford, A., ed., *International and Comparative Criminal Justice and Urban Governance*. Cambridge: Cambridge University Press, 214–250.
Lacey, N. (2013). Punishment, (Neo)Liberalism and Social Democracy. *In*: Simon, J. and Sparks, R., eds, *The Sage Handbook of Punishment and Society*. London: SAGE, 260–280.
Lange, P. and Regini, M. ([1989] 2010). *State, Market and Social Regulation*. Cambridge: Cambridge University Press.
Lazar, M. (2013). Testing Italian Democracy. *Comparative European Politics*, 11, 317–336.
Legge 20 maggio 1970, n. 300.
Legge 14 febbraio 2003, n. 20.
Legge 10 dicembre 2014, n. 188.
Lévy, R. (2007). Pardons and Amnesties as Policy Instruments in Contemporary France.

In: Tonry, M., ed., *Crime, Punishment and Politics in Comparative Perspective.* Chicago: University of Chicago Press, 551–590.
Loader, I. (2010). For Penal Moderation. *Theoretical Criminology*, 14, 349–367.
Melossi, D. (2003). 'In a Peaceful Life'. Migration and the Crime of Modernity in Europe/Italy. *Punishment and Society*, 5, 371–397.
Melossi, D. (2015). *Crime, Punishment and Migration.* London: Sage.
Melossi, D. and Pavarini, M. (1977). *Carcere e Fabbrica.* Bologna: Il Mulino.
Menichelli, F. (2015). The National Picture: The Reconfiguration of Sovereignty, the Normalization of Emergency and the Rise to Prominence of Urban Security in Italy. *European Journal of Criminology*, 12, 263–276.
Mingione, E. (1994). Life Strategies and Social Economies in the Postfordist Age. *International Journal of Urban and Regional Research*, 18, 24–45.
Mingione, E. (1995). Labour Market Segmentation and Informal Work in Southern Europe. *European Urban and Regional Studies*, 2, 121–143.
Mingione, E. (2009). Family, Welfare and Districts. The Local Impact of New Migrants in Italy. *European Urban and Regional Studies*, 16, 225–236.
Mingione, E. and Morlicchio, E. (1993). New Forms of Urban Poverty in Italy: Risk Path Models in the North and South. *International Journal of Urban and Regional Research*, 17, 413–427.
Molina, O. and Rhodes, M. (2007). The Political Economy of Adjustment in Mixed Market Economies: A Study of Spain and Italy. In: Hancké, B., Rhodes, M. and Thatcher, M., eds, *Beyond Varieties of Capitalism.* Oxford: Oxford University Press, 223–252.
Nelken, D. (1994). Whom Can You Trust? The Future of Comparative Criminology. In: Nelken, D., ed., *The Futures of Criminology.* London: Sage, 220–243.
Nelken, D. (1996). The Judges and Political Corruption in Italy. *Journal of Law and Society*, 23, 95–112.
Nelken, D. (2005). When is a Society Non-punitive? The Italian Case. In: Pratt, J., ed., *The New Punitiveness.* Cullompton: Willan, 218–235.
Nelken, D. (2014). Of Rights and Favours. *Law and Society Review*, 48, 275–228.
OECD. Union Members and Employees.
Paci, M. (1987). Pubblico e privato nel sistema Italiano di welfare. In: Lange, P. and Regini, M., eds, *Stato e Regolazione Sociale.* Bologna: Il Mulino, 271–293.
Paci, M. (2009). Il regime corporativo di welfare tra resistenza e cambiamento. Alcune riflessioni sui casi Italiano e Francese. *Rassegna Italiana di Sociologia*, 50, 279–299.
Pasquino, G. (1995). La Partitocrazia. In: Pasquino, G., ed., *La Politica Italiana Dizionario Critico 1945–95.* Roma: Editori Laterza, 341–354.
Pasquino, G. (2002). *Il sistema politico italiano.* Bologna: Bononia University Press.
Pavarini, M. (1994). The New Penology and Politics in Crisis: The Italian Case. *British Journal of Criminology*, 34, 49–61.
Pizzorno, A. (1997). Le trasformazioni del sistema politico italiano, 1976–92. In: Barbagallo, F., ed., *Storia dell'Italia Repubblicana: III. L'Italia nella crisi mondiale. L'ultimo ventennio: 2. Istituzioni, politiche, culture.* Torino: Giulio Einaudi Editore, 301–344.
Prospero, M. (2015). *Il nuovismo realizzato.* Roma: Bordeaux edizioni.
Rebuffa, G. (2007). Antichi vizi e nuovi interessi del corporativismo. *il Mulino*, 1, 14–20.
Regini, M. (1997). Social Institutions and Production Structure. The Italian Variety of

Capitalism in the 1980s. *In*: Crouch, C. and Streeck, W., eds, *Political Economy and Modern Capitalism: Mapping Convergence and Diversity*. London: Sage, 102–116.

Reiner, R. (2007). *Law and Order. An Honest Citizen's Guide to Crime and Control*. Cambridge: Polity Press.

Reyneri, E. (1987). Il mercato del lavoro italiano tra controllo statale e regolazione sociale. *In*: Lange, P. and Regini, M., eds, *Stato e Regolazione Sociale*. Bologna: Il Mulino, 151–176.

Reyneri, E. ([1989] 2010). The Italian Labor Market: Between State Control and Social Regulation. *In*: Lange, P. and Regini, M., eds, *State, Market and Social Regulation. New Perspectives on Italy*. Cambridge: Cambridge University Press, 129–145.

Rusche, G. ([1933] 1978). Labor Market and Penal Sanction: Thoughts on the Sociology of Criminal Justice. *Crime and Social Justice*, 10, 2–8.

Rusche, G. and Kirchheimer, O. (1939). *Punishment and Social Structure*. New York: Morningside Heights: Columbia University Press.

Salvati, M. (2000). *Occasioni Mancate. Economia e politica in Italia dagli anni '60 a oggi*. Roma: Laterza.

Saraceno, C. (1994). The Ambivalent Familism of the Italian Welfare State. *Social Politics*, 1, 60–82.

Savelsberg, J. (1994). Knowledge, Domination and Criminal Punishment. *The American Journal of Sociology*, 99, 911–943.

Savelsberg J. (1999). Knowledge, Domination and Criminal Punishment Revisited: Incorporating State Socialism. *Punishment and Society*, 1, 45–70.

Schmidt V and Gualmini E. (2013). The Political Sources of Italy's Economic Problems: Between Opportunistic Political Leadership and Pragmatic, Technocratic Leadership. *Comparative European Politics* 11, 360–382.

Smith, P. (2013). Punishment and Meaning: The Cultural Sociological Approach. *In*: Simon, J. and Sparks, R., eds, *The SAGE Handbook of Punishment and Society*. London: Sage, 114–128.

Streeck, W. (2008). *Re-Forming Capitalism*. Oxford: Oxford University Press.

Tonry, M. (2007). Determinants of Penal Policy. *Crime and Justice*, 36, 1–48.

Treccani, Istituto dell'Enciclopedia Italiana (2010). Lottizzazione. In: *Il Vocabolario della Lingua Italiana Treccani*. Roma: Edizioni Treccani.

Trento, S. (2012). Continuità e cambiamento nel capitalismo italiano. *il Mulino*, 3, 439–447.

Trigilia, C. and Burroni, L. (2009). Italy: Rise, Decline and Restructuring of a Regionalized Capitalism. *Economy and Society*, 38, 630–635.

Urbinati, N. and Ragazzoni, D. (2016). *La vera Seconda Repubblica*. Milano: Raffaello Cortina Editore.

Wacquant, L. (2009a). *Prisons of Poverty*. Minneapolis: University of Minnesota Press.

Wacquant, L. (2009b). *Punishing the Poor: the neoliberal government of social insecurity*. Durham: Duke University Press.

Zedner, L. (2002). Dangers of Dystopia in Penal Theory. *Oxford Journal of Legal Studies*, 22, 341–366.

Zincone, G. (2006). The Making of Policies: Immigration and Immigrants in Italy. *Journal of Ethnic and Migration Studies*, 32, 347–375.

Chapter 8

'A return to Gulags'?
Explaining trends in post-Soviet prison rates

Gavin Slade

Introduction

In *Crime Control as Industry*, Nils Christie posed the question: 'In view of the attempts to create a market economy in the former USSR, why not a resumed use of Gulags there as well?' (2000, p. 15) At the time, Christie had some justification for asking this question. Prison rates across the former Soviet region had been rising through the 1990s outstripping even the high rates of the Soviet period. Yet, the year 2000 was a peak. Since then, decarceration has almost uniformly taken hold. Thus, rather than taking Christie's question rhetorically, this chapter seeks to take the question at face value and ask: why has there not been a return to Gulags – understood as rising prison rates and mass incarceration – in the region?

During a 'punitive turn' over the last 30 years, the prison in North America and Western Europe has regained a central position in the political and economic landscape of many countries (Garland 2001; Wacquant 2009). There is a growing scholarly literature on the rise of the penal state in other parts of the world too (Wacquant 1999a, 1999b, 2009; Melossi *et al.* 2011; Müller 2012). This is often framed in terms of flows from the global North to the global South (Carrington *et al.* 2016). Growing punitiveness in Latin America and parts of Africa is in part produced by the flow of expertise, discourses and technologies from a global penal centre in North America and Western Europe. These accounts emphasize how these flows act as a corollary to the broader spread of neo-liberal political ideology, the shrinking of the state and punitive solutions to the issue of growing social marginality. Eastern Europe and post-Soviet Eurasia has largely been left out of this debate as a region of study. While some studies of prisons and punishment in the region exist (see King 1994; Oleinik 2003; Piacentini 2004, 2013; King and Piacentini 2005; Pallot and Piacentini 2012) these focus solely on Russia and do not aim to explicitly engage the political economic framework.

Taking a wider lens that encompasses the entire post-Soviet region, this chapter aims to investigate how prison rates have diverged in the region despite a common cultural and political heritage bequeathed by the Soviet Union. All countries started out with a particular Soviet inheritance: high incarceration rates, a particular philosophy and culture of punishment, similar recent history and identical justice institutions. While many trends in the region follow a pattern, the differences in the quantity and quality of punishment across the region give rise to important questions concerning the effects of socio-economic conditions, and the evolution of political and judicial institutions across the area, as well as preferences among policy-making elites.

To explore this, the chapter takes the two most divergent cases in terms of prison rates in the decade 2000–2010: Georgia (quickest increasing use of prison) and Kazakhstan (quickest decreasing use of prison). These case studies provide some support to the general tenets of the political economy approach to understanding penal policy. However, the chapter makes the argument that market liberalization and a deregulated labour market do not fully explain penal policy choices among Georgian and Kazakh elites. Instead, the chapter provides evidence that these elites were in each case deliberately using prison rates to signal state capacity to deliver certain goods to these recently liberalized economies; which goods these were depended on the position of the economies of Georgia and Kazakhstan within the global economy. In Georgia, a fragile state with few natural resources, the state wished to signal security and credible guarantees of corruption-free market competition. In Kazakhstan, a stable state with developed extractive industries, the state rather used prison rates to signal commitment to internationally agreed human rights norms, and thus security against reputational damage for serious investors.

Before coming to the case studies, the chapter will provide an overview of trends in incarceration in the former Soviet Union, establishing that since 2000 the broad trend has been towards decarceration but there has been significant divergence in the rates of this change. The chapter then goes on to consider theories that would help to explain these divergences. It then applies these theories to the cases of Georgia and Kazakhstan, the two most divergent cases of prison rates in the region in the 2000s.

Incarceration after the Gulag

In 1991, the Soviet Union collapsed. The 15 successor states were bequeathed pieces of an almighty penal apparatus. The Soviet Gulag had comprised hundreds of camp complexes, special settlements, colonies, pre-trial and holding facilities as well as prisoner trains that criss-crossed a continent-wide system of punishment. As Piacentini (2013, p. 159) writes: 'in [the Russian penal system's] sheer scale, its geographical shape, its landscape domination, brutalizing history and the culture of punishment and politics … it is unique'. Nils Christie (2000, p. 31) similarly wrote that 'Russia is the great incarcerator of Europe'. Reduction of incarceration and reform of the Gulag's institutions has been a constant theme since independence in Russia and across the post-Soviet region.

Former Soviet states launched into diverging attempts at democratization and the creation of a market economy in the 1990s. The successor countries immediately looked to integrate in global governance structures. Slowly, throughout the 1990s, many former Soviet states became part of European and international infrastructure in respect of human rights signing up to the Council of Europe and European Court of Human Rights, placing a moratorium on the death penalty, and becoming signatories to the UN's Optional Protocol on the Convention Against Torture (Bowring 2013). At differing speeds, new penal codes were written and new criminal procedural codes were adopted across the region. In some countries, such as Russia in 1998, responsibility for the prison system was shifted from the Ministry of Interior to the Ministry of Justice to lock in greater humanization of the system. Despite these historic changes, at a time of liberal market reform and democratization, prison rates rose above those seen in the undemocratic command economy of the Soviet Union.

This was in part due to the economic and social turmoil caused by the Soviet collapse. Across the region, crime increased dramatically. The types of offence and the profiles of victim and offender changed markedly as property rights and wealth were redistributed, class structures became fluid, and normative expectations were shifted. In the early 1990s, there were marked jumps in crime across Central and Eastern Europe, particularly in violent crime and homicide (Lotspeich 1995; Zvekic et al. 1998; Pridemore 2006).

Yet, as King and Piacentini (2005, p. 269) note in line with research from the US (Tonry 1995; Gairsborough and Mauer 2000; Zimring 2006), increases in incarceration rates, at least in Russia, did not correlate with levels of criminality and cannot be fully explained simply on this basis. Relative to crime levels, the use of prison in Russia in the 1990s was 30 times higher than in England and Wales (King and Piacentini 2005). Thus, reform to the size and functioning of the penal system remained a question up to the present day. In the 2000s, further major penal reform was planned across the region from Lithuania to Georgia, Russia and Kazakhstan, promoting both decarceration through alternative sentencing and physical reform to the penal system's Soviet-era infrastructure. Since 2000, states across the region, with some exceptions, have been decarcerating. Yet, by 2015, post-Soviet countries still made up eight out of the top ten incarcerators in Europe as Table 8.1 shows.

This is a static picture. A further graph (Figure 8.1) is given showing how incarceration rates increased in the 1990s but have been decreasing since then in some cases already falling below 1991 levels. Trends across selected countries of the region are shown. The selected countries show trends that have been fairly stable across the region. First, all former Soviet countries had an increase in the prison rate in the 1990s. Second, this increase for all countries peaked around 1998–2001. Third, with the exception of Georgia, the prison population across all former Soviet states has shown a clear downward trend throughout the 2000s and 2010s but at widely differing rates. These three observations elicit the central question that this chapter aims to address: Why is it that since the peak in

Table 8.1 Top ten incarcerators in Europe per 100,000 of the population in 2015

Ranking	Title	Prison population rate
1	Russian Federation	441
2	Belarus	314
3	Georgia	263
4	Lithuania	254
5	Turkey	238
6	Azerbaijan	236
7	Latvia	224
8	Moldova (Republic of)	222
9	Estonia	217
10	Czech Republic	213

Source: International Centre for Prison Studies

incarceration rates around 1998–2001 some countries have decarcerated so much quicker than others? In terms of this question, Georgia and Kazakhstan emerge as particularly interesting for comparison. Georgia is the only country in the region to increase its incarceration rates in the 2000s, growing its prison population by 300 per cent between 2003 and 2010 and not joining in the decarceration trend until 2013. Kazakhstan is the leading penal reformer in the region; it reduced its prison population by almost 50 per cent between 2000 and 2014.

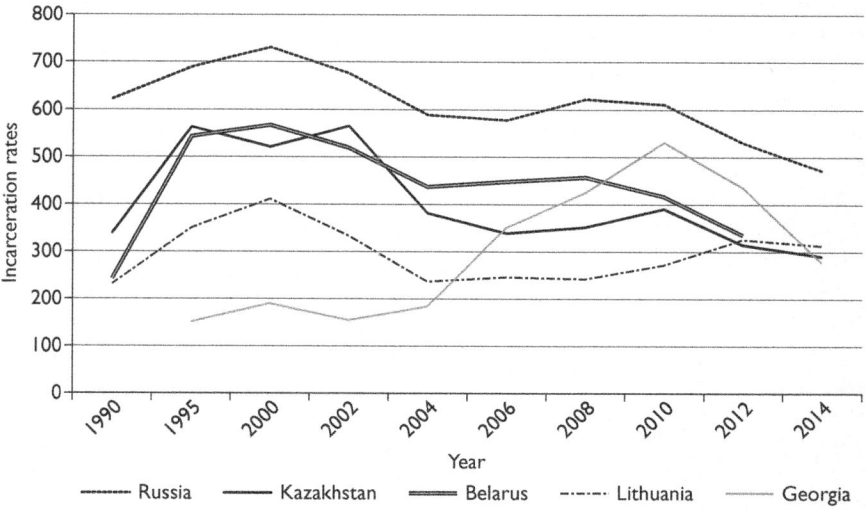

Figure 8.1 Prison rates in selected post-Soviet countries across time.
Source: International Centre for Prison Studies.

I will utilize these two cases in the chapter to help answer the question stated above, focusing on the decade 2000–2010 when the greatest divergence between Georgia and Kazakhstan occurred. In answering the question above, the chapter interrogates a political economic explanation for the divergence. Comparing the two most divergent cases, Georgia and Kazakhstan, shows that a political economic approach is helpful but cannot on its own explain the widely different rates of change in prison populations. Certainly, labour market conditions are worse in Georgia than in Kazakhstan. Yet, both countries on most measures are highly liberalized market economies. Thus, I will argue that the divergent dynamics of Georgia and Kazakhstan's prison rates are the direct result of policy preferences that are shaped by the positioning of the two countries in the wider global economy. These preferences were acted upon in the 2000s through superpresidential and autocratic executive bodies in both countries. Positioning in the global economy produces pressures to generate credible signals to domestic and outside actors; the strength of the executive over policy in both cases enables these signals to be made at speed. Prison rates were constitutive of this signalling in both cases. In the 2000s, both governments utilized scores in the International Centre for Prison Studies' World Prison Brief to signal different state capacities to different audiences.

Before considering Georgia and Kazakhstan, the chapter considers in more depth theoretical approaches for explaining variation in prison rates with a focus on a political economic approach. The following section considers this approach and the importance of the political-institutional context in which political economic choices are made.

Theorizing the use of prison in the former Soviet Union

The cases of the post-Soviet region allow us to explore the political economic approach to punishment (Rusche and Kirchheimer [1939] 1968) as the countries begin from a common starting point and have since diverged along political economic variables as well as the institutional contexts in which policy-makers work. All of the post-Soviet states inherited the same sets of institutions, all had spent decades under the Soviet yoke with an ideology that rejected the notion of a law-governed state, embraced a criminology that saw the bases of criminal activity as class exploitation, and punishment as a matter of collective and individual re-socialization as well as a cornerstone of the command economy (Slade and Light 2015). This suggests that the post-Soviet region might be considered something of a natural experiment in the political economy of punishment in showing how divergence in economic and institutional change has impacted concrete policy decisions including those around criminal justice.

As Figure 8.1 showed, general trends in incarceration tend to follow similar patterns in the region, perhaps revealing intertwined economic fortunes and the latent pressures of institutional and cultural legacies. Yet, decarceration has been a broad trend in the region since 2000 and the rates of this change in prison populations diverge significantly across states; this must be accounted for. In doing so first, we should note that none of the former Soviet countries are somehow beholden to their penal history, though many legacies exist here that in principle would make decarceration unlikely. For example, King and Piacentini (2005) as well as Christie (2000) identify inertial pressures within the Russian prison system that present obstacles to decarceration. These pressures would fully apply to a country such as Kazakhstan too. These include administrative structures and traditions designed for a large prison population; a penal system designed for production that had no competition in the command system; and a lack of resources to make reforms. Moreover, a capacious understanding of incarceration as a way of solving the Soviet Union's ills was a cultural and political frame the newly independent states took possession of; it did not need importing from anywhere else (Piacentini and Slade 2015).

Despite such factors, decarceration is now the observable trend. Moreover, variation in prison rates across the region does not appear to correlate well with legacies. Thus, Kazakhstan, the most impressive decarcerator for the past decade, had the largest penal inheritance of all the former Soviet states and had the highest rates of incarceration with the exception of Russia. Of 700,000 prisoners in the collapsing Soviet Union, 100,000 were in Kazakhstan, drawn from across the Union (General Prosecutor of Kazakhstan 2013). Georgia and the Baltic States on the Gulag periphery inherited much less in terms of penal infrastructure but have been much slower to decarcerate. We should, therefore, move beyond Soviet legacies to explain prison rates in the region today.

Second, while there is some basis to see in the early liberal market reforms of the 1990s the structural changes that predict an increase in severity and predictability of punishment, this should be treated with care. Certainly, spiralling prison rates in the 1990s occurred as neo-liberalization and 'shock therapy' were embraced. Thus, some blame the global mobility of particular political economic policies and systems of expertise for the woes that former Soviet countries have experienced (Cohen 2001). As Wacquant (1999b, 2009) has argued, these systems radiated outwards from a penal centre, most obviously the US. Karstedt (2002, p. 120) has also made the same point: 'models are adopted from … [the US] not because of coercion or constraint but because they come with a particular image of success'. And Downes (2001, p. 56) writes of mass incarceration:

> having gone this route alone, the US is actively exporting it … It may be more, not less, difficult for other societies to resist its appeal when the USA is both its role model and advocate, both in the 'law and order' and other political and economic respects.

On the other hand, Müller (2012, p. 63), writing of Latin America, observes 'the undeniable impact and attractiveness of American policies (economic, penal, welfare), political ideas and ideologies, as well as their demonstrative effect on other countries' while cautioning that analysts must identify 'local variations in penal statecraft'. Similarly, Melossi et al. (2011) argue that more academic emphasis should be put on the reception of policy ideas, their elective affinities with elements of local cultures of punishment and their transformation in the process of reception by local institutions.

In many countries of the former Soviet Union, these cautionary remarks about the overgeneralization of 'Americanization' (Peck 2003) remain highly pertinent for a number of reasons. For example, in Christie's (2000) gloomy outlook for Russia's penal system, he expects increasing use of imprisonment due to insidious 'Western' economic thinking and functionalism in governing social marginality, a penal populism that would demonize criminals as culpable for society's woes, and a law and order politics pushed by external advice on such things as a war on drugs. This has simply not happened. Thus, the cases of the region suggest that neo-liberalization of the economy does not inevitably lock in high incarceration rates.

The region then presents a puzzle. Both historical factors and positioning in the global flow of expertise and economic influence would suggest a return to 'Gulags' – rising and pervasive mass incarceration. After 2000 however this has not been the case. The failed predictions of the early 2000s demonstrate that the former Soviet Union occupies a contentious position for the emerging debates on Northern and Southern criminologies about who receives what from whom. 'The North/South divide' write Carrington et al. (2016, p. 2) 'refers to the divide between the metropolitan states of Western Europe and North America, on the one hand, and the countries of Latin America, Africa, Asia and Oceania, on the other', it is a 'metaphor for power relations' between a centre and a periphery. Eastern Europe is conspicuous in its absence here. One claim that this chapter makes is that the region offers opportunities to more rigorously probe these global power relations. Certainly, on the face of it the region shows us, in line with Müller (2012) and Melossi et al. (2011), that while acknowledging the impact of global flows of political economic ideologies, expertise and the influence of history, we must identify the local variation in political and cultural factors in the region. This would help explain why, rather than locking in high prison rates in an inevitable neo-liberal economic system against the backdrop of Soviet legacies, post-Soviet states since 2000 have taken diverging, and often quickly decarcerating, paths in terms of their prison rates. In taking on this task further, the chapter now utilizes the political economic approach and then brings in an analysis of policy-making through a comparison of the two most divergent cases in the region – Georgia and Kazakhstan.

A straightforward statement of the political economy approach to punishment is given by De Giorgi (2012, p. 43) following the classic work of Rusche and Kirchheimer ([1939] 1968): 'the emergence or demise of different penal practices cannot be ascribed to the ideas of reformers: penal change is ultimately determined by the conditions of labour and the labour market'. De Giorgi further acknowledges however, that this structural approach must also take into account the ways in which structural determinants are mediated by punishment's highly symbolic and cultural aspects as well as the political-institutional contexts in which penal policy is made and reformers work.

The challenge of understanding the array of political-institutional contexts has been taken up in the comparative approach of Lacey (2008) and Cavadino and Dignan (2005). These works highlight that while structural determinants might play a key role in explaining punishment trends, closer attention needs to be paid to political-institutional frameworks that dictate production regimes, labour markets, education and productivity, and disparities of wealth. Based on the work of Hall and Soskice (2001) concerning varieties of capitalism, Cavadino and Dignan (2005) found significant differences in the use of incarceration between liberal market economies (LMEs), such as the US and UK, and co-ordinated market economies (CMEs) such as Germany, the Netherlands and France. The former tend to produce much more exclusionary penal policies and higher incarceration rates.

Countries of the post-Soviet region do not fall neatly into one or the other group. However, David Lane and Martin Myant's edited collection on varieties of capitalism in post-communist countries (2007) analyses cases across the region along such variables as the form of coordination of activities by firms, the extent of private ownership, price and trade liberalization, capital accumulation and provision of credit, domestic and foreign investment and levels of income redistribution and inequality. Lane (2005, 2008; Lane and Myant 2007) suggests that rather than market capitalism emerging in the region, the former Soviet states went through a period of 'chaotic capitalism' in the 1990s where little was regulated and market mechanisms and private property did not function smoothly.

Coming out of this period, three broad groupings of states in the wider post-communist region have emerged (Lane 2007, p. 33). First, a 'continental type' co-ordinated market economy in places such as Hungary, the Czech Republic and Slovakia; second, a 'hybrid state/market uncoordinated capitalism' in the former Soviet space outside the Baltic States, particularly in Russia and Kazakhstan; third, a set of 'laggards' that simply preserve for the most part the Soviet statist economy, Belarus and Uzbekistan being good examples. Lane and Myant also position the post-Soviet republics into three groups based on 'low', 'medium' or 'high' levels of privatization given the share of Gross Domestic Product (GDP) accounted for by the private sector. Most countries are in the 'medium' category with only the Baltic States in the 'high' group.

The chapter will compare Kazakhstan and Georgia in the 2000s along some of the variables derived from these theoretical reflections. First, the chapter looks at conditions in the labour market, particularly unemployment, inequality, labour productivity and levels of poverty. Second, the structure of the economy in these two countries is discussed focusing on variables that determine the variety of capitalism they belong to. These variables are the percentage of GDP produced by the private sector and the level of foreign direct investment. Third, the political-institutional environment is considered in terms of the power of the executive to shape and force policy through. The chapter finds that these factors do not of themselves explain the vastly diverging paths of prison rates in Georgia and Kazakhstan in the 2000s. Finally, the chapter turns to how economic and institutional conditions structured policy preferences towards incarceration very differently in the two cases focusing in particular on the strength of the state and the type of investment opportunities the two countries offered in the international market.

Comparing Georgia and Kazakhstan

Turning first to the labour market, Georgia's indicators in the 2000s were much worse than Kazakhstan. Unemployment in Georgia increased, while it dropped dramatically in Kazakhstan. According to Georgian government figures, which are most likely significantly understated, unemployment increased from 12.6 per cent in 2004 to 16.9 per cent in 2009 (Georgian Office of Statistics 2010). Over the entire decade 2000–2010, a 5 per cent increase was recorded. In contrast, Kazakhstan saw a quick decrease of 7 per cent in unemployment figures as the economy grew (World Bank 2016). Thus, by the end of the decade Kazakhstan boasted a 6 per cent unemployment rate and Georgia a 16 per cent rate. Moreover, job security and conditions were poorer in Georgia; incredibly flexible labour laws raised concerns of the International Labour Organisation and the EU over workers' rights (Ryan 2011). As a result, the minimum wage as a percentage of the average wage collapsed in Georgia during the 2000s, while in Kazakhstan the value of the minimum wage was maintained albeit at comparatively low levels by international standards (Arias *et al.* 2014).

However, in terms of labour productivity both countries saw improvements through the decade. More productive labourers, it is supposed, create greater costs on increasing prison rates as prison removes industrious workers from the economy. As Lacey (2008) argues, increases in productivity and education of the workforce produces pressure to build inclusionary penal policies rather than exclusionary ones. Yet, Georgia outperformed Kazakhstan on this particular variable. In Georgia the average annual productivity growth in the period 2000–2007 was around 10 per cent and 7 per cent in Kazakhstan. Wages also increased in line with productivity in both countries as both economies grew relatively rapidly (Arias *et al.* 2014).

These indicators did not necessarily translate into poverty reduction. The principle of less eligibility assumes that prison rates should increase and prison conditions worsen the greater the number of economically marginal people. In Georgia, the human development index slowed in the 2000s (MacFarlane 2011). Gini coefficient scores, with 100 representing perfect inequality, stood at 42 in Georgia up from 39 in 2001 and 29 in Kazakhstan down from 35 in 2001. Both are then highly unequal countries by international standards but Kazakhstan's indicators are improving. In Georgia, by 2010, almost 20 per cent of the population lived on less that $1.90 a day, virtually the same percentage as ten years earlier. The European Commission (2008) stated of Georgia that: 'no progress can be reported as regards poverty reduction or social welfare'. Statistics on social spending show that while spending on social protection, education and health nominally improved on 2003 levels, it slumped as a percentage of government spending in a time of record budget revenues and GDP growth. Meanwhile, in contrast in Kazakhstan, poverty levels dipped dramatically through the decade as the economy grew rapidly and unemployment decreased. By 2010, those living on less that $1.90 a day stood at less than 1 per cent, down from 15 per cent at the start of the decade (World Bank 2016).

What varieties of capitalism have Georgia and Kazakhstan moved towards since 2000? Kazakhstan, similarly to Russia, went on a path of quick economic liberalization that brought social upheaval and poverty in the 1990s. However, as the state reconsolidated by the early 2000s it had maintained a hold on some major enterprises in strategic sectors. Moreover, while legislation suggested Kazakhstan was a LME, a lack of enforcement of laws and statist intervention in the creation of jobs and protection of key industries suggest otherwise. As such Kazakhstan represented a 'state-led LME' run on the directives of an unchallenged and authoritarian presidential administration, 'rather than a fully independent legal system' (Charman 2007, p. 180). Still, the private sector made up 65 per cent of GDP in 2005, a 40 per cent increase on ten years earlier. Moreover, Kazakhstan was the first country in the Commonwealth of Independent States to be granted full market status by the US in 2002 (Junisbai and Junisbai 2005). It also has the highest rating by credit agencies in the region outside the Baltic States. Foreign direct investment is a critical element of the Kazakh economy and remains consistently higher than countries such as Russia as a percentage of GDP. Such investment made up almost 10 per cent of GDP on average across the 2000s (EBRD 2013).

In contrast, Georgia between 1991 and 2003 had an uncoordinated, chaotic market the regulation of which was used primarily to serve the corrupt interests of divided ruling elites. The state made an 'almost total retreat … from the provision of public welfare' (Christophe 2007, p. 183). Thus Georgia did not fit at that time with the easy categories that a 'varieties of capitalism' approach allows. However, Georgia moved to a highly liberalized market economy after a US-backed 'colour revolution' in 2003. Kakha Bendukidze, Minister of the Economy between 2004 and 2008 and a renowned billionaire and libertarian, created a very liberal visa and tax regime. As part of these reforms, Free Industrial Zones were set up in parts of the country, bureaucracy was massively reduced, and low flat tax rates were created. The World Bank survey on ease of doing business put Georgia 12th in the world for 2010 (World Bank 2009). Under President Mikheil Saakashvili (2004–2013), a mass privatization scheme brought in impressive revenues, foreign direct investment increased to average almost 10 per cent of GDP annually, just as in Kazakhstan, and the state budget swelled. By 2005, similarly to Kazakhstan, Georgia was one of the most liberalized economies in the region with a score of four out of five on the EBRD's privatization index and an estimated 75 per cent of GDP coming from the private sector (EBRD 2013).

Finally, in terms of the political and institutional context in which policy-making occurred in the 2000s, both countries were marked by a weakness of democratic checks and balances, though this was true of Kazakhstan to a much greater degree. Georgia between 2004 and 2012 could be classified as a fragile democracy or a competitive authoritarian regime. Freedom House defined it as a hybrid regime with elements of democratic procedure and authoritarian governance (Freedom House 2010). Saakashvili made constitutional amendments on first taking office that transferred great powers to the president's office and the process of policy-making gradually became more opaque and executive driven. Georgia's super-presidential system was not as repressive as Kazakhstan's regime however. Freedom House defines Kazakhstan as a 'consolidated authoritarian regime'. President Nursultan Nazarbayev has ruled the country since independence and is president for life. Policy is driven through a patrimonial system dominated by the presidential administration.

Table 8.2 summarizes the variables discussed above across the two cases. The outcome variable concerning prison rates is in the bottom row. On the face of it, Table 8.2 lends some support to Rusche and Kirchheimer's theory concerning the relationship between the labour market and punishment. Unemployment worsened in Georgia, poverty was not tackled and privatization and deregulation were a critical element of political economic policy in the 2000s. However, productivity improved increasing the costs on incarceration of potential workers. In contrast, in Kazakhstan labour market indicators improved drastically across the board. Institutionally however both countries were marked by similarities. Both were LMEs with important private sectors and depended on foreign investment. Both had policies made by elite groups in presidential administrations with little input from legislatures, parliamentary committees, ministries or the general public. Such top-down policy-making may account for the speed at which the two prison rates moved in the 2000s.

Table 8.2 introduces three more variables that have not yet been discussed. These concern state strength or stability, the presence of natural resources, and the criminal justice narrative that emerged in the two countries. While structural variables appear to correlate rather well with the diverging prison rates in the cases, they cannot be the whole story. For example, Ukraine, with a very similar economic profile to that of Georgia's did not increase its prison population over the 2000s. Thus, the aim of the following section is to establish the mechanism by which these structural variables might impact levels of incarceration. I will argue that the liberalization of the economy per se is not as important as, first, the positioning of the liberal economy within the world market, and subsequently the need to signal state capacity to deliver on certain goods. Such signalling is a political choice based on elite preferences.

Table 8.2 Variation across theoretically important factors in Georgia and Kazakhstan affecting prison rates

Variables in the 2000s	Georgia	Kazakhstan
Regime type[1]	Hybrid Regime	Consolidated Authoritarianism
Private sector share of GDP in 2010	75%	65%
FDI as share of GDP (annual average)[2]	9.1%	9.9%
Change in percentage of people in poverty[3]	0% (20% in 2010)	−15% (to <1% in 2010)
Inequality (change in Gini coefficient)	+3	−6
Labour productivity average annual increase[4]	10%	7%
Unemployment trend over decade[5]	+5% (to 16% in 2010)	−7% (to 6% in 2010)
Natural resources	Low	High
State fragility in 2010[6]	90.4 (Warning)	72.1 (Moderate)
Criminal justice policy and discourse	Zero tolerance	Humanization
Prison rates in 2000s[7]	+300%	−50%

Notes

1 Based on Freedom House definitions and scores in 2010. Available at: https://freedomhouse.org/report/nations-transit/2010/georgia & https://freedomhouse.org/report/nations-transit/2010/kazakhstan [accessed 11 August 2017].
2 FDI and private sector share of GDP taken from EBRD European Bank for Reconstruction and Development (ERBD), *Transition Indicators, 1991–2012*; *Structural Change Indicators, 1989–2008, 2003–2010*. Both available at: www.ebrd.com/what-we-do/economic-research-and-data/data/forecasts-macro-data-transition-indicators.html [accessed 11 August 2017].
3 Based on poverty line definition of people living on less than $1.90 a day. See World Bank data at: http://data.worldbank.org/indicator/SI.POV.DDAY?locations=KZ-GE [accessed 11 August 2017].
4 Taken from the World Bank data. See: Arias, O.S. et al. (2014). *Back to Work: Growing with Jobs in Europe and Central Asia*. Washington, DC: World Bank.
5 Unemployment as a percentage of the total workforce, calculated by the International Labour Organization and available at: http://data.worldbank.org/indicator/SL.UEM.TOTL.ZS?locations=KZ-GE [accessed 11 August 2017].
6 Scores from Fund for Peace. 2010. *Fragile States Index*. Available at: http://fsi.fundforpeace.org/rankings-2010-sortable.
7 Prison rates available at International Centre for Prison Studies. World Prison Brief, www.prisonstudies.org [accessed 11 August 2017].

Prison rates as a signal of state capacity

Georgia suffered one of the worst collapses of any of the post-Soviet states. It had one of the bloodiest transitions to independence. Two wars broke out with the secessionist regions of Abkhazia and South Ossetia through 1989–1993 and a low intensity civil war in 1992 and 1993. Industrial output declined by 90 per cent in the first years of independence under Eduard Shevardnadze. The state went virtually bankrupt. Disillusionment with post-independence politics, the lack of development and corruption and fraud brought about a peaceful revolution in 2003. Known as the Rose Revolution, this uprising brought to power Mikheil Saakashvili and his United National Movement (UNM) on a wave of huge popular support. On the back of this public confidence the new government had a window of opportunity to push through a raft of deep reforms (Wheatley 2005). The elites that came to power in the UNM were young, often western-educated and English-speaking.

Against the backdrop of endemic violence and corruption, Saakashvili made criminal justice a primary object of government intervention immediately. Upon taking office, Saakashvili began a highly public anti-corruption campaign. He introduced a policy of zero tolerance for minor crimes in 2006 (President's Office of Georgia 2006). Mandatory custodial sentencing as part of the zero tolerance policy was the primary cause for the subsequent surge in the prison population. Between 2003 and 2010, and particularly accelerating after 2006, the number of people incarcerated increased by 300 per cent. From some 6,000 inmates under Shevardnadze, the figure by 2010 stood at over 24,000. Other than the US, by the end of the 2000s, only three countries in the world incarcerated more of their citizens proportionately than Georgia (International Centre for Prison Studies 2012). This policy of mass incarceration was expensive. The Penitentiary Department budget for 2007 alone stood at roughly 0.5 per cent of total GDP for that year (Government of Georgia 2007; Ministry of Finance 2011). This figure stood at just 0.1 per cent in 2004. Yet, funds were also directly flowing into state coffers through the adoption of zero tolerance, plea-bargaining, fines and the confiscation of assets under anti-corruption legislation. After the change of government, a freedom of information request revealed that over 140 million lari ($70 million) had been transferred into the state budget in the period 2009 to 2012 from plea bargain agreements alone (Institute for the Development of Freedom of Information 2013)

Moreover, Georgia is a country with few natural resources; scrap metal is the biggest export. A reliance on attracting foreign capital against the background of a reputation for state weakness produced a strong economic incentive to signal that the state could tackle potential physical threats to investors and the risk corruption posed to property rights. The fight against corruption meant demonstrating that arbitrary and venal state interventions would not be taken against investors in favour of rent-seekers. The fight against corruption and the hard line on crime was signalled time and again with reference to international indicators.

At the European Parliament in 2010, Saakashvili referenced *The Economist* and the World Bank to flag up the liberalization of the economy and stated that: 'once the epicenter of the post-Soviet mafia, Georgia has made more progress against corruption than any other country in the world from 2004 to 2009, according to Transparency International' (Civil.ge 2010). Bendukidze promised a 'Hong Kong on the Black Sea' and Saakashvili frequently referred to Singapore as a model for Georgia (De Waal 2011). Thus, the capacity of the state to at once retreat from regulating the market and secure assets and property rights was being signalled. Success in anti-corruption measures, police reform and deregulation were promoted internationally. Advisors travelled the world to promote Georgian reforms; whole page adverts were taken out in *The Economist* encouraging investment; Georgia's de-bureaucratizing reforms were even brought up in the UK Parliament.

Thus, increasing prison rates internationally for Georgia were not an embarrassment but a signal of renewed state capacity, seriousness about corruption as a threat to property rights and state action on the issue of security. Thus, increasing prison rates was a policy preference enacted by elite individuals through a discourse of zero tolerance in weakly democratic institutions and shaped by the political and economic position of Georgia within the broader global economy.

In contrast to Georgia, despite the Soviet inheritance, incarceration rates in Kazakhstan have been in serious decline since the early 2000s. In 2000 there were 520 prisoners per 100,000 of the population, by 2014 this stood at 289. Whereas in much of the post-Soviet space declines in prison populations can occur through amnesties which powerfully expresses state power to enact 'enforced forgetting' (McEvoy and Mallinder 2012) and enables state-society bargaining in undemocratic regimes, Kazakhstan has eschewed the use of amnesty. Thus, policy-makers report that the decreases are part of a concerted policy to institutionalize the reduction of the prison population through consistent non-custodial sentencing and the development of and investments in viable alternatives to prison.

In contrast to Georgia, the Kazakh economy relies on extractive industries in mining and particularly in oil (Charman 2007). This has allowed for a much stronger position in the world economy. The funding of social protection can be made with oil revenues. As mentioned, employment indicators have improved greatly in the 2000s and investments in education between 2005 and 2011 went up six-fold (Milanovitch 2014). The penal factories of the Soviet camps are largely dormant now in Kazakhstan or have been re-roled to produce very basic goods. In colonies, work is now optional and taken up only by a minority of prisoners. As Christie notes (2000), penal labour can in no way compete in a market economy. Thus, given the uncompetitiveness of penal labour and the oil revenue-driven state interventions to integrate marginal social groups, the size of the prison population and average sentences of eight years made no sense economically.

The impetus to reduce prison rates undoubtedly came from the Presidential Administration of President Nazarbayev. This office laid out modernization plans to lift Kazakhstan into the top 50 leading world economies by 2050. In 2015, a 100-step programme was set out to achieve this with ten steps concerning criminal justice reform. In response to these pressures from above, in 2013, the General Prosecutor's office set out ten steps to reduce the prison population, based in the words of the General Prosecutor himself, 'on the advanced standards and innovations, successfully applied in countries abroad' (Daulabaev 2016, p. 18). There was clearly an incentive not to exclude large numbers of potentially productive workers in decrepit colonies that no longer played a role in Kazakhstan's modernizing economy. As the General Prosecutor put it a lack of penal reform had created 'an unjustifiable increase in expenditure' (Daulabaev 2016, p. 19). Number 34 of the President's 100 steps is to create new prisons based on public-private partnerships.

Thus, the economic waste of maintaining a large prison population during years of economic growth and investment in productivity created a drive to reduce the prison rate. In addition to this, the political elite had a strong incentive to attract investors by downplaying the human rights situation in a consolidated authoritarian regime. Contrary to Georgia, in Kazakhstan the state could funnel Foreign Direct Investment (FDI) into a developed energy sector in mining and oil that demanded high levels of productive labour. The energy sector attracts multinational firms that are extremely sensitive to reputational damage. Kazakh elites thus needed to show that the state had the capacity to protect firm reputation through the improvement of the human rights situation.

In doing so, there was an opportunity to utilize prison rates to signal to investors the state's capacity to adapt to international norms and avoid scandal. Policy documents and forum discussions among the top civil servants in charge of the process of prison rate reduction explicitly state this rationale. The 'ten steps to reduce the prison population' policy is largely based on Kazakhstan's image as a 'normal' country for investment and anxiety about the incarceration rate league table promoted through the International Centre for Prison Studies' World Prison Brief. This thinking among the Kazakh elite is in line with Heathershaw's (2013) argument that Central Asian states act out their legitimacy through participating in international networks and systems of rankings as 'global performance states'. As General Prosecutor Daulabaev argued:

> completing these measures [reducing incarceration] will allow us to take our country out of the top 50 leading countries by prison rates … and in the long term to compare with indicators from advanced European countries … a low prison rate will bring about not only a smaller budget expenditure, but show the effectiveness of criminal justice, the security of society, and the investment attractiveness of the state.
>
> (Daulabaev 2016, p. 19)

Human rights turn out to be a signal of state capacity to work within accepted international norms generating both foreign direct investment and creating healthier state budgets

Conclusion

This chapter has attempted to explore the question 'why not resumed use of Gulags' in the post-Soviet region? As Nils Christie formulated it, the question was premised on the idea that the development of liberal markets would lead to increasing incarceration rates in this world area. The chapter has shown that in fact incarceration rates have varied among the countries of the region. Furthermore, overall there has been a trend towards decarceration after a peak in 2000. In exploring the variation that the region offers, the chapter has provided evidence for some of the key tenets of an approach which sees penal policy as part of political economy. Incarceration rates appear to correlate well with the conditions of the labour market. The case studies of Georgia and Kazakhstan showed that the type of market economy and its organization do appear to impact on, or at least correlate with, decisions to pursue exclusionary or inclusionary penal policies.

Yet, the chapter has argued that penal policy preferences among the elite must be understood not as following simply from the liberalization of the economy but also from the position of the economy in world markets and state capacities to enable competitiveness within those markets. Thus, economically, the Georgian elite in the 2000s engaged in creating a predictable framework, following a decade of state fragility, for an LME based on foreign direct investment, tax-free zones, and flexible workers rights. As a corollary of that a zero tolerance crime control policy increased incarceration rates dramatically. The mechanism linking these developments is an incentive to signal state capacity for preventing corruption and insecurity. This mechanism need not be inferred as it was stated many times publically by Georgian policy-makers. In Kazakhstan, the economy was liberalized and FDI promoted in a stable state with a resource-rich economy and an improving labour market. As a corollary, prison rates slumped in the 2000s. Again, the mechanism linking the two was the need to signal capacity this time for sensitivity to brand reputation and international image in terms of obeying accepted human rights norms. Again, elites were explicit about this preference. In both cases, the International Centre for Prison Studies prison rate league tables made a convenient proxy for such capacities.

The cases of Kazakhstan and Georgia reveal the on-going importance of the global and the local in understanding the political economy of punishment. Future pathways for research in the former Soviet Union might look to develop more robust statistical analyses across more cases to examine the interrelationships between economic variables and prison rates. In addition, future research should investigate not only rates of imprisonment but also the conditions of incarceration; the latter is much harder to measure comparatively and changes take place at a slower rate. Moreover, while this chapter has found much evidence for a political economic and institutionalist approach to post-Soviet punishment, culture may provide a vital further dimension for comparative analysis. In particular, the elites who make decisions on penal policy in the region are more and more often drawn from among those who only faintly remember the Soviet past. Thus, the particular attitudes, values and cultures of internationally mobile civil servants shopping for 'best practice' policies or 'tried and tested' reforms must factor into the adoption and direction of incarceration in the region.

Acknowledgements

The author would like to thank Barbara Junisbai for sharing her knowledge (and data) on Kazakhstan; Laura Piacentini and Alexei Trochev for enlightening conversations on the data presented here; and the participants of the workshop held at University of A Coruna in September 2014 on the political economy of punishment today: visions, debates and challenges.

Bibliography

Arias, O.S. et al. (2014). *Back to Work: Growing with Jobs in Europe and Central Asia*. Washington, DC: OECD.
Bowring, B. (2013). *Law, Rights and Ideology in Russia: Landmarks in the Destiny of a Great Power*. London: Routledge.
Carrington, K., Hogg, R. and Sozzo, M. (2016). Southern Criminology. *British Journal of Criminology*, 56 (1), 1–20.
Cavadino, M. and Dignan, J. (2005). *Penal Systems: A Comparative Approach*. London: Sage.
Charman, K. (2007). Kazakhstan: A State-led Liberalized Market Economy? *In*: D. Lane and M. Myant, eds, *Varieties of Capitalism in Post-Communist Countries*. London: Palgrave Macmillan, 165–182.
Christie, N. (2000). *Crime Control as Industry: Towards Gulags, Western Style*. Hove: Psychology Press.
Christophe, B. (2007). Georgia: Capitalism as Organized Chaos. *In*: D. Lane and M. Myant, eds, *Varieties of Capitalism in Post-Communist Countries*. London: Palgrave Macmillan, 183–200.
Civil.ge. 2010. Saakashvili's Speech to the European Parliament. Available from: www.civil.ge/eng/article.php?id=22883 [accessed 20 January 2017].
Cohen, S.F. (2001). *Failed Crusade: America and the Tragedy of Post-communist Russia*. New York: WW Norton & Company.
Daulabaev, K. (2016). *10 Steps to Reducing the Prison Population: Address to the Prison Forum of Kazakhstan*. Astana: General Prosecutor's Office.
De Giorgi, A. (2012). The Political Economy of Punishment. *In*: J. Simon and R. Sparks, eds, *The Sage Handbook of Punishment and Society*. London: Sage, 40–59.
De Waal, T. (2011). *Georgia's Choices: Charting a Future in Uncertain Times*. Vol. 5. Washington, DC: Carnegie Endowment for International Peace.
Downes, D. (2001). The Macho Penal Economy: Mass Incarceration in the United States – a European Perspective. *In*: D. Garland, ed., *Mass Imprisonment: Social Causes and Consequences*. London: Sage, 51–69.
European Bank for Reconstruction and Development (EBRD) (2013). *Transition Indicators, 1991–2012; Structural Change Indicators, 1989–2008, 2003–2010*. Available

from: www.ebrd.com/what-we-do/economic-research-and data/data/forecasts-macro-data-transition-indicators.html [accessed 1 December 2016].

European Commission (2008). Implementation of the European Neighbourhood Policy 2007: Georgia Progress Report, SEC (2008), 393 (3 April 2008). Available from: http://ec.europa.eu/world/enp/pdf/progress2008/sec08_393_en.pdf [accessed 12 April 2017].

Freedom House. 2010. Nations in Transition. Available at: https://freedomhouse.org/report/nations-transit/2010/georgia [accessed 11 August 2017].

Gainsborough, J. and Mauer, M. (2000). *Diminishing Returns: Crime and Incarceration in the 1990s*. Washington, DC: The Sentencing Project.

Garland, D. (1990). *Punishment and Modern Society: A Study in Social History*. Oxford: Oxford University Press.

Garland, D. (2001). *The Culture of Control. Crime and Social Order in Contemporary Society*. Oxford: Oxford University Press.

Georgian Office of Statistics (2010). Crime and Unemployment Rates (2003–2009). Available from: www.geostat.ge/index.php?action=0&lang=eng [accessed 28 March 2011].

General Prosecutor of Kazakhstan (2013). Presentation of the Deputy General Prosecutor. Available from: http://prokuror.gov.kz/rus/novosti/press-releasy/vystuplenie-zamestitelya-generalnogo-prokurora-zhakipa-asanova-na-prezentacii [accessed 12 January 2017].

Government of Georgia (2007). *Georgia's Democratic Transformation: An Update Since the Rose Revolution*. Tbilisi: Ministry of Foreign Affairs of Georgia.

Hall, P.A. and Soskice, D., eds (2001). *Varieties of Capitalism: The Institutional Foundations of Comparative Advantage*. Oxford: Oxford University Press.

Heathershaw, J. (2013). The Global Performance State: A Reconsideration of the Central Asian 'Weak State'. *In*: M. Reeves, J. Rasanayagam, and J. Beyer, eds, *Performing Politics in Central Asia: Ethnographies of the State*. Bloomington: Indiana University Press, 39–61.

International Centre for Prison Studies (2012). World Prison Brief. Available from: www.prisonstudies.org/info/worldbrief/wpb_country.php?country=122 [accessed 10 May 2011].

Institute for the Development of Freedom of Information (2013). Transfers to the State Budget from Plea Bargains. Available from: https://idfi.ge/en/for-the-first-time-the-amountstransferred-to-the-state-budget-through-the-use-of-plea-bargaining-agreements [accessed 16 January 2017].

Junisbai, B. and Junisbai, A. (2005). The Democratic Choice of Kazakhstan: A Case Study in Economic Liberalization, Intraelite Cleavage, and Political Opposition. *Demokratizatsiya*, 13 (3), 373–392.

Karstedt, S. (2002). Durkheim, Tarde and Beyond. *Criminology and Criminal Justice*, 2 (2), 111–123.

King, R.D. (1994). Russian Prisons after Perestroika-End of the Gulag. *British Journal of Criminology*, 34 (S1), 62–82.

King, R.D. and Piacentini, L. (2005). The Russian Correctional System during the Transition. *In*: A. Pridemore, ed., *Ruling Russia: Law, Crime and Justice in a Changing Society*. Oxford: Rowman & Littlefield, 261–281.

Lacey, N. (2008). *The Prisoners' Dilemma: Political Economy and Punishment in Contemporary Democracies*. Cambridge: Cambridge University Press.

Lane, D. (2005). Emerging Varieties of Capitalism in Former State Socialist Societies. *Competition & Change*, 9 (3), 227–247.

Lane, D. (2008). From Chaotic to State-led Capitalism. *New Political Economy*, 13 (2), 177–184.
Lane, D.S. and Myant, M.R., eds (2007). *Varieties of Capitalism in Post-communist Countries*. Basingstoke: Palgrave Macmillan, 13–39.
Lotspeich, R. (1995). Crime in the Transition Economies. *Europe-Asia Studies*, 47 (4), 555–589.
MacFarlane, S.N. (2011). Post-Revolutionary Georgia on the Edge? *Chatham House Briefing Paper* REPBP2011/01. Available from: www.chathamhouse.org.uk/files/18919_bp0311_macfarlane.pdf [accessed 18 May 2011].
McEvoy, K. and Mallinder, L. (2012). Amnesties in Transition: Punishment, Restoration, and the Governance of Mercy. *Journal of Law and Society*, 39 (3), 410–440.
Melossi, D., Sozzo, M. and Sparks, R., eds (2011). *Travels of the Criminal Question: Cultural Embeddedness and Diffusion*. London: Bloomsbury Publishing.
Milanovitch, M. (2014). *Reviews of National Policies of Education: Secondary Education in Kazakhstan*. Paris: OECD.
Ministry of Finance (2011). Georgia Statistical Databases (2003–2011). Available from: www.mof.ge/3855 [accessed 20 May 2011].
Müller, M.M. (2012). The Rise of the Penal State in Latin America. *Contemporary Justice Review*, 15 (1), 57–76.
Oleinik, A. (2003). *Organized Crime, Prison and Post-Soviet Society*. Aldershot: Ashgate.
Pallot, J. and Piacentini, L. (2012). *Gender, Geography, and Punishment: The Experience of Women in Carceral Russia*. Oxford: Oxford University Press.
Peck, J. (2003). Geography and Public Policy: Mapping the Penal State. *Progress in Human Geography*, 27 (2), 222–232.
Piacentini, L. (2004). *Surviving Russian Prisons*. Milton: Willan Publishing.
Piacentini, L. (2013). The Russian Penal System. *In*: V. Ruggiero and P. Ryan, eds, *Punishment in Europe*. London: Palgrave Macmillan, 157–182.
Piacentini, L. and Slade, G. (2015). Architecture and Attachment: Carceral Collectivism and the Problem of Prison Reform in Russia and Georgia. *Theoretical Criminology*, 19 (2), 179–197.
President's Office of Georgia. (2006). State of the Nation Address. Available from: www.president.gov.ge/index.php?lang_id=GEO&sec_id=228&info_id=2686 [accessed 20 May 2011].
Rusche, G. and Kirchheimer, O. ([1939] 1968) *Punishment and Social Structure*. New York: Columbia University Press.
Ryan, T. (2011). Seeing Georgia through Rose Colored Glasses. *Huffington Post*. Available from: www.huffingtonpost.com/timothy-ryan/seeing-georgia-through-ro_b_862495.html [accessed 18 May 2011].
Slade, G. and Light, M. (2015). Crime and Criminal Justice after Communism: Why Study the Post-Soviet Region? *Theoretical Criminology*, 19 (2), 147–158.
Tonry, M. (1995). *Malign Neglect: Race, Crime, and Punishment in America*. New York: Oxford University Press.
Wacquant, L. (1999a). Urban Marginality in the Coming Millennium. *Urban Studies*, 36 (10), 1639–1647.
Wacquant, L. (1999b). How Penal Common Sense Comes to Europeans: Notes on the Transatlantic Diffusion of the Neoliberal Doxa. *European Societies*, 1 (3), 319–352.
Wacquant, L. (2009). *Punishing the Poor: The Neoliberal Government of Social Insecurity*. Durham: Duke University Press.

Wheatley, J. (2005). *Georgia from National Awakening to Rose Revolution: Delayed Transition in the Former Soviet Union*. Aldershot: Ashgate.

World Bank. (2009) *Georgia – Poverty Assessment*. Available from: www-wds.worldbank.org/external/default/WDSContentServer/WDSP/IB/2009/04/29/000350881_20090429111740/Rendered/PDF/444000ESW0P1071C0Disclosed041281091.pdf [accessed 25 May 2011].

World Bank (2016) Data Analytics: Unemployment & Poverty Headcount Indicators. Available from: http://data.worldbank.org/indicators [accessed 03 January 2017].

Zimring, F.E. (2006). *The Great American Crime Decline*. New York: Oxford University Press.

Zvekic, U. (1998). *Criminal Victimisation in Countries in Transition*. Vol. 61. Rome: UNICRI.

Chapter 9

Inclusion's dark side

The political economy of irregular migration in Greece

Leonidas K. Cheliotis

Scholars and non-governmental organisations grappling with issues of immigration from disadvantaged parts of the world today have increasingly engaged in public efforts to critique the ways in which immigrants, be they regular or irregular, with or without papers, are mistreated by affluent regions and countries. Explicitly or implicitly, the aim of such critique has been to promote progressive change by giving as wide coverage as possible to research and other reports highlighting the injustices inflicted upon disadvantaged migrant populations. The underlying and commonly unstated premise of these interventions in the public sphere has been that humans, all of us, have a natural capacity for empathy, and that knowledge of the suffering of others is bound to animate our universal empathetic predisposition, which in its turn will trigger a sense of moral obligation to intervene and remedy the suffering at issue. In other words, if affluent societies previously failed to bring an end to the injustices suffered by poor migrants on their soil or en route to their shores, it is not because of compassion fatigue, whereby repeated exposure to maladies drains us emotionally and desensitises us morally. Nor is it because of perceived inability practically to lend a hand of help to suffering others. If affluent societies previously failed to take action against the injustices suffered by poor migrants, it is because this suffering remained largely unknown; it is because it remained more or less invisible.

In what follows, I seek, first, to problematise the notion that the suffering of poor migrants has necessarily been invisible to affluent societies around the world, a notion predicated on the perception that destitute migrants have been physically excluded from entering such societies in the first instance; and second, to account for the fact that large segments of affluent societies have either tolerated or even contributed to migrant suffering at and inside their borders, drawing attention to the politico-economic functions that poor migrants in general and irregular migrants in particular are so often made to serve once they find themselves inside the borders of 'host' states. In the process of developing and substantiating my argument, I focus on developments that have taken place in Greece between the early 1990s, at which time migration policy started taking shape in the country in order to deal with what was already a rapidly growing influx of foreigners and especially undocumented migrants, and the beginning of

2015, when a coalition government led by the left-wing Syriza party assumed power against the backdrop of a 'refugee crisis' mounting in various parts of the globe and manifesting itself particularly acutely by European standards in Greek border areas.[1] Substantively, although, as explained in detail elsewhere and briefly elaborated below, the politico-economic functions poor migrants may play in 'host' states can extend wider, I single out for analysis and dissect the issue of irregular migrant exploitation in the labour market. In so doing, I point to ways in which apparently unrelated state policies and practices regarding matters of migration, welfare, employment and criminal justice, as well as certain manifestations of anti-migrant violence by non-state actors, may act in combination with one another to this end.

Irregular migration as 'entrapment'

Many critical reports and commentaries on policies and practices regarding matters of immigration, and especially regarding the array of national and international efforts to manage the flows of poor immigrants into the advanced economies of the West, have relied on the notion of physical or geographical exclusion. Thus, regions and nation-states have been described as impermeable 'fortresses', as striving to solidify their borders against migration from impoverished or otherwise disadvantaged parts of the globe, in order to meet a range of political imperatives. This claim appears to contain a significant element of truth when one considers, for instance, that irregular migrants have increasingly been forced by border regimes to navigate border zones where they are bound to face serious threats to health and life that are not only environmental, but are also meted out by state actors (see, e.g. Albahari 2015; Basaran 2015; Bigo 2015; Migreurop 2016).

In practice, however, as argued by such scholars as Andreas (2009), Anderson (2010), De Giorgi (2010) and Rahola (2011), borders can be far more permeable than usually assumed, and they are thus better described as points of variable intensity than as rigid structures. To the extent that the permeability of borders has been recognised in the literature, efforts to explain it have duly extended beyond practical factors that may undermine effective border control as such (e.g. extensive borderlands or limited availability of financial resources) to the role played by governing elites inside and across nation-states in adopting policies and promoting practices that essentially enable the mass import of exploitable migrant labour according to domestic market needs and dominant political interests. What these political economy accounts essentially tell us is that what is at stake in the context of affluent 'host' states is not so much their 'inclusion' or 'exclusion' of migrants than the terms on which migrants are actually included. So-called 'exclusionary' border control policies and practices may be to a significant extent imperfect by design, and the failure to fully and permanently exclude poor migrants from national territories may, in fact, be driven by the pursuit of important economic and political imperatives domestically (as well as internationally).[2]

Greece is a case that readily lends itself to this kind of interpretation. For one, Greece has become the main point of entry for irregular migration into the European Union, which is at least in part why both the estimated absolute number and the proportional population share of irregular migrants living on Greek soil have persistently stood at exceptionally high levels by European standards ever since Greece first became a country of net immigration in the 1990s. At the same time, the country's extensive informal labour market has urgently needed and absorbed large cohorts of workers without papers, and there is also evidence to suggest that successive Greek governments, both of the centre-right and the centre-left, have played a key role in the maintenance of what they have portrayed in apocalyptic terms as the excessive size of the irregular migrant population in the country, not just in terms of allowing permeable borders, but also – and this is a point largely overlooked by pertinent scholarship, whether on Greece or other jurisdictions – in the sense of restricting outflows.

On the one hand, at least up until 2015, when a 'refugee crisis' was declared in Europe in light of the rapid rise in the number of people reaching the continent in an effort to flee violence and other adversities in their homelands, Greece had failed for decades to engage in systematic efforts to police its borders effectively. It is true that policing the country's borders is practically an exceptionally difficult task, given not only their extensiveness (Greece having the longest coastline in Europe, for example), but also European accords that have served to swell irregular migration routes into Europe and Greece in particular (see further Xenakis and Cheliotis 2017). It is notable, however, that Greek authorities have long made limited use of access to European Union funding to enhance the efficacy of border controls (see further Cheliotis 2013).

On the other hand, Greek governments have also effectively restricted both voluntary and forced outflow for those already inside Greek borders without papers, either actively, through new restrictive legislation, or passively, in the sense of leaving unfavourable legal structures and bureaucratic arrangements more or less intact. While Greece has ratified a number of key international and European treaties that guarantee fundamental rights for all, it has been reluctant to grant legal status to refugees, asylum seekers and migrants more generally. Although Greek state officials have often openly endorsed this stance, portraying it as a deterrent against irregular migration into Greece (see, e.g. Baldwin-Edwards 2014), it has rather served to discourage transit migration from within Greece herself on to continental Europe, not least by raising fears of being caught in the process of irregular border-crossing or thereafter (see further Papadopoulou-Kourkoula 2008, pp. 82–90). That this outcome has been consistent with pan-European political pressures (see, e.g. Zaiotti 2011) does not negate the point that it has been in considerable measure one of Greece's own making and in line with the interests of key constituencies domestically.

Thus, Greece has maintained one of the lowest rates of refugee recognition in Europe and one of the highest rates of pending asylum cases in the world, having long failed to establish an effective and timely system for processing applications, rather having kept asylum decisions within the purview of an ill-equipped and generally unsympathetic national police force for decades. In a similar vein, regularisation in Greece has been substantively narrow and procedurally perverse. In the vast majority of cases, regularisation is effectively reduced to seeking a renewable residence or work permit of very short duration. The process of regularisation, including renewal of temporary permits, has meanwhile been fraught with a series of grave challenges over the years. Information about the application process itself is usually limited and unclear, formal eligibility criteria have been increasingly stringent, and deeply unfair financial impediments are in place, including, most notably, excessively high application fees and, for the purposes of renewing a work permit, the legal requirement that applicants themselves assume the burden of paying their social insurance contributions when their employer has refused or otherwise failed to do so. Lengthy delays are also common in the assessment and subsequent stages of applications as a consequence of complex bureaucratic procedures, inadequate training and poor staffing levels, while decision-making has often been found to be arbitrary and inconsistent. Practically, the best-case scenario for most migrants seeking regularisation is to find themselves in limbo, shifting between regular and irregular status with long breaks filled with uncertainty and anxiety in between (see further Cheliotis 2017). Efforts inside Greece to apprehend and deport irregular migrants have meanwhile been known to be of limited efficiency and effectiveness, so much so that the annual rates of apprehensions and deportations have both followed an overall downward trend over the years. While, moreover, voluntary repatriation schemes for undocumented migrants have remained little used, the legal maximum length of administrative detention of irregular migrants has undergone repeated extensions (see further Cheliotis 2013).

As Carr (2012, p. 108) argues, therefore, for irregular migrants Greece has been a 'trap' (see also Anderson 2000, pp. 49–56). Yet neither the fact that irregular migrants may find themselves entrapped in a given country, nor the desperate predicament with which they are typically faced as a result of poverty and attendant needs, suffice to explain the degree and longevity of their exploitability as labourers. It is to this issue that I now turn.

Greece's informal economy and the role of immigration

Greece has a 'semi-peripheral' national economic structure that relies on its comparatively large informal economy, itself estimated to account for around 25 per cent of GDP, one of the highest proportions in the EU-27 (Schneider 2012), to bring together low-skill labour and employers seeking to fill vacancies in private households and small or medium-sized enterprises specialising in farming, construction, industry or service activities (Cheliotis and Xenakis 2010). Yet the size of Greece's informal economy does not in itself suffice to account for the fact that migrants in the country have been afforded ample opportunities for informal employment over the last two-and-a-half decades or so. This has been primarily due to a mixture of broader social, economic and cultural contingencies.

On one hand, the construction boom of the 1990s, the expansion of export-oriented labour-intensive farming, and the upsurge in the number of dual-income nuclear families against the backdrop of persistently minimal levels of state welfare provision for the elderly and young children, have heightened demand for a wide range of poorly paid low-skill and menial labour traditionally supplied for the most part outside the boundaries of the formal economy (e.g. building, fruit-picking, domestic care work). On the other hand, the spread of a cultural trope that grossly undermines the symbolic status of such labour, essentially equating it with failure and backwardness in the context of a country desperate to achieve a bourgeois notion of 'modernisation' (see, e.g. Herzfeld 2004), has combined with widespread knowledge of the exploitative conditions Greek employers tend to impose upon informal workers, to discourage Greek nationals from continuing to fill these crucial niches, many of them rather choosing unemployment, even under conditions of financial crisis (see further Triandafyllidou 2013; also Cavounidis 2006; Lawrence 2007; Demoussis *et al.* 2010)

Migrants in desperate financial need have lent themselves as readily accessible replacements for the resigning Greek workforce, as vividly captured in images of them congregating in public squares in the early morning hours, waiting for passing employers to hire them for day labour (see, e.g. Lawrence 2007, p. 62). Their being foreign migrants in a society with deeply entrenched racist attitudes, however, has additionally allowed for the intensification of exploitation in the workplace. Research on wage differentials in Greece points in this direction, given that the wages of migrant workers have been found to be systematically and significantly lower than those of their Greek counterparts, not only because migrants are usually pushed into low-paid jobs regardless of their skills and prior experience, but also in good part as a result of discriminatory practices against them within their occupations (see further Lianos *et al.* 1996; Fakiolas 1999; Demoussis *et al.* 2010; Drydakis and Vlassis 2010). Although successive waves of migrants have varied both by the main country or region of origin and, to a significant degree, by the niches they have respectively occupied in Greece's informal labour market (during the 1990s, for example, Albanians were predominant in unskilled farm work and the construction industry, while since the 2000s Chinese have usually filled gaps in retail stores and trade, and Bangladeshis in restaurants), exploitation has remained a common feature of migrant employment in the Greek informal economy.

There is no denying that numerous small- and medium-size Greek employers have profited through exploitation of informal migrant labour over the years. The list of beneficiaries would be incomplete, however, were it not to extend to governing elites both of the centre-right and the centre-left, who have concurrently sought to retain and expand their electoral clienteles by sustaining the conditions for such exploitation to occur (see further Cheliotis 2013, 2017). In what follows, I go on to explore the nature of the conditions of migrant labour exploitation in the Greek informal economy, the ways in which they may relate to one another, and the role of government in their emergence and reproduction.

Irregular status and exploitation in Greece's informal economy

Although, as I argued earlier, poverty is a positive correlate of migrant labour exploitability, it cannot alone account for the level and durability of exploitation migrants commonly suffer in the Greek informal labour market. That is to say, in and of itself, poverty does not always permanently prevent migrants from engaging in individual and collective worker resistance, be it in the form of raising grievances and initiating bargaining with current employers, changing employer or occupation, or opting for self-employment (see, e.g. Maroukis et al. 2011). Such prospects are far from inconsequential for business, insofar as they can afflict employers with adjustment costs associated with finding and training replacements, especially when opportunities for securing reserves happen to be limited (due, for example, to the specialist nature of skills required in certain occupations, or temporary labour shortages in geographically isolated locations).

Curiously, the ways in which migrant labour exploitability is maintained and, indeed, enhanced inside the borders of so-called 'host' countries have yet to receive sufficiently comprehensive scholarly attention, above and beyond the role poverty plays in the process. Pertinent research has so far tended towards either focusing on unjust welfare and employment policies that are designed to keep migrants socio-politically weak, for example through systematically restricting their access to welfare and labour rights, or on aggressive criminal justice and cognate policies that target poor migrants and threaten them into acceptance of unfair conditions of work (see, e.g. Bigo 2002; Melossi 2003; Calavita 2005; Lawrence 2007; Brotherton and Barrios 2011; Sawyer and Blitz 2011). However important this body of work may be, I suggest it can be advanced through investigating, first, the functional equivalence and aggregate effect of seemingly unrelated state policies and practices regarding matters of welfare, employment and criminal justice, insofar as they bolster, simultaneously as well as cumulatively, poor migrants' exploitability in the labour market; and second, the contributions state policies and practices in other areas (e.g. migration) and certain patterns of behaviour by non-state actors (e.g. street-level manifestations of anti-migrant violence performed by private citizens or political formations) may additionally make to the same outcome, whether by design or coincidence.[3] Indeed, unless one pays attention to these and related themes, one risks undermining both the multiplicity of bases of migrant labour exploitability and the complexity and intensity of the issue, thereby ultimately overlooking the full scope and downplaying the intricate and persistent nature of the political and policy interventions required to overturn it (see further Cheliotis 2017).

In the Greek case, poor migrants' exploitation in the labour market cannot be adequately explained without considering the consequences that stem from the irregular status so commonly cast upon them. State policies and practices that have kept large swathes of underprivileged migrants irregular have not just served to entrap an ample pool of likely labourers inside the country's borders. They have effectively restricted those migrants' prospects for paid employment to the informal economy, where wages can freely be shrunk well below the legal minimum and layoffs go entirely unchecked, while concurrently depriving them both of trade union rights and any welfare entitlements that would soften the sanction of dismissal and the strains of unemployment more generally.[4] Meanwhile, the very enormity of the irregular population as such has meant that a sufficiently large 'reserve army' of workers is usually at hand, thereby enhancing the exploitability of those already in wage labour by further accentuating their sense of expendability. In sum, state policies and practices that produce and sustain irregularity promote labour exploitation in that they facilitate both the depression of wages in themselves and the conditions that make depressed wages more likely to be accepted by workers. As I explain below, however, these conditions extend to anti-migrant violence.[5]

Although violence against migrants has been alarmingly common in Greece, this has been especially so against those lacking regular status. Such violence has been carried out routinely on a large scale by the state itself, through criminal and administrative justice institutions (from the police and conventional prisons to immigration detention centres), but also, on smaller scales, by non-state actors such as private citizens and political groups of the far-right. Indeed, in important respects, state and non-state actors may be bound together by strong ties of mutual dependence and support. Just as, for example, Greek state authorities often rely on information from members of the public in order to be able to initiate and carry through proceedings of arrest, detention and deportation against individuals residing or working in the country without papers, so too they tend to tolerate violence perpetrated by non-state actors against irregular migrants, as attested by the impunity with which the police and the judiciary have typically responded to such cases, not to mention that the police have also actively discouraged irregular migrants from reporting their victimisation in the first instance, effectively forewarning them of deportation should they proceed to do so (see further Cheliotis 2017). In this context, Greek employers have been afforded opportunities to further strengthen their control and buttress their exploitation over undocumented workers by recourse to violence against them, whether threatened or enacted. Thus, for instance, irregular migrants have commonly been subject to blackmail by employers who threaten either to report the undocumented status of troublesome employees to the police, in which case the deportation machinery would be set in motion against the individuals concerned, or, more boldly, directly to exercise or order physical violence against them, including by calling upon the 'rent-a-mob' services of the neo-fascistic party Chrysi Avyi ('Golden Dawn') (see further Reyneri 2001; Lawrence 2007; Papaioannou 2013; Chrysochoou 2014; Cheliotis 2017).

To the extent that the plight of irregular migrants in Greece has not only been known or directly visible to the country's mainstream public, but has often even involved members of the latter as either instigators or perpetrators, the all too common assumption of a universal human capacity for empathy in wait only for triggers from the external environment appears ripe for retirement. The immediate question concerns the ways in which passive tolerance and active promotion of the injustices suffered by irregular migrants have become possible.

The discursive bases of irregular migrants' labour exploitation in the Greek informal economy

According to research on responses to violence, although the empathic emotions that are necessary to induce a sense of responsibility for remedial action cannot be animated when the pain of others remains in obscurity, there is no guarantee that empathy will actually be called forth as soon as the pain of others comes to the surface. Humans do have a natural capacity for empathy, but the expression of empathy is a matter of culture and the politics that shape it. To put the point differently: whether or not empathy is shown to suffering others is largely dependent on the culture that defines the meaning that those others and their condition have for us.

In particular, a crucial precondition of empathy is that sufferers are deemed worthy of empathic reaction, and that failure to react empathically to their predicament is considered to be discordant with dominant moral principles. Conversely, if sufferers carry individual or collective labels that dress their plight in the clothes of deservedness and necessity, empathy towards them is unlikely to emerge; here exhibition of empathy may in fact be prohibited by the moral strictures of the day. Stereotypes that justify the imposition of pain on others and prevent empathic intervention to remedy their misfortune may be durable even against direct, physical visibility of the misfortune at issue, and this regardless of whether or how one may be related to victims (e.g. through kith or kin; see further Vetlesen 2005; also Cheliotis 2010). This being the case, direct, visible suffering can be inflicted upon poor migrants, or can be tolerated, so long as victims have previously been given labels that render their suffering justifiable or normal. But what kind of discourse has such power and under what conditions can it be so influential?

In Greece, dominant political, media and public discourse has typically employed dramatic language to misrepresent migrants as an undifferentiated mass that poses a variety of serious threats to Greek society, from ethno-cultural disintegration and health deterioration to unemployment and, most notably, crime, often also associating these purported threats to one another. Nowhere is the constructed nexus between migration and crime more acute, however, than in the case of irregular migrants, who, before anything else, are ascribed a criminal label by mere dint of the irregular status essentially thrust upon them.[6] Unsurprisingly, the most extreme messages have come from Chrysi Avyi, which has not only castigated irregular migrants for their purported role in rising crime rates and falling living standards for the Greek majority, but has also advocated cracking down on irregular migration by laying landmines along the Greek-Turkish mainland borders and placing special forces in the area with a licence to shoot at will. Yet the electoral popularity of this discourse has encouraged centrist parties to intensify their own anti-migrant rhetoric, and indeed, to co-opt the far-right agenda in so doing (Karamanidou 2015). To give only a flavour of this, in 2012, in a series of highly publicised parliamentary speeches and media appearances, centre-right Minister of Citizen Protection Nikos Dendias highlighted what he called the 'unbelievable number of foreigners participating in serious crime', linking irregular immigrants more specifically to homicide, drug trafficking and other forms of lawbreaking, as well as to urban squalor. Due to irregular immigration, Dendias opined, Greece 'is being lost. Never since the coming of the Dorians, 4,000 years ago, has the country been subject to an invasion of such magnitude.... This is a bomb at the foundations of society and the state' (see further Xenakis and Cheliotis 2013).

It is not difficult to see how this discourse has found great appeal in the context of a strongly nationalistic society with deeply entrenched racist attitudes and a markedly declining birth rate, not to mention the intensification of socioeconomic insecurities among large segments of the public since the outbreak of the financial crisis in 2009 (see further Cheliotis and Xenakis 2010, 2011; Xenakis and Cheliotis 2013).[7] But if we are to adequately explain why the Greek public has come to hold views or fall for political narratives that blatantly misrepresent a population of weaker others, then we need to appreciate the role of anti-migrant discourse in helping to authorise or otherwise promote policies, practices and behaviours that effectively serve the economic interests of many average Greeks by heightening the exploitability of irregular migrants in the country's informal labour market, even while calling for their exclusion from local communities and Greek national territory altogether.

Concluding remarks: beyond exclusion/inclusion

From the politico-economic perspective taken in my analysis of the Greek case, migrant inclusion can assume forms and perform functions that are no less unjust or inhumane than those of unequivocally exclusionary strategies of migration control. Indeed, it is the various forms that inclusion takes which require more systematic unpicking for the injustices of migration to be fully grasped.

What this implies for scholarly and other accounts that seek to sensitise and call to action broader publics is that they ought to advocate an end not simply to exclusion, but to unjust forms of inclusion as well. The discourse of exclusion reaffirms the desirability of the 'inside', and so forecloses critical analysis of the political order. As this chapter's account of irregular migrants' labour exploitation in Greece suggests, the transition from exclusion to inclusion, the horizontal move from 'outside' to 'inside', cannot be taken at face value as a remedy to injustice, which is always a problem of vertical, top-down social relations (see further Allen 2005a, 2005b). At the same time, progressive interventions in the field of symbolic politics need to consider the mutual complementarity and cumulative effect of different forms of inequality that migrants may face in an affluent 'host' society. Such a holistic approach would help to guard against partial responses that might unwittingly leave existing structures of inequality effectively unchallenged. This, admittedly, could only be a first step in challenging such structures, given the powerful politico-economic interests that underpin them.

Notes

1 This temporal span was necessary partly due to limitations of space, and partly because at the time of writing the Syriza-led coalition had been in office for too short a period for its policies on migration and other social issues to be conclusively assessed.
2 Indeed, just as some affluent states may be willing to relax their national borders in order to 'import' cheap foreign labour, other, weaker states may be willing to boost their own economies by facilitating emigration, relaxing their own borders and even promoting the production of suitably flexible labourers willing to emigrate overseas (see, e.g. Ong 2006).
3 Significant, if partial, steps towards this direction have already been taken by such scholars as Andreas (2009), Wacquant (2009a, 2009b), Anderson (2010), Mezzadra and Neilson (2013) and De Giorgi (2010).
4 Like their regularised counterparts, irregular migrants do not have the right to public protest, either, although there have been instances where they have engaged in organised protest action against the unjust and exploitative conditions they commonly endure in their capacity as workers (see, e.g. Karyotis and Skleparis 2016).
5 Although regularised migrants may also seek to secure wage labour in the informal economy when employment opportunities are limited for them in the country's formal economy, they are comparatively less vulnerable to exploitation than their irregular counterparts, insofar as they can have access to protections from which the latter are categorically excluded. This goes a long way towards explaining why the overwhelming majority of migrants working in Greece's informal economy have been irregular.
6 Indeed, the criminal label so commonly attached to irregular migrants has tended to persist even whey have managed gradually to be absorbed by the legal economy (see further Xenakis 2011).
7 It would be wrong to assume that anti-migrant political discourse has merely been responsive to public attitudes. As explained in detail elsewhere, governing parties have sought to generate and inflame anti-migrant sentiment among the Greek public, and to deploy the aggressive penal and cognate policies and practices such sentiment promotes, as a convenient means of managing the electoral challenges of disaffection that their increasingly regressive socio-economic policies and their continuing impunity towards grand political corruption have produced among the public; disaffection that has become all the more pervasive and acute since the financial crisis hit Greece in 2009 and harsh austerity measures ensued to meet the requirements of successive bailouts. For example, the widely publicised intensification in the use of immigration

detention in the name of security has helped to deflect and appease a range of anxieties and frustrations among lower- and middle-class segments of the population, from heightened concerns relating to personal and family finances, to increased anger with political elites, to a spreading sense of national humiliation before foreign audiences. This, indeed, is an additional politico-economic function anti-migrant discourse and attendant policies and practices have performed in Greece (see further Cheliotis and Xenakis 2010, 2011; Xenakis and Cheliotis 2013, 2017).

References

Albahari, M. (2015). *Crimes of Peace: Mediterranean Migrations at the World's Deadliest Border*. Philadelphia: University of Pennsylvania Press.
Allen, D. (2005a). A Reply to Bader and Orwin. *In*: M.S. Williams and S. Macedo, eds, *Political Exclusion and Domination*. New York: New York University Press, 179–181.
Allen, D. (2005b). Invisible Citizens: Political Exclusion and Domination in Arendt and Ellison. *In*: M.S. Williams and S. Macedo, eds, *Political Exclusion and Domination*. New York: New York University Press, 29–76.
Anderson, B. (2010). Migration, Immigration Controls and the Fashioning of Precarious Workers. *Work, Employment and Society*, 24 (2), 300–317.
Andreas, P. (2009). *Border Games: Policing the US–Mexico Divide*. 2nd ed. Ithaca: Cornell University Press.
Baldwin-Edwards, M. (2014). Greece. *In*: M. Baldwin-Edwards and A. Kraler, eds, *Regularisations in Europe*. Amsterdam: European Commission/Amsterdam University Press, 297–330.
Basaran, T. (2015). The Saved and the Drowned: Governing Indifference in the Name of Security. *Security Dialogue*, 46 (3), 205–220.
Bigo, D. (2002). Security and Immigration: Toward a Critique of the Governmentality of Unease. *Alternatives*, 27 (Special Issue), 63–92.
Bigo, D. (2015). Death in the Mediterranean Sea: The Results of the Three Fields of Action of European Union Border Controls. *In*: Y. Jansen, R. Celikates and J. De Bloois, eds, *The Irregularization of Migration in Contemporary Europe*. Lanham: Rowman & Littlefield, 55–70.
Brotherton, D.C. and Barrios, L. (2011). *Banished to the Homeland: Dominican Deportees and their Stories of Exile*. New York: Columbia University Press.
Calavita, K. (2005). *Immigrants at the Margins: Law, Race, and Exclusion in Southern Europe*. Cambridge: Cambridge University Press.
Cavounidis, J. (2006). Migration and Policy Trends. *In*: M. Petmesidou and E. Mossialos, eds, *Social Policy Developments in Greece*. Aldershot: Ashgate, 358–379.
Carr, M. (2012). *Fortress Europe: Dispatches from a Gated Continent*. London: Hurst.
Cheliotis, L.K. (2010). The Sociospatial Mechanics of Domination: Transcending the 'Exclusion/Inclusion' Dualism, *Law & Critique*, 21 (2), 131–145.
Cheliotis, L.K. (2013). Behind the Veil of Philoxenia: The Politics of Immigration Detention in Greece. *European Journal of Criminology*, 10 (6), 725–745.
Cheliotis, L.K. (2017). Punitive Inclusion: The Political Economy of Irregular Migration in the Margins of Europe. *European Journal of Criminology*, 14 (1), 78–99.
Cheliotis, L.K. and Xenakis, S. (2010). What's Neoliberalism Got To Do with It? Towards a Political Economy of Punishment in Greece. *Criminology and Criminal Justice*, 10 (4), 353–373.

Cheliotis, L.K. and Xenakis, S. (2011). Crime, Fear of Crime and Punitiveness. *In*: L.K. Cheliotis and S. Xenakis, eds, *Crime and Punishment in Contemporary Greece: International Comparative Perspectives*, Bern: Peter Lang, 1–43.

Chrysochoou, X. (2014). *Severe Forms of Labour Exploitation: Supporting Victims of Severe Forms of Labour Exploitation in Having Access to Justice in EU Member States: Greece, 2014*. Vienna: European Union Agency for Fundamental Rights. Available from: http://fra.europa. eu/sites/default/files/fra_uploads/severe-labour-exploitation-country_el.pdf [accessed 1 November 2015].

De Giorgi, A. (2010). Immigration Control, Post-Fordism, and Less Eligibility: A Materialist Critique of the Criminalization of Immigration Across Europe. *Punishment and Society*, 12 (2), 147–167.

Demoussis, M., Giannakopoulos, N. and Zografakis, S. (2010). Native-immigrant Wage Differentials and Occupational Segregation in the Greek Labour Market. *Applied Economics*, 42 (8), 1015–1027.

Drydakis, N. and Vlassis, M. (2010). Ethnic Discrimination in the Greek Labour Market: Occupational Access, Insurance Coverage and Wage Offers. *The Manchester School*, 78 (3), 201–218.

Fakiolas, R. (1999). Socio-economic Effects of Immigration in Greece. *Journal of European Social Policy*, 9 (3), 211–229.

Herzfeld, M. (2004). *The Body Impolitic: Artisans and Artifice in the Global Hierarchy of Value*. Chicago: The University of Chicago Press.

Karamanidou, L. (2015). Political Parties and Immigration in Greece: Between Consensus and Competition. *Acta Politica*, 50 (4), 442–460.

Karyotis, G. and Skleparis, D. (2016). Resistance to the Criminalization of Migration: Migrant Protest in Greece. *In*: R. Furman, G. Lamphear and D. Epps, eds, *The Immigrant Other: Lived Experiences in a Transnational World*. New York: Columbia University Press, 266–281.

Lawrence, C.M. (2007). *Blood and Oranges: Immigrant Labor and European Markets in Rural Greece*. Oxford: Berghahn.

Lianos, T.P., Sarris, A.H. and Katseli, L.T. (1996). Illegal Immigration and Local Labour Markets: The Case of Northern Greece. *International Migration*, 34 (3), 449–484.

Maroukis, T., Iglicka, K. and Gmaj, K. (2011). Irregular Migration and Informal Economy in Southern and Central-Eastern Europe: Breaking the Vicious Cycle? *International Migration*, 49 (5), 129–156.

Melossi, D. (2003). 'In a Peaceful Life': Migration and the Crime of Modernity in Europe/Italy. *Punishment and Society*, 5 (4), 371–397.

Mezzadra, S. and Neilson, B. (2013). *Border as Method, or, the Multiplication of Labor*. Durham: Duke University Press.

Migreurop (2016) *Europe's Murderous Borders*. Available from: www.migreurop.org/IMG/pdf/Rapport-Migreurop-nov2009-en-final.pdf [accessed 8 November 2016].

Ong, A. (2006). *Neoliberalism as Exception: Mutations in Citizenship and Sovereignty*. Durham: Duke University Press.

Papadopoulou-Kourkoula, A. (2008). *Transit Migration: The Missing Link between Emigration and Settlement*. Basingstoke: Palgrave Macmillan.

Papaioannou, K. (2013). *The 'Clean Hands' of Chrysi Avyi: Applications of Nazi Purity*. Athens: Metaichmio [in Greek].

Rahola, F. (2011). The Detention Machine. *In*: S. Palidda, ed., *Racial Criminalization of Migrants in the 21st Century*. Aldershot: Ashgate, 95–106.

Reyneri, E. (2001). Migrants in Irregular Employment in the Mediterranean Countries of the European Union. *International Migration Papers*, No. 41. Geneva: ILO.

Sawyer, C. and Blitz, B.K. (2011). *Statelessness in the European Union: Displaced, Undocumented, Unwanted*. Cambridge: Cambridge University Press.

Schneider, F. (2012). Size and Development of the Shadow Economy of 31 European and 5 Other OECD Countries from 2003 to 2012: Some New Facts, Working Paper. Available from: www.econ.jku.at/members/Schneider/files/publications/2012/ShadEcEurope31_March%202012.pdf [accessed 13 July 2012].

Triandafyllidou, A. (2013). Migration policy in Southern Europe: Challenges, Constraints and Prospects. *In*: LSE IDEAS, ed., *A Strategy for Southern Europe*. London: LSE IDEAS. Available from: www.lse.ac.uk/IDEAS/publications/reports/pdf/SR017/Triandafyllidou.pdf [accessed 1 January 2016].

Vetlesen, A.J. (2005). *Evil and Human Agency: Understanding Collective Evildoing*. Cambridge: Cambridge University Press.

Wacquant, L. (1999). 'Suitable Enemies': Foreigners and Immigrants in the Prisons of Europe. *Punishment and Society*, 1 (2), 215–222.

Wacquant, L. (2009a). *Prisons of Poverty*. Expanded ed. Minneapolis: University of Minnesota Press.

Wacquant, L. (2009b). *Punishing the Poor: The Neoliberal Government of Social Insecurity*. Durham: Duke University Press.

Xenakis, S. (2011). Organised Crime and Political Violence. *In*: L.K. Cheliotis and S. Xenakis, eds, *Crime and Punishment in Contemporary Greece: International Comparative Perspectives*. Bern: Peter Lang, 241–287.

Xenakis, S. and Cheliotis, L.K. (2013). Crime and Economic Downturn: The Complexity of Crime and Crime Politics in Greece since 2009. *British Journal of Criminology*, 53 (5), 719–745.

Xenakis, S. and Cheliotis, L.K. (2017, forthcoming). Carceral Modernation and Janus Face of International Pressure: A Long View of Greece's Engagement with the European Convention of Human Rights. *Crime, Law & Social Change*.

Zaiotti, R. (2011). *Cultures of Border Control: Schengen and the Evolution of European Frontiers*. Chicago: The University of Chicago Press.

Chapter 10

Reflections on Spanish policies of migration control

A political economic reading on the punishment of migrants

José A. Brandariz-García

Introduction: the political economic analysis of policies of migration control

One striking feature of the analyses on migration control and bordered penality is the wide variety of perspectives upon which they are founded, encompassing legal, political, cultural and social viewpoints. This field of study also includes a prolific line of analysis that interprets migration enforcement through an economic lens. This comes as no surprise since human mobility is most frequently understood as a pivotal factor in the shaping of the labour force. Likewise, a critical representation underpinning migration policies is one in which the immigrant is portrayed above all as a worker (Aparicio Wilhelmi 2010; Calavita 2005; De Giorgi 2006).

The study of migration control policies from an economic perspective has evolved along disparate lines of inquiry (see e.g. Preston and Perez 2006; Facchini and Testa 2015). This chapter delves into the economic account by considering a theoretical framework that has been notably fruitful for developing materialist and critical analyses on penality: the Political Economy of Punishment (from now on, PEofP). Some authors (De Giorgi 2006, 2010; Melossi 2013a, 2013b, 2015) have already undertaken this type of analytical endeavour. In line with their contributions, this chapter intends to examine the policies of migration control in Spain through the lens of the PEofP.

There are some good reasons to employ Spain as a national case study. One of them is the sheer magnitude of the migration phenomenon experienced in Spain throughout the first decade of the century, when the country was a top-priority destination for international migrations (Arango *et al.* 2011). The consequences of this process of mobility are especially noteworthy: according to the Spanish National Statistics Institute (hereafter INE), the number of foreign-born residents grew by 348.5 per cent between 2000 and 2010. They accounted for 3.6 per cent of the whole population in 2000 (2.2 per cent as regards non EU-15 born population), compared with 14.0 per cent in 2010 (9.0 per cent in the case of non EU-27 born population). There is no shortage of academic literature dealing with the economic effects of this immigration phenomenon of the 2000s

(Conde-Ruiz *et al.* 2008; Godenau 2012; González *et al.* 2009; Oficina Económica del Presidente 2006). In particular, a wide range of academic works has analysed migration enforcement in Spain from the standpoint of its economic determinants and consequences (Brandariz García 2011; Calavita 2005; Romero 2010). However, the unique shift in Spanish migration control policies requires further reflection, since the enforcement of the various instruments of bordered penality, encompassing both the penal and civil detention of migrants and the deportation regime, has remarkably declined since the onset of the Great Recession (Fernández Bessa 2016), as will be examined in the fourth section of this chapter.

This chapter assumes that the analysis of migration penality requires an economic perspective and aims to develop this viewpoint in line with the theoretical framework of the PEofP. The chapter seeks thereby to reflect on the strengths and pitfalls of that framework to grasp migration control policies. To that end, the chapter begins by considering the various lines of development of the PEofP, focusing especially on the topics of less eligibility and discipline of the workforce, to test their interpretative value with regard to the Spanish case. This first part of the text is centred on the expansion and peak of the migration cycle between 2000 and 2009. The analysis subsequently approaches the marked changes in migration penality set in motion since the beginning of the Great Recession. The chapter concludes by delving into the shortcomings of an economic account of the relation between penality and migration. The reflection highlights the pressing need to supplement economy-driven interpretations with perspectives that regard, among other points, both the sovereign components inherent to migration control and the processes of othering and racialisation underlying this realm of punishment. The investigation of a subfield of the criminal justice system with numerous contradictions requires including such lines of inquiry.

Political economy of punishment and policies of migration control

The central tenet of the PEofP framework assumes that the analysis of penality, in its concrete forms and expressions, cannot be disconnected from the evolution of the modes of production, since punishment practices are essentially determined by economic conditions (Rusche and Kirchheimer [1939] 2003, pp. 5–6). In Georg Rusche and Otto Kirchheimer's seminal work, this assumption led to the conclusion that the evolution of the labour market, i.e. the demand of living labour, has a most prominent influence on the extension and intensity of punishment, and even on the specific forms of penality (Rusche [1933] 1978, p. 4).

The original and more 'orthodox' developments of the PEofP framework supported the hypothesis of a direct correlation between unemployment rate and prison population rate (Greenberg 1977; Inverarity and McCarthy 1988; Jankovic 1977; see also Chiricos and Delone 1992; Michalowski and Carlson

2006), an analytic perspective that was eventually contested (De Giorgi 2006, 2013; Melossi 1993, 2001, 2003a; see also Aviram 2015). That hypothesis is unsuitable to examine the migration control policies in Spain, since over the first decade of the century migration penality featured a distinct rise in punitiveness, whereas the unemployment rate of the foreign population remained essentially stable, as can be seen in Table 10.1. The number of foreigners incarcerated in Spanish prisons rose by 202 per cent from 2000 to 2009, while the prison population of Spanish citizens increased by 35.5 per cent over the same period. Consequently, foreign inmates accounted for 19.9 per cent of the whole prison population in 2000 (equal to an incarceration rate of 656 inmates per 100,000 foreigners residing in Spain) compared with 35.7 per cent in 2009 (or 503 inmates per 100,000 foreign inhabitants) (Source: INE). In addition, Spanish Home Office data show that 1,226 irregular migrants were deported in 2000 with the number of forced repatriations climbing to 28,865 in 2009 (*Source*: Eurostat). Moreover, it is estimated[1] that 2,727 migrants were held in detention centres in 2000 compared with 17,203 detainees being held in 2009 (Fernández Bessa 2013, 2016). In contrast to these increases, the unemployment rate of the foreign population remained constant between 2002 (14.3 per cent, 15.4 per cent with regard to non-EU foreigners) and 2008 (14.7 per cent, 15.3 per cent in the case of non-EU foreigners) (Source: INE).

A body of scholar literature has elaborated on PEoP from the viewpoint of the concept of 'business cycles' (Barlow *et al.* 1993; Brion 2015; Melossi 1985, 2002, 2003a, 2013b; Vanneste 2000, 2001), in line with the well-known economic theories known as 'business cycles' (Schumpeter 1939) and 'long waves' (Kondratiev [1925] 1984). With regard to the relation between economy and punishment, business cycles may be divided in two different periods: first, a stage of economic growth and improvement of the conditions of the workforce, coupled with moderate penality; second, a phase of economic stagnation and an increase in the level of exploitation, featuring a rise in punitiveness (Melossi 1985, 2003a). At first glance, this thesis appears to be suitable to explain Spanish policies of migration control that may be neatly split into two different phases (2000–2009 and 2009–2015). However, the conclusions of that PEofP thesis

Table 10.1 Evolution of the unemployment rate of the foreign population and evolution of the foreign prison population rate, 2000–2009

	2000	2001	2002	2003	2004	2005	2006	2007	2008	2009
Unemployment rate (Foreign population)	–	–	14.3	17.9	14.1	13.8	12.3	12.6	14.7	28.4
Foreign prison population rate	19.9	23.3	25.9	27.1	29.1	30.5	32.2	34.2	35.6	35.7

Source: INE.

stand at odds with the features of those two periods of bordered penality, since no inverse correlation between economic expansion and a rise in punitiveness is shown. On the contrary, the analysis of those two periods shows a direct correlation.

One particularly insightful analytical framework in the field of PEofP, put forth by Dario Melossi (1993, 2003a), claims that the crucial explaining variable of the evolution of penality is not the unemployment rate, but the 'performance' of the economic system regarding the level of exploitation of the workforce (see also Hale 2013). Melossi claims therefore that higher severity of labour conditions co-varies with higher punitiveness. This perspective seems unable to analyse migration control in the Spanish case. Even though more accurate data on the labour conditions of the migrant workforce are still needed, Table 10.2 indicates that the mounting punitiveness of the decade (2000–2009) did not correspond with increased exploitation of the living labour (Jiménez Franco 2015). In fact, while the migrant population has faced severe working conditions, those conditions arguably remained quite constant throughout the decade.

To sum up, the data illustrate that the rising punitiveness (in general terms and vis-à-vis the migrant population) of the first decade of the century coincided with both a period of economic growth and stability in the level of workforce exploitation.

Less eligibility and discipline in policies of migration control

The PEofP framework has driven the elaboration of other theoretical lines that may be suitable to grasp migration penality in Spain. In particular, the concept of 'less eligibility' and the notion of discipline of the workforce, both of which relate punishment with social and labour policies, should be taken into account. In fact, several authors (De Giorgi 2006, 2010, González Sánchez 2014, Melossi 2013a, 2013b) have recently drawn on these concepts to examine European policies of migration control. The approach of this chapter essentially agrees with the perspective developed by those authors.

The notion of 'less eligibility', coined by Jeremy Bentham at the dawn of the nineteenth century (Dean 2010, Sieh 1989), was revisited by Rusche and Kirchheimer ([1939] 2003, p. 94, 108, 139ff.) to explain the evolution of penality from an economic viewpoint, particularly in Rusche's article of 1933 (Rusche [1933] 1978, pp. 3–4). They interpreted the role of the principle of less eligibility within the technologies of power from two different perspectives (De Giorgi 2010, 2013; Garland 1990; Melossi 2003a). From a negative viewpoint, the concept of less eligibility implies that the conditions of punishment, and especially prison conditions, cannot be better than the living standard of the less favoured segment of the working class (see also Pratt 2002). More interestingly, from a positive perspective the notion of less eligibility means that penality should be severe enough to discourage the rejection of waged labour. Therefore,

Table 10.2 Evolution of prison population rate and evolution of certain economic and labour variables, 2000–2009

Year	Prison pop. rate	Year-on-year GDP growth	GINI Index	Shadow Economy size (% GDP)	Wage share (% GDP)	Unemploym. rate	Temporary work rate	Part-time work rate	Social spending (% GDP)
2000	113	+4.5	–	26.3	47.2	–	–	–	–
2001	118	+3.3	–	23.0	47.1	–	–	–	19.7
2002	126	+2.7	–	21.4	46.8	11.5	32.1	8.3	20.0
2003	134	+3.2	31.0	19.8	46.6	12.0	31.4	8.4	20.3
2004	140	+3.4	32.2	18.2	46.3	11.5	31.8	8.9	20.3
2005	141	+3.8	31.9	15.5	45.4	10.2	31.9	12.7	20.6
2006	145	+4.1	31.9	13.5	45.2	9.0	33.2	12.3	20.5
2007	150	+3.2	31.9	14.5	45.6	8.4	31.8	12.5	20.8
2008	161	–1.4	31.9	17.8	47.2	9.6	30.0	12.1	22.2
2009	165	–3.0	33.0	21.1	47.3	17.2	25.2	13.0	25.4

Sources: Eurostat (social spending and GINI Index data); INE; Pickhardt and Sardà 2015 (shadow economy data).

penality should promote the subjection of the lower or more unbridled sectors of the working class to the exploitation of salaried labour.

This reading of the governing of the working classes in terms of less eligibility is closely related to the concept of discipline. The PEofP account insightfully claims that the penal system contributes to disciplining working class individuals into a workforce (Rusche and Kirchheimer [1939] 2003, pp. 44ff., see also Wacquant 2009). In other words, penality is aimed at enabling the availability and willingness of those individuals to be subjected to the requirements of the production regime. This interpretation has been thoroughly developed by Michel Foucault, especially in his books *Discipline and Punish* ([1975] 1977) and *The Punitive Society* ([2013] 2015; see also Foucault [2003] 2006), but it is also a pivotal conclusion of the renowned Dario Melossi and Massimo Pavarini's work, *The Prison and the Factory* ([1977] 1981).[2]

Both the concept of less eligibility and the notion of disciplining individuals into a workforce greatly facilitate the understanding of the shift in Spanish policies of migration control. In effect, in line with Alessandro De Giorgi's compelling analysis on the variety of Global North countries (2006, 2010), recent Spanish migration penality can be grasped from the standpoint of the transformation of the economic system commonly termed as post-Fordism (Boyer and Durand 1998; Brenner and Glick 1991; Marazzi 2011). With its emphasis on just-in-time production, the post-Fordist regime of accumulation unavoidably depends on the availability of living labour in conditions of utmost flexibility. Therefore, migrant workforce has become essential for the current production system (Calavita 2003; Melossi 2013a; Sciurba 2009). Indeed, the massive availability of a hyper-flexible and highly exploitable migrant workforce, along with the phenomenon of deficit spending based on the secondary circuit of accumulation, was the key explaining variable of the Spanish cycle of economic growth between 1994 and 2007 (López Hernández and Rodríguez López 2010; Rodríguez 2003).

The massive influx of migrants into the post-Fordist production regime has led to extraordinary levels of exploitation, precarity, subalternity and vulnerability of the migrant population (Calavita 2005). Like in other European Union (EU) countries, the percentage of employed migrants in Spain working on a temporary contract was higher (42.8 per cent in 2009) than that of the domestic workforce. Migrant workers also earn lower average wages (29 per cent lower than those of native workers in 2007), work much overtime, have to endure geographical mobility to find work, and face considerable exposure to the black labour market (42.6 per cent of the migrant workforce was active in the black labour market in 2004). Furthermore, the hardships of the migrant labour market have been exacerbated by the Spanish workfare regime, which has led to the emergence of ethnic segmentations within the labour market and subsequent upward labour mobility for the Spanish workforce (Carrasco Carpio 2008; Colectivo Ioé 2008; Pajares 2010). All of these factors are consistent with the concept of less eligibility. In effect, the analysis of the subordination of migrants within the Spanish production regime unveils a pattern of less eligibility fuelled by the legal status of the migrant as a whole, but especially by the apparatuses of migration control (De Giorgi 2010; Melossi 2013a), most prominent among them being *imm-carceration* and the deportation regime.

Consequently, and in spite of their declared goals of exclusion, the policies of migration enforcement have actually generated effects of differential and subordinated inclusion (Calavita 2003; Mezzadra and Neilson 2013; Romero 2010). Therefore, stale metaphors such as 'Fortress Europe' appear flawed, to the extent that European and Spanish borders have worked as a selective filter, rather than as an impregnable rampart (Brighenti 2009; Huysmans 2006; Mezzadra and Neilson 2013). In this sense, the policies of migration control, instead of ending irregular migration flows, have led to administering them (Cuttitta 2008; Guild and Bigo 2005; Romero 2010) As a result, the massive influx of migrants has become a massive economic insertion of exploited migrant living labour in accordance with the needs of an increasingly post-Fordist regime of accumulation.

Spanish policies in this field have integrated elements of normalisation, i.e. of subjection of the migrant workforce to a condition of conspicuous subalternity (De Giorgi 2010). From this perspective, the disciplinary character of those policies cannot be more apparent (Mezzadra 2006; Rodríguez 2003; Patel and Tyrer 2011). These effects of normalisation, though, do not operate at the level of the individual subject. On the contrary, deportation, civil detention and *imm-carceration*, with all their selectivity, are not directly geared towards the discipline of the foreign individual, but to the normalisation – especially through the deterrent effects of the condition of *deportability* – of the entire migrant population (Calavita 2003; De Giorgi 2010; Dingeman-Cerda and Bibler Coutin 2012). That is not a minor caveat. Taking into account Michel Foucault's ([1976] 1979, [1997] 2003, see also Lemke 2011) analysis on the differences between disciplinary and bio-political apparatuses of power, a wide bio-political pattern of government of migrant individuals' lives, which frames them as a distinct group of population, has been developing in the field of migration penality (Brandariz García 2011; Valverde 2008). Sandro Mezzadra and Brett Neilson (2013, pp. 168ff.) have convincingly analysed the somehow conflicting coexistence of disparate technologies of power in the government of borders and immigrants by understanding these political regimes as 'sovereign machines of governmentality'[3] (see also Pratt 2005). In sum, Spanish migration control policies during the first decade of the century (i.e. 2000–2009), which have incorporated a rationale of less eligibility and especially goals of discipline of the migrant workforce, have operated as a sovereign machine of governmentality. Yet, this model of bordered penality has been sharply modified by the emergence of the financial crisis, which has changed the conditions of economic insertion of the foreign population and, consequently, the practices of migration enforcement.

The Spanish policies of migration control since the onset of the Great Recession: managerialism on the rise

The Great Recession has significantly influenced the Spanish criminal justice system, by fuelling both the decline of the correctional population and the debasement of the prisoners' living conditions (Brandariz García 2014, Jiménez Franco 2015). Yet, the impact of the already long-lasting economic crisis has been even more prominent in the domain of migration penality (Brandariz García and Fernández Bessa 2017; Fernández Bessa 2013, 2016).

An effect of the grave economic downturn and the rapidly increasing unemployment has been the apparent lack of demand for the migrant workforce, which has endured notably high unemployment rates since 2009 (López-Sala 2013). This dispensability has only partially been counterbalanced by the return of migrants to their countries of origin, since this process of repatriation (or migration to a third country) has been fairly insignificant, with the exception of 2014, as can be seen in Table 10.3.

In line with what occurred during the first decade of the century, the relation between the evolution of the unemployment rate and the evolution of punitiveness has not followed the path foreseen by the former elaborations of the PEofP framework. In contrast to the sharp increase of unemployment rates, the policies of migration control have recently undergone a process of stark contraction. As illustrated by the data in Table 10.4, the foreign prison population rate, the number of migration law-based arrests, the number of enforced deportations, and the number of migrants held in detention centres have constantly declined between 2009 and 2015.

The recent evolution of the policies of migration law enforcement appears puzzling from a politico-economic account of penality. The recessive economic cycle and its dire consequences in terms of unemployment, impoverishment and growing inequality have not led to a rise of punitiveness, but to a prominent

Table 10.3 Evolution of the unemployment rate of the non EU-born population and evolution of the non EU-born resident population, 2009–2016 (%)

Year	Non EU-born population unemployment rate	Non EU-born population	Year-on-year evolution of non EU-born population
2009	30.2	8.9	+7.3
2010	32.7	9.0	+2.0
2011	32.4	9.0	+1.0
2012	38.7	9.1	+1.1
2013	42.2	9.1	−0.7
2014	40.8	9.0	−1.9
2015	30.9	8.5	−5.6
2016	26.3	8.5	−0.0

Source: INE.

Table 10.4 Evolution of the foreign prison population and evolution of migration law-enforcement activities, 2009–2015

Year	Foreign prison population rate (%)	Migration law-based police arrests	Enforced deportations	Migrants held in detention centres
2009	35.7	103,904	28,865	17,203
2010	35.6	86,060	21,955	11,915
2011	34.8	90,425	23,350	13,241
2012	33.4	59,570	18,865	11,325
2013	31.6	49,389	17,285	9,020
2014	30.3	42,245	15,150	7,286
2015	29.4	36,327	13,315	6,930

Sources: INE (2009–2014 foreign prison population rates); Spanish Prison Service (2015 foreign prison population rate); Spanish Home Office; Eurostat.[1]

Note
1 The data on the quantity of enforced deportations have been published by Eurostat (ec.europe.eu/eurostat; Accessed 8 April 2016). The data on the number of migrant individuals held in detention centres and of migration law-based arrests have been provided by Cristina Fernández Bessa (University of Barcelona), who obtained them from the Spanish Home Office.

decline of the penal apparatuses. Moreover, migration control policies cannot continue to be aimed at setting up a regime of less eligibility and discipline of the workforce, since migrant living labour is understood as rather dispensable in the current economic phase (Melossi 2013a, 2013b).

A new rationale of scarcity has been consolidating in the field of migration control, in line with Hadar Aviram's (2015) recent claim about the contraction of the US prison population. The available data allow one to conclude that managerialism is on the rise in Spanish migration penalty (Brandariz García and Fernández Bessa 2017; Fernández Bessa 2016). In this realm, migration law-based policing, the deportation apparatus and the circuit prison-detention facility-deportation have become more targeted, aiming to manage scarce resources, to achieve efficiency and to coordinate the operation of the various law enforcement agencies.

More precisely, Spanish bordered penality has evolved in recent years along two different albeit interconnected lines (Brandariz García and Fernández Bessa 2017). First, the Spanish government has fostered the enforcement of the so-called 'qualified deportations', i.e. criminal law-related returns (Fernández Bessa 2016; Sainz de la Maza Quintanal 2015). Table 10.5 shows that the enforcement of both criminal deportation orders (Article 89 of the Spanish Penal Code) and administrative deportation orders based on criminal records (Article 57.2 of the Spanish Foreigners' Law) has constantly increased since 2008–2009 even though the total number of forced repatriations has consistently dropped. The gradual oversight of the enforcement of administrative deportation orders based on the civil offence of irregular stay in the country (Articles 53, 57.1 of the

Table 10.5 Evolution of the various legal categories of enforced deportations, 2008–2014

Year	Administrative removals: irregular Stay	Administrative removals: criminal records	Administrative removals: others	Criminal deportations
2008	9,003 (84.8%)	343 (3.2%)	636 (6.0%)	634 (6.0%)
2009	11,223 (84.5%)	395 (3.0%)	214 (1.6%)	1,446 (10.9%)
2010	8,642 (75.4%)	856 (7.5%)	157 (1.4%)	1,799 (15.7%)
2011	7,608 (67.0%)	1,284 (11.3%)	165 (1.4%)	2,301 (20.3%)
2012	6,148 (60.7%)	1,395 (13.8%)	278 (2.7%)	2,309 (22.8%)
2013	5,218 (58.1%)	1,394 (15.5%)	267 (3.0%)	2,105 (23.4%)
2014	4,029 (52.4%)	1,451 (18.9%)	300 (3.8%)	1,916 (24.9%)

Source: Spanish Home Office.[1]

Note
1 The data included in this table have been provided by Cristina Fernández Bessa (University of Barcelona), who obtained them from the Spanish Home Office.

Spanish Foreigners' Law) has been essentially consistent with a governmental rhetoric that has unambiguously portrayed deportees as menacing criminal aliens (Ulloa Rubio 2012).

Second, the Spanish Home Office has remarkably ameliorated the performance of its policies and practices of migration control. Specifically, it has promoted the enforcement of the so-called 'express deportations', i.e. repatriations in which the deportable migrant is immediately transferred after his or her arrest directly from the police station (or from a correctional facility) to the transportation of return site, thereby avoiding the resource-consuming confinement in a detention centre (Martínez Escamilla 2013; Sainz de la Maza Quintanal 2015). For these purposes, the Spanish National Police has decisively improved the planning of transportations of return. The contribution of the EU has been critical in this regard, for the Union has prompted a cost-effective policy of joint flights of removal, initiated by Directive No. 2003/110/EC of 25 November 2003 and Council Decision No. 2004/573/EC of 29 April 2004 and subsequently coordinated by Frontex (Barbero 2010; Fernández Bessa 2016; see also Walters 2016). This thorough reorganisation of the logistical details of the deportation regime in turn has led the Spanish Home Office to develop much more targeted practices of migration law policing. The scheduling of a deportation flight destined for a certain country on a certain date leads the police to carry out arrests of deportable foreigners of the given nationality to load the carrier (Campaña Estatal por el Cierre de los CIE 2014). In sum, since the onset of the economic crisis Spanish policies of migration penality have evolved in line with a rationale of 'cheap on (migration) crime', to borrow Hadar Aviram's (2015) expression. Migration enforcement has become much more efficient, resource-saving and expedited (Brandariz García and Fernández Bessa, 2017). All of these developments are evidently consistent with a managerial model of penality (see Raine 2005; Vigour 2006; Wood and Shearing 2006). In fact, the field of migration control has become a laboratory for the introduction of managerial rationales and practices within the Spanish criminal justice system (see also De Giorgi 2006; Guild 2009; Koulish 2010).

A variety of reasons may contribute to explicate the managerial turn of the Spanish policies of migration enforcement. First, the deportation regime is a remarkably cost-intensive subfield of the criminal justice system (Calavita 2003, 2005; García España 2007), which has become particularly burdensome in an era of public spending cuts and recessive penality. Second, the pre-Great Recession model of migration penality was especially inefficient, since a significant number of deportation orders remained unenforced, and a wide percentage of irregular migrants held in detention facilities were not deported (Brandariz García 2011; Monclús Masó 2008; Silveira Gorski 2003). This former inefficiency has assisted in promoting the current managerial turn. Third, the comparatively high exposure to public scrutiny of this field of penal policies and the criticisms raised against the Government by non-governmental organisations (NGOs) and institutions (Martínez Escamilla 2013; Campaña Estatal por el Cierre de los CIE 2014) have also contributed to a performance-enhancing model of migration control. However, there is another pivotal reason that should not be neglected. The managerial turn cannot be disconnected from the prominent role of the EU institutions within the field of migration control. EU political and administrative culture is much more prone to managerial public policies (Haar and Walters 2004) than Spanish Administration has traditionally been. The EU has not only provided political, technical, and financial assistance to the arena of migration control, but it has also injected a managerial rationale into Spanish punitive policies (Brandariz García and Fernández Bessa, 2017).

Yet, the managerial turn of Spanish policies of migration control cannot be easily grasped from the theoretical framework of the PEofP. Both Andrew Scull's (1977) reference to decarceration and punishment in the community and Rusche and Kirchheimer's ([1939] 2003, p. 7) highly criticised allusions to the influence of fiscal conditions on the evolution of penality appear to be unsuitable to explain the current situation, since for obvious historical reasons they could not consider the profound and multi-faceted transformation brought about by managerial penality.

The conflictual relation of political economic and sovereign accounts on the punishment of migrants: processes of othering, racialisation and penality

A body of literature (De Giorgi 2006, 2013; Garland 1990; Melossi 1985, 2003a) has compellingly claimed that PEofP analyses should reinforce their symbolic, cultural, social and political dimensions in order to elaborate an insightful account of penality. This perspective can also be found in Rusche's work ([1933]

1978, p. 3), which highlighted the limitations of an economic understanding of punishment. The unbalanced weighing of economic determinations on the evolution of penality in Rusche and Kirchheimer's seminal book was also criticised by early reviewers such as Ernst Burgess, Thorsten Sellin and Edwin Sutherland (De Giorgi 2013; Melossi 2003a, 2015). Hence, the conclusion of the aforementioned body of contemporary scholarship can hardly be regarded as innovative. Nevertheless, in the realm of migration enforcement, the hybridisation of the analytical viewpoint is particularly needed, since a political economic reading in this area of penality is insufficient.

As has been previously examined, the policies and tools of border control facilitate the exploitation of the migrant workforce within both the informal economy and the criminal markets (Melossi 2015; Mosconi 2010). However, these measures of control can only partly be explained from the perspective of capitalist accumulation. A range of authors (Arrighi 2007; Koulish 2010; Žižek 2009; see though Brown 2014; De Lissovoy 2015) has convincingly emphasised that the free mobility of workers would be the best border policy for the interests of capital, to the extent that it would enable a general reduction of wages and therefore of production costs.

Consequently, an analysis of bordered penality requires taking into account perspectives that to some extent stand in contrast with the needs of the regime of accumulation. In this sense, at least two additional points should be regarded: the sovereign traits of the policies of migration control and the development of processes of othering and the role of racialisation.

The policies of migration penality are difficult to grasp without considering their sovereign contours (Brown 2014; Huysmans 2006; Weber 2013),[4] i.e. their ability to self-perpetuate state power and to govern pivotal elements of sovereignty, such as territory and population. These political goals may lead to subordinate economic concerns in the realm of border control. Sovereign features are especially apparent in three interrelated consequences of bordered penality. First, migration control assists to reinforce, at least symbolically and performatively, state sovereignty and the capability of state agencies to govern social problems (Brown 2014; Fernández Bessa 2008; Patel and Tyrer 2011). Second, the sovereign rationale underlies the contribution of the policies of migration control to scapegoating certain groups of foreign population for various social evils (Bauman 2003; Calavita 2003; Rodier 2012). Migration enforcement is thus geared towards the maintenance of social order and the strengthening of social cohesion (Balibar [2001] 2004; Bauman 1998; Calavita 2005; see though Tsoukala 2002). Third, sovereign power-based policies of migration control contribute to the governing of the population by setting boundaries between human groups, that is, by building identities, most critical among them national identities (Bosworth and Guild 2008; Fekete 2009; Melossi 2014, 2015).

The shaping of patterns of belonging, i.e. identities, does entail the simultaneous production of processes of othering (Ferrell *et al.* 2008; Huysmans 2006; Mouffe 2005). Indeed, resorting to a 'constitutive exterior' (Derrida 1988) is a crucial mode of constructing identities. Consequently, the apparatus of migration control is founded upon and reproduces patterns of otherness (Castel 2009; Koulish 2010; Stumpf 2006). In the field of border control a critical instrument to construct alterity is obviously racism and the processes of racialisation. Whether based on allegedly biological traits or cultural features (Brah 1996; Fekete 2009; Patel and Tyrer 2011), racism has constituted a pivotal apparatus aimed at dividing population groups, reinforcing social stratification and reproducing power and exploitation throughout the last centuries (Foucault [1997] 2003). The analysis of racism allows an economic reading, which highlights the role racism plays in producing ethnic stratifications of the workforce (Akers Chacon and Davis 2006; Balibar and Wallerstein 1991; Harvey 2014). However, the consequences of the dynamics of discrimination and subordination fuelled by processes of racialisation go far beyond the economic realm and cannot be subsumed within it.

In Spain race and racism are largely absent in the public debate. The national Spanish narrative conceal the disgraceful fact that the construction of Spain as a nation led to the expulsion of Jews and Muslims (fifteenth to seventeenth centuries), to the genocidal annihilation of native populations in the Americas and to a centuries-long discrimination of Roma communities. However, this biased narrative has not immunised Spanish society from racism and the persistence of post-colonial traits. The dynamics of racial discrimination have gained momentum since the onset of the recent period of immigration at the beginning of the 2000s, as can be ascertained from the data of the periodical surveys carried out by the Spanish Centre of Sociological Research (CIS, from its initials in Spanish) (Colectivo Ioé 2008; Daunis Rodríguez 2008; Fernández Bessa *et al.* 2008). Processes of racialisation are also embedded within the operation of the Spanish criminal justice system. A conspicuous example is the widespread use of racial profiling in the domain of policing (Barbero González and Fernández Bessa 2013; Bradford *et al.* 2013; García España *et al.* 2016). Most notably, the Spanish Constitutional Court (ruling No. 13/2001, of 29 January 2001) upheld that physical traits and skin colour are legally valid criteria to guide immigration law policing. The operation of the deportation regime has been racially biased as well. An analysis on the nationalities most affected by deportation enforcement illustrates that Spanish migration penalty has been oriented by processes of racialisation (Fernández Bessa 2016).

To sum up, dynamics of othering and deeply entrenched racial stereotypes are inherent components of migration enforcement (Harris 2006; Melossi 2003b; Tonry 2011) that need to be taken into account in order to grasp bordered penality. As the Algerian-French sociologist Abdelmayek Sayad ([1999] 2004) cogently pointed out, the selective and biased operation of the criminal justice system against migrant individuals shows that the foreigner, beyond his or her unlawful behaviour, is held liable for a sort of 'underlying' offence deriving from a condition of alienness. This offence is founded upon a persistent stigma of alterity that strengthens the blameworthiness of the illicit act (Bosworth and

Guild 2008; Melossi 2013a, 2015). The migrant violates therefore both the legal norm and the underlying informal rule that requires reinforced obedience and a harmless conduct of individuals depicted as aliens (Monclús Masó 2008). These rooted processes of othering have little to do with the need to secure a constant supply of economic, obedient and useful migrant workforce. However, they should inevitably be taken into account to grasp the disparate and somehow contradictory contours of migration control.

Notes

1 Unfortunately, the data on immigration law enforcement, especially those related to the first years of the century, are only partially reliable in the Spanish case (Martínez Escamilla 2013).
2 On the connection between the PEoP theoretical framework and Foucauldian analyses see Melossi 2002, 2003.
3 Assuming a post-Foucauldian analytical framework, Mezzadra and Neilson (2013: 174–175) define this notion by pointing out that:

> What we can call with Achille Mbembe (2003) the 'necropolitical' effects of governmental processes of border and migration management—that is, the thousands of often unreported deaths that occur every year across the world's borderscapes— are the shocking material reminder of the sovereign powers that interrupt this vision of liberal governmentality. While they dramatically show that the dream of a just-in-time and to-the-point migration is precisely a dream, they also point to the necessary supplement that is needed to keep the biopolitical border working. To grasp both the processes of governmentalization of borders and migration management and this necessary supplement, we introduce the concept of a sovereign machine of governmentality.

Moreover, Mezzadra and Neilson (2013, p. 206) emphasise that the sovereign measure of deportation is inscribed within a variety of governmental processes, crucial among them the logistical coordination that enables the efficient return of unwanted aliens.
4 On the concept of sovereign technologies of power see Foucault [1997] 2003, [2004] 2007.

References

Akers Chacon, J. and Davis, M. (2006). *No One is Illegal*. Chicago: Haymarket Books.
Aparicio Wilhelmi, M. (2010). Desde los márgenes. Diversidad cultural, democracia e inclusión social. In: S. Palidda, J.A. Brandariz, A. Iglesias and J.A. Ramos, eds, *Criminalización racista de los migrantes en Europa*. Granada: Comares, 57–77.
Arango, J., Aja, E. and Oliver, J. (2011). *Inmigración y crisis económica: Impactos actuales y perspectivas de futuro*. Barcelona: CIDOB.
Arrighi, G. (2007). *Adam Smith in Beijing*. London: Verso.
Aviram, H. (2015). *Cheap on Crime: Recession-Era Politics and the Transformation of American Punishment*. Oakland: University of California Press.
Balibar, E. ([2001] 2004). *We, the People of Europe? Reflections on Transnational Citizenship*. Princeton: Princeton University Press.
Balibar, E. and Wallerstein, I. (1991). *Race, Nation, Class: Ambiguous Identities*. Verso: London.

Barbero, I. (2010). *Las transformaciones del Estado y del Derecho ante el control de la inmigración.* Zarautz: Ikuspegi.

Barbero González, I. and Fernández Bessa, C. (2013). Beyond surveillance: Racial profiled detention practices in everyday life. *In*: W.R. Webster, G. Galdon, N. Zurawski, K. Boersma, B. Sagvari, C. Backman, and C. Leleux, eds, *Living In Surveillance Societies: The State of Surveillance.* Seattle: CreateSpace, 295–304.

Barlow, D.E., Hickman-Barlow, M. and Chiricos, T.G. (1993). Long Economic Cycles and the Criminal Justice System in the US. *Crime, Law and Social Change*, 19 (2), 143–69.

Bauman, Z. (1998). *Work, Consumerism and the New Poor.* Philadelphia: Open University Press.

Bauman, Z. (2003). *City of Fears, City of Hopes.* London: Goldsmith's College.

Bosworth, M. and Guild, M. (2008). Governing through Migration Control. *The British Journal of Criminology*, 48 (6), 703–719.

Boyer, R. and Durand, J.P. (1998). *L'après Fordisme.* Paris: Syros.

Bradford, B., J.G. Añón, J.A. García Sáez, A.G. Cuenca and A.L Ferreres (2013). Identificación policial por perfil étnico en España: Informe sobre experiencias y actitudes en relación con las actuaciones policiales. València: Tirant lo Blanch.

Brah, A. (1996). *Cartographies of Diaspora: Contesting identities.* London: Routledge.

Brandariz García, J.A. (2011). *Sistema penal y control de los migrantes: Gramática del migrante como infractor penal.* Granada: Comares.

Brandariz García, J.A. (2014). La evolución de la penalidad en el contexto de la *Gran Recesión*: La contracción del sistema penitenciario español. *Revista de Derecho penal y Criminología*, 12, 309–342.

Brandariz García, J.A. and Fernández Bessa, C. (2017). The Managerial Turn: The Transformation of the Spanish Policies of Migration Control Since the Onset of the Great Recession. The Howard Journal of Crime and Justice, 56 (2), 198–219.

Brenner, R. and Glick, M. (1991). The Regulation Approach: Theory and History. *New Left Review*, 188, 45–119.

Brighenti, A.M. (2009). *Territori migranti. Spazio e controllo della mobilità globale.* Verona: Ombre corte.

Brion, F. (2015). Quand l'Etat crée une logique d'enfermement de 'l'étranger'. *In*: A. Medhoune, A. Medhoune, S. Lausberg, M. Martinello and A. Rea, eds, *L'immigration marocaine en Belgique.* Bruxelles: Couleur Livres, 135–146.

Brown, W. (2014). *Walled States, Waning Sovereignty.* New York: Zone Books.

Calavita, K. (2003). A 'Reserve Army of Delinquents'. The Criminalization and Economic Punishment of Immigrants in Spain. *Punishment & Society*, 5 (4), 399–413.

Calavita, K. (2005). *Immigrants at the Margins.* Cambridge: Cambridge University Press.

Campaña Estatal por el Cierre de los CIE (2014). *Paremos los vuelos: Las deportaciones de inmigrantes y el boicot a Air Europa.* Oviedo: Cambalache.

Carrasco Carpio, C. (2008). Mercado de trabajo e inmigración. *In*: A. Izquierdo Escribano, ed., *El modelo de inmigración y los riesgos de exclusión.* Madrid: Foessa, 213–257.

Castel, R. (2009). *La montée des incertitudes.* Paris: Seuil.

Chiricos, T. and Delone, M. (1992). Labour Surplus and Imprisonment: A Review and Assessment of Theory and Evidence. *Social Problems*, 39 (4), 421–446.

Colectivo Ioé (2008). *Inmigrantes, nuevos ciudadanos: ¿Hacia una España plural e intercultural?* Madrid: Funcas.

Conde-Ruiz, J.I., García, J.R. and Navarro, M. (2008). Inmigración y crecimiento regional en España. Fedea (www.fedea.net/documentos; accessed 20 April 2016).
Cuttitta, P. (2008). The Case of the Italian Southern Sea Borders: ¿Cooperation across the Mediterranean? *Documentos CIDOB Migraciones*, 17, 45–62.
Daunis Rodríguez, A. (2008). La gestación de la xenofobia: mitos y (pre)juicios de la inmigración. *In*: N. Sanz Mulas, ed., *Dos décadas de reformas penales*. Granada: Comares, 113–144.
Dean, M. (2010). *Governmentality*. 2nd ed. London: Sage.
De Giorgi, A. (2006). *Re-thinking the Political Economy of Punishment: Perspectives on Post-Fordism and Penal Politics*. Aldershot: Ashgate.
De Giorgi, A. (2010). Immigration Control, Post-Fordism, and Less Eligibility. A Materialist Critique of the Criminalization of Immigration across Europe. *Punishment & Society*, 12 (2), 147–167.
De Giorgi, A. (2013). Punishment and Political Economy. *In*: J. Simon and R. Sparks, eds, *The SAGE Handbook of Punishment and Society*. London: Sage, 40–59.
De Lissovoy, N. (2015). Injury and Accumulation: Making Sense of the Punishing State. *Social Justice*, 42 (2), 52–69.
Derrida, J. (1988). *Limited Inc*. Evanston: Northwestern University Press.
Dingeman-Cerda, M.K. and Bibler Coutin, S. (2012). The Ruptures of Return. Deportation's Confounding Effects. *In*: C. Kubrin, M.S. Zatz and R. Martínez Jr., eds, *Punishing Immigrants*. New York: New York University Press, 113–137.
Facchini, G. and Testa, C. (2015) The Political Economy of Migration Enforcement: Domestic versus Border Control. *CESifo Economic Studies*, 61 (3–4), 701–721.
Fekete, L. (2009). *A Suitable Enemy*. London: Pluto Press.
Fernández Bessa, C. (2008). El Estado español como punta de lanza del control y exclusión de la migración en Europa. *In*: VVAA, *Frontera Sur: Nuevas políticas de gestión y externalización del control de la inmigración en Europa*. Barcelona: Virus, 135–158.
Fernández Bessa, C. (2013). Il panorama dei Centri di Internamento per Stranieri in Spagna: Dal controllo delle frontieri alla gestione della criminalità. *Antigone*, 8 (1), 68–91.
Fernández Bessa, C. (2016). *El dispositiu de deportació: Anàlisi criminològica de la detenció, internament I expulsió d'immigrants en el context espanyol*. Thesis (PhD). University of Barcelona. Available from: diposit.ub.edu [accessed 20 April 2016].
Fernández Bessa, C., Ortuño Aix, J.M. and Manavella Suárez, A. (2008). Los efectos de la cultura de la emergencia en la criminalización de los inmigrantes. *In*: L.M. Puente Aba, M. Zapico Barbeito and L. Rodríguez Moro, eds, *Criminalidad organizada, terrorismo e inmigración*. Granada: Comares, 225–258.
Ferrell, J., Hayward, K. and Young, J. (2008). *Cultural Criminology*. London: Sage.
Foucault, M. ([1975] 1977). *Discipline and Punish: The Birth of the Prison*. New York: Pantheon Books.
Foucault, M. ([1976] 1979). *The History of Sexuality. Volume 1: An Introduction*. London: Allen Lane.
Foucault, M. ([1997] 2003). *Society Must Be Defended*. New York: Picador.
Foucault, M. ([2003] 2006). *Psychiatric Power*. New York: Picador.
Foucault, M. ([2004] 2007). *Security Territory, Population*. New York: Picador.
Foucault, M. ([2013] 2015). *The Punitive Society*. London: Palgrave MacMillan.
García España, E. (2007). Extranjeros presos y reinserción: Un reto del siglo XXI. *In*: A.I. Cerezo Domínguez and E. García España, eds, *La prisión en España. Una perspectiva criminológica*. Granada: Comares, 101–134.

García España, E., Arenas García, L. and Miller, J. (2016). *Identificaciones policiales y discriminación racial en España: Evaluación de un programa para su reducción*. València: Tirant lo Blanch.
Garland, D. (1990). *Punishment and Modern Society: A Study in Social Theory*. Chicago: University of Chicago Press.
Godenau, D. (2012). El papel de la inmigración en la economía española. *Documento de Trabajo ODF* 7 (www.iefweb.org; accessed 20 April 2016).
González, C.I., Conde-Ruiz, J.I. and Boldrin, M. (2009). Immigration and Social Security in Spain. *Documentos de Trabajo FEDEA*, 26, 1–42.
González Sánchez, I. (2014). *La penalidad neoliberal: Aumento de presos y reconfiguración del Estado en España (1975–2008)*. Thesis (PhD). Complutense University of Madrid. Available from: eprints.ucm.es [accessed 20 April 2016].
Greenberg, D. (1977). The Dynamics of Oscillatory Punishment Processes. *The Journal of Criminal Law and Criminology*, 68 (4), 643–651.
Guild, E. (2009). *Security and Migration in the 21st Century*. Cambridge: Polity Press.
Guild, E. and Bigo, D. (2005). Policing at a Distance: Schengen Visa Policies. In: D. Bigo and E. Guild, eds, *Controlling Frontiers: Free movement into and within Europe*. Farnham: Ashgate, 203–227.
Haahr, J.H. and Walters, W. (2004). *Governing Europe: Discourse, Governmentality and European Integration*. Abingdon: Routledge.
Hale, C. (2013). Economic Marginalization, Social Exclusion, and Crime. In: C. Hale, K. Hayward, A. Wahidin and E. Wincup, eds, *Criminology*. 3rd ed. Oxford: Oxford University Press, 289–307.
Harris, D.A. (2006). US Experiences with Eacial and Ethnic Profiling: History, Current Issues, and the Future. *Critical Criminology*, 14 (3), 213–239.
Harvey, D. (2014). *Seventeen Contradictions and the End of Capitalism*. New York: Oxford University Press.
Huysmans, J. (2006). *The Politics of Insecurity: Fear, Migration and Asylum in the EU*. Abingdon: Routledge.
Inverarity, J. and McCarthy, D. (1988). Punishment and Social Structure Revisited: Unemployment and Imprisonment in the United States, 1948–1984. *Sociological Quarterly*, 29 (2), 263–279.
Jankovic, I. (1977). Labor Market and Imprisonment. *Crime and Social Justice*, 8, 17–31.
Jiménez Franco, D. (2015). *Trampas y tormentos: Para una ecología del castigo en el reino de España*. Madrid: La Caída.
Kondratiev, N. ([1925] 1984). *The Long Wave Cycle*. New York: Richard and Snyder.
Koulish, R.E. (2010). *Immigration and American Democracy: Subverting the Rule of Law*. New York: Routledge.
Lemke, T. (2011). *Biopolitics*. New York: New York University Press.
López Hernández, I. and Rodríguez López, E. (2010). *Fin de ciclo: Financiarización, territorio y sociedad de propietarios en la onda larga del capitalismo hispano (1959–2010)*. Madrid: Traficantes de Sueños.
López-Sala, A. (2013). Managing Uncertainty: Immigration Policies in Spain during Economic Recession (2008–2011). *Migraciones Internacionales*, 7 (2), 39–69.
Marazzi, C. (2011). *Capital and Affects: The Politics of the Language Economy*. New York: Semiotext(e).
Martínez Escamilla, M., ed., (2013). *Mujeres en el CIE: Género, inmigración e internamiento*. Donostia-San Sebastián: Gakoa.

Melossi, D. (1985). Punishment and Social Action: Changing Vocabularies of Punitive Motive within a Political Business Cycle. *Current Perspectives in Social Theory*, 6, 169–197.
Melossi, D. (1993). Gazette of Morality and Social Whip: Punishment, Hegemony, and the Case of the USA, 1970–92, *Social and Legal Studies*, 2 (3), 259–279.
Melossi, D. (2001). The Cultural Embeddedness of Social Control: Reflections on the Comparison of Italian and North-American Cultures Concerning Punishment. *Theoretical Criminology*, 5 (4), 403–424.
Melossi, D. (2002). Discussione a mo' di prefazione: Carcere, postfordismo e ciclo di produzione della 'canaglia'. *In*: A. De Giorgi, *Il governo dell'eccedenza: Postfordismo e controllo della moltitudine*. Verona: Ombre corte, 7–24.
Melossi, D. (2003a). Introduction to the Transaction Edition: The Simple 'Heuristic Maxim' of an 'Unusual Human Being'. *In*: G. Rusche and O. Kirchheimer, *Punishment and Social Structure*. New Brunswick: Transaction, ix–xiv.
Melossi, D. (2003b). 'In a Peaceful Life'. Migration and the Crime of Modernity in Europe/Italy. *Punishment & Society*, 5 (4), 371–397.
Melossi, D. (2013a). Punishment and Migration between Europe and the USA: A Transnational 'Less Eligibility'? *In*: J. Simon and R. Sparks, eds, *The SAGE Handbook of Punishment and Society*. London: Sage, 416–433.
Melossi, D. (2013b). People on the Move: From the Countryside to the Factory/Prison. *In*: K. Franko Aas and M. Bosworth, eds, *The Borders of Punishment: Migration, Citizenship, and Social Exclusion*. Oxford: Oxford University Press, 273–290.
Melossi, D. (2014). The Borders of the European Union and the Processes of Criminalization of Migrants. *In*: Body-Gendrot, S., Hough, M., Kerezsi, K., Lévy, R. and Snacken, S., eds, *The Routledge Handbook of European Criminology*. Abingdon: Routledge, 499–513.
Melossi, D. (2015). *Crime, Punishment and Migration*. London: Sage.
Melossi, D. and Pavarini, M. ([1977] 1981). *The Prison and the Factory: Origins of the Penitentiary System*. Macmillan: London.
Mezzadra, S. (2006). *Diritto di fuga: Migrazioni, cittadinanza, globalizzazione*. Verona: Ombre corte.
Mezzadra, S. and Neilson, B. (2013). *Border as Method, or, the Multiplication of Labor*. Durham: Duke University Press.
Michalowski, R. and Carlson, S. (2006). Unemployment, Imprisonment, and Social Structures of Accumulation: Historical Contingency in the Rusche-Kirchheimer Hypothesis. *Criminology*, 37 (2), 217–250.
Monclús Masó, M. (2008). *La gestión penal de la inmigración*. Buenos Aires: Del Puerto.
Mosconi, G. (2010). La seguridad de la inseguridad. Retóricas y giros de la legislación italiana. *In*: S. Palidda, J.A. Brandariz, A. Iglesias and J.A. Ramos, eds, *Criminalización racista de los migrantes en Europa*. Granada: Comares, 321–343.
Mouffe, C. (2005). *On the Political*. Abingdon: Routledge.
Oficina económica del Presidente (2006). Inmigración y economía española: 1996–2006. (www.redri.org; accessed 20 April 2016).
Pajares, M. (2010). *Inmigración y mercado de trabajo. Informe 2010*. Madrid: Ministerio de Trabajo e Inmigración.
Patel, T.G. and Tyrer, D. (2011). *Race, Crime and Resistance*. London: Sage.

Pickhardt, M. and Sardà, J. (2015). Size and Causes of the Underground Economy in Spain: A Correction of the Record and New Evidence from the MCDR Approach. *European Journal of Law and Economy*, 39 (2), 403–429.
Pratt, A. (2005). *Securing Borders: Detention and Deportation in Canada*. Vancouver: UBC Press.
Pratt, J. (2002). *Punishment and Civilization*. London: Sage.
Preston, P. and Perez, M.P. (2006). The Criminalization of Aliens: Regulating Foreigners. *Critical Criminology*, 14 (1), 43–66.
Raine, J.W. (2005). Courts, Sentencing, and Justice in a Changing Political and Managerial Context. *Public Money and Management*, 25 (5), 291–298.
Rodier, C. (2012). *Xénophobie business*. Paris: La Découverte.
Rodríguez, E. (2003). *El gobierno imposible*. Madrid: Traficantes de Sueños.
Romero, E. (2010). *Un deseo apasionado de trabajo más barato y servicial. Migraciones, fronteras y capitalismo*. Oviedo: Cambalache.
Rusche, G. ([1933] 1978). Labor Market and Penal Sanction: Thoughts on the Sociology of Punishment. *Social Justice*, 10, 2–8.
Rusche, G. and Kirchheimer, O. ([1939] 2003). *Punishment and Social Structure*. New Brunswick: Transaction.
Sainz de la Maza Quintanal, E. (2015). *'Ultima ratio': El proceso de expulsión de inmigrantes en situación irregular en España*. Thesis (PhD). Complutense University of Madrid. Available from: eprints.ucm.es [accessed 20 April 2016].
Sayad, A. ([1999] 2004). *The Suffering of the Immigrant*. Cambridge: Polity.
Schumpeter, J. (1939). *Business Cycles: A Theoretical, Historical and Statistical Analysis of the Capitalist Process*. New York: McGraw-Hill.
Sciurba, A. (2009). *Campi di forza: Percorsi confinati di migranti in Europa*. Verona: Ombre corte.
Scull, A. (1977). *Decarceration: Community Treatment and the Deviant*. Englewood Cliffs: Prentice Hall.
Sieh, E.W. (1989). Less Eligibility: The Upper Limits of Penal Policy. *Criminal Justice Policy Review*, 3 (2), 159–183.
Silveira Gorski, H.C. (2003). Inmigración y derecho: la institucionalización de un sistema dual de ciudadanía. *In*: R. Bergalli Russo, ed., *Sistema penal y problemas sociales*. Valencia: Tirant lo Blanch, 539–577.
Stumpf, J. (2006). The Crimmigration Crisis: Immigrants, Crime, and Sovereign Power. *American University Law Review*, 56 (2), 367–419.
Tonry, M. (2011). *Punishing Race*. New York: Oxford University Press.
Tsoukala, A. (2002). Le traitement médiatique de la criminalité étrangère en Europe. *Déviance et Société*, 26 (1), 61–82.
Ulloa Rubio, I. (2012). El desafío de garantizar la seguridad pública: El modelo de seguridad pública. *Seguridad y ciudadanía: Revista del Ministerio del Interior*, 7–8, 13–24.
Valverde, M. (2008). Beyond Discipline and Punish: Foucault's Challenge to Criminology. *Carceral Notebooks*, 4, 201–223.
Vanneste, C. (2000). L'èvolution de la population pénitentiaire belge de 1830 à nos jours: comment e pourquoi? Des logiques socio-économiques a leur traduction pénale. *Revue de droit pénal et de criminology*, 6, 689–723.
Vanneste, C. (2001). *Les Chiffres des Prisons*. Paris: L'Harmattan.
Vigour, C. (2006). Justice: L'introduction d'une rationalité managériale comme euphémisation des enjeux politiques. *Droit et société*, 63–64, 425–455.

Wacquant, L. (2009). *Punishing the Poor: The Neoliberal Government of Social Insecurity*. Durham: Duke University Press.
Walters, W. (2016). The Flight of the Deported: Aircraft, Deportation and Politics. *Geopolitics*, 21 (2), 435–453.
Weber, L. (2013). *Policing Non-Citizens*. London: Routledge.
Wood, J. and Shearing, C. (2006). *Imagining Security*. Cullompton: Willan.
Žižek, S. (2009). *First as Tragedy, Then as Farce*. London: Verso.

Index

Page numbers in *italics* denote tables, those in **bold** denote figures.

academic field 76
accumulation: of capital 4, 6, 27, 74, 77, 192, 229; primitive 79, 110
Africa 185, 191; *see also* South Africa
agency 76; and structure 77
alienation 40
Amable, B. 124, 128, 130, 131
amnesties 179n2; Italy 162; post-Soviet region 198
Andersen, R. 122
anomie 40
Argentina, incarceration rates *56*
Ascoli, U. 177, 178
Asiatic model of capitalism 124
asylum cases, Greece 207–8
Atkinson, A.B. 123
Attica prison revolt (1971) 26, 33n6, 33n7
austerity 11, 131
Australia 137–59; Corrective Services Administrators' Council 155; drugs offences 140, 141; electoral system 149; female incarceration rate 138; female offenders 141; homicide rates 140; immigration 151; incarceration rates *see* Australian incarceration rates; judiciary 150–1; as liberal market economy (LME) 44, 151, 156; media 150, 156; neoliberalism 39, 137, 143, 156; offender rates 140–1, 153, 154; parole system 150–1; physical assault offences 140; public order offences 140; remand rates 138; sexual offences 140; social-democratic tradition 137, 156; theft offences 140; victimisation rates 139–40, 141; *see also* indigenous Australians; *and individual jurisdictions*

Australian Bureau of Statistics (ABS) 138, 153, 154
Australian incarceration rates 9, 13, *48*, 52, 54, 59n13, 137, 138, 140, 141, **143, 144,** 146, 147, 156; and education levels 148, 149; and income inequity 148, 149; indigenous population 138, 154–5; and inequality 147, 149; and political dominance 149–50; and public opinion 150; and unemployment rates 147–8, 149
authority, destructuration of 25–9
Aviram, H. 10, 226, 227
Azerbaijan *188*

Bagnasco, A. 166
bail system, New South Wales (NSW) 151
Baltic States 190, 192; *see also* Estonia; Latvia; Lithuania
Barker, V. 151
base/structure and superstructure 39
Bauman, Z. 30
Beckett, K. 41, 142, 150
Belarus *188,* **188**
Belgium 9, 13, 128–9; coal prices 110; and Depression (1929–1939) 129–30; economic cycles and prisoner population 108–12; economic security/insecurity 111, 112; and Great Recession (2007–2009) 130, 131; incarceration rates (and income inequality 13, 112–14, **114, 115–17,** 118, 128, 129; and political dominance 118–19, **119, 120,** 121); social welfare 111, 128; trade unions 111, 128; unemployment rate 112; and varieties of

capitalism approach 128–9; wheat prices 110
Bell, D. 29
Bendukidze, K. 194
Bentham, J. 4, 24, 28, 221
bio-politics 224
Black Panthers 31
Blousons gang 31
Bobbio, N. 118
body: and habitus 78–9; political economy of 4
Bolivia, incarceration rates 56
border control policies 206–7; exclusionary 206; outflow restrictions, Greece 207–8; see also migration control policies
Bourdieu, P. 12, 69–81; bureaucratic field 12, 71, 72, 73–6, 80; habitus 12, 72, 76–80; symbolic power 70–3; see also field(s)
Bourgois, P. 31
Braverman, H. 28
Brazil 9; incarceration rates 56
Britain see United Kingdom
Brown, D. 153
bureaucracy/bureaucratization 7, 8, 42, 46, 53
bureaucratic field 12, 71, 72, 73–6, 80
Burgess, E. 229
Burroni, L. 166, 168, 169
business cycles: and Spanish migration control policies 220–1; see also economic cycle theory; economic cycles

California 10, 29
Canada 46, 51, 54, 59n16, 146, 153
capital 75, 80; accumulation of 4, 6, 27, 74, 77, 192, 229; juridical 75; symbolic 75, 76
capitalism 3, 4, 6, 7, 12, 23–4, 65, 66, 67, 69, 79–80; Fordist 37, 163; post-Fordist 6, 14, 37, 160, 163–4, 168, 169–70, 223; see also varieties of capitalism
Carr, M. 208
Carrington, K. 191
Carter, B. 31
Cavadino, M. and Dignan, J. 7–8, 12, 13, 38–43, 46, 49, 50, 53, 125, 126, 133n16, 137, 139, 141, 142, 143, 144, 145, 156, 163, 167, 176, 177, 192
centralization 7
centre vote, Belgium 118, 119, **120**

Chile 56; incarceration rates 56
Christian Democracy party, Italy 173, 177
Christie, N. 185, 186, 190, 191, 198, 200
Chrysi Avyi ('Golden Dawn') 212, 213
circulation, sphere of 24, 27, 30
civil service 46, 47, 74
class 31, 69; see also working class
class struggle 12, 23–5, 25–6, 29, 30, 32, 66, 72
clientelism, Italy 167, 171, 172, 175–7
coal prices, Belgium 110
Cohen, S. 29
Colombia, incarceration rates 56
Colombo, S. 166, 168, 169
colonialism 153, 156
common law 47
Communist Party of France (PCF) 28
Communist Party of Italy (PCI) 177
communitarian ethos 41
community service, Spain 99
comparative research 7–8, 12, 125–8, 192; contributions, limitations and challenges 48–57; see also Cavadino, M. and Dignan, J.; Lacey, N.
Comparative Welfare States Data Set 118, 132n11
consensual democracies 58n11, 126, 128, 149
conservative corporatism (CCE) 7, 41, 44, 49, 124, 128, 142, 176; and incarceration rates 39, 126, 133n16, 142, 144–5
constitutional structure 8, 46–7, 149, 150
consumption 37
continental European model of capitalism 124, 128
continental legal system 47
continental welfare regimes 46
convergence thesis 123, 124, 125
coordinated market economies (CME) 8, 44, 45, 46, 47, 48, 49, 51, 52, 56, 58n11, 123, 124, **125**, 126, 128, 132n13, 147, 149, 151, 164, 167, 169, 170, 172, 177, 192
corporatism 5, 126, 127
corporatist economies (CEs) 40, 41, 42, 49, 52; oriental (OCE) 7, 39, 49, 124, 126, 142; see also conservative corporatism (CCE); social democratic corporatism (SDCE)
corruption: anti-corruption, Georgia 186, 197–8, 200; Italy 173

Council of Europe 187
credit 130, 192
crime 40; and destitution 2–3, 121–2; fear of 10; and incarceration 40; and political economy 2
crime rates: Germany 101n3; and Great Recession 9–10; and incarceration rates 67; Spain 101n3
crime waves 5
criminalization 8, 31, 47; of immigrants 11; of indigenous Australians 153–4; of poverty 76
critical criminology 5, 65
Crouch, C. 166
cultural factors/attitudes 6, 7, 40–1, 42, 46, 51, 200–1
culturalist turn 5–6, 50
Czech Republic *188*, 192

Daulabaev, K. 199
Davis, A. 33n11
De Cecco, M. 166, 167
De Giorgi, A. 6, 38, 39, 43, 57, 67, 68, 160, 161, 162–4, 169, 170, 191–2, 223
deaths in custody 50
decarceration 29; Georgia 188, 190, 198; Kazakhstan 188, 190, 198–9; post-Soviet region 185, 187, 189–90, 191, 200
delinquency 29, 31
democratization, post-Soviet region 187
Dendias, N. 213
deportation regime, Spain 219, 220, 225, 226–7, 228, 230
Depression (1929–1939) 2, 129; Belgium and 129–30; fine systems in Germany and 13, 88, 90–5, 99, 100, 101n6, 101–2n7
deprivation, relative 40
deregulation 130, 164; labour market 168, 169
destitution 2–3
destructuration of authority 25–9
detention centres, and Spanish migration control policies 219, 220, 225
detention rates *see* incarceration rates
deterrence 2, 107
deviance, sociology of 2
Dignan, J. *see* Cavadino, M. and Dignan, J.
discipline 3, 4, 23, 24–5, 27, 29, 30–2, 66, 221; and Spanish migration control policies 15, 219, 223, 224, 226; and technology 27

Dobb, M. 23
domination, relations of 71, 72, 73, 74, 75, 79, 81
Downes, D. 142, 190
doxa 79
drug offences 10; Australia 140, 141
Durkheim, É. 15n1, 69, 70, 75, 77, 79, 81
Dutschke, R. 25, 28

Eastern Europe 9, 185; see also post-Soviet region; *and individual countries*
economic crisis and recession *see* Depression; Great Recession
economic cycle theory 108, 109
economic cycles: and prisoner population in Belgium 108–12; and Spanish migration control policies 220–1
economic field 76
economic security/insecurity 121–2; Belgium 111, 112
Economist, The 198
Ecuador, incarceration rates *56*, 59n18
education level, and incarceration rates, Australia 148, 149
electoral systems 8, 42, 45–6, 53, 58–9n11, 149
elites 41–2; penal 7, 41, 42, 53
employment 123; full 3; *see also* unemployment
Engels, F. 32
England and Wales 39, 44, 142; incarceration rates *48*, 54, 59n13, **144**, 146, 165
equality 40, 118; *see also* inequality
Esping-Andersen, G. 7, 38, 46, 55, 124, 126, 128, 142, 175
Estonia *188*
European Court of Human Rights (ECHR) 10, 187
European Social Survey (ESS) 126
European Union (EU): incarceration rates 9; penal policies 10; and Spanish migration control policies 227, 228
exclusion 6, 39, 124, 126, 142, 147; of immigrants 171–2, 176, 177, 206
exploitation 3, 11, 24, 66, 69, 79, 221; of migrants in Greek informal economy 209–13

factories 4, 23, 25, 28, 29
family ties, Italy 167, 170, 175
fear of crime 10, 121–2

Index 241

Feeley, M. 29
female incarceration rate, Australia 138
female offenders, Australia 141
Ferrara, M. 175
field(s) 75–6, 77, 78, 80; academic 76; bureaucratic 12, 71, 72, 73–6; economic 76
financial sector 131
fine systems and economic depressions 13, 87–106; default imprisonment 88, 89–90, 92, 93, 94, 95, 97, 99, 100; Germany during Great Depression 13, 88, 90–5, 99, 100, 101n6, 101–2n7; Spain during Great Recession of 13, 88, 95–7, 98, 100
Finland 9, 39, 44, 142; incarceration rates 48, 49, 97
"first-past-the-post" electoral systems 42, 45, 149
Fordism 37, 163
foreign direct investment: Georgia 194, 195, 196, 200; Kazakhstan 194, 195, 196, 199, 200
Foucault, M. 4, 12, 23, 24, 25–6, 33n5, 223, 224; *illégalismes* 29, 31; and Marx/Marxist tradition 15n4, 26–9
France 9, 39, 142, 175; Communist Party (PCF) 28; incarceration rates 48, 49, 145
Frankfurt School 28
Franzece, R. 113
Freedom House 195
Freiberg, A. 150, 151
full employment 3

Gallo, Z. 160, 161, 162, 170
Garland, D. 25, 28, 55, 67, 163, 164, 170
Garrett, G. 123
Georgia 14, 186, 191; anti-corruption 186, 197–8, 200; as competitive authoritarian regime 195; criminal justice policy and discourse 196, 197–8, 200; decarceration 188, 190, 198; foreign direct investment 194, 196, 200; incarceration rates 186, 188, 195, 196, 197, 198, 200; inequality 193, 194, 196; labour market 189, 193, 195; labour productivity 193, 196; as liberal market economy (LME) 195, 200; natural resources 186, 196, 197; poverty 193, 194, 195, 196; privatization 194–5, 196; Rose Revolution (2003) 197; state capacity 198; state fragility in 2010 196;

unemployment rate 193, 195, 196; and varieties of capitalism approach 194–5; wages 193; zero tolerance discourse 197, 198, 200
Germany 9, 39, 44, 46, 47, 89, 142, 164, 175; crime rates 101n3; fines system and Great Depression 13, 88, 90–5, 99, 100, 101n6, 101–2n7; Imperial Penal Code 90–1, 95; incarceration rates 48, 49, 97, 145, 165; prison sentences (1920s/1930s) 91–2, 93, 94, 95
Gini index 112, 113, 127, 132n5, 147, 148, 149, 157n5, 193
globalization 37, 108, 122, 123, 165
Goffman, A. 31
govermentality 224
Gramsci, A. 4
Great Recession (2007–2009) 8–11, 129; Belgium and 130, 131; fine systems in Spain and 13, 88, 95–7, 98, 100; and incarceration rates 9; and neoliberal model 130–1; and Spanish migration control policies 225–8
Greece, irregular migrants 14, 205–6; anti-migrant discourse 212–13, 214–15n7; asylum cases 207–8; exploitation in labour market 209–13; and informal economy 207, 208–13; outflow restrictions ('entrapment') 207–8; refugee recognition 207; violence against 210, 211–12
Group of Twenty (G20) 9

habitus 12, 72, 76–80; corporal dimension of 78–9; primary and secondary 78
Hall, P. 8, 44, 56, 123, 124, 126, 128, 147, 160, 164, 192
Hall, S. 3
Hansen, K. 142
Harcourt, B.E. 28
heterogeneity thesis 123–4, 125
hierarchical market economy (HME) 56
Hirst, P.Q. 3
homicide rates, Australia 140
house arrest, Spain 99
Huggins, J. 31
human rights: Kazakhstan 186, 199, 200; post-Soviet region 187
'humonetarianism' 10
Hungary 192
Husserl, E. 71
hysteresis 77

identity building, and migration control policies 229–30
ideology 27, 68, 79
illégalismes 29, 31
immigrants/immigration 6, 10, 31; Australia 151; criminalization of 11; exclusion of immigrants 171–2, 176, 177, 206; integration of immigrants 47, 151; invisibility of suffering of migrants 205; *see also* Greece, irregular migrants; migration control policies
imprisonment rate *see* incarceration rates
incarceration rates 4, 29, 31, 37, 41, *48*, 49, 54, 97, 126–8, 160; and class struggle 30; and conservative corporatism 39, 126, 133n16, 142, 144–5; and crime rates 67; decline in 49; and education level, Australia 148; and Great Recession 9; and income inequality *see* income inequality; Latin America 55–6; and neoliberalism 39, 126, 133n16, 142, 144, 145, 146, 156, 190; and oriental corporatism 39, 126; and political dominance *see* political dominance; post-Soviet region *see* post-Soviet region; and punitiveness 49–50; and social democratic corporatism 39, 126, 133n16, 142, 145, **146**; and unemployment 5, 67, 89, 126, 127, 148, 219–20; *see also under individual countries*
inclusion 39, 124, 126, 142, 147, 163; migrants and unjust forms of 31, 206–8, 213–14, 224; subordinate 30–2
income disparity indicator 113, 132n8
income inequality 123, 192
income inequality and incarceration rates 126–8; Australia 148, 149; Belgium 13, 112–14, **114**, **115–17**, 118, 128, 129
indigenous Australians 13, 143, 152–5, 156–7; criminalization of 153–4; incarceration rates 138, 154–5; offender rate 153, 154, 155; overrepresentation in criminal justice system 137, 142, 153, 154; (post)colonialism and offending behaviour 156–7; recidivism rate 155; rehabilitation of offenders 155; urbanisation of 152
individualism 40, 47, 142, 147, 165
Indonesia 9
inequality 5, 6, 11, 40, 121, 122, 126, 130, 131; Australia 147; Georgia 193, 194, *196*; Kazakhstan 193–4, *196*; and Left–Right voting 118, 119; *see also* income inequality
inflation rate 126
informal economy 229; Greece, and irregular migrants 207, 208–13
institutional dimensions 6, 7, 42, 43, 44, 51, 53; Italy 172–4
institutional racism 154
interactionism 5
interest groups 126; Italy 176
International Centre for Prison Studies 189, 199, 200
International Crime Victim Surveys 143
International Labour Organisation 193
Ireland 9
Italy 4, 10, 14, 39, 89, 142, 160–84; amnesties and pardons 162; Cassa *Integrazione Guadagni* (CIG) 170; clientelism/patronage relations 167, 171, 172, 175–7; family as welfare surrogate 167, 170, 175; as hybrid political economy 160, 165–9, 171, 172, 174, 177, 178, 179; incarceration rates *48*, 49, 97, 145, 162; industrial transformation 166–7; informal social controls 162, 170, 172, 178; institutional structure 172–4; interest groups 176; labour flexibility 168, 169; labour market 168, 170, 175; law/legal norms 174, 178; *lottizzazione* process 173; migrants' exclusions 171–2, 176, 177; as mixed-market economy (MME) 167, 168, 170; political factors and penality in 14, 161, 172–4, 177–8, 178–9; political parties 173–4, 177; and post-Fordist narratives 14, 168, 169–70, 178; punitive/moderate duality 14, 162, 172, 174, 178; service sector 166–7; small and medium-sized enterprises (SMEs) 166, 170; *Tangentopoli* corruption scandal 173; three Italies analysis 166; trade unions 167, 168, 173; welfare reform 168; welfare state 14, 174–8, 179

Japan 9, 39, 55, 142; incarceration rates *48*, 49
judiciary 8, 47; Australia 150–1; relationship with government 47, 150; selection and tenure 47, 53, 150
juridical capital 75

Karstedt, S. 190
Kazakhstan 14, 186, 191, 192; as consolidated authoritarian regime 195; criminal justice policy and discourse *196*, 198–9; decarceration 188, 190, 198–9; foreign direct investment 194, 195, *196*, 199, 200; and human rights 186, 199, 200; incarceration rates 186, 190, 195, *196*, 200; inequality 193–4, *196*; labour market 189, 193, 195, 200; labour productivity 193, *196*; as liberal market economy (LME) 194, 195; natural resources 186, *196*, 198, 200; oil and mining sector 198, 199; poverty 193–4, *196*; privatization 194, 195, *196*; state fragility in 2010 *196*; unemployment rate 193, 194, *196*; wages 193
Keynesian economics 111, 131
Killias, M. 127
King, R.D. 187, 190
Kirchheimer, O. 2–3, 4, 6, 11, 12, 13, 23, 37, 43, 65, 66, 69, 87–90, 93, 97, 100, 101n2, 107, 128, 133n20, 163, 191, 219, 221, 228, 229
Kondratiev cycles 108, 109, 220
Koulinsky, A. 113

labelling 2, 70
labour: post-Fordist 163–4; power 24, 25; scarcity 163, 165; surplus 163, 165, 169
labour flexibility 169, 223; Italy 168, 169; Spain 223
labour market 2, 4, 23, 37, 66–7, 69, 75, 87, 89, 107, 163, 200, 219; deregulation 168, 169; Georgia 189, 193, 195; Italy 168, 170, 175; Kazakhstan 189, 193, 195, 200
labour productivity: Georgia 193, *196*; Kazakhstan 193, *196*
labour-force participation 5
Lacey, N. 8, 12, 13, 38, 42, 43–8, 49, 51, 52–3, 54–5, 125, 126, 137, 141–2, 146–7, 149, 150, 151, 156, 160, 162, 163, 164–5, 170, 171, 192
Lane, D. 192
Lange, P. 173
Lappi-Seppälä, T. 125, 126, 127
Latin America 60n25, 185, 190–1; capitalisms 56–7; incarceration rates 55–6, *56*; *see also individual countries*
Latvia *188*

law 65, 66, 68; common 47; Italy 174, 178
left/right division and incarceration rates: Australia 149–50; Belgium 118–19, **119**, **120**, 121, 126
legal syllogism 2, 67
legal systems 47
legitimation 72, 73, 81, 122, 127
less eligibility concept 2, 66, 107, 193, 221, 223; and Spanish migration control policies 15, 219, 223–4, 226
Leterme, Y. 131
liberal market economies (LME) 8, 44, 45, 46, 47, 51, 52, 54, 55, 56, 58n11, 123, 124, **125**, 126, 128, 132n13, 147, 149, 151, 156, 164, 165, 167, 192, 195, 200
liberal welfare regimes 46, 142
Lijphart, A. 126, 128, 149
Lithuania *188*, **188**
Loader, I. 53, 73
lottizzazione process, Italy 173
Luxemburg, R. 25

Mc Ara, L. 53
managerialism, and Spanish migration control policies 15, 226–8
Marx, K. 3–4, 15n4, 24, 30, 52, 65, 67, 69, 70, 71, 75, 81, 110; and Foucauldian analysis 26–9
Marxism 1, 2, 3, 4, 5, 25, 39, 43, 44, 67, 68; crisis of 5–6
mass imprisonment 11, 31, 79
materialist analysis 65, 68, 70–3, 76, 80
Matthews, R. 49
media 41, 42–3, 50, 73, 142; Australia 150, 156
Mediterranean model of capitalism 174
Melossi, D. 3, 5, 66, 67, 79, 80, 110, 122, 133n20, 191, 221, 223
mental hospitals 25
Mexico 56
Mezzadra, S. 231n3
migration 48, 110; irregular, as 'entrapment' 206–8; *see also* Greece, irregular migrants; immigrants/immigration; migration control policies; vagrancy
migration control policies 14–15, 206–8, 218; identity building and 229–30; othering processes 15, 229–31; racialisation 15, 230; scapegoating of populations and 229; sovereign traits of 229–31; *see also* Spanish migration control policies

Mills, C.W. 31
mixed-market economy (MME), Italy as 167, 168, 170
Moldova, Republic of *188*
Molina, O. 166, 167, 168, 169, 175
Monti, M. 168
Müller, M.M. 190–1
Myant, M. 192

national identity 229–30
nationality 69
natural resources: Georgia 186, *196*, 197; Kazakhstan 186, *196*, 198, 200
Nazarbayev, N. 195, 198
Neilson, B. 231n3
Nelken, D. 39, 51, 53, 138, 139, 170
neodevelopmentalism 56
neoliberal penality thesis 48
neoliberalism (NE) 6, 7, 11, 37, 39–41, 42, 44, 52, 54, 76, 123, 125, 142, 156, 164, 185; and Great Recession 130–1; and incarceration rates 39, 126, 133n16, 142, 144, 145, 146, 156, 190; and minority overrepresentation in prisons 152–3; post-Soviet region 190, 191
Netherlands 9, 39, 44, 59n19, 142, 144; incarceration rates *48*, 49, 52, 59n19, 60n20, 97, 144, **145**
New Left 28
New South Wales (NSW): bail system 151; female offenders 141; immigration 151; incarceration rates 137, **143**, 146 (and education level 148; and income inequity 148; indigenous 154; and inequality 147, 149; and unemployment rate 148, 149); indigenous offender rate 153, 154; indigenous population 152; offender rates 140, 153, 154; parole system 151; victimisation rates 139
New Zealand 39, 42, 44, 58n6, 142; incarceration rates *48*, 54, 59n13, **144**
nomination 72, 73
non-custodial sentences 10, 50
'non-non-nons' 11
North/South divide 191
Northern Territory: female offenders 141; immigration 151; incarceration rates 137, 138, 146 (and education level 148; female 138; and income inequity 148; indigenous 138, 154; and inequality 147; and unemployment 148); indigenous offender rate 153, 154; indigenous population 152; offender rates 140, 141, 153, 154; physical assault offences 140; remand rate 138; victimisation rates 139, 141

obedience 12, 30, 31
offender rates, Australia 140–1, 153, 154
oil, Kazakhstan 198, 199
oil crisis (1973) 111–12
O'Malley, P. 93, 156
Organisation for Economic Co-operation and Development (OECD) 112, 113
oriental corporatism (OCE) 7, 39, 49, 124, 126, 142
othering processes, and migration control policies 15, 229–31
'others'/outsiders, institutional capacity for integration of 8, 47, 151

Panopticon/panopticism 24, 25, 27, 28
Paraguay, incarceration rates *56*
parole 10, 50; Australia 150–1
Pashukanis, E. 29, 65, 68
patronage relations, Italy 167, 171, 172, 175–7
Pavarini, M. 3, 66, 79, 223
Pease, K. 127–8
penal differences 48–9, 52
penal elites 7, 41, 42, 53
penal welfarism 41
Penn, W. 23, 32–3n3
Peru, incarceration rates *56*
phenomenology 71
physical assault offences, Australia 140
Piacentini, L. 186, 187, 190
Pizzorno, A. 173
police 68, 73
political dominance and incarceration rates 126; Australia 149–50; Belgium 118–19, **119**, **120**, 121, 126
political factors 6, 7, 41–2, 43, 45–6, 50, 52–3; and Italian penality 14, 161, 172–4, 177–8, 178–9
political parties 42; Italy 173–4, 177; Leftist 127; *see also names of individual parties*
politicians 41, 42
Portugal 9
Positivist School 1
post-colonialism 153, 156

post-Fordism 6, 14, 37, 160, 163–4, 168, 169–70, 178, 223
post-Soviet region 14, 185–93; amnesties 198; decarceration 185, 187, 189–90, 191, 200; democratization 187; human rights 187; incarceration rates 185–9; liberal market reform 187, 190; neoliberalization 190, 191; privatization 192; varieties of capitalism in 192; *see also* Georgia; Kazakhstan
Poulantzas, N. 68
poverty 111, 153, 171; criminalization of 76; and fine systems 88, 95; Georgia 193, 194, 195, *196*; irregular migrants 208, 210; Kazakhstan 193–4, *196*
power 74; concentration of 127; symbolic 70–3, 80
power relations, global 191
pragmatism 5
Pratt, J. 151
pressure groups 45–6
primitive accumulation 79, 110
prison rates *see* incarceration rates
prison sentences: Germany (1920s/1930s) 91–2, 93, 94, 95; Spain 95, 96, *97*, 98
prisons/prison systems 3, 68, 73; US 9
privatization 11; Georgia 194–5, *196*; Kazakhstan 194, 195, *196*; post-Soviet region 192
probation 50
production 23, 69; modes of 24, 65–6, 160, 219; post-Fordist 37, 164; sphere of 24, 25, 27, 30
productive surplus 164
productive system 67, 68, 73, 80, 81n3, 82n15
profit 24
property crime 9
proportional representation (PR) electoral systems 42, 45, 46, 59n11, 149
Protestant ethic 24
public opinion 41, 42–3, 45, 46, 50, 142, 150
public order offences, Australia 140

Quakers 23, 32n3
Queensland 152; female offenders 141; immigration 151; incarceration rates 137, 138, **143**, 146 (and education level 148; female 138; indigenous 138, 154; and inequality 147; and unemployment rate 148); indigenous offender rate 153, 154; indigenous population 152; offender rates 140, 141, 153, 154; victimisation rates 139

race 31, 69
racialization 152–3; and migration control policies 15, 230
racism 230; institutional 154
Rasphuis 23, 32n3
Real Socialism 6
recidivism rate, indigenous Australians 155
refugees, Greece 207
Regini, M. 166, 168, 169, 173
rehabilitation 29; indigenous Australian offenders 155
Reiner, R. 16n6
relative deprivation 40
remand rates, Australia 138
Reyneri, E. 166, 169
Rhodes, M. 166, 167, 168, 169, 175
Right vote, Belgium 118, 119, **120**, 121, 128, 129
rights 66; *see also* human rights
Rios, V. 31
risk 29
Roberts, L.D. 150
Rose Revolution (2003), Georgia 197
Rusche, G. 2–3, 4, 6, 11, 12, 13, 23, 37, 43, 65, 66, 69, 87–90, 93, 97, 100, 107, 108, 126, 127, 128, 133n20, 163, 191, 195, 219, 221, 228–9
Russia 9, 186, 187, *188*, **188**, 191, 192

Saakashvili, M. 194, 195, 197, 198
Salvati, M. 177
Savelsberg, J. 42
Savio, M. 28
Sayad, A. 230
Scandinavia 7, 9, 142, 151; *see also* Finland; Sweden
scapegoating, and migration control policies 229
Schneider, B.R. 56
Scotland 55, 58n6, 58n11, 59n11, 59n15
Scull, A. 228
selectivity of penality 6
Sellin, T. 2, 229
sentencing 41, 50; community service 99; house arrest 99; non-custodial 10, 50; suspended 99, 100; *see also* fine systems; prison sentences

service economy 45, 169; Italy 166–7
sexual offences, Australia 140
Shevardnadze, E. 197
Simon, John 26
Simon, Jonathan 29, 31
single-issue pressure groups 45–6
Slovakia 192
small and medium-sized enterprises (SMEs), Italy 166, 170
social control 3, 4, 12, 29–30, 40, 142, 163, 165; informal 41, 142, 162, 165, 170, 172, 178
social democracy 28; Australia 137, 156
social democratic corporatism (SDCE) 7, 41, 44, 49, 124, 142; and incarceration rates 39, 126, 133n16, 142, 145, **146**
social democratic welfare regimes 46, 142
social surplus 164
social welfare models 46, 124, 142; Belgium 111, 128; Italy 168; *see also* welfare state
Soskice, D. 8, 44, 56, 123, 124, 126, 128, 147, 160, 164, 192
South Africa 9, 39, 55, 142; incarceration rates *48*, 54, 59n13, 138, 144
South Australia: female offenders 141; immigration 151; incarceration rates 137, **143**, 146 (and education level 148; indigenous 138, 154; and inequality 147; and unemployment rate 148, 149); indigenous offender rate 153, 154; indigenous population 152; offender rates 140, 141, 153, 154; remand rate 138; victimisation rates 139, 141
sovereignty, and migration control policies 229–31
Soviet Union 185–6; collapse of 186, 187; *see also* post-Soviet region
Spain 9; community service 99; crime rates 101n3; fines system and Great Recession 13, 88, 95–7, *98*, 99, 100; foreign prison population rate 225, *226*; foreign-born population 218, 220, *225*; house arrest 99; incarceration rate 97, 220, *222*, 225, *226*; labour flexibility 223; migrant workforce 221, 223–4; Penal Code 95, 96; prison sentences 95, 96, *97*, *98*; suspended sentences 99, 100; unemployment rate 96, 220, *222*, 225; *see also* Spanish migration control policies
Spanish migration control policies 15, 218–19; and business cycles 220–1;

deportation regime 219, 220, 225, 226–7, 228, 230; detention centres 219, 220, 225; differential and subordinated inclusion effects 224; and discipline of workforce 219, 223, 224, 226, 230; EU institutions and 227, 228; and Great Recession 225–8; and less eligibility concept 15, 219, 223–4, 226; managerialism and 15, 226–8; racialization in 230
Sparks, R. 53
Stalinism 28
state 38, 68–9, 72, 73–6
state sovereignty, and migration control policies 229–31
stop-and-search practices 73
structural unemployment 112
structuralism 76–7, 80
structure, and agency 77
structure of the economy 45
struggles: in bureaucratic field 74, 75, 76; *see also* class struggle
subjectivism 77
subordinate inclusion 30–2
subordination 12, 30, 32
Sumner, C. 122
surplus value 3, 23, 25, 27
suspended sentences, Spain 99, 100
Sutherland, E. 229
Sutton, J. 5, 7, 125, 126, 127, 133n20
Sweden 9, 39, 44, 142, 151; incarceration rates *48*, 49, 97
symbolic analysis 68, 70–3, 80
symbolic capital 75, 76
symbolic power 70–3, 80
symbolic violence 12, 72, 75, 79
Syriza 206

Tangentopoli corruption scandal, Italy 173
tax cuts 130, 131
taxonomical approaches 53–5
Taylor, J. 3
technology, and discipline 27
terrorism 10
theft offences, Australia 140
Thompson, E.P. 28, 79
Torreggiani v. Italy (2013) 10
total institutions 25, 29, 153
trade unions 5, 126, 127; Belgium 111, 128; Italy 167, 168, 173
transatlantic consensus 123
Trigilia, C. 168, 169

Trump, D. 11
Turkey 9, *188*

Ukraine 195
unemployment 31, 123, 163; structural 112
unemployment benefits 5, 126
unemployment rates 2, 4, 6, 11, 37, 69, 107–8; Australia 147–8; Belgium 112; Georgia 193, 195, *196*; and incarceration 5, 67, 89, 126, 127, 148, 219–20; Kazakhstan 193, 194, *196*; Spain 96, 220, *222*, 225
unionization *see* trade unions
United Kingdom (Britain) 4, 6, 38, 46, 47, 89, 164; *see also* England and Wales; Scotland
United National Movement (UNM), Georgia 197
United Nations (UN) Optional Protocol on the Convention Against Torture 187
United States (USA) 1, 2, 4, 6, 31, 37–8, 39, 44, 46, 52, 54, 58n9, 89, 125, 142, 164; export of policy ideas 190–1; incarceration rates 5, 9, 29, *48*, 54, 59n13, 97, 144, 145, 160, 190; penal policy 10–11; prison downsizing 9, 10; unemployment rates 5
Uruguay, incarceration rates *56*
USSR *see* Soviet Union

vagrancy 110, 111
varieties of capitalism 8, 44, 56, 108, 123–4, 125, 128, 129, 160, 164–5, 178, 192; Georgia/Kazakhstan 194–5; *see also* coordinated market economies (CME); hierarchical market economy (HME); liberal market economies (LME)
Venezuela, incarceration rates *56*
victimisation rates, Australia 139–40, 141
Victoria, Australia 59n16, 151, 152; female incarceration rate 138; female offenders 141; immigration 151; incarceration rates 51, 137, 138, **143**, 146, 156; (and education level 148; indigenous 138, 154; and inequality 147, 149; and unemployment rate 148, 149); indigenous population 152; parole system 151; victimisation rates 139
violence: against irregular migrants, Greece 210, 211–12; physical 75; symbolic 12, 72, 75, 79
violent crime 9, 40

Wacquant, L. 16n6, 48, 68, 70, 71, 73, 74, 76, 125, 137, 152–3, 155, 171, 190
wage-bargaining 126
wages 2, 3, 29, 111, Georgia 193; Kazakhstan 193; stagnation 130
Walmsley, R. 144
Walton, P. 3
warehousing 29
Weatherburn, D. 153
Weber, M. 24, 28, 69, 70, 71, 75, 81
welfare state 8, 40, 46, 163; Italy 14, 174–8, 179
Western Australia: female offenders 141; immigration 151, incarceration rates 137, **143**, 146 (and education level 148; and income inequity 148, 149; indigenous 138, 154; indigenous females 138; and inequality 147, 149; and unemployment rate 148); indigenous population 152; offender rates 140; parole system 151; victimisation rates 139, 141
Western, B. 142
wheat prices, Belgium 110
Wisman, J.D. 130
women *see* female incarceration rate; female offenders
workhouses 23–4, 32–3n3
working class 2, 3, 4, 25, 30, 79
World Bank 194
World Prison Statistics Archive 144
World Values Survey 122
World Wealth and Income Database 113

Young, J. 52

zero tolerance discourse, Georgia 197, 198, 200

Taylor & Francis eBooks

Helping you to choose the right eBooks for your Library

Add Routledge titles to your library's digital collection today. Taylor and Francis ebooks contains over 50,000 titles in the Humanities, Social Sciences, Behavioural Sciences, Built Environment and Law.

Choose from a range of subject packages or create your own!

Benefits for you
- Free MARC records
- COUNTER-compliant usage statistics
- Flexible purchase and pricing options
- All titles DRM-free.

Benefits for your user
- Off-site, anytime access via Athens or referring URL
- Print or copy pages or chapters
- Full content search
- Bookmark, highlight and annotate text
- Access to thousands of pages of quality research at the click of a button.

REQUEST YOUR FREE INSTITUTIONAL TRIAL TODAY

Free Trials Available
We offer free trials to qualifying academic, corporate and government customers.

eCollections – Choose from over 30 subject eCollections, including:

Archaeology	Language Learning
Architecture	Law
Asian Studies	Literature
Business & Management	Media & Communication
Classical Studies	Middle East Studies
Construction	Music
Creative & Media Arts	Philosophy
Criminology & Criminal Justice	Planning
Economics	Politics
Education	Psychology & Mental Health
Energy	Religion
Engineering	Security
English Language & Linguistics	Social Work
Environment & Sustainability	Sociology
Geography	Sport
Health Studies	Theatre & Performance
History	Tourism, Hospitality & Events

For more information, pricing enquiries or to order a free trial, please contact your local sales team:
www.tandfebooks.com/page/sales

Routledge
Taylor & Francis Group

The home of
Routledge books

www.tandfebooks.com